300
Sensational
Soups

Carla Snyder & Meredith Deeds

Robert
ROSE

To our parents

*Barbara Tatum, whose homemade soups were loved by family, friends and
countless restaurant diners who never left a drop in the bottom of their bowls*

and

*Gene and Linda Ferguson, with gratitude for the limitless bowls of nourishing soup
that really did help us to grow up of sound body and strong moral fiber.*

300 Sensational Soups
Text copyright © 2008 Carla Snyder and Meredith Deeds
Photographs copyright © 2008 Robert Rose Inc.
Cover and text design copyright © 2008 Robert Rose Inc.

For complete cataloguing information, see page 375.

Disclaimer
The recipes in this book have been carefully tested by our kitchen and our tasters. To the best of our knowledge, they
are safe and nutritious for ordinary use and users. For those people with food or other allergies, or who have special
food requirements or health issues, please read the suggested contents of each recipe carefully and determine whether
or not they may create a problem for you. All recipes are used at the risk of the consumer.

We cannot be responsible for any hazards, loss or damage that may occur as a result of any recipe use.

For those with special needs, allergies, requirements or health problems, in the event of any doubt, please
contact your medical adviser prior to the use of any recipe.

Design and Production: Joseph Gisini/PageWave Graphics Inc.
Editor: Sue Sumeraj
Recipe Tester: Jennifer MacKenzie
Proofreader: Sheila Wawanash
Indexer: Gillian Watts
Photography: Colin Ericson
Food Styling: Kathryn Robertson and Kate Bush
Prop Styling: Charlene Ericson

We acknowledge the financial support of the Government of Canada through the Book Publishing Industry
Development Program (BPIDP) for our publishing activities.

Published by Robert Rose Inc.
120 Eglinton Avenue East, Suite 800, Toronto, Ontario, Canada M4P 1E2
Tel: (416) 322-6552 Fax: (416) 322-6936
www.robertrose.ca

Printed and bound in Canada

3 4 5 6 7 8 9 FP 16 15 14 13 12

Contents

▲▽▲▽▲▽▲▽▲▽▲▽▲▽▲▽▲▽▲▽▲▽▲▽▲▽▲▽

Introduction

▲▼

Soup is not just another meal — it's comfort in a bowl, love on a spoon, satisfaction simmering on the stove. Nothing makes a house feel more like a home than a pot of freshly made soup. And all this goodness comes together so easily. Whether you make it all from scratch, starting from the stock up, or you purchase stock and a few other ingredients for a quick and easy meal, soup will never fail you.

While 300 soups is a lot of recipes, there is no end to the possible combinations. You'll find that many of the recipes can be made with items that are already in your pantry or refrigerator and can be cooked and on your table in under an hour.

Our book begins with the Stock Basics chapter, which has recipes for the foundation of all soups: stocks. Here we guide you through the ins and outs of making your own stock. You'll be surprised at how easy it is and what a flavorful difference it makes. We include many different kinds of stocks, such as mushroom, veal and roasted vegetable, as well as the more familiar chicken and beef stock recipes. We hope you'll experiment, using some of the more unusual stocks in place of beef or chicken stock in your soups.

To make the book easy to use, we've divided the soup recipes among 10 chapters, such as Fresh from the Garden Vegetable Soups, Hearty Soups for Meat Lovers and Chow Down Chowders, so you'll always know where to turn when you crave a particular type of soup.

Because soup is embraced by every culture, we've included a comprehensive selection of international soups: iconic soups such as French Onion, Mulligatawny, Pasta Fagiole and Tortilla Soup, as well as some you might not be familiar with but will soon come to love, such as Vatapá, a Brazilian black bean soup, or African Peanut Soup, made with coconut milk and sweet potatoes.

While you may be accustomed to thinking of soup as an appetizer or a main course, soup also makes an excellent dessert! Our Just Dessert Soups chapter includes more than 20 recipes for mouth-watering dessert soups made with fresh fruits and chocolate.

And because we think almost every soup benefits from a garnish, we've included an entire chapter of toppings and garnishes called Gilding the Lily. For instance, Split Pea Soup is wonderful on its own, but when paired with Pumpernickel Croutons, it becomes something truly special. We hope you'll look at this chapter every time you make soup and experiment with all the possibilities.

We loved feeding our families these comforting soups, and we hope that once you begin cooking with our recipes, these soups will become your family's new favorites as well.

Soup Stocks

▲▽▲▽▲▽▲▽▲▽▲▽▲▽▲▽▲▽▲▽▲▽▲▽▲▽▲▽▲▽

Stock Basics

▲▽

In a perfect world, everyone would make soup with homemade stock. Stock, made from scratch, with quality ingredients, can elevate a soup from simple to sublime. And the good news is, stocks are much easier to make than most home cooks think. Though stocks can cook for hours, most of that time is not hands-on. And, of course, your home will smell heavenly whenever you have stock simmering on the stove.

If you're going to make stock, it makes sense to make it in large quantities. For that reason, we've made the investment in an extra-large stockpot that holds multiple gallons. But if you don't have a large enough pot, you can make stock in two pots or cut the recipe in half.

The terms "stock" and "broth" are often used interchangeably in cookbooks. While both are made from simmering water with meaty bones and aromatics, there is a distinct difference between the two. A stock is the foundation of a dish. It can be reduced and used in any number of ways, from soups and stews to complex sauces. A broth can be served on its own or with simple additions such as noodles or vegetables, and is more highly seasoned than stock. Due to the level of seasoning in broth, it is not intended to be reduced significantly because it can become overly seasoned or salty.

Purchased broth is an alternative that many cooks turn to when time is of the essence. While it will save you time in the kitchen, it will never approach the depth of flavor of a homemade stock. There are a few good reasons homemade stock is superior to purchased. The most glaring difference is the amount of salt found in purchased broth. Manufacturers often add large amounts of salt to their broths as a way to mask a lack of flavor. Sometimes you will find artificial colorings in broth, as well as a chemical aftertaste.

That being said, there are a few stocks and broths on the market that we've found to be superior to others. We had good results when using Swanson's broths, especially the low-sodium organic varieties sold in the aseptic (or cardboard) containers. Recently, Swanson's has introduced a product called Cooking Stock, which we also like. It has a nice depth of flavor and can be successfully reduced, which makes it great for both soup and sauces. We never use a store-bought broth or stock that isn't low-sodium, and we're careful not to buy those with artificial colors or flavors. We don't recommend bouillon cubes, because of their salty nature and off-flavors.

If you are looking to save time but still want the big flavors of homemade stock, try our Quick Chicken Stock recipe (page 11). It uses store-bought stock as its base, with added chicken bones and vegetables, which are cooked together for a short time.

Though we don't always call for the stocks in this chapter in our recipes, we wanted to give you as many options as possible. You can certainly substitute any stocks that appeal to you or that you have ready in your freezer. For instance, if you are making a mushroom soup and want a heartier flavor, you can substitute beef stock or chicken stock for mushroom stock. If you want to make a vegetarian version of a soup, use any of the meatless stocks, such as vegetable stock or miso stock.

Preparing Chicken Stock

Chicken stock is made the same way that your grandma made chicken soup, only instead of a whole chicken, we like to use chicken bones and necks. There is a whole world of flavor trapped inside these trimmings that most people just throw away. A peek inside our freezers reveals bags of breast bones, leg bones and backs from chickens that we either cut up or boned out. We gather bones until we have enough to make a big pot of stock (because it is just as easy to make a lot of stock as a little), then store the stock in the freezer for future use.

Preparing Meat Stock

Make sure to get beef or veal bones that aren't too large; if they are, have your butcher cut them into small pieces. A huge leg bone, kept in one piece, won't give off the same amount of flavor as the same bone cut into smaller sections. The increased surface area of the cut bones will result in increased flavor. Although we don't typically make our beef or veal stock with all oxtail, a few thrown in with the other bones adds to the "meaty" taste, and their gelatinous quality helps to create a smooth finish.

Preparing Fish Stock (Fumet)

Just like a good chicken, beef or veal stock, a good fish stock begins with bones, or fish frames and heads. You will need to become good friends with your local fishmonger, or the fish guy at your supermarket, to get the inside track on when whole fish are delivered. If they know you want them, the fish can be filleted and the bones frozen for your future use. Once you have acquired about 6 lbs (3 kg), you will have enough to make a nice batch of stock for your freezer.

The best fish for fumet are small, light-fleshed fish, such as snapper, rock fish, bass, cod or haddock. Salmon gives fumet a decidedly salmony taste that won't work for many soups. Grouper, tuna, swordfish and the like are large fish, so it is difficult to break them down into pieces, and once you do, it is difficult to remove the blood from their larger bones. If you can get fish heads, don't hesitate to use them, as they contain big flavor. Of course, the bones should smell like the sea and should have no fishy smell.

Once you have your fish bones and heads, they must be cleaned of all blood and skin. That means cutting out the gills of the fish heads, because they are full of blood, and cutting the fins from the frames and discarding them. Blood will give your fumet a bitter quality, as will the fins. Inspect the base of the head, where the vertebrae used to be connected. There is often a large blood clot there that should be removed. Once you have discarded the gills and fins, cut the frames into smaller pieces and soak them for 30 minutes in a bowl of ice-cold water with a lemon squeezed in. This acidic water will help to remove any lingering blood in the bones or head. Drain well and pat them dry with paper towels before using.

Once the stock is made, it is a good idea to reduce it so that it can be stored easily (see right). Reducing a fumet also adds flavor.

Straining Stock

The best tool for this job is a chinois, or China cap strainer, with a very fine mesh, but your best strainer with the finest mesh will work fine. Set up a large pot with the strainer over it and ladle the stock through the strainer, dumping out the solids after you've pushed as much liquid from them as possible with the back of the ladle.

Degreasing Stock

There are a few ways to degrease stock, but our favorite uses a large, shallow serving spoon. Run the lip of the spoon just under the grease-slicked top of the stock, discarding the grease into a throw-away container.

Remove as much of the grease as possible for the best-looking, clearest stock.

Reducing and Storing Stock

We reduce stock for two reasons: so that we can store it efficiently and for a richer, fuller flavor. After degreasing, we return the stock to medium heat and boil it until the volume is reduced by about three-quarters. That sounds like a lot, but the more the stock is reduced, the more space you'll have in your freezer. Highly reduced stock also keeps longer than less-reduced stock.

Stock can be made ahead and refrigerated for up to 4 days or frozen for up to 4 months. When you want to use it, just add water in increments until it tastes right to you. With reduced chicken, meat and vegetable stocks, we begin by adding 2 parts water to 1 part stock. With reduced fish stock, we use a 1 to 1 ratio of stock and water. If that tastes too strong, add a little more water until you get the flavor just right.

White Chicken Stock

When you don't want your soup to be muddied by a darker stock, and the flavor of the soup is to be light and fresh, white chicken stock is a good choice as the base.

Tips

Before making this recipe, be sure to review "Stock Basics" on page 6.

Chicken backs and necks can be found in most grocery stores. If you don't see them in the freezer case, ask the meat department where they can be found, or if they can order some for you.

If you prefer to cook your stock longer, you can simmer it for up to 8 hours. It will have a more concentrated flavor and a slightly lower yield.

Makes about 40 cups (10 L), or 10 cups (2.5 L) reduced

12 lbs	chicken parts (necks, backs, breast bones, wings, etc.)	6 kg
2 lbs	onions, quartered	1 kg
1 lb	carrots, quartered	500 g
4	stalks celery, quartered	4
3	leeks, green tops only	3
1	head garlic, halved	1
1	bunch parsley, stems only	1
2	bay leaves	2
1 tbsp	whole black peppercorns	15 mL
1 tbsp	dried thyme	15 mL

1. In an extra-large stockpot, combine chicken parts, onions, carrots, celery, leeks, garlic, parsley stems, bay leaves, peppercorns and thyme. Add about 12 quarts (12 L) cold water, or as much as is needed to cover the bones and vegetables by at least 2 inches (5 cm). Heat over medium-low heat until the stock begins to give off a little bubble every now and then, about 1 hour. Skim the scum as it forms on the surface and discard. Watch to make sure the pot doesn't boil and reduce the heat accordingly. Cook at a very low simmer (you will see a bubble every 10 seconds or so) for 4 hours.
2. Strain, degrease and, if desired, reduce stock (see page 8).

Brown Chicken Stock

▲▽▲

Brown chicken stock is our all-purpose most-used stock. It is brown because we brown the bones in a hot oven before adding them to the vegetables in the stockpot. The flavor of brown chicken stock is more robust than that of white chicken stock. We compare the two stocks to a poached chicken breast (white stock) and a roasted chicken breast (brown stock). The beauty of hearty brown stock is that it can stand in for beef or veal stock in a pinch.

▲▽▲▽▲▽▲▽▲▽▲

Tips

Before making this recipe, be sure to review "Stock Basics" on page 6.

Save the parsley leaves and the white part of the leeks for another recipe.

If you prefer to cook your stock longer, you can simmer it for up to 8 hours. It will have a more concentrated flavor and a slightly lower yield.

Makes about 40 cups (10 L), or 10 cups (2.5 L) reduced

- Preheat oven to 425°F (220°C)
- Baking sheets

12 lbs	chicken parts (necks, backs, breast bones, wings, etc.)	6 kg
2 lbs	onions, quartered	1 kg
1 lb	carrots, quartered	500 g
4	stalks celery, quartered	4
3	leeks, green tops only	3
1	head garlic, halved	1
1	tomato, halved	1
1	bunch parsley, stems only	1
2	bay leaves	2
1 tbsp	whole black peppercorns	15 mL
1 tbsp	dried thyme	15 mL

1. Arrange chicken bones on baking sheets, leaving space between them so they will brown nicely. Roast in preheated oven until golden brown, about 40 minutes.
2. In an extra-large stockpot, combine chicken bones, onions, carrots, celery, leeks, garlic, tomato, parsley stems, bay leaves, peppercorns and thyme. Add about 12 quarts (12 L) cold water, or as much as is needed to cover the bones and vegetables by at least 2 inches (5 cm). Heat over medium-low heat until the stock begins to give off a little bubble every now and then, about 1 hour. Skim the scum as it forms on the surface and discard. Watch to make sure the pot doesn't boil and reduce the heat accordingly. Cook at a very low simmer (you will see a bubble every 10 seconds or so) for 4 hours.
3. Strain, degrease and, if desired, reduce stock (see page 8).

Quick Chicken Stock

▲▽

Sometimes we want the flavor of homemade chicken stock but don't have time to make it. That's when we compromise and make this quick version, cooking a good canned stock with extra chicken bones and vegetables. The result is a better-than-canned-flavor chicken stock in less than an hour.

▲▽▲▽▲▽▲▽▲▽

Tip

Before making this recipe, be sure to review "Stock Basics" on page 6.

Makes about 14 cups (3.5 L)

16 cups	store-bought chicken stock	4 L
2 lbs	chicken parts (necks, backs, breast bones, wings, etc.)	1 kg
2	onions, sliced	2
2	cloves garlic, crushed	2
1	carrot, sliced	1
1	stalk celery, sliced	1
6	whole black peppercorns	6
3	parsley stems	3
1	bay leaf	1
½ tsp	dried thyme	2 mL

1. In a large stockpot, combine stock, chicken parts, onions, garlic, carrot, celery, peppercorns, parsley stems, bay leaf and thyme; bring to a simmer over medium-low heat. Cook at a very low simmer for 45 minutes.
2. Strain and degrease stock (see page 8).

Chinese Chicken Stock

▲▼▲▼▲▼▲▼▲▼▲▼▲▼▲▼▲▼▲▼▲▼▲▼▲▼▲▼▲▼▲▼▲▼▲▼▲▼▲

With the simple additions of lemongrass, star anise, green onions, cinnamon and ginger, everyday chicken stock becomes an exotically flavored base for wonton soup, egg drop soup, hot-and-sour soup and even Thai soups. But don't put any limits on your creativity — use this stock whenever you want that little extra something-something.

▲▼▲▼▲▼▲▼▲▼

Tip
Before making this recipe, be sure to review "Stock Basics" on page 6.

Makes about 14 cups (3.5 L)

16 cups	chicken stock (homemade or store-bought)	4 L
2 lbs	chicken parts (necks, backs, breast bones, wings, etc.)	1 kg
6	green onions, sliced	6
2	cloves garlic, crushed	2
2	stalks lemongrass, bulbs sliced	2
1	carrot, sliced	1
1	stalk celery, sliced	1
6	whole black peppercorns	6
3	parsley stems	3
2	whole star anise	2
1	thumb-sized knob gingerroot, sliced	1
1	stick cinnamon, about 4 inches (10 cm) long	1
1	bay leaf	1
½ tsp	dried thyme	2 mL

1. In a large stockpot, combine stock, chicken parts, green onions, garlic, lemongrass, carrot, celery, peppercorns, parsley stems, star anise, ginger, cinnamon, bay leaf and thyme; bring to a simmer over medium-low heat. Cook at a very low simmer for 45 minutes.
2. Strain and degrease stock (see page 8).

Japanese Chicken Stock

▲▽▲▽▲▽▲▽▲▽▲▽▲▽▲▽▲▽▲▽▲▽▲▽▲▽▲▽▲▽▲▽▲▽▲▽▲▽▲

By adding kombu (seaweed), ginger, soy sauce and bonito flakes (dried fish flakes) to basic chicken stock, we have created a perfect base for Japanese noodle soups.

▲▽▲▽▲▽▲▽▲

Tips

Before making this recipe, be sure to review "Stock Basics" on page 6.

Before using the kombu, remove dirt and sand by wiping the surface with a slightly damp kitchen towel.

Makes about 14 cups (3.5 L)

16 cups	chicken stock (homemade or store-bought)	4 L
2 lbs	chicken parts (necks, backs, breast bones, wings, etc.)	1 kg
2	onions, sliced	2
2	cloves garlic, crushed	2
2	pieces kombu (dried kelp), each about 4 inches (10 cm) square	2
1	carrot, sliced	1
1	stalk celery, sliced	1
1 cup	dried bonito flakes (katsuobushi)	250 mL
6	whole black peppercorns	6
3	parsley stems	3
1	thumb-sized knob gingerroot, sliced	1
1	bay leaf	1
½ tsp	dried thyme	2 mL
2 tbsp	soy sauce	25 mL

1. In a large stockpot, combine stock, chicken bones, onions, garlic, kombu, carrot, celery, bonito flakes, peppercorns, parsley stems, ginger, bay leaf, thyme and soy sauce; bring to a simmer over medium-low heat. Cook at a very low simmer for 45 minutes.
2. Strain and degrease stock (see page 8).

Beef Stock

▲▽

There is no equal to hearty homemade beef stock. The difference it can make to a beef or even vegetable soup can be the difference between an okay bowl and something truly special. Canned beef stock tends to taste more like salt than beef and will never come close to giving you the depth of flavor you get by browning bones and simmering them with hearty veggies for hours, until they have given their all to the rich liquid.

▲▽▲▽▲▽▲▽▲▽▲

Tips

Before making this recipe, be sure to review "Stock Basics" on page 6.

Save the parsley leaves and the white part of the leeks for another recipe.

If you prefer to cook your stock longer, you can simmer it for up to 8 hours. It will have a more concentrated flavor and a slightly lower yield.

Makes about 24 cups (6 L), or 6 cups (1.5 L) reduced

- Preheat oven to 450°F (230°C)
- Rimmed baking sheets

8 lbs	beef bones (necks, shanks, knuckles, oxtails or a mixture of these), cut into 2-inch (5 cm) pieces	4 kg
4	cloves garlic, crushed	4
3	onions, quartered	3
3	carrots, quartered	3
3	stalks celery, quartered	3
2	tomatoes, halved	2
3	leeks, green tops only	3
2	bay leaves	2
1	bunch parsley, stems only	1
2 tsp	whole black peppercorns	10 mL
1 tsp	whole allspice	5 mL

1. Arrange beef bones on baking sheets, leaving space between them so they will brown nicely. Roast in preheated oven for 25 minutes. Remove from the oven and scatter garlic, onions, carrots, celery and tomatoes around the bones. Continue to roast for 20 minutes or until bones and vegetables are well browned. Transfer to an extra-large stockpot, pouring off and discarding any accumulated fat.
2. While the baking sheets are still hot, deglaze them by pouring 1 cup (250 mL) water onto the sheets and scraping up any brown bits. Pour into the stockpot.
3. Add about 8 quarts (8 L) cold water, or as much as is needed to cover the bones and vegetables by at least 2 inches (5 cm). Add leeks, bay leaves, parsley stems, peppercorns and allspice. Heat over medium-low heat until the stock begins to give off a little bubble every now and then, about 1 hour. Skim the scum as it forms on the surface and discard. Watch to make sure the pot doesn't boil and reduce the heat accordingly. Cook at a very low simmer (you will see a bubble every 10 seconds or so) for 4 hours.
4. Strain, degrease and, if desired, reduce stock (see page 8).

Veal Stock

▲▼▲▼▲▼▲▼▲▼▲▼▲▼▲▼▲▼▲▼▲▼▲▼▲▼▲▼▲▼▲▼▲▼▲▼▲▼▲

Veal stock is a lovely thing to have on hand. Its mellow but rich nature is the perfect base for soups that would be overwhelmed by the deep flavor of a hearty beef stock but need more than the lighter flavor of a simple chicken stock.

▲▼▲▼▲▼▲▼▲▼▲

Tips

Before making this recipe, be sure to review "Stock Basics" on page 6.

If veal bones are not readily found at your grocery store, ask your butcher. They are more expensive than chicken or beef bones but contain more collagen, which makes for a gelatinous, velvety stock.

If you prefer to cook your stock longer, you can simmer it for up to 8 hours. It will have a more concentrated flavor and a slightly lower yield.

Makes about 24 cups (6 L), or 6 cups (1.5 L) reduced

8 lbs	veal bones (necks, shanks, knuckles, oxtails or a mixture of these), cut into 2-inch (5 cm) pieces	4 kg
2 lbs	onions, quartered	1 kg
1 lb	carrots, quartered	500 g
4	stalks celery, quartered	4
3	leeks, green tops only	3
2	tomatoes, halved	2
1	head garlic, halved	1
1	bunch parsley, stems only	1
2	bay leaves	2
½ cup	tomato paste	125 mL

1. In an extra-large stockpot, combine veal bones, onions, carrots, celery, leeks, tomatoes, garlic, parsley stems, bay leaves and tomato paste. Add about 8 quarts (8 L) cold water, or as much as is needed to cover the bones and vegetables by at least 2 inches (5 cm). Heat over medium-low heat until the stock begins to give off a little bubble every now and then, about 1 hour. Skim the scum as it forms on the surface and discard. Watch to make sure the pot doesn't boil and reduce the heat accordingly. Cook at a very low simmer (you will see a bubble every 10 seconds or so) for 4 hours.
2. Strain, degrease and, if desired, reduce stock (see page 8).

Fish Stock (Fumet)

AVAVAVAVAVAVAVAVAVAVAVAVAVAVAVAVAVAVAVAVAVAVAVA

No purchased fish stock will be as good as what you can make in an hour, with only about 15 minutes of hands-on time.

AVAVAVAVAVA

Tip

Before making this recipe, be sure to review "Stock Basics" on page 6.

Makes about 16 cups (4 L), or 4 cups (1 L) reduced

2 tbsp	olive oil	25 mL
6 lbs	fish bones and heads, fins and gills discarded, soaked (see page 7)	3 kg
3	onions, chopped	3
2	stalks celery, chopped	2
2	leeks, white and light green parts only, chopped	2
2	cloves garlic, crushed	2
8	parsley stems	8
8	whole black peppercorns	8
1	bay leaf	1
1 tsp	salt	5 mL
½ tsp	dried thyme	2 mL
16 cups	water	4 L
1 cup	dry white wine	250 mL
1 tsp	freshly squeezed lemon juice	5 mL

1. In a large stockpot, heat oil over medium heat. Add fish bones and heads, onions, celery and leeks; cover and cook for 3 minutes. Add garlic, parsley stems, peppercorns, bay leaf, salt, thyme, water, wine and lemon juice; bring to a boil. Reduce heat and simmer for 30 minutes.
2. Strain and, if desired, reduce stock (see page 8).

Shellfish Stock

▲▼▲▼▲▼▲▼▲▼▲▼▲▼▲▼▲▼▲▼▲▼▲▼▲▼▲▼▲▼▲▼▲▼▲▼▲▼▲

Because it can be difficult to find fish frames (bones), shellfish stock is our stock of choice when making fish- or seafood-based soups. We always buy shrimp with the shells on, so that we have a supply of shrimp shells in the freezer for this quick stock.

We turn to this stock time and time again because it's relatively easy to make (especially compared to fumet), and so much tastier than store-bought shellfish or fish stock.

▲▼▲▼▲▼▲▼▲▼▲

Tip
Lobster or crab shells are also a good addition to shellfish stock.

Makes 5 to 6 cups (1.25 to 1.5 L)

2 tbsp	olive oil	25 mL
1	small onion, diced	1
1	clove garlic, crushed	1
1	small carrot, diced	1
½	stalk celery, diced	½
5	whole black peppercorns	5
1	bay leaf	1
¼ tsp	dried thyme	1 mL
	Shells from about 3 lbs (1.5 kg) shrimp	
1 cup	dry white wine	250 mL
2 cups	chicken stock (homemade or store-bought)	500 mL
2 cups	water	500 mL
1 cup	bottled clam juice	250 mL

1. In a large soup pot, heat oil over medium-high heat. Add onion and sauté until onion starts to soften, about 2 minutes. Add garlic, carrot and celery; sauté until vegetables start to soften, about 3 minutes. Add peppercorns, bay leaf, thyme and shrimp shells; sauté until shells turn pink, 1 to 2 minutes.
2. Add wine and cook until reduced by half, about 5 minutes. Add stock, water and clam juice; bring to a boil. Reduce heat and simmer for 40 minutes.
3. Strain stock through a fine-mesh strainer (see page 8).

Ichiban Dashi

▲▽

Dashi is a simple soup stock flavored with kelp and dried bonito flakes (a type of tuna). It's the base for many Japanese dishes, including Miso Soup (page 333).

Makes 6 cups (1.5 L)

4	pieces kombu (dried kelp), each about 6 inches (15 cm) square	4
6 cups	water	1.5 L
1 cup	dried bonito flakes (katsuobushi)	250 mL

1. Line a strainer with cheesecloth and set it over a large bowl.
2. Remove dirt and sand from kombu by wiping the surface with a slightly damp kitchen towel. Place kombu and water in a large soup pot over medium-low heat and bring to a simmer. (Do not let boil, as kombu can become slimy and unpleasant.)
3. Once the kombu has come to the surface, remove it with a slotted spoon and discard. Immediately add bonito flakes. After 10 seconds, remove from heat and skim off any foam. Let stand until bonito flakes begin to sink to the bottom of the pot. Pour stock through the lined strainer, discarding solids.

Miso Stock

Miso pastes are made from a combination of fermented soybeans and white rice. The most common miso found in North American groceries is white miso, which is brownish yellow in color, not white as you would assume. It has a delicate, nutty, salty flavor that we find most appealing. Brown and red miso pastes are more strongly flavored and a good bit saltier.

It is surprising how much like chicken stock good miso can taste. It is a terrific substitute for vegetable stock and is easy to keep on hand in the refrigerator.

Tips

Miso stock is most likely to be called for in vegetarian or vegan soups, but it can be used in place of vegetable or chicken stock in any soup recipe.

We like to boost the flavor of many soups with a tablespoon (15 mL) or so of white miso paste, even when we're using a meat stock.

Makes 8 cups (2 L)

8 cups	water	2 L
1 cup	white miso paste	250 mL
3	green onions, thinly sliced	3

1. In a pot, bring water to a simmer over medium-high heat. Whisk in miso paste and green onions; reduce heat and simmer for 5 minutes.
2. Strain stock through a fine-mesh strainer (see page 8).

Vegetable Stock

▲▽

Make sure to use or freeze this stock soon after you make it, as vegetable stock loses its flavor quickly. This light stock makes a suitable substitute for chicken stock.

▲▽▲▽▲▽▲▽▲▽

Tip
Save the white part of the leeks for another recipe.

Makes about 16 cups (4 L), or 4 cups (1 L) reduced

3	onions, quartered	3
3	leeks, green tops only	3
3	stalks celery, quartered	3
3	carrots, quartered	3
3	tomatoes, coarsely chopped	3
2	cloves garlic, crushed	2
1	parsnip, quartered	1
1	bulb fennel, quartered	1
1 cup	mushrooms (including stems)	250 mL
6	sprigs parsley	6
6	whole black peppercorns	6
2	bay leaves	2
20 cups	water	5 L

1. In a large stockpot, combine onions, leeks, celery, carrots, tomatoes, garlic, parsnip, fennel, mushrooms, parsley, peppercorns, bay leaves and water; bring to a boil over medium heat. Reduce heat and simmer for 1 hour.
2. Strain and, if desired, reduce stock (see page 8).

Roasted Vegetable Stock

▲▽▲

This hearty, more deeply flavored vegetable stock is a nice addition to robust soups or a good substitute for beef stock.

▲▽▲▽▲▽▲▽▲▽

Tip

When cutting vegetables for other uses, save the ends and other trimmings in a sealable plastic bag in the freezer to have on hand when you're ready to make stock.

Makes about 16 cups (4 L), or 4 cups (1 L) reduced

- Preheat oven to 425°F (220°C)
- 2 large baking sheets

3	onions, quartered	3
3	leeks, green tops only	3
3	stalks celery, quartered	3
3	carrots, quartered	3
1	parsnip, quartered	1
1 cup	mushrooms (including stems)	250 mL
3 tbsp	olive oil	45 mL
6	sprigs parsley	6
6	whole black peppercorns	6
2	bay leaves	2
2	cloves garlic	2
20 cups	water	5 L
2 tbsp	tomato paste	25 mL

1. Combine onions, leeks, celery, carrots, parsnip and mushrooms on baking sheets. Drizzle with olive oil and toss to coat. Spread out vegetables evenly, leaving space between them so they will brown nicely. Roast in preheated oven, stirring at least once to ensure even browning, for 45 minutes or until well browned.
2. In a large stockpot, combine roasted vegetables, parsley, peppercorns, bay leaves, garlic, water and tomato paste; bring to a boil over medium heat. Reduce heat and simmer for 1 hour.
3. Strain and, if desired, reduce stock (see page 8).

Mushroom Stock

▲▽▲

Mushroom stock is the beef stock of the vegetarian world. Dried mushrooms give this stock a rich flavor that is perfect for mushroom soup, or for any vegetable soup where heartier flavors are welcome.

▲▽▲▽▲▽▲▽▲▽▲

Tip

To clean mushrooms, you can either rinse them quickly in water or wipe them with a damp paper towel. Mushrooms will be much happier in your refrigerator if you store them in a paper bag.

Makes about 16 cups (4 L), or 4 cups (1 L) reduced

3	onions, quartered	3
3	leeks, green tops only	3
3	stalks celery, quartered	3
3	carrots, quartered	3
2	cloves garlic	2
4 cups	mushrooms (including stems), sliced (about 1½ lbs/750 g)	1 L
½ oz	dried porcini mushrooms	15 g
6	sprigs parsley	6
6	whole black peppercorns	6
2	bay leaves	2
20 cups	water	5 L

1. In a large stockpot, combine onions, leeks, celery, carrots, garlic, mushrooms, porcini mushrooms, parsley, peppercorns, bay leaves and water; bring to a boil over medium heat. Reduce heat and simmer for 1 hour.
2. Strain and, if desired, reduce stock (see page 8).

Chilled Soups

▲▽▲▽▲▽▲▽▲▽▲▽▲▽▲▽▲▽▲▽▲▽▲▽▲▽▲▽▲▽

Almond Gazpacho

▲▽▲▽▲▽▲▽▲▽▲▽▲▽▲▽▲▽▲▽▲▽▲▽▲▽▲▽▲▽▲▽▲▽▲

We can't think of any other soup that is as sophisticated, unusual and striking in appearance as this white gazpacho. The subtle flavors of almond, sherry vinegar and a hint of garlic are beautifully paired with the cool sweetness of green grapes, which make a gorgeous garnish against the stark whiteness of the soup. Use top-notch olive oil for this soup, and you won't be disappointed.

▲▽▲▽▲▽▲▽▲▽▲

Tip

Chilled soups will stay cold for much longer in chilled bowls.

Serves 6

3 cups	cubed stale French bread (crusts removed)	750 mL
1 cup	water	250 mL
1 cup	whole blanched almonds	250 mL
½ tsp	salt	2 mL
1 tsp	minced garlic	5 mL
1 tbsp	sherry vinegar	15 mL
⅓ cup	mild extra-virgin olive oil	75 mL
2 cups	ice water	500 mL
	Green grapes, halved	
	Extra-virgin olive oil	

1. Soak bread in water for 5 minutes, then squeeze dry, discarding soaking water.
2. In a food processor, process almonds and salt until as smooth as possible. Add garlic, vinegar and bread; pulse until combined. With the motor running, add oil in a slow stream through the feed tube, then add ice water and blend well.
3. Force purée through a fine sieve into a bowl, pressing firmly on solids. Discard solids. Cover soup and refrigerate until cold, about 3 hours. Taste and adjust seasoning with salt and vinegar, if necessary.
4. Ladle into chilled bowls and garnish each with several grape halves and a drizzle of olive oil.

Chilled Green Apple Soup

We especially liked tart Granny Smith apples in this recipe, but you could use Mutsu, if you prefer. This soup is as good warm as it is cold.

Tip

If you want to serve this soup hot, reheat in a saucepan over medium-low heat until heated through.

Serves 6

¼ cup	unsalted butter	50 mL
2	onions, thinly sliced	2
1	stick cinnamon, about 4 inches (10 cm) long	1
½ tsp	salt	2 mL
½ tsp	ground cardamom	2 mL
4	Granny Smith apples, peeled and diced	4
1 cup	dry white wine	250 mL
3 cups	chicken stock	750 mL
2 cups	unsweetened apple cider	500 mL
3	whole cloves	3
1	strip orange peel, about 2 inches (5 cm) long	1
½ cup	whipping (35%) cream	125 mL
	Freshly ground black pepper	
	Cheesy Croutons (optional, see recipe, page 369), made with Cheddar cheese	
	Oven-Dried Apple Slices (optional, see recipe, page 367)	

1. In a large pot, melt butter over medium heat until sizzling. Add onions, cinnamon stick, salt and cardamom; sauté until onions are lightly browned, 7 to 8 minutes. Add apples and sauté for about 2 minutes or until they begin to soften. Add wine and cook until reduced by half, about 5 minutes. Add stock and cider; bring to a boil.
2. Push the pointed ends of the cloves into the orange peel and add it to the soup. Reduce heat and simmer for about 25 minutes or until apples are tender and flavors are blended. Discard cinnamon stick, orange peel and cloves.
3. Using an immersion blender, or in a food processor or blender in batches, purée soup until smooth. Transfer to a bowl and stir in cream. Season with salt and pepper to taste. Cover and refrigerate until cold, about 3 hours, or overnight. Taste and adjust seasoning with salt and pepper, if necessary.
4. Ladle into chilled bowls and garnish with croutons or apple slices, if desired.

Chilled Curried Pear Soup

▲▼▲▼▲▼▲▼▲▼▲▼▲▼▲▼▲▼▲▼▲▼▲▼▲▼▲▼▲▼▲▼▲▼▲

The sweetness of pears blends beautifully with the complex spices of India.

▲▼▲▼▲▼▲▼▲▼

Tip

To trim leeks, cut off and discard the root end and the dark green tops (or save the tops for stock). Cut leeks lengthwise and wash under running water to remove any grit or dirt. Then cut as directed in the recipe.

Serves 6

6 tbsp	unsalted butter, divided	90 mL
6 cups	diced peeled pears (about 6)	1.5 L
2 cups	chopped onions	500 mL
2 cups	sliced leeks, white and light green parts only	500 mL
1 tsp	minced garlic	5 mL
3 tbsp	all-purpose flour	45 mL
2 tbsp	curry powder (store-bought or see recipe, opposite)	25 mL
6 cups	chicken stock	1.5 L
½ cup	dry white wine	125 mL
¼ tsp	salt	1 mL
Pinch	freshly ground black pepper	Pinch

Yogurt Garnish

¼ cup	sliced green onions	50 mL
1 tbsp	liquid honey	15 mL
1 tsp	toasted sesame oil	5 mL
⅓ cup	plain yogurt	75 mL
	Salt and freshly ground black pepper	

1. In a large pot, melt 5 tbsp (75 mL) of the butter over medium-high heat. Add pears, onions, leeks and garlic; sauté for 2 minutes. Reduce heat to medium and sauté for 1 minute. Sprinkle with flour and curry powder; sauté for 5 minutes or until pears are soft.

2. Gradually whisk in stock and wine; simmer for 15 minutes, reducing heat if necessary, until soup is velvety and slightly thickened. Season with salt and pepper.

3. *Meanwhile, prepare the garnish:* In a small skillet, heat the remaining butter over medium-high heat. Add green onions and sauté for 2 minutes. Add honey and sesame oil; sauté for 1 minute. Remove from heat and stir in yogurt. Season with salt and pepper to taste. Set aside.

4. Using an immersion blender, or in a food processor or blender in batches, purée soup until smooth. Cover and refrigerate until cold, about 3 hours, or overnight. Taste and adjust seasoning with salt and pepper, if necessary.

5. Ladle into chilled bowls and top with yogurt garnish. Draw a chopstick or knife through the yogurt to create a decorative swirl.

Tip

Making your own curry powder guarantees a fresh, lively character in your dishes. Purchased curry powder may have been sitting on your grocer's shelf for a long time, which reduces its flavor.

Curry Powder

Makes about ½ cup (125 mL)

- Preheat oven to 375°F (190°C)
- Baking sheet

1	dried ancho or pasilla chile pepper	1
1	stick cinnamon, about 4 inches (10 cm) long	1
1 tbsp	coriander seeds	15 mL
1 tbsp	cumin seeds	15 mL
1 tbsp	cardamom seeds	15 mL
1 tbsp	fenugreek seeds	15 mL
1 tsp	mustard seeds	5 mL
1 tbsp	ground turmeric	15 mL
1 tsp	ground ginger	5 mL

1. On baking sheet, toss chile pepper, cinnamon stick, coriander seeds, cumin seeds, cardamom seeds, fenugreek seeds and mustard seeds. Toast in preheated oven until fragrant, about 5 minutes. Let cool, then grind spices with a mortar and pestle or in a spice mill. Stir in turmeric and ginger. Store in an airtight container and use within a few weeks for best results.

Cold Thai-Style Mango Coconut Soup with Mango Relish

▲▽

Mango and coconut are a match made in heaven; when combined with Thai red curry paste, the flavors in this soup are to die for.

▲▽▲▽▲▽▲▽▲▽▲

Tip

When shopping for mangos, choose fragrant fruit that yields slightly when pressed.

Serves 4 to 6

2 tsp	olive oil	10 mL
1	onion, diced	1
2 tsp	Thai red curry paste	10 mL
2	large mangos, peeled and quartered	2
1 tbsp	light brown sugar	15 mL
2 tsp	grated gingerroot	10 mL
½ tsp	salt	2 mL
1	can (14 oz/400 mL) unsweetened coconut milk	1
1¼ cups	water	300 mL
½ cup	plain yogurt	125 mL
2 tbsp	freshly squeezed lime juice	25 mL

Mango Relish

1	large mango, diced	1
2 tbsp	light brown sugar	25 mL
2 tbsp	chopped fresh basil	45 mL

1. In a skillet, heat oil over medium heat. Add onion and sauté until softened, about 6 minutes. Add curry paste and sauté for 1 minute.
2. In a food processor or blender, purée onion mixture, mangos, brown sugar, ginger and salt until smooth. Add coconut milk, water, yogurt and lime juice; process to combine. Transfer to a bowl, cover and refrigerate until cold, about 3 hours, or overnight. Taste and adjust seasoning with salt, if necessary.
3. *Prepare the relish:* In a small bowl, combine mango, brown sugar and basil. Let stand for 15 minutes.
4. Ladle soup into chilled bowls and top each with a dollop of mango relish.

Summer Melon Soup with Crème Fraîche

▲▽▲

Because melon is the star of this dish, it really needs to be juicy and sweet. Make this soup at the peak of summer, when local melons are ripe and cheap.

▲▽▲▽▲▽▲▽▲▽▲

Tip

Honey rock melons have orange flesh, while honeydews are green.

Variation

Try making this soup with cantaloupe, but use 2 melons, since they are usually smaller.

Serves 6

1	honey rock or honeydew melon, peeled, seeded and cut into chunks	1
¼ cup	extra-virgin olive oil	50 mL
	Salt and freshly ground black pepper	
⅓ cup	crème fraîche or sour cream	75 mL
¼ cup	finely chopped fresh mint	50 mL

1. In a food processor or blender, in batches if necessary, purée melon until smooth. With the motor running, add oil through the feed tube or hole in lid and process until combined. Season with salt and pepper to taste. Transfer to a bowl, cover and refrigerate until cold, about 3 hours. Taste and adjust seasoning with salt and pepper, if necessary.
2. Ladle into chilled bowls and garnish with crème fraîche and mint.

Chilled Nectarine Soup with Mint

▲▼

When nectarines are at their peak of flavor, there is no finer fruit. We liked this slightly sweet-tart soup thick and rich, but if you want it to be thinner, just add some orange juice.

▲▼▲▼▲▼▲▼▲▼

Tip

Greek yogurt is strained so that it is thicker and richer than most domestic yogurt. If you can't find Greek yogurt, lay a coffee filter in a strainer and place it over a bowl. Pour the yogurt into the strainer and place in the refrigerator for 2 to 3 hours. The whey will drain from the yogurt, leaving it thicker.

Serves 4

2 lbs	nectarines (about 5), chopped	1 kg
1 cup	plain yogurt (preferably Greek yogurt, see tip, at left)	250 mL
2 tsp	liquid honey (approx.)	10 mL
1 tsp	freshly squeezed lemon juice (approx.)	5 mL
1 tbsp	chopped fresh mint	15 mL
¼ tsp	salt	1 mL
Pinch	cayenne pepper	Pinch
	Mint leaves	

1. In a food processor or blender, purée nectarines, yogurt, honey, lemon juice, mint, salt and cayenne until smooth, adding more honey and/or lemon juice to taste. Transfer to a bowl, cover and refrigerate until cold, about 3 hours. Taste and adjust seasoning with honey, lemon juice, salt and cayenne, if necessary.
2. Ladle into chilled bowls and garnish with mint leaves.

Chilled Yogurt Soup with Roasted Red Pepper and Pesto Swirls

▲▽

While developing the recipe for this soup, we were concerned that the yogurt might overwhelm the flavors of the other ingredients. To our surprise and delight, just the opposite was true. Instead of dominating, the yogurt seemed to carry the flavors of the onion, garlic, red peppers and pesto even further, making this one of our new favorite soups.

▲▽▲▽▲▽▲▽▲▽▲

Tip

To roast peppers, lay halved seeded peppers on a baking sheet and broil until skins char and blacken. Transfer to a heatproof bowl and cover with plastic wrap. When cool enough to handle, scrape off the blackened skins with the back of a knife. Don't worry about a little bit of black remaining on the peppers.

Serves 6

2 tbsp	olive oil	25 mL
½ cup	minced onion	125 mL
1	clove garlic, minced	1
4 cups	chicken or vegetable stock	1 L
3 cups	plain yogurt	750 mL
½ tsp	salt	2 mL
¼ tsp	freshly ground black pepper	1 mL
2	roasted red bell peppers (see tip, at left)	2
1 tbsp	balsamic vinegar	15 mL
¼ cup	pesto (store-bought or see recipe, page 363)	50 mL

1. In a skillet, heat oil over medium heat. Add onion and sauté until lightly browned, about 10 minutes. Add garlic and sauté for 1 minute. Add stock and bring to a boil. Reduce heat and simmer for about 5 minutes to blend the flavors. Let cool to room temperature.
2. Using an immersion blender, or in a food processor or blender in batches, purée soup until smooth. Add yogurt, salt and pepper; pulse until just blended. Transfer to a bowl, cover and refrigerate until cold, about 3 hours. Taste and adjust seasoning with salt and pepper, if necessary.
3. In a food processor or blender, pulse red peppers and vinegar until smooth.
4. Ladle soup into chilled bowls and top each with a dollop of pesto and a dollop of red pepper purée. Swirl a knife around the bowl to create a marbled effect.

Cold Avocado Soup

▲▼▲

This soup is quick and easy to prepare, though it requires some chilling time, so take advantage of perfectly ripe avocados and serve it often, either as is or using one of the variations.

▲▼▲▼▲▼▲▼▲▼

Tip

Ripe avocados yield slightly to gentle pressure.

Variations

Serve with a dollop of salsa and crushed corn chips, or top with sautéed scallops or crab salad.

Pair this soup with Bloody Mary Soup (page 39). Just pour each into a pitcher and pour simultaneously into chilled serving bowls. Half the soup will be green avocado and the other half red bloody Mary. We liked it garnished with corn chips and a few shrimp.

Serves 6 to 8

4	avocados, halved	4
3 cups	cold water	750 mL
¼ cup	whipping (35 %) cream	50 mL
1 tsp	salt	5 mL
1 tsp	liquid honey	5 mL
1 tsp	white wine vinegar	5 mL
Pinch	cayenne pepper	Pinch
	Lightly whipped cream	

1. In a food processor or blender, purée avocados, cold water, cream, salt, honey, vinegar and cayenne until velvety and smooth. Transfer to a bowl and lay plastic wrap directly on the surface of the soup to keep it from discoloring. Refrigerate until cold, about 3 hours. Taste and adjust seasoning with salt, honey, vinegar and cayenne, if necessary.
2. Ladle into chilled bowls and garnish with whipped cream.

Chilled Curried Pear Soup
(page 26)
Overleaf: Cold Thai-Style Mango
Coconut Soup with Mango Relish
(page 28)

Guacamole Soup

▲▽▲

Familiar guacamole flavors undergo a mouth-watering transformation in this rich and refreshing soup. It's the perfect starter for a Mexican-themed dinner party.

▲▽▲▽▲▽▲▽▲▽

Tip

Chile peppers contain oils that can cause chemical burns on your skin. When seeding and chopping them, always wear latex, plastic or rubber gloves.

Serves 4 to 6

1	serrano chile pepper, seeded and coarsely chopped	1
1	clove garlic	1
½ cup	tightly packed fresh cilantro leaves	125 mL
2	avocados, halved	2
2 cups	chicken or vegetable stock	500 mL
¼ cup	freshly squeezed lime juice	50 mL
½ tsp	salt	2 mL
1 cup	diced seeded tomatoes	250 mL
	Crispy Tortilla Strips (see recipe, page 372)	

1. In a food processor or blender, process chile pepper, garlic and cilantro until finely chopped, scraping down the sides of the bowl once or twice as necessary. Add avocados, stock, lime juice and salt; process until smooth. Transfer to a bowl, cover and refrigerate until cold, about 3 hours. Taste and adjust seasoning with salt, if necessary.
2. Ladle into chilled bowls and garnish with tomatoes and tortilla strips.

Silky Cream of Corn Soup with Chipotle (page 59)

Overleaf: Carrot, Celery and Leek Soup with Cornbread Dumplings (page 53)

Chilled Carrot Soup with Dill

▲▼▲▼▲▼▲▼▲▼▲▼▲▼▲▼▲▼▲▼▲▼▲▼▲▼▲▼▲▼▲▼▲▼▲▼▲

This carrot soup is brought to life by the addition of cardamom, gingerroot and carrot juice. You'll love it cold, but it's also great heated, with a big slice of peasant bread on the side.

▲▼▲▼▲▼▲▼▲▼

Tip

If you want to serve this soup hot, reheat in a saucepan over medium-low heat until heated through.

Variation

Try substituting passion fruit juice for the carrot juice. You'll be surprised by how good it is.

Serves 4

¼ cup	unsalted butter	50 mL
1	onion, sliced	1
1 lb	carrots, thinly sliced	500 g
½ tsp	ground cardamom	2 mL
⅓ cup	dry white wine	75 mL
1	knob gingerroot (about 1 inch/2.5 cm), minced	1
2 cups	carrot juice	500 mL
2 cups	chicken stock	500 mL
½ tsp	salt	2 mL
Pinch	freshly ground black pepper	Pinch
2 tsp	freshly squeezed lemon juice	10 mL
¼ cup	snipped fresh dill	50 mL

1. In a heavy saucepan, melt butter over medium heat. Add onion and sauté until softened, about 6 minutes. Add carrots and cardamom; sauté for 2 minutes. Add wine and ginger; cook until wine has evaporated, about 5 minutes. Add carrot juice, stock, salt and pepper; bring to a boil. Cover, reduce heat to low and simmer gently until carrots are tender, about 20 minutes.
2. Using an immersion blender, or in a food processor or blender in batches, purée soup until smooth. Transfer to a bowl and stir in lemon juice. Taste and adjust seasoning with salt and pepper, if necessary. Cover and refrigerate until cold, about 3 hours. Taste and adjust seasoning, if necessary.
3. Ladle into chilled bowls and garnish with dill.

Cold Cucumber Soup with Yogurt and Mint

▲▼▲▼▲▼▲▼▲▼▲▼▲▼▲▼▲▼▲▼▲▼▲▼▲▼▲▼▲▼▲▼▲▼▲▼▲▼▲

Nothing beats this summertime favorite for its cooling and refreshing personality. We like to use English (hothouse) cucumbers, as they are less bitter and have fewer seeds, but regular cucumbers will work fine in a pinch. Be sure to add the garnish: it is pretty and gives a nice texture to the finished soup.

▲▼▲▼▲▼▲▼▲

Tip

The easiest way to seed a cucumber is to halve it lengthwise and scrape the seeds from the flesh with a spoon.

Serves 6 to 8

2	green onions, chopped	2
2 lbs	English cucumbers, peeled, seeded and chopped	1 kg
2 cups	cold water	500 mL
1½ cups	Greek yogurt (see tip, page 30)	375 mL
1½ tsp	salt	7 mL
1½ tsp	granulated sugar	7 mL
¼ tsp	cayenne pepper	1 mL
¼ tsp	freshly ground black pepper	1 mL
2 tsp	freshly squeezed lemon juice	10 mL

Garnish

1 cup	diced seeded peeled English cucumber	250 mL
2 tbsp	chopped fresh mint	25 mL
Pinch	salt	Pinch
Pinch	freshly ground black pepper	Pinch

1. In a food processor or blender, in batches, purée green onions, cucumbers and cold water until smooth. Transfer to a large bowl and whisk in yogurt, salt, sugar, cayenne, black pepper and lemon juice. Taste and adjust seasoning with salt and black pepper, if necessary. Cover and refrigerate until cold, about 3 hours. Taste and adjust seasoning, if necessary.
2. *Prepare the garnish:* In a bowl, combine cucumber, mint, salt and pepper. Cover and refrigerate until ready to use, for up to 3 hours.
3. Ladle soup into chilled bowls and top with cucumber garnish.

Chilled Pea Soup with Cilantro Swirl

▲▼▲▼▲▼▲▼▲▼▲▼▲▼▲▼▲▼▲▼▲▼▲▼▲▼▲▼▲▼▲▼▲▼▲▼▲

It's amazing how good a soup made from a few bags of frozen peas can be. The light green color is gorgeous with the darker green swirl. Take a picture — this soup looks like a shot from a glossy food magazine.

▲▼▲▼▲▼▲▼▲▼

Tip

We're sure this soup couldn't be better even if you used freshly shucked spring peas, but do use the frozen early (or baby) peas, as they will have a better flavor than older, larger varieties.

Serves 6

¼ cup	unsalted butter	50 mL
1	small onion, minced	1
2 lbs	frozen peas, thawed	1 kg
1 tsp	granulated sugar	5 mL
½ tsp	salt	2 mL
Pinch	freshly ground white pepper	Pinch
4 cups	chicken or vegetable stock	1 L
1 cup	half-and-half (10%) cream	250 mL
½ cup	whipping (35%) cream	125 mL
Pinch	ground nutmeg	Pinch
Pinch	cayenne pepper	Pinch
	Cilantro Swirl (see variation, page 363)	

1. In a large pot, melt butter over medium heat. Add onion and sauté until softened, about 6 minutes. Add peas, sugar, salt and pepper; sauté for 2 minutes or until peas are heated through. Add stock and bring to a boil. Reduce heat and simmer for 10 minutes to blend the flavors.
2. Transfer to a food processor or blender, in batches, and purée until smooth and silky. Return to the pot and add half-and-half and whipping cream. Bring back to a simmer and add nutmeg and cayenne. Transfer to a bowl, cover and refrigerate until cold, about 3 hours. Taste and adjust seasoning with salt and pepper, if necessary.
3. Ladle into chilled bowls and drizzle Cilantro Swirl into the center of the soup. Draw a chopstick or knife through the center to create a decorative swirl.

Gazpacho

▲▼▲▼▲▼▲▼▲▼▲▼▲▼▲▼▲▼▲▼▲▼▲▼▲▼▲▼▲▼▲▼▲▼▲▼▲

We like to think of gazpacho as liquid salad in a bowl. For this soup to sing, it needs to have a balance of sweet, sour and salty. Depending on the sweetness or acidity of the tomatoes, you may need to add a little more vinegar or salt to balance the flavors.

▲▼▲▼▲▼▲▼▲

Tip
Because the quality of tomatoes can vary widely, be sure to taste your soup with a discerning palate and remedy any flavor deficiency with more salt, pepper or vinegar — or even a touch of honey, if necessary.

Variation
We love to add chilled cooked shrimp or crab as a garnish when serving this soup as a luncheon entrée.

Serves 6

5 cups	water, divided	1.25 L
2 lbs	tomatoes (about 7 medium)	1 kg
1 cup	cubed baguette or country-style bread (crusts removed)	250 mL
1 cup	chopped seeded peeled cucumber	250 mL
¾ cup	diced green bell pepper	175 mL
¾ cup	chopped red onion	175 mL
1	clove garlic, minced	1
3 tbsp	sherry vinegar	45 mL
2 tsp	salt	10 mL
¼ tsp	freshly ground black pepper	1 mL
¼ cup	extra-virgin olive oil	50 mL
	Buttery Croutons (see recipe, page 368) or Garlic Croutons (see variation, page 368)	

1. In a large saucepan, bring 4 cups (1 L) of the water to a simmer over medium-high heat. Cut an X into the skin on the bottom of each tomato and drop them 3 or 4 at a time into the simmering water. Blanch tomatoes for 1 minute, then remove with a slotted spoon to a bowl of cold water to stop the cooking. It should be easy to peel off the skin. Discard the skin and cut each tomato in half.

2. Set up a large bowl with a strainer over it and squeeze the tomatoes so that the seeds and juice run into the strainer. Discard the seeds and drop the tomato halves into the bowl with the juice. Add bread, cucumber, green pepper, red onion, garlic, vinegar, salt, pepper and the remaining water.

3. Transfer to a food processor or a blender, in batches if necessary, and purée until smooth. Pour into a large bowl and whisk in olive oil. Taste and adjust seasoning with salt, pepper and vinegar, if necessary. Cover and refrigerate until cold, about 3 hours. Taste and adjust seasoning, if necessary.

4. Ladle into chilled bowls and garnish with croutons.

Yellow Tomato Gazpacho
with Cilantro Oil

We like this soup as an easy and light alternative to traditional Spanish gazpacho. With no bread or olive oil, it's low in fat — but it's big in flavor.

Tip

If yellow tomatoes are not available, red ones work just as well. Do wait, though, for tomatoes to be in season, as that is when this soup will shine.

Serves 6

1	yellow bell pepper, chopped	1
½	English cucumber, peeled, seeded and chopped	½
1½ lbs	yellow tomatoes (about 5 medium), chopped	750 g
½ cup	chopped sweet onion (such as Vidalia)	125 mL
1 tsp	minced garlic	5 mL
2 tbsp	sherry vinegar	25 mL
	Salt and freshly ground black pepper	
	Cilantro Oil (see recipe, page 362)	

1. In a food processor or blender, in batches if necessary, process yellow pepper, cucumber, tomatoes, onion and garlic until almost smooth. Transfer to a bowl and stir in vinegar. Season to taste with salt and pepper. Cover and refrigerate until cold, about 3 hours. Taste and adjust seasoning with vinegar, salt and pepper, if necessary.
2. Ladle into chilled bowls and drizzle with Cilantro Oil.

Bloody Mary Soup

▲▽▲▽▲▽▲▽▲▽▲▽▲▽▲▽▲▽▲▽▲▽▲▽▲▽▲▽▲▽▲▽▲▽▲▽▲▽▲

We used the bloody Mary as inspiration for this spicy, tomato-based soup. Have fun with the add-ins: anything from pickled vegetables to shrimp and crab makes a great garnish.

▲▽▲▽▲▽▲▽▲▽▲

Tips

San Marzano tomatoes are thought by many to be the best sauce tomatoes in the world. They hail from a small town of the same name near Naples. San Marzano's volcanic soil is thought to filter impurities from the water and render tomatoes with thick flesh, fewer seeds and a stronger taste.

Salad shrimp, also known as bay shrimp, can be found in the freezer section. They are cooked tiny shrimp that need only a thaw in the refrigerator. We give them a rinse in cold water to freshen them up.

Variation

Instead of shrimp, garnish with cooked crabmeat and diced avocado, or crumbled crispy bacon and chopped green onions.

Serves 6 to 8

2	cans (each 28 oz/796 mL) San Marzano tomatoes, with juice	2
1 cup	beef or chicken stock (approx.)	250 mL
¼ cup	chopped green onions	50 mL
¼ cup	Worcestershire sauce	50 mL
¼ cup	vodka	50 mL
2 tbsp	prepared horseradish	25 mL
2 tbsp	liquid honey	25 mL
1 tbsp	freshly squeezed lemon juice	15 mL
2 tsp	salt	10 mL
2 tsp	celery salt	10 mL
1 tsp	freshly ground black pepper	5 mL
1 lb	chilled salad shrimp	500 g
¼ cup	chopped fresh cilantro	50 mL

1. In a food processor or blender, in batches, purée tomatoes with juice, stock, green onions, Worcestershire sauce, vodka, horseradish, honey, lemon juice, salt, celery salt and pepper until smooth. Transfer to a large pitcher, taste and adjust seasoning with salt and pepper. Thin with more stock or water, if desired. Cover and refrigerate until cold, about 3 hours. Taste and adjust seasoning, if necessary.
2. Pour into chilled bowls and garnish with shrimp and cilantro.

Shrimp Cocktail Soup
with Horseradish Cream

You can make this a completely no-cook soup if you buy the shrimp already cooked and add them in at the end, but we love the way the halved shrimp curl and look so pretty in this colorful cold soup.

▲▼▲▼▲▼▲▼▲▼

Tip
Chilled soups will stay cold for much longer in chilled bowls.

Serves 6 to 8

8 cups	chilled vegetable cocktail (such as V8)	2 L
¼ cup	Worcestershire sauce	50 mL
2 tbsp	prepared horseradish	25 mL
2 tbsp	freshly squeezed lemon juice	25 mL
1 tsp	celery salt	5 mL
1 tsp	cracked black pepper	5 mL
1 lb	medium shrimp, peeled and halved lengthwise	500 g
	Juice of 1 lemon	
2 tbsp	minced fresh chives	25 mL

Horseradish Cream

½ cup	whipping (35%) cream	125 mL
1 tbsp	prepared horseradish	15 mL
	Salt and freshly ground black pepper	

1. In a large pitcher, combine vegetable juice, Worcestershire sauce, horseradish, 2 tbsp (25 mL) lemon juice, celery salt and pepper. Taste and adjust seasoning with celery salt, pepper, lemon juice or horseradish, if necessary. Cover and refrigerate until cold, about 3 hours. Taste and adjust seasoning, if necessary.

2. Meanwhile, bring a large pot of salted water to a boil. Add shrimp and lemon juice. Cover, remove from heat and let stand for 3 minutes. Drain shrimp and plunge into an ice bath to cool quickly. Drain again and pat dry. The shrimp will have curled into attractive corkscrew shapes. Cover and refrigerate until ready to serve, for up to 3 hours.

3. *Prepare the horseradish cream:* In a bowl, beat cream with a whisk or mixer until thick. Fold in horseradish and salt and pepper to taste. Cover and refrigerate until ready to serve, for up to 24 hours.

4. Pour soup into chilled bowls and garnish with shrimp and horseradish cream. Sprinkle with chives.

Vichyssoise

▲▼▲▼▲▼▲▼▲▼▲▼▲▼▲▼▲▼▲▼▲▼▲▼▲▼▲▼▲▼▲▼▲▼▲

Vichyssoise is a fancy name for a simple potato soup served cold. But it's versatile: sophisticated when served cold, it can be an excellent comfort food when served hot.

▲▼▲▼▲▼▲▼

Tips

Sometimes the soup will thicken as it cools. If it is too thick, thin it with chicken stock or milk until it is the right texture. Remember to taste for seasoning after thinning — it might need adjustment.

If you want to serve this soup hot, reheat in a saucepan over medium-low heat until heated through.

Serves 6

¼ cup	unsalted butter	50 mL
2	leeks (white part only), thinly sliced	2
1	onion, minced	1
½ tsp	salt	2 mL
6 cups	chicken or vegetable stock	1.5 L
3 lbs	baking potatoes, peeled and diced	1.5 kg
1	bay leaf	1
1 cup	half-and-half (10%) cream	250 mL
¼ cup	whipping (35%) cream	50 mL
1 tbsp	freshly squeezed lemon juice	15 mL
Pinch	freshly ground white or black pepper	Pinch
Pinch	ground nutmeg	Pinch
Pinch	cayenne pepper	Pinch
2 tbsp	minced fresh chives	25 mL

1. In a large pot, melt butter over medium-high heat until sizzling. Add leeks, onion and salt; sauté until softened, about 5 minutes. Add stock, potatoes and bay leaf; bring to a boil. Reduce heat and simmer until potatoes are tender, about 20 minutes. Discard bay leaf.

2. Using an immersion blender, or in a food processor or blender in batches, purée soup until smooth. Transfer to a bowl and stir in half-and-half, whipping cream, lemon juice, white pepper, nutmeg and cayenne. Cover and refrigerate until cold, about 3 hours. Taste and adjust seasoning with salt and white pepper, if necessary.

3. Ladle into chilled bowls and garnish with chives.

Zucchini Vichyssoise
with Tarragon Pesto

▲▼▲▼▲▼▲▼▲▼▲▼▲▼▲▼▲▼▲▼▲▼▲▼▲▼▲▼▲▼▲▼▲▼▲▼

The anise flavor of tarragon is subtle in this beautiful pale green soup that is delicious cold in the summer, when zucchini is at its peak, or hot in the winter when you need a breath of summer to get you through the bleak, cold days.

▲▼▲▼▲▼▲▼▲▼▲

Tips

Use caution when blending hot liquids. It's best to cover the top of the food processor or blender with a towel to prevent any hot soup from splattering out.

If you want to serve this soup hot, reheat in a saucepan over medium-low heat until heated through.

Serves 6

2 tbsp	unsalted butter	25 mL
1	onion, chopped	1
1 lb	baking potatoes, peeled and diced	500 g
4	sprigs fresh tarragon	4
2	cloves garlic, chopped	2
6 cups	chicken stock	1.5 L
2 lbs	small zucchini (about 5 inches/13 cm long), cut into ½-inch (1 cm) cubes	1 kg
½ cup	cold whipping (35%) cream	125 mL
2 tbsp	freshly squeezed lemon juice	25 mL
	Salt and freshly ground black pepper	
	Tarragon Pesto (see recipe, page 363)	

1. In a large pot, melt butter over medium heat. Add onion and sauté until softened, about 6 minutes. Add potatoes, tarragon and garlic; sauté for 1 minute. Add stock and bring to a boil. Reduce heat and simmer for 15 minutes. Add zucchini and simmer, covered, until potatoes and zucchini are very tender, about 10 minutes. Discard tarragon.

2. Using an immersion blender, or in a food processor or blender in batches, purée soup until smooth. Transfer to a bowl and stir in cream, lemon juice and salt and pepper to taste. Let cool to room temperature. Cover and refrigerate until cold, about 4 hours, or for up to 2 days. Taste and adjust seasoning with salt and pepper, if necessary.

3. Ladle into chilled bowls and garnish each with a dollop of Tarragon Pesto.

Fresh from the Garden Vegetable Soups

▲▼▲▼▲▼▲▼▲▼▲▼▲▼▲▼▲▼▲▼▲▼▲▼▲▼▲

continued on next page

Cream of Artichoke Soup

▲▼▲▼▲▼▲▼▲▼▲▼▲▼▲▼▲▼▲▼▲▼▲▼▲▼▲▼▲▼▲▼▲▼▲▼▲▼▲

No need to worry about the prickly leaves of fresh artichokes for this easy-to-make soup. We use a generous amount of frozen artichoke hearts to give it its rich, earthy flavor.

▲▼▲▼▲▼▲▼▲

Tip

Use caution when blending hot liquids. It's best to cover the top of the food processor or blender with a towel to prevent any hot soup from splattering out.

Serves 6 to 8

2 tbsp	olive oil	25 mL
2	leeks, white part only, chopped	2
2	cloves garlic, minced	2
2	packages (each 8 oz/250 g) frozen artichoke hearts, thawed	2
1	small potato, peeled and chopped	1
6 cups	chicken stock	1.5 L
1 tsp	chopped fresh thyme	5 mL
½ tsp	salt	2 mL
¼ tsp	freshly ground black pepper	1 mL
Pinch	ground nutmeg	Pinch
Pinch	cayenne pepper	Pinch
½ cup	whipping (35%) cream	125 mL
1 tbsp	freshly squeezed lemon juice	15 mL
	Lemon and Chive Compound Butter (see recipe, page 367)	

1. In a large, heavy pot, heat oil over medium heat. Add leeks and garlic; sauté until softened, about 6 minutes. Add artichokes, potato, stock, thyme, salt, black pepper, nutmeg and cayenne; reduce heat and simmer until vegetables are tender, about 20 minutes.
2. Using an immersion blender, or in a food processor or blender in batches, purée soup until smooth. Return to the pot, if necessary. Stir in cream and lemon juice; reheat over medium heat, stirring often, until steaming. Do not let boil. Taste and adjust seasoning with salt and pepper, if necessary.
3. Ladle into heated bowls and garnish each with a slice of compound butter.

Cream of Asparagus Soup

▲▽▲

Simple soups are sometimes the best, and this is the perfect example. Asparagus, when in season and at its prime, doesn't need much help to be extraordinary. We've taken that to heart with a soup that lets the asparagus shine.

▲▽▲▽▲▽▲▽▲▽▲

Tip
Soup will stay hot much longer in a heated bowl.

Serves 4 to 6

2 lbs	asparagus	1 kg
2 tbsp	unsalted butter	25 mL
1	onion, chopped	1
2 tbsp	all-purpose flour	25 mL
4 cups	chicken stock	1 L
½ cup	whipping (35%) cream	125 mL
1 tsp	freshly squeezed lemon juice	5 mL
	Salt and freshly ground black pepper	
	Buttery Croutons (see recipe, page 368) or Lemon and Chive Compound Butter (see recipe, page 367)	

1. Trim off the tough bottoms of the asparagus and peel stalks. Rinse spears, pat dry and cut into 1½-inch (4 cm) pieces, reserving tips separately. Set aside.
2. In a large pot, melt butter over medium heat. Add onion and sauté until softened, about 6 minutes. Sprinkle with flour and sauté for 2 minutes.
3. Gradually whisk in stock. Add asparagus spears and bring to a boil. Reduce heat and simmer, stirring occasionally, until asparagus is very soft, about 25 minutes.
4. Meanwhile, in a saucepan of boiling salted water, cook asparagus tips until just tender-crisp, about 2 minutes. Drain and plunge tips into cold water to refresh, changing water as necessary as it warms up. Set aside.
5. Using an immersion blender, or in a food processor or blender in batches, purée soup until smooth. Return to the pot, if necessary. Stir in cream and reheat over medium heat, stirring often, until steaming. Do not let boil. Reduce heat to low and stir in lemon juice. Season with salt and pepper to taste.
6. Ladle into heated bowls and garnish with asparagus tips and croutons or a slice of compound butter.

Lemony Cream of Asparagus Soup

This light, clean-flavored soup blends the springtime flavors of lemon and asparagus beautifully.

Tip

We like to use a Microplane grater to grate citrus zest.

Serves 6 to 8

1½ lbs	asparagus	750 g
5 cups	chicken stock	1.25 L
½ cup	minced shallots	125 mL
1	baking potato, peeled and cut into small dice	1
	Finely grated zest of 2 lemons	
¾ cup	whipping (35%) cream	175 mL
¼ cup	freshly squeezed lemon juice	50 mL
	Salt and freshly ground black pepper	
	Additional grated lemon zest	

1. Trim off the tough bottoms of the asparagus and peel stalks. Rinse spears, pat dry and cut into 1½-inch (4 cm) pieces, reserving tips separately. Set aside.
2. In a large pot, bring stock to a boil. Add asparagus tips and cook until just tender, about 2 minutes. Remove with a slotted spoon and set aside.
3. Add asparagus spears, shallots, potato and lemon zest to the stock and bring to a simmer. Simmer, stirring occasionally, until potato is very soft, about 25 minutes.
4. Using an immersion blender, or in a food processor or blender in batches, purée soup until smooth. Return to the pot, if necessary. Stir in cream and reheat over medium heat, stirring often, until steaming. Do not let boil. Reduce heat to low and stir in lemon juice. Season with salt and pepper to taste.
5. Ladle into heated bowls and garnish with asparagus tips and lemon zest.

Hot Guacamole Soup
with Cumin and Cilantro

We are crazy for avocados, so we had to come up with a hot avocado soup for those times when a cold soup simply won't do. We've kept it simple so as not to muddy the irresistible flavor of this hearty staple.

Tip

The challenge in making this soup lies in finding perfectly ripe avocados. This is definitely a dish to plan ahead for, since most avocados found in the grocery store are as hard as rocks. Luckily, they ripen beautifully on your kitchen counter in a few days. Ripe avocados should yield slightly when pressed.

Serves 6

3	avocados, halved	3
6 cups	chicken or vegetable stock, divided	1.5 L
2 tbsp	olive oil	25 mL
3	cloves garlic, minced	3
1 tsp	ground cumin	5 mL
½ tsp	salt	2 mL
	Freshly ground black pepper	
½ cup	sour cream	125 mL
¼ cup	chopped fresh cilantro	50 mL
2 tbsp	freshly squeezed lime juice	25 mL
	Crispy Tortilla Strips (see recipe, page 372)	
	Pico de Gallo Salsa (see recipe, page 364)	

1. In a food processor or blender, purée avocados and half the stock until smooth. Set aside.
2. In a large pot, heat oil over medium-high heat. Add garlic and cumin; sauté until garlic is fragrant and softened, about 2 minutes. Add avocado mixture, the remaining stock, salt and pepper to taste. Reduce heat to medium and bring almost to a simmer, stirring often. Be careful not to let the soup boil or the thickened avocado will scorch the bottom of the pan. Whisk in sour cream, cilantro and lime juice; heat for 1 minute. Taste and adjust seasoning with salt and pepper, if necessary.
3. Ladle into heated bowls and garnish with tortilla strips and salsa.

Cream of Broccoli Soup with Bacon Bits

▲▼▲▼▲▼▲▼▲▼▲▼▲▼▲▼▲▼▲▼▲▼▲▼▲▼▲▼▲▼▲▼▲▼▲▼▲

Even the kids will eat their broccoli when you make it into this hearty, satisfying soup. We start out with everyone's favorite, bacon, and fry it up, leaving some of its flavor in the pot to help out the soup. We make it even better by adding a bit of half-and-half cream to smooth out the rough edges.

▲▼▲▼▲▼▲▼▲▼

Tip

Use the tender green part of the broccoli stalk, about 3 inches (7.5 cm) down from where it branches out. The lower part of the stalk can be used in vegetable stock.

Serves 6 to 8

2 tbsp	olive oil	25 mL
6	slices bacon, chopped	6
3	cloves garlic, minced	3
1	onion, chopped	1
1 tbsp	all-purpose flour	15 mL
6 cups	chicken or vegetable stock	1.5 L
1½ lbs	broccoli florets and stalks (about 3 large stalks), chopped (about 4 cups/1 L)	750 g
2	potatoes, peeled and diced	2
2 tsp	dried tarragon	10 mL
½ cup	half-and-half (10%) cream	125 mL
1 tsp	cider vinegar	5 mL
Pinch	cayenne pepper	Pinch
Pinch	ground nutmeg	Pinch
	Salt and freshly ground black pepper	

1. In a large pot, heat oil over medium-high heat. Add bacon and cook until crisp, about 5 minutes. Remove with a slotted spoon to a plate lined with paper towels.
2. Pour off all but 2 tbsp (25 mL) of the fat in the pot. Add garlic and onion; sauté for 1 minute. Sprinkle with flour and sauté for 2 minutes.
3. Gradually whisk in stock. Add broccoli, potatoes and tarragon; bring to a boil. Reduce heat and simmer, stirring often, until vegetables are tender, about 10 minutes. Add cream, vinegar, cayenne and nutmeg. Season with salt and black pepper to taste.
4. Ladle into heated bowls and garnish with reserved bacon.

Broccoli Buttermilk Soup

▲▽▲▽▲▽▲▽▲▽▲▽▲▽▲▽▲▽▲▽▲▽▲▽▲▽▲▽▲▽▲▽▲▽▲▽▲

We especially like the tang that buttermilk gives this soup. The addition of toasted bread and a drizzle of olive oil makes this light green soup a little more substantial for hearty eaters and lets the fresh green flavor of the broccoli really shine through.

▲▽▲▽▲▽▲▽▲▽

Tip

Be careful not to let the soup boil after adding the buttermilk, or it will curdle.

Serves 6

1½ lbs	broccoli (about 3 large stalks)	750 g
2 tbsp	unsalted butter	25 mL
1	onion, chopped	1
½ tsp	salt	2 mL
½ tsp	dried thyme	2 mL
4 cups	chicken or vegetable stock	1 L
1	bay leaf	1
2 cups	buttermilk	500 mL
Pinch	cayenne pepper	Pinch
Pinch	ground nutmeg	Pinch
	Freshly ground black pepper	
	Spicy Mustard Croutons (see recipe, page 370) or Buttery Croutons (see recipe, page 368)	

1. Cut the broccoli florets from the stalks and trim them into smaller pieces. Measure out 1 cup (250 mL) of the florets and set the remainder aside. Peel and thinly slice the stalks and set aside separately from the florets.
2. In a saucepan of boiling water, blanch the 1 cup (250 mL) florets until tender-crisp, about 2 minutes. Drain and plunge florets into ice water to set the color. Pat dry and set aside to use as garnish.
3. In a large pot, melt butter over medium-high heat. Add onion, salt and thyme; sauté until onion is softened, about 3 minutes. Add broccoli stalks, stock and bay leaf; bring to a boil. Reduce heat and simmer until broccoli is almost tender, about 8 minutes. Add uncooked broccoli florets and simmer for 3 minutes. Discard bay leaf.
4. Using an immersion blender, or in a food processor or blender in batches, purée soup until smooth. Return to the pot, if necessary. Stir in buttermilk and reheat over medium heat, stirring often, until steaming. Do not let boil. Season with cayenne, nutmeg and salt and black pepper to taste.
5. Ladle into heated bowls and garnish with reserved broccoli florets and croutons.

Creamy Cabbage and Bacon Soup

▲▼▲▼▲▼▲▼▲▼▲▼▲▼▲▼▲▼▲▼▲▼▲▼▲▼▲▼▲▼▲▼▲▼▲▼▲▼▲

If you're having any trouble getting in touch with your inner leprechaun, one bowl of this deeply Irish soup will have you sitting in clover.

▲▼▲▼▲▼▲▼▲

Tip

We've made some suggestions for garnishes, but feel free to look through the toppings and garnishes chapter (pages 361–374) and mix and match to your heart's delight.

Serves 4

4	slices bacon, chopped	4
2 tbsp	unsalted butter	25 mL
1	onion, chopped	1
1	leek, white and light green parts only, sliced	1
6 cups	chopped savoy cabbage	1.5 L
½ tsp	salt	2 mL
¼ tsp	freshly ground black pepper	1 mL
4 cups	chicken stock	1 L
2 cups	diced peeled potatoes	500 mL
1 cup	whipping (35%) cream	250 mL
	Pumpernickel Croutons (see variation, page 368) or Buttery Croutons (see recipe, page 368)	
	Chopped fresh chives	

1. In a large pot, cook bacon over medium heat, stirring occasionally, until it renders its fat, about 5 minutes. Add butter, onion and leek; sauté until softened, about 6 minutes. Add cabbage, salt and pepper; cover and cook, stirring occasionally, until cabbage is tender, about 10 minutes. Add stock and potatoes; bring to a boil. Reduce heat and simmer until potatoes are tender, about 20 minutes. Add cream and simmer, stirring occasionally, until soup achieves a creamy texture, about 10 minutes.
2. Using an immersion blender, or in a food processor or blender in batches, process soup, leaving the texture a bit chunky. Return to the pot, if necessary. Reheat over medium heat, stirring occasionally, until steaming. Do not let boil. Taste and adjust seasoning with salt and pepper, if necessary.
3. Ladle into heated bowls and garnish with croutons and chives.

Curry-Spiced Carrot Soup

▲▽▲

Carrots provide a great background flavor for assertive spices. We've imbued this bright orange soup with the colorful flavors of the East, using curry powder easily procured from our local grocery store. If you can find an Indian market, by all means get your spices there — they will be fresher and more flavorful.

▲▽▲▽▲▽▲▽▲

Tip

You can use store-bought curry powder or make your own, using our recipe on page 27.

Serves 6

2 tbsp	unsalted butter	25 mL
2 tbsp	olive oil	25 mL
2	onions, finely chopped	2
1½ lbs	carrots (about 8 medium), chopped	750 g
1 tbsp	curry powder	15 mL
½ tsp	salt	2 mL
6 cups	chicken or vegetable stock	1.5 L
½ cup	long-grain white rice	125 mL
2 tsp	freshly squeezed lemon juice	10 mL
	Freshly ground black pepper	
1 cup	half-and-half (10%) cream	250 mL
¼ cup	minced fresh cilantro	50 mL
	Cheesy Croutons (see recipe, page 369), made with Gruyère cheese	

1. In a large pot, heat butter and olive oil over medium-high heat. Add onion and sauté until softened, about 6 minutes. Add carrots, curry powder and salt; sauté until carrots start to soften, about 5 minutes. Add stock and bring to a boil. Add rice, reduce heat and simmer until carrots and rice are tender, about 20 minutes.
2. Using an immersion blender, or in a food processor or blender in batches, purée soup until smooth. Return to the pot, if necessary, and stir in lemon juice and salt and pepper to taste. Stir in cream and reheat over medium heat, stirring occasionally, until steaming. Do not let boil.
3. Ladle into heated bowls and garnish with cilantro and croutons.

Carrot, Celery and Leek Soup with Cornbread Dumplings

▲▼▲▼▲▼▲▼▲▼▲▼▲▼▲▼▲▼▲▼▲▼▲▼▲▼▲▼▲▼▲▼▲▼▲

We love recipes like this for their hearty, stick-to-your-ribs personality. The sweet leeks and carrots shine next to the tender cornbread dumplings, which soak up flavor from the stock and vegetables. Make this comforting, rich soup on a cold and stormy winter day and you won't want to stop eating it.

▲▼▲▼▲▼▲▼▲

Variation

This recipe turns into a pot pie with the addition of chicken or turkey. You can poach a few chopped breasts in the stock with the vegetables or simply add leftover cooked chicken or turkey just before topping with the dumplings.

Serves 6

2 tbsp	olive oil	25 mL
2 tbsp	unsalted butter	25 mL
3	leeks, white part only, thinly sliced	3
6	carrots (about 12 oz/375 g), thinly sliced	6
2	stalks celery, thinly sliced	2
½ tsp	each salt and dried thyme	2 mL
Pinch	each freshly ground black pepper and cayenne pepper	Pinch
6 cups	chicken or vegetable stock	1.5 L
1 cup	half-and-half (10%) cream	250 mL
¼ cup	minced fresh flat-leaf (Italian) parsley	50 mL

Cornbread Dumplings

1 cup	all-purpose flour	250 mL
¼ cup	stone-ground cornmeal	50 mL
1 tsp	baking powder	5 mL
¼ tsp	each baking soda and salt	1 mL
2	eggs, beaten	2
½ cup	buttermilk	125 mL
2 tbsp	unsalted butter, melted	25 mL
½ cup	frozen corn kernels, thawed	125 mL

1. In a large pot, heat oil and butter over medium-high heat. Add leeks and sauté until starting to soften, about 2 minutes. Add carrots, celery, salt, thyme, black pepper and cayenne; sauté until vegetables start to soften, about 5 minutes. Add stock, cream and parsley; bring to a simmer. Reduce heat and simmer, stirring occasionally, while you assemble the dumplings.
2. *Prepare the dumplings:* In a large bowl, combine flour, cornmeal, baking powder, baking soda and salt.
3. In another bowl, whisk together eggs, buttermilk and butter. Pour over dry ingredients, along with corn. Using a large spatula, fold the dry ingredients into the wet just until mixed. (Don't overmix, or the dumplings will be heavy and tough.) Drop dumpling batter by tablespoonfuls (15 mL) into simmering soup. Cover, reduce heat to low and simmer until vegetables are tender and dumplings are cooked through, about 20 minutes.
4. Ladle into heated bowls.

Carrot, Parsnip and Celery Root Soup with Porcini Mushrooms

▲▽▲▽▲▽▲▽▲▽▲▽▲▽▲▽▲▽▲▽▲▽▲▽▲▽▲▽▲▽▲▽▲▽▲▽▲▽▲

Root vegetables have a sweet, earthy flavor that pairs well with mushrooms, especially dried porcinis. Though difficult to find fresh, dried porcinis are easily found in the produce section of most grocery stores. Once hydrated, you have tasty mushrooms *and the* tasty mushroom liquid *to add even more mushroom flavor to your soup.*

▲▽▲▽▲▽▲▽▲

Tips

Filtering the mushroom liquid removes any dirt that may have been loosened from the mushrooms as they soaked.

To prepare celery root, use a sharp vegetable peeler or a paring knife to remove the outer layer. You'll need a large, sharp knife to cut it into cubes.

Serves 6 to 8

¼ oz	dried porcini mushrooms	7 g
1 cup	boiling water	250 mL
3 tbsp	olive oil	45 mL
2	cloves garlic, minced	2
1	onion, chopped	1
1	stalk celery, chopped	1
1 tsp	dried marjoram	5 mL
1 tsp	dried thyme	5 mL
1 cup	dry white wine	250 mL
1 cup	whipping (35%) cream	250 mL
6 cups	vegetable or chicken stock	1.5 L
2	carrots, cut into 1-inch (2.5 cm) cubes	2
2	parsnips, cut into 1-inch (2.5 cm) cubes	2
1	sweet potato, peeled and cut into 1-inch (2.5 cm) cubes	1
1	celery root (celeriac), cut into 1-inch (2.5 cm) cubes	1
1	leek, white and light green parts only, thinly sliced	1
1	bay leaf	1
1 tsp	salt	5 mL
¼ tsp	freshly ground black pepper	1 mL
Pinch	ground nutmeg	Pinch
Pinch	cayenne pepper	Pinch
¼ cup	minced fresh flat-leaf (Italian) parsley	50 mL
1 tsp	freshly squeezed lemon juice	5 mL
	Gingery Crème Fraîche Swirl (see variation, page 365)	

Tips

To trim leeks, cut off and discard the root end and the dark green tops (or save the tops for stock). Cut leeks lengthwise and wash under running water to remove any grit or dirt. Then cut as directed in the recipe.

When we instruct you to cut vegetables to a certain size, it's because we think size really does matter in the recipe. In some recipes, we like disciplined dice because the vegetables cook more evenly, and we think the uniformly chopped vegetables make for a nice texture and a more attractive soup.

1. In a small bowl, soak mushrooms in boiling water until softened, about 30 minutes. Using a slotted spoon, gently lift mushrooms from liquid and swish in a bowl of cold water to remove any clinging sand or dirt. Chop and set aside. Pour mushroom liquid through a sieve lined with a coffee filter into a small bowl and set aside.

2. In a large pot, heat oil over medium-high heat. Add garlic, onion, celery, marjoram and thyme; sauté until vegetables are softened, about 3 minutes. Add wine and cook until reduced by half, about 5 minutes. Add cream and cook until reduced by half, about 5 minutes. Add stock, reserved mushroom liquid, mushrooms, cubed carrots, parsnips, sweet potato, celery root, leek, bay leaf and salt; bring to a boil. Partially cover, reduce heat to low and simmer gently until vegetables are tender, about 25 minutes.

3. Using an immersion blender, pulse the soup in 3 or 4 quick spurts to partially blend it, leaving it chunky (or process half the soup in a food processor or blender in batches, then return to the pot). Season with black pepper, nutmeg, cayenne and salt to taste. Stir in parsley and lemon juice.

4. Ladle into heated bowls and drizzle Gingery Crème Fraîche Swirl into the center of the soup. Draw a chopstick or knife through the crème to create a marbling effect.

Roasted Cauliflower Soup with Bacon

▲▽▲

It would be easy to skip the roasting step and just throw the cauliflower into the pot raw, but in our opinion cauliflower is one of those vegetables that benefits greatly from being roasted. The oven browning brings out its sweetness and concentrates its flavor like no soak in a liquid ever could. Add salty bacon, and you've got a no-holds-barred flavor-fest going on in your mouth. Finally, we decided to thicken it with bread, which Grandma would definitely have approved of.

▲▽▲▽▲▽▲▽▲▽

Tip

Seasoning with a little bit of vinegar at the end of cooking heightens the flavor of the soup. Although most home cooks think only in terms of salt and pepper when it comes to adjusting the seasoning in their dishes, we've found that a little acid goes a long way toward making a soup taste just right.

Serves 6

- Preheat oven to 400°F (200°C)
- Rimmed baking sheet

1	head cauliflower, cut into 2-inch (5 cm) pieces	1
⅓ cup	olive oil, divided	75 mL
8	slices bacon, chopped	8
1	onion, finely chopped	1
3 tbsp	finely chopped garlic	45 mL
6 cups	chicken or vegetable stock	1.5 L
3 cups	torn French or Italian bread (crusts removed)	750 mL
1 tsp	paprika	5 mL
Pinch	cayenne pepper	Pinch
2 tsp	white wine vinegar	10 mL
½ tsp	salt	2 mL
¼ tsp	freshly ground black pepper	1 mL
2 tbsp	minced fresh flat-leaf (Italian) parsley	25 mL

1. On baking sheet, combine cauliflower and 2 tbsp (25 mL) of the olive oil; toss to coat evenly and spread in a single layer. Roast in preheated oven until soft and brown around the edges, about 20 minutes. Set aside.
2. In a large pot, heat the remaining oil over medium heat. Add bacon and cook until crisp. Remove with a slotted spoon to a plate lined with paper towels.
3. Pour off all but about 3 tbsp (45 mL) of the fat in the pot. Add onion and garlic; sauté for 2 minutes. Add cauliflower, stock, bread, paprika and cayenne; bring to a boil. Reduce heat and simmer until cauliflower is tender, about 10 minutes. Stir in vinegar.
4. Using an immersion blender, or in a food processor or blender in batches, purée soup until smooth. Return to the pot, if necessary, and season with salt and black pepper.
5. Ladle into heated bowls and garnish with parsley and bacon.

Cream of Cauliflower Soup

▲▽▲▽▲▽▲▽▲▽▲▽▲▽▲▽▲▽▲▽▲▽▲▽▲▽▲▽▲▽▲▽▲▽▲▽▲

Rich and silky cream of cauliflower soup gets its luxurious texture from a classic French technique called liaison. By whisking eggs into the warm liquid and heating just until the eggs thicken the soup, an unmistakably velvety texture is created.

▲▽▲▽▲▽▲▽▲

Tip

An immersion blender is one of our favorite kitchen tools. Because it can be immersed in the soup, it saves you from transferring hot liquids from the pot to a blender or food processor. Look for one that has a detachable blade unit for easy cleaning.

Serves 6

3 tbsp	unsalted butter	45 mL
3	slices bacon, chopped	3
1 cup	onion, finely chopped	250 mL
⅓ cup	all-purpose flour	75 mL
4 cups	chicken or vegetable stock	1 L
1 cup	water	250 mL
1	small head cauliflower, florets only, cut into 1-inch (2.5 cm) pieces	1
1½ cups	milk	375 mL
1½ tsp	salt	7 mL
¼ tsp	freshly ground white pepper	1 mL
¼ tsp	ground nutmeg	1 mL
2	egg yolks, lightly beaten	2
½ tsp	freshly squeezed lemon juice	2 mL
Pinch	cayenne pepper (optional)	Pinch
¼ cup	minced fresh parsley or chives (optional)	50 mL

1. In a large pot, melt butter over medium-high heat. Add bacon and onion; sauté until onion is translucent, about 4 minutes. Sprinkle with flour, reduce heat to medium and sauté for 2 minutes.

2. Gradually whisk in stock and water; increase heat to high and bring to a boil, stirring often. Add cauliflower, reduce heat and simmer, stirring often, until cauliflower is tender, about 20 minutes.

3. Using an immersion blender, or in a food processor or blender in batches, purée soup until smooth. Return to the pot, if necessary. Stir in milk, salt, white pepper and nutmeg; bring to a simmer over medium heat. Remove from heat and let cool for 10 minutes.

4. Gradually whisk 1 cup (250 mL) of the soup into the beaten eggs. Slowly pour back into the pot, stirring constantly. Simmer, stirring constantly, for about 3 minutes. Do not let boil, or the eggs will curdle. Stir in lemon juice and cayenne (if using). Taste and adjust seasoning with salt, white pepper, nutmeg and cayenne, if necessary.

5. Ladle into heated bowls and garnish with parsley or chives, if desired.

Chestnut Soup with Truffle Oil

Chestnuts have a nice meaty flavor on their own, but when you garnish them with truffle oil, you've hit the flavor jackpot.

Tip

Truffle oil is usually an olive oil infused with the flavor of truffles. The scent of truffle is hard to describe; it's kind of mushroomy, but deeper. Look for truffle oil in the oil section of your local grocery store or at specialty food stores.

Serves 6

2 tbsp	unsalted butter	25 mL
⅔ cup	minced shallots	150 mL
⅓ cup	minced celery	75 mL
3	cans (each 8 oz/250 g) whole chestnuts, drained	3
5 cups	chicken stock	1.25 L
½ cup	whipping (35%) cream	125 mL
½ tsp	salt	2 mL
	Freshly ground black pepper	
2 tbsp	truffle oil (see tip, at left)	25 mL
	Minced fresh flat-leaf (Italian) parsley	

1. In a large pot, melt butter over medium heat. Add shallots and celery; sauté until softened, about 3 minutes. Add chestnuts and stock; bring to a boil. Reduce heat and simmer for about 20 minutes to blend the flavors.
2. Using an immersion blender, or in food processor or blender in batches, purée soup until smooth. Return to the pot, if necessary. Stir in cream, salt and pepper to taste; bring to a simmer over medium heat, stirring occasionally.
3. Ladle into heated bowls and garnish with a drizzle of truffle oil and parsley.

Silky Cream of Corn Soup with Chipotle

▲▼▲

We made this soup in the summer with fresh local corn and thought it tasted like summer in a bowl. But even if you make it in the winter, using frozen corn, it will still taste great.

▲▼▲▼▲▼▲▼▲

Tip

If you use fresh corn, you'll need about 4 ears. Throw the cobs in the soup as it cooks; they will give up even more corn flavor. Just fish them out before puréeing. For almost-fresh flavor, use frozen white corn. It has more taste and better texture than the larger yellow kernels.

Serves 6 to 8

¼ cup	olive oil	50 mL
1 cup	chopped onion	250 mL
¼ cup	chopped celery	50 mL
2	cloves garlic, minced	2
½ tsp	dried oregano	2 mL
4 cups	fresh or frozen corn kernels (see tip, at left)	1 L
4 cups	chicken or vegetable stock	1 L
1 cup	milk	250 mL
½ tsp	salt	2 mL
¼ tsp	freshly ground black pepper	1 mL
¼ tsp	chipotle chile powder or cayenne pepper	1 mL
¼ cup	torn fresh basil	50 mL
	Garlic Croutons (see variation, page 368)	

1. In a large pot, heat oil over medium-high heat. Add onion and celery; sauté until starting to soften, 2 to 3 minutes. Add garlic and oregano; sauté until garlic is fragrant, about 1 minute. Add corn and stock; bring to a boil. Reduce heat and simmer until corn is tender and flavors are blended, about 20 minutes.
2. Using an immersion blender, pulse the soup in 3 or 4 quick spurts to partially blend it, leaving it chunky (or process half the soup in a food processor or blender in batches, then return to the pot). Stir in milk, salt, black pepper and chipotle powder; bring to a simmer over medium heat, stirring often. Taste and adjust seasoning with salt, black pepper and chipotle powder, if necessary.
3. Ladle into heated bowls and garnish with basil and croutons.

Garlic Soup with Aïoli

▲▼▲▼▲▼▲▼▲▼▲▼▲▼▲▼▲▼▲▼▲▼▲▼▲▼▲▼▲▼▲▼▲▼▲

Garlic soup is peasant food at its best. Almost every Western cuisine has a version of bread soup made famous by wives, mothers and grandmothers as a way to use up stale bread. Their soups were probably made with water, but we like the richness the stock imparts to this family favorite.

▲▼▲▼▲▼▲▼▲▼

Tips

Simple soups enriched with bread can sometimes have a slippery feel in your mouth. If you find this unpleasant, purée the soup in a food processor or blender before adding to the eggs to make it smooth and silky.

Make sure to let the soup cool as directed before adding it to the eggs. The eggs may curdle if the soup is too hot.

Serves 6

⅓ cup	olive oil	75 mL
3 cups	torn French or Italian bread (crusts removed)	750 mL
3 tbsp	finely chopped garlic	45 mL
6 cups	chicken or vegetable stock	1.5 L
1 tsp	paprika	5 mL
3	eggs, lightly beaten	3
½ tsp	salt	2 mL
¼ tsp	freshly ground black pepper	1 mL
2 tbsp	minced fresh flat-leaf (Italian) parsley	25 mL
	Aïoli (see recipe, page 362)	

1. In a large pot, heat oil over medium heat. Add bread and garlic; sauté until garlic is soft, but not brown, and bread has begun to color and crisp, about 2 minutes. Add stock and paprika; bring to a boil. Reduce heat and simmer for 20 minutes. Remove from heat and let cool for 10 minutes.
2. Whisk soup to break up the bread. Gradually whisk 2 cups (500 mL) of the soup into the beaten eggs. Slowly pour back into the pot, stirring constantly, and reheat over medium heat. Do not let boil, or the eggs will curdle. Season with salt and pepper.
3. Ladle into heated bowls and garnish with parsley and aïoli.

Garlic Soup with Pesto and Cabbage

▲▽▲▽▲▽▲▽▲▽▲▽▲▽▲▽▲▽▲▽▲▽▲▽▲▽▲▽▲▽▲▽▲▽▲▽▲▽▲

Here we've paired the great taste of garlic with cabbage and basil. We've given you a recipe for pesto because it works so well in flavoring many different soups, but feel free to buy some already made at the grocery store. It will taste almost as good.

▲▽▲▽▲▽▲▽▲▽▲

Tip

Because adding delicate eggs to a pot of hot soup would result in scrambled eggs, we use a technique called tempering. By gradually adding hot soup to the eggs, the temperature of the eggs rises slowly, so that when they eventually make it into the soup, they are already hot and stay fluid and velvety.

Serves 6

⅓ cup	olive oil	75 mL
1	onion, chopped	1
1	carrot, chopped	1
1	stalk celery, chopped	1
2 cups	thinly sliced napa cabbage	500 mL
3 tbsp	finely chopped garlic	45 mL
6 cups	chicken or vegetable stock	1.5 L
1 cup	torn French or Italian bread (crusts removed)	250 mL
1 tsp	paprika	5 mL
2	eggs, lightly beaten	2
½ tsp	salt	2 mL
¼ tsp	freshly ground black pepper	1 mL
¼ cup	pesto (store-bought or see recipe, page 363)	50 mL
2 tbsp	thinly sliced fresh basil	25 mL

1. In a large pot, heat oil over medium heat. Add onion, carrot, celery, cabbage and garlic; sauté until starting to soften, about 5 minutes. Add stock, bread and paprika; bring to a boil. Reduce heat and simmer for 20 minutes. Remove from heat and let cool for 10 minutes.
2. Whisk soup to break up the bread. Gradually whisk 2 cups (500 mL) of the soup into the beaten eggs. Slowly pour back into the pot, stirring constantly, and reheat over medium heat. Do not let boil, or the eggs will curdle. Season with salt and pepper. Whisk in pesto.
3. Ladle into heated bowls and garnish with basil.

Mushroom and Thyme Soup

▲▼▲

This simple soup is infused with deep mushroom flavor. Although thyme is a key ingredient, it serves more to draw out the flavor of mushrooms than to stand on its own.

▲▼▲▼▲▼▲▼▲▼

Tip

Shiitake stems are too tough to eat, but they make a wonderful addition to vegetable stock.

Serves 4 to 6

¼ cup	unsalted butter	50 mL
1	onion, chopped	1
1 lb	mushrooms, thinly sliced	500 g
6 oz	shiitake mushrooms, stems removed and caps thinly sliced	175 g
2 tbsp	all-purpose flour	25 mL
1½ tsp	dried thyme	7 mL
½ tsp	salt	2 mL
¼ tsp	freshly ground black pepper	1 mL
5 cups	chicken stock	1.25 mL
1 cup	dry white wine	250 mL
	Garlic Croutons (see variation, page 368)	

1. In a large pot, melt butter over medium heat. Add onion, mushrooms and shiitake mushrooms; sauté until mushrooms are browned, 10 to 15 minutes. Sprinkle with flour, thyme, salt and pepper; sauté for 2 minutes.
2. Gradually whisk in stock and wine; bring to a boil. Reduce heat and simmer, stirring occasionally, for 30 minutes to blend the flavors.
3. Ladle into heated bowls and garnish with croutons.

Three-Mushroom Soup with Risotto Cakes

▲▽

If you like mushrooms, you'll love this soup. We combined an assortment of wild and dried mushrooms that pack a wallop of mushroomy flavor. Once we paired this soup with a crispy on the outside, silky smooth on the inside mushroom risotto cake, all our testers agreed: this soup could be the star of any restaurant's menu.

▲▽▲▽▲▽▲▽▲▽

Tips

Filtering the mushroom liquid removes any dirt that may have been loosened from the mushrooms as they soaked.

Use shallow soup bowls (soup plates) so the risotto cakes don't sink to the bottom.

Serves 6

½ oz	dried porcini mushrooms	15 g
1 cup	boiling water	250 mL
¼ cup	olive oil	50 mL
1	onion, chopped	1
2	cloves garlic, minced	2
1 lb	mixed wild (exotic) mushrooms (such as cremini, porcini, shiitake or oyster), sliced	500 g
½ tsp	chopped fresh thyme (or a pinch of dried)	2 mL
½ tsp	salt	2 mL
1 cup	dry white wine	250 mL
4 cups	chicken stock	1 L
2 cups	beef stock	500 mL
1 tbsp	freshly squeezed lemon juice	15 mL
Pinch	cayenne pepper (optional)	Pinch
	Freshly ground black pepper	
	Wild Mushroom Risotto Cakes (see recipe, page 373)	
1 tbsp	minced fresh chives	15 mL

1. In a small bowl, soak porcini mushrooms in boiling water until softened, about 30 minutes. Using a slotted spoon, gently lift mushrooms from liquid and swish in a bowl of cold water to remove any clinging sand or dirt. Chop and set aside. Pour mushroom liquid through a sieve lined with a coffee filter into a small bowl and set aside.

2. In a large pot, heat oil over medium-high heat. Add onion and sauté until starting to soften, about 2 minutes. Add porcini mushrooms and sauté for 2 minutes. Add garlic, wild mushrooms, thyme and salt; sauté until mushrooms release their liquid, about 10 minutes. Add wine and cook until most of the liquid has evaporated, about 5 minutes.

3. Add chicken stock, beef stock and reserved mushroom liquid; bring to a boil. Reduce heat and simmer until mushrooms are soft and flavors are blended, about 20 minutes. Add lemon juice and cayenne (if using). Season with salt and black pepper to taste.

4. Ladle into heated bowls and top each with a risotto cake. Garnish with chives.

Creamy Mushroom Soup

▲▼▲

If you're looking for big mushroom flavor, this soup is for you. Almost 2 lbs (1 kg) of mushrooms are combined with cream and Madeira, and practically nothing else. Need we say more?

▲▼▲▼▲▼▲▼▲

Tip

To clean mushrooms, you can either rinse them quickly in water or wipe them with a damp paper towel. Mushrooms will be much happier in your refrigerator if you store them in a paper bag.

Serves 4 to 6

3 tbsp	unsalted butter	45 mL
2 tbsp	olive oil	25 mL
3	cloves garlic, minced	3
1	onion, chopped	1
1½ lbs	mushrooms, sliced	750 g
4 oz	shiitake mushrooms, stems removed and caps thinly sliced	125 g
¼ cup	all-purpose flour	50 mL
5 cups	chicken stock	1.25 L
¼ cup	Madeira	50 mL
3	sprigs fresh thyme	3
½ cup	whipping (35%) cream	125 mL
	Salt and freshly ground black pepper	
	Buttery Croutons (see recipe, page 368)	

1. In a large, heavy pot, heat butter and oil over medium heat. Add garlic and onion; sauté for 2 minutes. Add mushrooms and shiitake mushrooms; sauté until liquid from mushrooms has evaporated, about 10 minutes. Sprinkle with flour and sauté for 2 minutes.

2. Gradually whisk in stock, Madeira and thyme; simmer, stirring occasionally, until slightly thickened, about 10 minutes. Add cream and simmer for 10 minutes. Season with salt and pepper to taste.

3. Ladle into heated bowls and garnish with croutons.

Roasted Yellow Pepper Soup with Cilantro Cream (page 71)

Overleaf: Sweet Potato, Coconut and Gingerroot Soup (page 77)

Cream of Wild Mushroom Soup

▲▽▲▽▲▽▲▽▲▽▲▽▲▽▲▽▲▽▲▽▲▽▲▽▲▽▲▽▲▽▲▽▲▽▲▽▲▽▲

We like to serve this rich, deeply flavored soup as a main course. Its intense mushroom flavor should take center stage and would be best served simply with a crisp green salad and crusty bread.

▲▽▲▽▲▽▲▽▲▽

Tip

If not using homemade chicken stock, be sure to purchase a low-sodium brand.

Serves 6 to 8

½ oz	dried porcini mushrooms	15 g
1 cup	boiling water	250 mL
6 tbsp	unsalted butter	90 mL
¾ cup	sliced shallots	175 mL
3	cloves garlic, minced	3
3 cups	sliced stemmed shiitake mushrooms	750 mL
3 cups	sliced cremini mushrooms	750 mL
3 cups	sliced oyster mushrooms	750 mL
3 tbsp	all-purpose flour	45 mL
1 cup	dry white wine	250 mL
7 cups	chicken stock	1.75 L
½ tsp	salt	2 mL
¼ tsp	freshly ground black pepper	1 mL
½ cup	whipping (35%) cream	125 mL
1 tsp	freshly squeezed lemon juice	5 mL
	Chopped fresh chives	
	Garlic Croutons (see variation, page 368)	

1. In a small bowl, soak porcini mushrooms in hot water until softened, about 30 minutes. Using a slotted spoon, gently lift mushrooms from liquid and swish in a bowl of cold water to remove any clinging sand or dirt. Chop and set aside. Pour mushroom liquid through a sieve lined with a coffee filter into a small bowl and set aside.

2. In a large pot, melt butter over medium-high heat. Add shallots and garlic; sauté until shallots are translucent, about 6 minutes. Add porcini, shiitake, cremini and oyster mushrooms; sauté until starting to soften, about 4 minutes. Sprinkle with flour and sauté for 2 minutes.

3. Gradually whisk in wine and cook, stirring, until most of the liquid has evaporated, about 5 minutes. Gradually stir in stock and reserved mushroom liquid; bring to a boil, stirring often. Add salt and pepper, reduce heat and simmer, stirring occasionally, until mushrooms are tender, about 10 minutes.

4. Using an immersion blender, or in a food processor or blender in batches, purée soup until smooth. Return to the pot, if necessary, and stir in cream and lemon juice. Reheat over medium heat, stirring often, until steaming. Do not let boil. Taste and adjust seasoning with salt and pepper, if necessary.

5. Ladle into heated bowls and garnish with chives and croutons.

Cream of Roasted Turnip Soup with Baby Bok Choy and Five Spices (page 88)

Overleaf: Butternut Squash Soup with Nutmeg Cream (page 79)

Tortellini and Mushrooms in Parmesan Stock

▲▽▲

Parmigiano-Reggiano is one of our favorite cheeses. Although it can be pricy, its flavor is nutty, rich and a world away from anything you'll shake out of a container. Because it can be costly, it makes sense to use every last crumb. Our favorite way to use the rind is to add it to soups, and no soup deserves it more than this one. The browned mushrooms and Parmesan flavor give this soup an earthy taste that reminds us of a perfect fall day.

Serves 6

2 tbsp	olive oil	25 mL
1 lb	mushrooms, sliced	500 g
3 tbsp	chopped shallots	45 mL
4	large cloves garlic, thinly sliced	4
1	Parmigiano-Reggiano cheese rind, about 3 by 3 inches (7.5 by 7.5 cm)	1
8 cups	chicken stock	2 L
	Salt and freshly ground black pepper	
1	package (9 oz/275 g) fresh cheese tortellini	1
¼ cup	finely chopped fresh parsley	50 mL
	Additional finely chopped fresh parsley	

1. In a large pot, heat oil over medium-high heat. Add mushrooms and shallots; sauté until mushrooms have released their liquid and are browned, about 6 minutes. Add garlic, cheese rind and stock; bring to a boil. Partially cover, reduce heat to low and simmer gently for 30 minutes. Discard rind. Season with salt and pepper to taste.
2. Add tortellini and simmer, partially covered, until tender to the bite, about 8 minutes. Stir in parsley.
3. Ladle into heated bowls and garnish with parsley.

Vidalia Onion Soup

▲▽▲

The Vidalia onion's sweet nature is the highlight of this soup. We use chicken stock instead of beef and adorn it only with buttered croutons, keeping the soup light, a pleasing departure from the heavier French Onion Soup.

▲▽▲▽▲▽▲▽▲▽▲

Tip

Soup will stay hot much longer in a heated bowl.

Serves 6

3 tbsp	unsalted butter	45 mL
2 tbsp	vegetable oil	25 mL
3	large Vidalia onions, finely chopped	3
1½ tbsp	granulated sugar	22 mL
1 tsp	salt	5 mL
¾ cup	dry white wine	175 mL
5 cups	chicken stock	1.25 L
1 tsp	white wine vinegar	5 mL
	Freshly ground black pepper	
¼ cup	finely chopped green onions	50 mL
	Buttery Croutons (see recipe, page 368)	

1. In a large pot, heat butter and oil over medium heat. Add onions, sugar and salt; cook, stirring occasionally, until onions are soft and pale golden, 15 to 20 minutes. Stir in wine and cook until most of the liquid has evaporated, about 5 minutes.
2. Add stock and bring to a boil. Reduce heat and simmer for 5 minutes. Stir in vinegar and season with salt and pepper to taste.
3. Ladle into heated bowls and garnish with green onions and croutons.

Creamy Three-Onion Soup with Crispy Shallots

▲▼▲▼▲▼▲▼▲▼▲▼▲▼▲▼▲▼▲▼▲▼▲▼▲▼▲▼▲▼▲▼▲▼▲▼▲▼▲

Anyone who loves the true flavor of onion will love this soup. No bread, no cheese, no wine, just onion and more onion, topped off with — you guessed right — more onion.

▲▼▲▼▲▼▲▼▲

Tip

To trim leeks, cut off and discard the root end and the dark green tops (or save the tops for stock). Cut leeks lengthwise and wash under running water to remove any grit or dirt. Then cut as directed in the recipe.

Serves 6

3 tbsp	unsalted butter	45 mL
3	leeks, white and light green parts only, thinly sliced	3
2	onions, thinly sliced	2
2	cloves garlic, minced	2
4 cups	beef stock	1 L
1 cup	water	250 mL
4	sprigs fresh thyme	4
1 cup	whipping (35%) cream	250 mL
2 tbsp	red wine vinegar	25 mL
	Salt and freshly ground black pepper	
	Crispy Shallots (see recipe, page 367)	

1. In a large pot, melt butter over medium heat. Add leeks, onions and garlic; sauté until browned, about 15 minutes. Add stock, water and thyme; bring to a boil. Cover, reduce heat to low and simmer gently for 30 minutes to blend the flavors. Discard thyme sprigs.
2. Using an immersion blender, or in a food processor or blender in batches, purée soup until smooth. Return to the pot, if necessary. Stir in cream, vinegar and salt and pepper to taste; reheat over medium heat, stirring often, until steaming. Do not let boil.
3. Ladle into heated bowls and garnish with Crispy Shallots.

Parsnip and Apple Soup with Thyme

▲▽

Parsnips and tart apple make a surprisingly good team in this fresh from the orchard soup that tastes great hot or cold.

▲▽▲▽▲▽▲▽▲▽

Tips

If you want to serve this soup cold, transfer it to a bowl, cover and refrigerate for 3 hours. Serve in chilled bowls.

If serving the soup chilled, it may be necessary to thin it with a little extra chicken stock to achieve the desired texture.

Serves 6

¼ cup	unsalted butter	50 mL
1	onion, sliced	1
½ tsp	salt	2 mL
1 lb	parsnips, sliced	500 g
1 lb	sweet-tart apples (such as Braeburn, Mutsu or Crispin), peeled and diced	500 g
1	baking potato, peeled and diced	1
2 cups	unsweetened apple cider or apple juice	500 mL
2 cups	chicken stock	500 mL
½ cup	whipping (35%) cream	125 mL
2 tsp	cider vinegar	10 mL
1 tsp	minced fresh thyme	5 mL
	Freshly ground black pepper	
	Sprigs of fresh thyme (optional)	

1. In a large pot, melt butter over medium heat. Add onion and sauté until softened, about 6 minutes. Add salt and sauté for 1 minute. Add parsnips and apples; sauté for about 3 minutes to warm them up. Add potato, cider and stock; bring to a boil. Reduce heat and simmer until parsnips and potato are tender, about 20 minutes.

2. Using an immersion blender, or in a food processor or blender in batches, purée soup until smooth. Return to the pot, if necessary, and stir in cream, vinegar and thyme. Reheat over medium heat, stirring often. Season with salt and pepper to taste.

3. Ladle into heated bowls and garnish with thyme sprigs, if desired.

Roasted Red Pepper Soup

Although you can use jarred roasted peppers for this soup, we like to buy fresh peppers when they are in season and the price is right, roast them in large quantities and freeze them. That way, we can make this soup whenever we want.

▲▽▲▽▲▽▲▽▲▽▲

Tip

Sour cream is a good substitute if crème fraîche is not available.

Serves 6 to 8

1 tbsp	olive oil	15 mL
1	onion, chopped	1
3	cloves garlic, chopped	3
1 cup	dry white wine	250 mL
6	roasted red bell peppers (see tip, page 31), diced	6
4 cups	chicken or vegetable stock	1 L
½ tsp	salt	2 mL
¼ tsp	freshly ground black pepper	1 mL
	Crème fraîche (see tip, at left)	
	Minced fresh chives	

1. In a large pot, heat oil over medium heat. Add onion and sauté until softened, about 6 minutes. Add garlic and sauté for 1 minute. Add wine and cook until reduced by half, about 5 minutes. Add red peppers, stock, salt and pepper; bring to a boil. Reduce heat and simmer for 20 minutes to blend the flavors.

2. Using an immersion blender, or in a food processor or blender in batches, purée soup until smooth. Return to the pot, if necessary. Taste and adjust seasoning with salt and pepper, if necessary.

3. Ladle into heated bowls and garnish with crème fraîche and chives.

Roasted Yellow Pepper Soup with Cilantro Cream

▲▼

Roasting the peppers gives this lovely golden soup a vibrant flavor. The green Cilantro Cream on top makes it as pretty as a picture.

▲▼▲▼▲▼▲▼▲▼

Tip
If not using homemade chicken stock, be sure to purchase a low-sodium brand.

Serves 4 to 6

2 tbsp	unsalted butter	25 mL
2	cloves garlic, minced	2
¼ cup	finely chopped shallots	50 mL
½ tsp	dried thyme	2 mL
½ tsp	salt	2 mL
¼ tsp	freshly ground black pepper	1 mL
6	roasted yellow bell peppers (see tip, page 31), coarsely chopped	6
5 cups	chicken stock (approx.)	1.25 L
	Freshly squeezed lemon juice	
	Cilantro Cream (see recipe, page 365)	

1. In a large pot, melt butter over medium-low heat. Add garlic, shallots, thyme, salt and pepper; sauté until shallots are softened, about 6 minutes. Add yellow peppers and stock; cover and simmer until peppers are very soft, 12 to 15 minutes.
2. Using an immersion blender, or in a food processor or blender in batches, purée soup until smooth, thinning with a little more stock, if necessary. Return to the pot, if necessary, and add lemon juice to taste. Taste and adjust seasoning with salt and pepper, if necessary.
3. Ladle into heated bowls and top each with a dollop of Cilantro Cream.

Potato Tarragon Soup

▲▽▲▽▲▽▲▽▲▽▲▽▲▽▲▽▲▽▲▽▲▽▲▽▲▽▲▽▲▽▲▽▲▽▲

This elegant, decidedly French version of potato soup certainly fits the bill served warm on a cold winter day, but is also wonderful and refreshing served cold.

▲▽▲▽▲▽▲▽▲▽▲

Tip

If you want to serve this soup cold, transfer it to a large bowl after puréeing it. Stir in the remaining ingredients and adjust the seasoning, then cover and refrigerate for 3 hours. Serve in chilled bowls and omit the compound butter.

Serves 6 to 8

2 tbsp	unsalted butter	25 mL
1	onion, chopped	1
2½ lbs	baking potatoes, peeled and cut into ½-inch (1 cm) dice	1.25 kg
2	cloves garlic, chopped	2
4	sprigs fresh tarragon	4
6 cups	chicken stock	1.5 L
½ cup	whipping (35%) cream	125 mL
2 tbsp	freshly squeezed lemon juice	25 mL
	Salt and freshly ground black pepper	
	Lemon and Tarragon Compound Butter (see variation, page 367)	

1. In a large pot, melt butter over medium heat. Add onion and sauté until softened, about 6 minutes. Add potatoes, garlic and tarragon; sauté for 1 minute. Add stock and bring to a boil. Reduce heat and simmer until potatoes are tender, about 20 minutes. Discard tarragon sprigs.
2. Using an immersion blender, or in a food processor or blender in batches, purée soup until smooth. Return to the pot, if necessary. Stir in cream, lemon juice and salt and pepper to taste; reheat over medium heat, stirring often, until steaming. Taste and adjust seasoning with salt and pepper, if necessary.
3. Ladle into heated bowls and garnish each with a slice of compound butter.

Potato and Celery Root Soup with Blue Cheese Croutons

▲▽▲▽▲▽▲▽▲▽▲▽▲▽▲▽▲▽▲▽▲▽▲▽▲▽▲▽▲▽▲▽▲▽▲▽▲▽▲

Celery root is not a vegetable that's commonly seen on the dinner table, which is too bad because its delicate celery flavor and light texture definitely deserve more attention. Here, we pair celery root with potatoes to give it nice body.

▲▽▲▽▲▽▲▽▲▽

Tip

To prepare celery root, use a sharp vegetable peeler or a paring knife to remove the outer layer. You'll need a large, sharp knife to cut it into cubes. Two medium or 1 large celery root will weigh about 1¼ lbs (625 g).

Serves 4 to 6

2 tbsp	unsalted butter	25 mL
1	onion, chopped	1
1¼ lbs	celery root (celeriac), cut into 1-inch (2.5 cm) cubes	625 g
2	large baking potatoes, peeled and cut into 1-inch (2.5 cm) cubes	2
5 cups	chicken stock (approx.)	1.25 L
2 cups	milk	500 mL
	Salt and freshly ground black pepper	
	Blue Cheese Croutons (see variation, page 369)	

1. In a large pot, melt butter over medium heat. Add onion and sauté until softened, about 6 minutes. Add celery root, potatoes and stock; bring to a boil. Reduce heat and simmer until vegetables are tender, about 30 minutes.
2. Using an immersion blender, or in a food processor or blender in batches, purée soup until smooth. Return to the pot, if necessary, and stir in milk. Thin with a little more stock, if necessary. Reheat over medium heat, stirring often, until steaming. Do not let boil. Season with salt and pepper to taste.
3. Ladle into heated bowls and garnish with croutons.

Potato and Leek Soup

Any kind of potato will work in this superbly simple soup, but we really love Yukon golds, as they are a little buttery in flavor. For a refreshing change of pace, try this soup cold in the summer.

Tip

If you want to serve this soup cold, transfer it to a large bowl after puréeing it. Stir in the remaining ingredients and adjust the seasoning, then cover and refrigerate for 3 hours. Serve in chilled bowls and omit the compound butter.

Serves 6

2 lbs	potatoes, peeled and diced	1 kg
2	leeks, white and light green parts only, sliced	2
6 cups	chicken stock	1.5 L
Pinch	ground nutmeg	Pinch
Pinch	cayenne pepper	Pinch
	Salt and freshly ground black pepper	
1 cup	whipping (35%) cream	250 mL
	Lemon and Chive Compound Butter (see recipe, page 367)	

1. In a large pot, bring potatoes, leeks and stock to a simmer over medium heat. Reduce heat and simmer until potatoes are tender, about 20 minutes.
2. Using an immersion blender, or in a food processor or blender in batches, purée soup until smooth. Return to the pot, if necessary, and bring to a simmer over medium heat. Add nutmeg, cayenne and salt and black pepper to taste. Stir in cream. Taste and adjust seasoning with salt and black pepper, if necessary.
3. Ladle into heated bowls and garnish each with a slice of compound butter.

Rosemary Roasted Potato and Parsnip Soup with Blue Cheese Croutons

▲▽▲▽▲▽▲▽▲▽▲▽▲▽▲▽▲▽▲▽▲▽▲▽▲▽▲▽▲▽▲▽▲▽▲▽▲▽▲

Roasting vegetables caramelizes their sugars and reduces their water content, making them sweeter and more flavorful than boiled or steamed vegetables. You can leave this classic farmhouse staple chunky or purée half of it, as we did, for a creamier rendition.

▲▽▲▽▲▽▲▽▲

Variation

Sauté 6 slices of bacon in the butter until crispy. Transfer to a plate lined with paper towels. Pour off all but 2 tbsp (25 mL) of the fat and sauté the leeks. Continue with recipe as directed and crumble the bacon over the soup as a garnish, with or without the croutons.

Serves 6

- Preheat oven to 400°F (200°C)
- Rimmed baking sheet

2 lbs	boiling potatoes, peeled and cut into 1-inch (2.5 cm) cubes	1 kg
2	parsnips, cut into 1-inch (2.5 cm) pieces	2
2 tbsp	olive oil	25 mL
1 tsp	salt	5 mL
¼ tsp	freshly ground black pepper	1 mL
1 tbsp	chopped fresh rosemary	15 mL
2 tbsp	unsalted butter	25 mL
2	leeks, white and light green parts only, sliced	2
5 cups	chicken stock (approx.)	1.25 L
2 cups	milk	500 mL
1 tsp	white wine vinegar	5 mL
2 tbsp	minced fresh flat-leaf (Italian) parsley	25 mL
Pinch	ground nutmeg	Pinch
Pinch	cayenne pepper	Pinch
	Blue Cheese Croutons (see variation, page 369)	

1. On baking sheet, combine potatoes, parsnips, olive oil, salt and black pepper; toss to coat evenly and spread out in a single layer. Roast in preheated oven for 20 minutes. Sprinkle with rosemary and roast until vegetables are tender and crispy brown around the edges, about 10 minutes.

2. In a large pot, melt butter over medium heat. Add leeks and sauté until softened, about 6 minutes. Add roasted vegetables and stock; bring to a boil. Reduce heat and simmer for 10 minutes to blend the flavors.

3. If desired, using an immersion blender, pulse the soup in 3 or 4 quick spurts to partially blend it, leaving it chunky (or process half the soup in a food processor or blender, then return to the pot). Stir in milk, vinegar, nutmeg and cayenne. Thin with a little more stock, if necessary. Reheat over medium heat, stirring often, until steaming. Do not let boil. Taste and adjust seasoning with salt and black pepper, if necessary.

4. Ladle into heated bowls and garnish with croutons.

Creamy Sweet Potato Soup
with Maple Cream

▲▽▲

Sweet potatoes make the most silky, velvety soups. With all the beta carotene, vitamins and minerals in this powerhouse of a potato, this soup packs more than just great flavor. We especially like to serve it as a starter to a simple meal of grilled chicken or pork. It's so good that we could almost eat it as dessert.

▲▽▲▽▲▽▲▽▲▽▲

Tip

Use caution when blending hot liquids. It's best to cover the top of the food processor or blender with a towel to prevent any hot soup from splattering out.

Serves 6, with leftovers

3 tbsp	olive oil	45 mL
1	small onion, chopped	1
1	leek, white part only, thinly sliced	1
2½ lbs	sweet potatoes, peeled and cut into 2-inch (5 cm) cubes	1.25 kg
6 cups	vegetable or chicken stock	1.5 L
1 tsp	salt	5 mL
1	stick cinnamon, about 4 inches (10 cm) long	1
¼ cup	whipping (35%) cream	50 mL
1 tbsp	cider vinegar	15 mL
½ tsp	ground cinnamon	2 mL
Pinch	ground nutmeg	Pinch
Pinch	ground cloves	Pinch
Pinch	cayenne pepper	Pinch
	Freshly ground black pepper	

Maple Cream

½ cup	whipping (35%) cream, divided	125 mL
3 tbsp	pure maple syrup	45 mL
Pinch	salt	Pinch

1. In a large pot, heat oil over medium-high heat. Add onion and leek; sauté until softened, about 3 minutes. Add sweet potatoes, stock, salt and cinnamon stick; bring to a boil. Cover, reduce heat to low and simmer gently until potatoes are very tender, about 40 minutes. Discard cinnamon stick.

2. Using an immersion blender, or in a food processor or blender in batches, purée soup until smooth. Return to the pot, if necessary. Stir in cream, vinegar, cinnamon, nutmeg, cloves, cayenne and salt and black pepper to taste; reheat over medium heat, stirring often, until steaming. Do not let boil.

3. *Prepare the maple cream:* In a bowl, using an electric mixer, whip cream until soft peaks form. Add maple syrup and salt; whip until well blended.

4. Ladle soup into heated bowls and top each with a dollop of maple cream.

Sweet Potato, Coconut and Gingerroot Soup

As simple as this soup is to make, the complex flavors of ginger and coconut milk will make it seem as though you've labored for hours.

Variation

For a spicy version, try adding 1 tbsp (15 mL) Thai red curry paste with the potatoes.

Serves 4 to 6

2 lbs	sweet potatoes, peeled and cut into 1-inch (2.5 cm) cubes	1 kg
1	knob gingerroot (about 2 inches/5 cm), cut into matchsticks	1
1	can (14 oz/400 mL) unsweetened coconut milk	1
3 cups	chicken stock	750 mL
½ tsp	salt	2 mL
Pinch	cayenne pepper	Pinch
	Freshly ground black pepper	
1 tbsp	freshly squeezed lime juice	15 mL
	Cilantro Cream (see recipe, page 365)	

1. In a large pot, bring sweet potatoes, ginger, coconut milk, stock, salt, cayenne and black pepper to a simmer over medium heat. Reduce heat and simmer until potatoes are tender, about 20 minutes.
2. Using an immersion blender, or in a food processor or blender in batches, purée soup until smooth. Return to the pot, if necessary, and stir in lime juice. Reheat if necessary. Taste and adjust seasoning with salt, cayenne and black pepper, if necessary.
3. Ladle into heated bowls and drizzle Cilantro Swirl into the center of the soup. Draw a chopstick or knife through the center to create a marbling effect.

Pumpkin Soup with Leeks and Ginger

▲▼▲

Make this soup when you need a fast dinner with stick-to-your-ribs staying power. We tested it with both fresh pumpkin and canned pumpkin and couldn't tell the difference, so we've called for canned for simplicity's sake. We love the balance of flavors: spicy ginger, subtle, oniony leeks and lightly sweet and savory pumpkin.

▲▼▲▼▲▼▲▼▲▼▲

Tip

Try serving this fall favorite as a starter to Thanksgiving dinner.

Serves 6

¼ cup	unsalted butter	50 mL
2	leeks, white part only, thinly sliced	2
1	clove garlic, minced	1
1 tbsp	grated gingerroot	15 mL
1 tsp	salt	5 mL
2 tbsp	liquid honey	25 mL
1	can (28 oz/796 mL) pumpkin purée (not pie filling)	1
4 cups	chicken or vegetable stock	1 L
1½ cups	half-and-half (10%) cream	375 mL
½ cup	whipping (35%) cream	125 mL
1 tsp	white wine vinegar	5 mL
Pinch	ground nutmeg	Pinch
Pinch	cayenne pepper	Pinch
	Freshly ground black pepper	
	Gingery Whipped Cream (see recipe, page 365)	

1. In a large pot, melt butter over medium heat. Add leeks and sauté until starting to soften, about 5 minutes. Add garlic, ginger, salt and honey; sauté until garlic and ginger are fragrant but not browning, about 2 minutes.
2. Add pumpkin and stock; bring to a boil. Reduce heat and simmer for about 20 minutes to blend the flavors. Stir in half-and-half cream, whipping cream, vinegar, nutmeg, cayenne and salt and black pepper to taste; reheat over medium heat, stirring often, until steaming. Do not let boil.
3. Ladle into heated bowls and top each with a dollop of Gingery Whipped Cream.

Butternut Squash Soup with Nutmeg Cream

▲▼▲▼▲▼▲▼▲▼▲▼▲▼▲▼▲▼▲▼▲▼▲▼▲▼▲▼▲▼▲▼▲▼▲▼▲▼

The flavor of freshly grated nutmeg in an unsweetened whipped cream makes a lovely complement to the sweet butternut squash soup.

▲▼▲▼▲▼▲▼▲

Tip

For best results when whipping, make sure the cream and your bowl and whip are cold.

Serves 6

¼ cup	unsalted butter	50 mL
1	butternut squash (about 2 lbs/1 kg), peeled and cut into 1-inch (2.5 cm) cubes	1
1	clove garlic, minced	1
1 cup	finely chopped onion	250 mL
1 tsp	salt	5 mL
½ tsp	ground coriander	2 mL
½ tsp	dried thyme	2 mL
Pinch	freshly ground black pepper	Pinch
5 cups	chicken or vegetable stock	1.25 L
½ cup	orange juice	125 mL
½ cup	whipping (35%) cream	125 mL
Pinch	freshly grated nutmeg (see tip, page 81)	Pinch
	Cayenne pepper	
	Soft baby sage leaves (optional)	

Nutmeg Cream

½ cup	cold whipping (35%) cream	125 mL
¼ tsp	freshly grated nutmeg	1 mL

1. In a large pot, melt butter over medium-high heat. Add squash, garlic and onion; sauté for 3 minutes. Reduce heat to medium and add salt, coriander, thyme and black pepper; sauté for 5 minutes. Add stock and orange juice; bring to a boil. Cover, reduce heat to low and simmer gently until squash is tender, about 30 minutes.

2. Using an immersion blender, or in a food processor or blender in batches, purée soup until smooth. Return to the pot, if necessary. Stir in cream, nutmeg and cayenne to taste; reheat over medium heat, stirring often, until steaming. Do not let boil. Taste and adjust seasoning with salt and black pepper, if necessary.

3. *Prepare the nutmeg cream:* In a bowl, using an electric mixer, whip cream until soft peaks form. Add nutmeg and whip until well blended.

4. Ladle soup into heated bowls and top each with a dollop of nutmeg cream. Garnish with sage leaves, if desired.

Curried Butternut Squash Soup with Toasted Coconut and Golden Raisins

▲▽

Try to make this soup in the fall, when squash is freshly picked, and you will be rewarded with the creamy, sweet flavors of autumn. The curry powder provides a little kick, and the toasted coconut and golden raisins give a nod to the complex flavors of India: spicy, sweet, savory and rich.

▲▽▲▽▲▽▲▽▲▽

Tip

To toast coconut, add it to a dry skillet and cook over medium heat, stirring constantly, until golden brown. Transfer to a heatproof plate to cool.

Serves 6

¼ cup	unsalted butter	50 mL
1	onion, finely chopped	1
2	cloves garlic, minced	2
1	butternut squash (about 3 lbs/1.5 kg), peeled and cut into 1-inch (2.5 cm) cubes	1
1	bay leaf	1
1 tbsp	curry powder	15 mL
1 tsp	salt	5 mL
½ tsp	dried thyme	2 mL
6 cups	vegetable stock	1.5 L
1 cup	half-and-half (10%) cream	250 mL
Pinch	ground nutmeg	Pinch
Pinch	cayenne pepper	Pinch
	Freshly ground black pepper	
½ cup	toasted sweetened shredded coconut (see tip, at left)	125 mL
⅓ cup	golden raisins, plumped in hot water for 10 minutes, then drained	75 mL

1. In a large pot, melt butter over medium-high heat. Add onion and sauté until starting to soften, about 2 minutes. Add garlic and squash; sauté until squash is slightly browned, about 10 minutes. Add bay leaf, curry powder, salt and thyme; sauté until curry is fragrant, about 2 minutes. Add stock and bring to a boil. Reduce heat and simmer until squash is tender, about 30 minutes. Discard bay leaf.
2. Using an immersion blender, or in a food processor or blender in batches, purée soup until smooth. Return to the pot, if necessary. Stir in cream, nutmeg, cayenne and salt and black pepper to taste; reheat over medium heat, stirring often, until steaming. Do not let boil.
3. Ladle into heated bowls and garnish with coconut and raisins.

Roasted Winter Squash and Apple Soup

▲▼▲▼▲▼▲▼▲▼▲▼▲▼▲▼▲▼▲▼▲▼▲▼▲▼▲▼▲▼▲▼▲▼▲▼▲

Any winter squash will work well in this soup. Have fun experimenting with different varieties from your market!

▲▼▲▼▲▼▲▼▲▼▲

Tip

Freshly grated nutmeg has a much more vibrant smell and taste than packaged ground nutmeg. We like to use our Microplane grater to grate whole nutmeg.

Serves 8

- Preheat oven to 425°F (220°C)
- Baking sheets, lined with parchment paper

2	acorn squash, halved and seeded (about 2 lbs/1 kg)	2
2 tbsp	unsalted butter	25 mL
1	large onion, chopped	1
1	Granny Smith apple, peeled and diced	1
4½ cups	chicken stock (approx.)	1.125 L
1	bay leaf	1
¼ tsp	ground nutmeg	1 mL
½ cup	whipping (35%) cream	125 mL
	Salt and freshly ground black pepper	
	Sour cream	
	Chopped fresh chives	

1. Place squash on prepared baking sheets, cut side down. Roast in preheated oven until tender, about 45 minutes. Let cool, then scoop out flesh.
2. In a large pot, melt butter over medium heat. Add onion and sauté until starting to brown, about 10 minutes. Add squash, apple, stock, bay leaf and nutmeg; bring to a boil. Reduce heat and simmer until apple is soft and flavors are blended, about 30 minutes.
3. Using an immersion blender, or in a food processor or blender in batches, purée soup until smooth. Return to the pot, if necessary. Season with salt and pepper to taste; bring to a simmer over medium heat, stirring often and thinning with more stock, if desired.
4. Ladle into heated bowls and garnish with sour cream and chives.

Spicy Winter Squash Soup
with Cheddar Chile Croutons

▲▽▲▽▲▽▲▽▲▽▲▽▲▽▲▽▲▽▲▽▲▽▲▽▲▽▲▽▲▽▲▽▲

Winter squashes are naturally likable. Both sweet and savory, there's something to please everyone. A serrano chile and a little cayenne bring an added element of heat to this party in a pot.

▲▽▲▽▲▽▲▽▲

Tip

Using two different types of squash gives this soup a nice flavor, but if it works better for you to use just one type, you will still get good results.

Serves 6 to 8

¼ cup	unsalted butter	50 mL
1	large onion, finely chopped	1
2	large cloves garlic, chopped	2
1	serrano or other hot green chile pepper, seeded and minced	1
6 cups	chicken stock	1.5 L
4 cups	cubed peeled butternut squash (1-inch/2.5 cm cubes)	1 L
4 cups	cubed peeled acorn squash (1-inch/2.5 cm cubes)	1 L
1 tsp	salt	5 mL
¼ tsp	freshly ground black pepper	1 mL
¼ tsp	cayenne pepper	1 mL
½ cup	whipping (35%) cream	125 mL
	Chile Cheddar Croutons (see recipe, page 370)	

1. In a large pot, melt butter over medium heat. Add onion and sauté until softened, about 6 minutes. Add garlic and serrano chile; sauté for 2 minutes. Add stock, butternut squash, acorn squash, salt, black pepper and cayenne; bring to a boil. Reduce heat and simmer until squash is very tender, about 30 minutes.
2. Using an immersion blender, or in a food processor or blender in batches, purée soup until smooth. Return to the pot, if necessary. Stir in cream and reheat over medium heat, stirring often, until steaming. Do not let boil. Taste and adjust seasoning with salt and black pepper, if necessary.
3. Ladle into heated bowls and garnish with croutons.

Pattypan and Summer Squash Soup with Avocado and Grape Tomato Salsa

▲▽▲

Pattypan squash are those round, yellow, spaceship-shaped squash that are available almost year-round. Just cut out the stem and dice them up as a welcome addition to the usual summer soups and stews.

▲▽▲▽▲▽▲▽▲▽▲

Tip

For a thicker texture, process half the soup in a blender or food processor, or use an immersion blender to thicken the soup.

Variation

Feel free to substitute zucchini for the summer squash, or try the new hybrid zucchini that is shaped like pattypan squash but is green. Your soup will be delicious.

Serves 6

¼ cup	olive oil	50 mL
1	large onion, finely chopped	1
1	stalk celery, diced	1
½ tsp	ground cumin	2 mL
1½ lbs	pattypan squash (about 2), diced	750 g
1½ lbs	summer squash (about 4), diced	750 g
1	sweet potato, peeled and diced	1
1 cup	dry white wine (such as Sauvignon Blanc or Chardonnay)	250 mL
1 tsp	salt	5 mL
6 cups	chicken or vegetable stock	1.5 L
¼ cup	whipping (35%) cream	50 mL
Pinch	cayenne pepper	Pinch
	Freshly ground black pepper	
	Avocado and Grape Tomato Salsa (see recipe, page 364)	
	Buttery Croutons (optional, see recipe, page 368)	

1. In a large pot, heat oil over medium-high heat. Add onion, celery and cumin; sauté until onion starts to soften, 2 to 3 minutes. Add pattypan and summer squash; sauté until starting to soften, about 5 minutes. Add sweet potato, wine and salt; cook until liquid has evaporated, about 3 minutes.

2. Add stock and bring to a boil. Reduce heat and simmer until vegetables are tender, about 20 minutes. Stir in cream, cayenne and salt and black pepper to taste.

3. Ladle into heated bowls and top each with a generous spoonful of salsa. Garnish with croutons, if desired.

Tomato Vodka Soup

▲▽▲▽▲▽▲▽▲▽▲▽▲▽▲▽▲▽▲▽▲▽▲▽▲▽▲▽▲▽▲▽▲▽▲▽▲▽▲

While vodka has been a popular addition to tomato sauce for some time now, it also works well in soup. It may not have occurred to you to mix your cocktail with your first course, but the vodka adds a lovely but subtle flavor.

▲▽▲▽▲▽▲▽▲▽

Tip

San Marzano tomatoes, imported from Italy, are thought by many to be the best canned tomatoes in the world. They hail from a small town of the same name near Naples, whose volcanic soil is thought to filter impurities from the water and render tomatoes with a thick flesh, fewer seeds and a stronger taste. Look for the words "San Marzano" on the label to be sure you're getting the best.

Serves 4 to 6

2 tbsp	olive oil	25 mL
2 tbsp	unsalted butter	25 mL
2	onions, chopped	2
2	cloves garlic, minced	2
2 tbsp	tomato paste	25 mL
1	can (28 oz/796 mL) plum (Roma) tomatoes, with juice	1
4 cups	chicken or vegetable stock	1 L
½ tsp	salt	2 mL
¼ tsp	freshly ground black pepper	1 mL
1 cup	whipping (35%) cream	250 mL
¼ cup	vodka	50 mL
1 tbsp	freshly squeezed lemon juice	15 mL
	Garlic Croutons (see variation, page 368)	

1. In a large pot, heat oil and butter over medium heat. Add onions and garlic; sauté until softened, about 6 minutes. Add tomato paste and sauté until paste turns a rusty brown, about 5 minutes. Add tomatoes with juice, stock, salt and pepper; bring to a boil. Reduce heat and simmer for 40 minutes.
2. Using an immersion blender, or in a food processor or blender in batches, purée soup until smooth. Return to the pot, if necessary, and reheat over medium heat until steaming. Stir in cream, vodka and lemon juice. Taste and adjust seasoning with salt and black pepper, if necessary.
3. Ladle into heated bowls and garnish with croutons.

Tomato and Rice Soup with Basil

This is a great recipe to turn to when you crave tomato soup but good fresh tomatoes aren't available. Canned tomatoes can have a lovely flavor, and in this soup we've upped the ante by adding tomato paste as well.

▲▽▲▽▲▽▲▽▲▽

Tip

Parmesan's rich, nutty flavor is a welcome addition to many soups. By far the best Parmesan is Parmigiano-Reggiano, made in Italy. While it's not cheap, the flavor is well worth the price. You should always buy your cheese in a large chunk and grate it yourself.

Serves 4

3 tbsp	unsalted butter	45 mL
½ cup	chopped onion	125 mL
¼ cup	chopped celery	50 mL
1 tsp	dried basil	5 mL
1	can (28 oz/796 mL) diced tomatoes, with juice	1
2 tbsp	tomato paste	25 mL
3 cups	chicken or vegetable stock	750 mL
½ cup	long-grain white rice	125 mL
½ tsp	salt	2 mL
¼ tsp	freshly ground black pepper	1 mL
Pinch	cayenne pepper (optional)	Pinch
½ cup	whipping (35%) cream	125 mL
½ cup	freshly grated Parmesan cheese	125 mL
½ cup	finely sliced fresh basil	125 mL

1. In a large pot, melt butter over medium-high heat. Add onion and celery; sauté for 2 minutes. Add dried basil and sauté for 1 minute. Add tomatoes with juice and tomato paste, stirring to incorporate the paste and break up the tomatoes. Reduce heat and simmer until liquid has reduced by half, 10 to 20 minutes.
2. Add stock and bring to a simmer. Add rice and simmer until tender, 15 to 20 minutes. Season with salt, black pepper and cayenne (if using). Stir in cream and bring to a simmer.
3. Ladle into heated bowls and garnish with cheese and fresh basil.

Roasted Tomato and Pesto Soup

▲▼▲▼▲▼▲▼▲▼▲▼▲▼▲▼▲▼▲▼▲▼▲▼▲▼▲▼▲▼▲▼▲▼▲

You'll be surprised at the difference roasting the cherry tomatoes makes. This easy step gives the soup a slightly sweet, deep tomato flavor that still manages to retain all of its freshness.

▲▼▲▼▲▼▲▼▲

Tip

If you're using a blender or food processor to purée hot soup, make sure not to fill the bowl more than one-third full. The buildup of pressure from the steam will sometimes blow the cover off, sending hot liquid flying.

Serves 6

- Preheat oven to 400°F (200°C)
- Rimmed baking sheet

6 cups	cherry tomatoes	1.5 L
3 tbsp	olive oil, divided	45 mL
1 tsp	salt	5 mL
½ tsp	freshly ground black pepper	2 mL
2 tbsp	unsalted butter	25 mL
6	cloves garlic, minced	6
1 cup	chopped onion	250 mL
¼ tsp	hot pepper flakes	1 mL
1	can (28 oz/796 mL) diced tomatoes, with juice	1
4 cups	chicken stock	1 L
½ tsp	dried thyme	2 mL
	Pesto (store-bought or see recipe, page 363)	

1. On baking sheet, combine cherry tomatoes, 2 tbsp (25 mL) of the oil, salt and pepper; toss to coat evenly and spread in a single layer. Roast in preheated oven until tomatoes are shriveled and have brown spots, 35 to 45 minutes.
2. In a large pot, heat butter and the remaining oil over medium heat. Add garlic, onion and hot pepper flakes; sauté until onion starts to brown, about 10 minutes. Add canned tomatoes with juice, stock, thyme and roasted tomatoes, including liquid on baking sheet; bring to a boil. Reduce heat and simmer for 40 minutes.
3. Using an immersion blender, or in a food processor or blender in batches, purée soup until smooth. Return to the pot, if necessary. Taste and adjust seasoning with salt and pepper, if necessary.
4. Ladle into heated bowls and swirl a dollop of pesto into each.

Cream of Roasted Tomato Soup with Grilled Cheese Croutons

▲▽▲

No need to dunk your grilled cheese sandwich anymore. We cut to the chase and threw the sandwich directly into the soup.

▲▽▲▽▲▽▲▽▲▽▲

Tip

An immersion blender is one of our favorite kitchen tools. Because it can be immersed in the soup, it saves you from transferring hot liquids from the pot to a blender or food processor. Look for one that has a detachable blade unit for easy cleaning.

Serves 6

- Preheat oven to 400°F (200°C)
- Rimmed baking sheet

6 cups	cherry tomatoes	1.5 L
3 tbsp	olive oil, divided	45 mL
1 tsp	salt	5 mL
½ tsp	freshly ground black pepper	2 mL
2 tbsp	unsalted butter	25 mL
2	cloves garlic, minced	2
1 cup	chopped onion	250 mL
1	can (28 oz/796 mL) diced tomatoes, with juice	1
4 cups	chicken stock	1 L
½ tsp	dried thyme	2 mL
1 cup	whipping (35%) cream	250 mL
	Grilled Cheese Croutons (see recipe, page 370)	

1. On baking sheet, combine cherry tomatoes, 2 tbsp (25 mL) of the oil, salt and pepper; toss to coat evenly and spread in a single layer. Roast in preheated oven until tomatoes are shriveled and have brown spots, 35 to 45 minutes.
2. In a large pot, heat butter and the remaining oil over medium heat. Add garlic and onion; sauté until softened, about 6 minutes. Add canned tomatoes with juice, stock, thyme and roasted tomatoes, including liquid on baking sheet; bring to a boil. Reduce heat and simmer for 40 minutes.
3. Using an immersion blender, or in a food processor or blender in batches, purée soup until smooth. Return to the pot, if necessary. Stir in cream and reheat over medium heat, stirring often, until steaming. Do not let boil. Taste and adjust seasoning with salt and pepper, if necessary.
4. Ladle into heated bowls and garnish with croutons.

Cream of Roasted Turnip Soup with Baby Bok Choy and Five Spices

▲▽

When turnips are roasted, they become so sweet and flavorful that we don't want to eat them any other way. We love the cute and tender baby bok choy lightly sautéed with Chinese five-spice powder.

▲▽▲▽▲▽▲▽▲▽

Tip

Five-spice powder is a blend of ground cloves, fennel seeds, cinnamon, star anise and Szechwan peppercorns. Most large grocery stores stock it, but if you can't find it, just use a mixture of the individual spices. It will still taste delicious.

Serves 6

- Preheat oven to 400°F (200°C)
- Rimmed baking sheet

1½ lbs	turnips, peeled and diced	750 g
¼ cup	olive oil, divided	50 mL
¾ tsp	salt, divided	3 mL
	Freshly ground black pepper	
1	large onion, finely chopped	1
5	heads baby bok choy, sliced	5
2	cloves garlic, minced	2
¼ tsp	five-spice powder (see tip, at left)	1 mL
6 cups	chicken or vegetable stock	1.5 L
½ cup	half-and-half (10%) cream	125 mL
2 tsp	freshly squeezed lemon juice	10 mL
Pinch	ground nutmeg	Pinch
Pinch	cayenne pepper	Pinch
2 tbsp	minced fresh chives	25 mL

1. On baking sheet, combine turnips, 2 tbsp (25 mL) of the oil, ½ tsp (2 mL) of the salt and black pepper to taste; toss to coat evenly and spread in a single layer. Roast in preheated oven until turnips are tender and begin to color, about 20 minutes.
2. In a large pot, heat the remaining oil over medium-high heat. Add onion and sauté until softened, about 3 minutes. Add bok choy, garlic, five-spice powder and the remaining salt; sauté until bok choy is tender, about 5 minutes. Transfer bok choy to a plate and keep warm.
3. Add stock to the pot and bring to a boil. Add turnips, reduce heat and simmer until turnips have flavored the liquid, about 10 minutes.
4. Using an immersion blender, or in a food processor or blender in batches, purée soup until smooth. Return to the pot, if necessary. Stir in cream, lemon juice, nutmeg and cayenne; reheat over medium heat, stirring often, until steaming. Do not let boil. Taste and adjust seasoning with salt and black pepper, if necessary.
5. Ladle into heated bowls and garnish with bok choy and chives.

Zucchini Soup with Tarragon and Sun-Dried Tomatoes

▲▽

We like this simple recipe for fast weekday dinners. Carnivores can grill a chicken breast to serve on the side, or you can just serve this fresh soup with a salad and bread.

▲▽▲▽▲▽▲▽▲▽

Tips

Sun-dried tomatoes can sometimes be found dried, not packed in oil. To use these tomatoes, simply immerse them in boiling water for 20 minutes. Don't throw out the water — it can be a tasty addition to the soup.

For extra zing, garnish with freshly grated Parmesan, crumbled feta or shredded Gruyère cheese.

Serves 6

¼ cup	olive oil	50 mL
⅓ cup	oil-packed sun-dried tomatoes, drained and chopped	75 mL
3	cloves garlic, minced	3
1	onion, finely chopped	1
2 lbs	zucchini, diced	1 kg
2	potatoes (about 10 oz/300 g), peeled and diced	2
6 cups	vegetable or chicken stock	1.5 L
2 tsp	dried tarragon	10 mL
¼ cup	minced fresh flat-leaf (Italian) parsley	50 mL
1 tbsp	freshly squeezed lemon juice	15 mL
1 tsp	salt	5 mL
¼ tsp	freshly ground black pepper	1 mL
	Buttery Croutons (see recipe, page 368)	

1. In a large pot, heat oil over medium-high heat. Add tomatoes, garlic and onion; sauté until onion is softened, about 3 minutes. Add zucchini and sauté until starting to soften, about 3 minutes. Add potatoes, stock and tarragon; bring to a boil. Reduce heat and simmer until vegetables are tender, about 20 minutes.
2. Using an immersion blender, pulse the soup in 2 or 3 quick spurts to partially blend it, leaving it chunky (or process about one-third of the soup in a food processor or blender in batches, then return to the pot). Stir in parsley, lemon juice, salt and pepper.
3. Ladle into heated bowls and garnish with croutons.

Zucchini Soup with Pancetta and Oven-Roasted Tomatoes

▲▽▲▽▲▽▲▽▲▽▲▽▲▽▲▽▲▽▲▽▲▽▲▽▲▽▲▽▲▽▲▽▲▽▲▽▲▽▲

Zucchini soup is one of our favorite ways to use up that most prolific of summer vegetables. When brown paper bags of zucchini arrive anonymously at your door, it must be August. So pairing zucchini with freshly picked tomatoes is a no-brainer. We like to roast sweet, juicy grape or cherry tomatoes to bring out the biggest flavor. They also look great sitting atop this incredibly simple soup.

▲▽▲▽▲▽▲▽▲▽▲

Tips

Pancetta is Italian bacon. While it isn't smoked like North American side bacon, it can be used interchangeably in most cases.

To chiffonade basil, lay the leaves in a pile and make narrow slices down through the layers. Because basil is a tender herb, it can become pasty and mushy if overly chopped.

Serves 6

- Preheat oven to 400°F (200°C)
- Rimmed baking sheet

2 cups	grape or cherry tomatoes	500 mL
3 tbsp	olive oil, divided	45 mL
1 tsp	salt, divided	5 mL
¼ tsp	freshly ground black pepper	1 mL
4 oz	pancetta or bacon, chopped	125 g
4	zucchini, diced	4
2	cloves garlic, minced	2
1	onion, minced	1
1 cup	dry white wine	250 mL
1 tsp	dried basil	5 mL
6 cups	chicken or vegetable stock	1.5 L
¼ cup	finely sliced (chiffonade) fresh basil (see tip, at left)	50 mL
	Freshly grated Parmigiano-Reggiano cheese	

1. On baking sheet, combine tomatoes, 1 tbsp (15 mL) of the oil, half the salt and the pepper; toss to coat evenly and spread in a single layer. Roast in preheated oven until tomatoes are shriveled and have brown spots, 35 to 45 minutes. Set aside.
2. Meanwhile, in a large pot, heat the remaining oil over medium-high heat. Add pancetta and sauté until golden brown and crispy, about 5 minutes. Add zucchini, garlic and onion; sauté until onion starts to soften, about 3 minutes. Add wine, dried basil and the remaining salt; cook until wine is reduced by half, about 5 minutes. Add stock and bring to a boil. Partially cover, reduce heat to low and simmer gently for about 20 minutes to blend the flavors. Taste and adjust seasoning with salt and pepper. Stir in fresh basil.
3. Ladle into heated bowls and garnish with roasted tomatoes and cheese.

Cream of Zucchini Soup with Roasted Grape Tomatoes

▲▼▲▼▲▼▲▼▲▼▲▼▲▼▲▼▲▼▲▼▲▼▲▼▲▼▲▼▲▼▲▼▲▼▲▼▲▼

Grape tomatoes are almost always good, even in the winter.

▲▼▲▼▲▼▲▼▲▼

Tip
Adding a potato to a vegetable soup with little or no starch is a great way to achieve a creamy texture without adding extra fat.

Serves 6

- Preheat oven to 400°F (200°C)
- Rimmed baking sheet

2 cups	grape tomatoes	500 mL
¼ cup	olive oil, divided	50 mL
	Salt and freshly ground black pepper	
1 cup	chopped onion	250 mL
3 cups	grated zucchini (about 2)	750 mL
2 tsp	dried tarragon	10 mL
1 tsp	salt	5 mL
6 cups	chicken or vegetable stock	1.5 L
1 cup	diced peeled potato	250 mL
½ cup	whipping (35 %) cream	125 mL
1 tsp	freshly squeezed lemon juice	5 mL

1. On baking sheet, combine tomatoes, 2 tbsp (25 mL) of the oil and salt and pepper to taste; toss to coat evenly and spread in a single layer. Roast in preheated oven until tomatoes are shriveled and have brown spots, 35 to 45 minutes. Set aside.
2. Meanwhile, in a large pot, heat the remaining oil over medium-high heat. Add onion and sauté until softened, about 3 minutes. Add zucchini, tarragon, salt and pepper to taste; sauté for 2 minutes. Add stock and potato; bring to a boil. Reduce heat and simmer until potato is tender, about 20 minutes.
3. Using an immersion blender, or in a food processor or blender in batches, purée soup until smooth. Return to the pot, if necessary. Stir in cream and lemon juice; reheat over medium heat, stirring often, until steaming. Do not let boil. Taste and adjust seasoning with salt and pepper, if necessary.
4. Ladle into heated bowls and garnish with roasted tomatoes.

Ratatouille Soup with Eggplant Roulade

▲▽▲▽▲▽▲▽▲▽▲▽▲▽▲▽▲▽▲▽▲▽▲▽▲▽▲▽▲▽▲▽▲▽▲▽▲

We made this soup with farmstand-fresh produce in the middle of August and were floored by how good it was. Now you know what to do with all those bags of zucchini and tomatoes that arrive on your doorstep in the black of night.

▲▽▲▽▲▽▲▽▲▽▲

Tips

Herbes de Provence is a blend of dried thyme, rosemary, sage, marjoram, summer savory, fennel seed and lavender. It can be purchased at large grocery stores, gourmet markets or online, and is definitely worth having in the pantry. We use it liberally whenever any of the individual herbs are called for, because it adds a more complex flavor than an individual herb can.

Use shallow soup bowls (soup plates) so the roulades don't sink to the bottom.

Serves 6

- Preheat oven to 375°F (190°C)
- Baking sheet, lined with parchment paper

¼ cup	olive oil	50 mL
1	large onion, chopped	1
2 tsp	herbes de Provence (see tip, at left) or a mixture of dried thyme and rosemary	10 mL
3	large zucchini, diced	3
3	cloves garlic, minced	3
2	Cubanelle peppers (or other mildly spicy peppers), diced	2
½ tsp	salt	2 mL
	Freshly ground black pepper	
5	tomatoes, chopped	5
¼ cup	minced fresh flat-leaf (Italian) parsley	50 mL
6 cups	chicken or vegetable stock	1.5 L
	Freshly grated Parmesan cheese	
	Additional minced fresh flat-leaf (Italian) parsley	

Eggplant Roulade

1	large eggplant, sliced lengthwise into six slices, each about ½ inch (1 cm) thick	1
¼ cup	olive oil	50 mL
	Salt and freshly ground black pepper	
1	egg yolk	1
⅔ cup	ricotta cheese	150 mL
¼ cup	freshly grated Parmesan cheese	50 mL
½ tsp	minced fresh thyme (or a pinch of dried)	2 mL
½ tsp	hot pepper flakes (optional)	2 mL

1. In a large pot, heat oil over medium-high heat. Add onion and herbes de Provence; sauté until onion starts to soften, about 2 minutes. Add zucchini, garlic, Cubanelle peppers, salt and pepper to taste; sauté until vegetables start to soften, about 3 minutes. Add tomatoes and parsley; sauté until some of the tomato juices have cooked off, about 5 minutes. Add stock and bring to a boil. Reduce heat and simmer until vegetables are tender and flavors are blended, about 30 minutes. Taste and adjust seasoning with salt and pepper, if necessary.

Variation

Add 1 lb (500 g) Italian sausage (bulk or with casings removed) to the hot oil and sauté until no pink remains, then continue with the recipe as directed.

2. *Meanwhile, prepare the eggplant roulade:* Arrange eggplant on prepared baking sheet. Brush with oil and sprinkle with salt and pepper to taste. Bake in preheated oven until tender, about 20 minutes.

3. In a bowl, combine egg yolk, ricotta, Parmesan, thyme and hot pepper flakes (if using). Season with salt and pepper to taste. Spread mixture over one side of each of the eggplant slices. Starting at one short edge, roll up jellyroll-style and place on baking sheet. Bake until eggplant is browned and cheese mixture is hot, about 10 minutes.

4. Ladle soup into heated bowls and add an eggplant roulade to each. Garnish with Parmesan and parsley.

Garden Vegetable Soup

No soup cookbook would be complete without a basic vegetable soup recipe. That said, we encourage you to forget the recipe and use whatever is in season, on sale or just hanging out in your fridge. Feel free to go out on your own; just keep in mind that heartier vegetables should go in first, so they can cook longer, and more tender vegetables should go in last to avoid mushy veggie syndrome.

Variation

Light soups like this can be made into more of a meal by adding Wild Mushroom Risotto Cakes (page 373), Italian Meatballs (page 368) or purchased crab cakes.

Serves 6 to 8

2 tbsp	unsalted butter	25 mL
1 tbsp	extra-virgin olive oil	15 mL
1	onion, chopped	1
1	can (28 oz/796 mL) diced tomatoes, with juice	1
6 cups	chicken or vegetable stock	1.5 L
2 cups	sliced carrots (¼-inch/0.5 cm slices)	500 mL
2 cups	diced peeled potatoes	500 mL
2 cups	chopped green beans (½-inch/1 cm pieces)	500 mL
2 cups	fresh or frozen corn kernels	500 mL
¼ cup	chopped fresh parsley	50 mL
	Salt and freshly ground black pepper	

1. In a large pot, heat butter and oil over medium heat. Add onion and sauté until softened, about 6 minutes. Add tomatoes with juice, stock, carrots and potatoes; bring to a boil. Reduce heat and simmer for 20 minutes. Add green beans and simmer for 5 minutes. Add corn and simmer until vegetables are just tender, about 5 minutes. Stir in parsley and season with salt and pepper to taste.
2. Ladle into heated bowls.

Vegetable Barley Soup

▲▼▲▼▲▼▲▼▲▼▲▼▲▼▲▼▲▼▲▼▲▼▲▼▲▼▲▼▲▼▲▼▲▼▲▼▲▼▲

It's hard to believe that a hearty, rich-tasting soup can be as good for you as it is delicious. Go ahead and dig in — this low-fat, high-fiber soup is sure to please.

▲▼▲▼▲▼▲▼▲

Tips

If not using homemade stock, be sure to purchase a low-sodium brand.

To make cheese curls, run a vegetable peeler down the side of a chunk of Parmigiano-Reggiano cheese until you have enough curls to garnish 6 to 8 bowls.

Serves 6 to 8

3 cups	water	875 mL
½ cup	pearl barley	125 mL
¼ oz	dried porcini mushrooms	7 g
½ cup	boiling water	125 mL
2 tbsp	olive oil	25 mL
2	stalks celery, thinly sliced	2
2	carrots, thinly sliced	2
1	large onion, chopped	1
12 oz	cremini mushrooms, thinly sliced	375 g
2	sprigs fresh thyme	2
6 cups	beef or vegetable stock	1.5 L
2 tbsp	dry sherry	25 mL
1 tsp	salt	5 mL
¼ tsp	freshly ground black pepper	1 mL
2 tsp	red wine vinegar	10 mL
¼ cup	minced fresh flat-leaf (Italian) parsley	50 mL
	Parmesan cheese curls (see tip, at left)	

1. In a saucepan, bring water and barley to a simmer over medium heat. Simmer, uncovered, until almost tender, 10 to 15 minutes. Drain and set aside.
2. Meanwhile, in a small bowl, soak porcini mushrooms in boiling water until softened, about 30 minutes. Using a slotted spoon, gently lift mushrooms from liquid and swish in a bowl of cold water to remove any clinging sand or dirt. Chop and set aside. Pour mushroom liquid through a sieve lined with a coffee filter into a small bowl and set aside.
3. In a large pot, heat oil over medium heat. Add celery, carrots and onion; sauté until golden, 6 to 8 minutes. Add cremini and porcini mushrooms; sauté until mushrooms have released their liquid and are browned, about 10 minutes. Add thyme, stock, reserved mushroom liquid, sherry, barley, salt and pepper; bring to a boil. Reduce heat and simmer, stirring occasionally, until vegetables and barley are tender, 10 to 15 minutes. Taste and adjust seasoning with salt and pepper, if necessary.
4. Ladle into heated bowls and garnish with parsley and cheese curls.

Roasted Summer Vegetable Soup

▲▽▲▽▲▽▲▽▲▽▲▽▲▽▲▽▲▽▲▽▲▽▲▽▲▽▲▽▲▽▲▽▲▽▲▽▲▽▲

We turn to this combination of summer vegetables time and time again. Whether we're tossing them into a pasta sauce, sautéing them for a side dish, or roasting them for a mouth-watering soup, eggplant, zucchini, tomatoes and corn are a team that never fails to win.

▲▽▲▽▲▽▲▽▲▽

Tip

When purchasing eggplants, look for those with shiny, smooth skin.

Serves 6

- Preheat oven to 425°F (220°C)
- 2 large rimmed baking sheets

10	cloves garlic, unpeeled	10
2	eggplants, cut into ½-inch (1 cm) dice	2
2	zucchini, cut into ½-inch (1 cm) dice	2
1	large onion, cut into 8 wedges	1
4 cups	cherry tomatoes	1 L
¼ cup	olive oil	50 mL
1 tsp	salt	5 mL
½ tsp	freshly ground black pepper	2 mL
6 cups	chicken stock, divided	1.5 L
2 cups	fresh or frozen corn kernels	500 mL
3	sprigs fresh thyme	3
	Pesto (store-bought or see recipe, page 363)	

1. On baking sheets, combine garlic, eggplants, zucchini, onion, tomatoes, oil, salt and pepper; toss to coat evenly and spread in a single layer. Roast in preheated oven, stirring occasionally, until vegetables are browned and tender, 35 to 45 minutes. Remove garlic cloves from pan, squeeze garlic from skins, mash into a paste and set aside. Discard skins.
2. Pour ¼ cup (50 mL) of the stock onto each baking sheet and scrape up any brown bits. Transfer stock and vegetables to a large pot and add the remaining stock, corn, thyme and roasted garlic; bring to a boil over medium heat. Reduce heat and simmer for 20 minutes to blend the flavors.
3. Ladle into heated bowls and swirl a dollop of pesto into each.

Roasted Mediterranean Vegetable Soup

▲▽▲

We've brought the taste of Morocco to your kitchen with this spicy, easy-to-make soup.

Roasted vegetables always taste so much better than boiled, because the oven dries them out a bit, resulting in less water but more flavor. It may seem like an extra step, but the result is worth the time.

▲▽▲▽▲▽▲▽▲▽▲

Tip

Harissa is a spicy North African condiment made from oil, chiles, garlic, cumin, coriander and sometimes cinnamon and dried mint. It can be found in a can or a jar at Middle Eastern grocers and at some large grocery stores. If you can't find it, make your own (see page 364). Harissa is also terrific rubbed onto grilled meats.

Serves 6 to 8

- Preheat oven to 425°F (220°C)
- Rimmed baking sheet

4	zucchini, chopped	4
2	eggplants, chopped	2
1	red bell pepper, chopped	1
1	red onion, chopped	1
¼ cup	olive oil, divided	50 mL
	Salt and freshly ground black pepper	
3	cloves garlic, minced	3
2 tbsp	harissa (see tip, at left)	25 mL
6 cups	chicken or vegetable stock	1.5 L
¼ cup	minced fresh flat-leaf (Italian) parsley	50 mL
	Grated zest and juice of 1 lemon	
½ cup	crumbled feta cheese	125 mL

1. On baking sheet, combine zucchini, eggplant, red pepper, red onion, 2 tbsp (25 mL) of the oil and salt and pepper to taste; toss to coat evenly and spread in a single layer. Roast in preheated oven until vegetables are browned and tender, 35 to 45 minutes.
2. In a large pot, heat the remaining oil over medium-high heat. Add garlic and sauté until fragrant, about 1 minute. Add roasted vegetables and harissa; sauté until harissa is fragrant, about 2 minutes. Add stock and bring to a boil. Reduce heat and simmer for about 20 minutes to blend the flavors.
3. Using an immersion blender, pulse the soup in 3 or 4 quick spurts to partially blend it, leaving it chunky (or process half the soup in a food processor or blender, then return to the pot). Stir in parsley, lemon zest and lemon juice. Taste and adjust seasoning with salt and pepper, if necessary (remember that the feta cheese used for garnish is on the salty side).
4. Ladle into heated bowls and garnish with feta cheese.

Hearty Harvest Roasted Vegetable Soup

▲▼▲

Roasting the vegetables gives this simple soup a totally different character and makes the flavors pop.

▲▼▲▼▲▼▲▼▲▼

Variation

Use chicken stock instead of vegetable stock and add 3 to 4 boneless chicken breasts, diced, to the soup. Simmer until chicken is no longer pink inside, 10 to 15 minutes.

Serves 6

- Preheat oven to 400°F (200°C)
- 2 large rimmed baking sheets

3	onions, cut into 1-inch (2.5 cm) slices	3
3	carrots, sliced	3
2	parsnips, sliced	2
2	zucchini, sliced	2
2	stalks celery, sliced	2
1	head fennel, sliced	1
1 cup	cubed winter squash (1-inch/2.5 cm cubes)	250 mL
¼ cup	olive oil	50 mL
1 tbsp	dried basil	15 mL
1 tsp	dried oregano	5 mL
½ tsp	salt	2 mL
½ tsp	freshly ground black pepper	2 mL
8 cups	vegetable stock	2 L
1	can (14 oz/398 mL) diced tomatoes, with juice	1
½ cup	freshly grated Parmesan cheese	125 mL
½ cup	minced fresh flat-leaf (Italian) parsley	125 mL
1 tbsp	balsamic vinegar	15 mL
Pinch	cayenne pepper (optional)	Pinch
	Additional freshly grated Parmesan cheese (optional)	

1. On baking sheets, combine onions, carrots, parsnips, zucchini, celery, fennel, squash, oil, basil, oregano, salt and black pepper; toss to coat evenly and spread in a single layer. Roast in preheated oven until lightly browned, 20 to 25 minutes.
2. Transfer vegetables to a large pot. Add stock and tomatoes with juice; bring to a simmer over medium heat. Simmer until vegetables are tender, about 30 minutes. Stir in cheese, parsley, vinegar and cayenne (if using). Taste and adjust seasoning with salt and black pepper, if necessary.
3. Ladle into heated bowls and garnish with cheese, if desired.

Beans, Beans and More Beans Soups

▲▽▲▽▲▽▲▽▲▽▲▽▲▽▲▽▲▽▲▽▲▽▲▽▲▽▲

Vegetarian Black Bean Chili Soup

You won't believe this soup contains no meat. Black beans and chili powder give it big flavor, and lots of add-ins make it fun, so when you're looking for a vegetarian bean soup that is sure to satisfy any appetite, this one is a winner.

Tip

Canned tomato sauce works well in this recipe, or use your favorite homemade sauce.

Variation

There is no end to the possible variations for this soup. Any kind of beans can be substituted, and vegetables such as celery, green pepper, yellow pepper or carrots can be added with the onions. At the end of cooking, you might try adding 1 to 2 cups (250 to 500 mL) of frozen corn or peas for great color.

Serves 6 to 8

¼ cup	olive oil	50 mL
2 cups	chopped onions	500 mL
4	cloves garlic, minced	4
1 cup	chopped red bell pepper	250 mL
2 tbsp	chili powder	25 mL
2 tsp	dried oregano	10 mL
1 tsp	ground cumin	5 mL
¼ tsp	cayenne pepper	1 mL
¼ tsp	chipotle chile powder (optional)	1 mL
3	cans (each 14 to 19 oz/398 to 540 mL) black beans, drained and rinsed	3
4 cups	vegetable stock	1 L
2 cups	tomato sauce	500 mL
1 tbsp	balsamic vinegar	15 mL
	Salt and freshly ground black pepper	
	Sour cream	
	Shredded Monterey Jack cheese	
	Chopped green onions	
	Chopped fresh cilantro	

1. In a large pot, heat oil over medium heat. Add onions and sauté until softened, about 6 minutes. Add garlic, red pepper, chili powder, oregano, cumin, cayenne and chipotle chile pepper (if using); sauté until peppers are tender, about 10 minutes.
2. Add beans, stock, tomato sauce and vinegar; bring to a boil. Reduce heat and simmer for about 30 minutes to blend the flavors. Season with salt and black pepper to taste.
3. Ladle into heated bowls and garnish with sour cream, cheese, onions and cilantro.

White Bean Chicken Chili Soup

▲▼▲▼▲▼▲▼▲▼▲▼▲▼▲▼▲▼▲▼▲▼▲▼▲▼▲▼▲▼▲▼▲▼▲▼▲

Sometimes we like a chili that is lighter in character but still hearty and filling. When that mood strikes, this is the chili to make. It comes together quickly and, as with all chilies, it is even better the next day.

▲▼▲▼▲▼▲▼▲

Tip

When making this recipe, we take advantage of the precooked rotisserie chicken found at almost any grocery store. One chicken usually yields about 3 cups (750 mL) meat.

Serves 6

3 tbsp	olive oil	45 mL
2	onions, chopped	2
2	cloves garlic, minced	2
2 tsp	ground cumin	10 mL
1 tsp	dried oregano	5 mL
¼ tsp	cayenne pepper	1 mL
2	cans (each 14 to 19 oz/398 to 540 mL) cannellini or white kidney beans, drained and rinsed	2
6 cups	chicken stock	1.5 L
3 cups	diced cooked chicken	750 mL
2 tbsp	white wine vinegar	25 mL
1 tsp	salt	5 mL
	Freshly ground black pepper	
2 cups	shredded Monterey Jack cheese	500 mL

1. In a large pot, heat oil over medium heat. Add onions and garlic; sauté for 1 minute. Add cumin, oregano and cayenne; sauté until onion starts to soften, about 2 minutes.
2. Add beans, stock, chicken, vinegar and salt; bring to a boil. Reduce heat and simmer for at least 20 minutes or until heated through. Season with salt and black pepper to taste.
3. Ladle into heated bowls and garnish with cheese.

Firehouse Chili Soup

▲▽▲

Quick to throw together, this beefy soup is sure to fire up hearty appetites.

▲▽▲▽▲▽▲▽▲▽▲

Tip

If you can't find Southwest-style tomatoes, regular canned diced tomatoes will also work.

Variations

Try using your favorite bulk sausage (or sausage meat removed from casings) instead of ground beef.

Substitute canned white kidney beans for the red kidney beans and ground turkey for the beef.

Serves 6 to 8

¼ cup	olive oil	50 mL
1 cup	chopped onion	250 mL
1 lb	lean ground beef	500 g
4	cloves garlic, minced	4
2	cans (each 14 to 19 oz/398 to 540 mL) red kidney beans, drained and rinsed	2
1	can (14 oz/398 mL) Southwest-style diced tomatoes, with juice	1
4 cups	beef stock	1 L
2 tbsp	chili powder (or to taste)	25 mL
1 tsp	dried oregano	5 mL
1 tsp	salt	5 mL
½ tsp	freshly ground black pepper	2 mL
1 tbsp	Worcestershire sauce	15 mL
2 tsp	balsamic vinegar	10 mL
1 cup	shredded Cheddar cheese (optional)	250 mL
1	avocado, diced (optional)	1

1. In a large pot, heat oil over medium heat. Add onion and sauté until softened, about 6 minutes. Add ground beef and garlic; sauté, breaking beef up with the back of a wooden spoon, until no longer pink, about 5 minutes. Drain any excess fat.

2. Add beans, tomatoes with juice, stock, chili powder, oregano, salt, black pepper, Worcestershire sauce and vinegar; bring to a boil. Cover, reduce heat to low and simmer gently for 30 minutes to blend the flavors. Taste and adjust seasoning with salt and black pepper, if necessary.

3. Ladle into heated bowls and garnish with cheese and avocado, if desired.

Aztec Chili Soup

▲▽

Meredith made this soup to share during her alma mater's San Diego State University Aztec football games. Adding hominy to this spicy soup gives it an earthy, rustic feel.

▲▽▲▽▲▽▲▽▲▽▲

Tip

Chile peppers contain oils that can cause chemical burns on your skin. When seeding and chopping them, always wear latex, plastic or rubber gloves.

Serves 6

1 tbsp	olive oil	15 mL
1	onion, chopped	1
1	serrano or other hot green chile pepper, seeded and minced	1
1½ lbs	lean ground beef	750 g
2 tbsp	chili powder	25 mL
2 tsp	ground cumin	10 mL
1 tsp	salt	5 mL
1	can (14 to 19 oz/398 to 540 mL) red kidney beans, drained and rinsed	1
1	can (28 to 32 oz/796 mL to 900 mL) crushed tomatoes	1
1	can (14 oz/398 mL) hominy	1
4 cups	chicken stock	1 L
2	green onions, chopped	2

1. In a large pot, heat oil over medium heat. Add onion and sauté until softened, about 6 minutes. Add serrano chile and sauté for 2 minutes. Add ground beef and sauté, breaking up with the back of a wooden spoon, until no longer pink, about 5 minutes. Drain any excess fat. Return to the heat and add chili powder, cumin and salt; sauté for 1 minute.
2. Add beans, tomatoes, hominy and stock; bring to a boil. Reduce heat and simmer for 20 minutes to blend the flavors.
3. Ladle into heated bowls and garnish with green onions.

Knock-Your-Socks-Off Chipotle Chili Soup

▲▽▲

Chipotle and black beans are often paired, probably because the earthy flavor of the beans holds up well against the smoky nature of chipotles. This soup would be the perfect one to serve on Super Bowl Sunday, with a big bowl of warm tortilla chips on the side.

▲▽▲▽▲▽▲▽▲▽▲

Tip
We prefer to use crushed tomatoes with added purée in this recipe, but if you can't find them, you can use regular crushed tomatoes or diced tomatoes with juice.

Serves 6 to 8

2 tbsp	vegetable oil	25 mL
1½ lbs	lean ground beef	750 g
6	cloves garlic, finely chopped	6
2	onions, finely chopped	2
¼ cup	chili powder	50 mL
1 tsp	salt	5 mL
½ tsp	freshly ground black pepper	2 mL
1	can (14 oz/398 mL) crushed tomatoes with added purée	1
6 cups	beef stock	1.5 L
3 tbsp	minced chipotle chile peppers in adobo sauce	45 mL
2	cans (each 14 to 19 oz/398 to 540 mL) black beans, drained and rinsed	2
	Cilantro Cream (see recipe, page 365)	
	Corn tortilla chips	

1. In a large pot, heat oil over medium heat. Add ground beef and sauté, breaking up with the back of a wooden spoon, until no longer pink, about 5 minutes. Drain any excess fat. Add garlic and onions; cook until softened, about 6 minutes. Add chili powder, salt and pepper; sauté for 2 minutes.
2. Add tomatoes, stock and chipotle chiles; bring to a boil. Reduce heat and simmer, stirring occasionally, for 1 hour. Add beans and simmer for 10 minutes. Taste and adjust seasoning with salt and pepper, if necessary.
3. Ladle into heated bowls and top each with a dollop of Cilantro Cream. Stick a few chips upright into the cream.

Chorizo Chili Soup with Chile Cheddar Croutons

▲▽▲▽▲▽▲▽▲▽▲▽▲▽▲▽▲▽▲▽▲▽▲▽▲▽▲▽▲▽▲▽▲▽▲▽▲

When you need good spicy soup fast, look no further than this recipe. We always have these ingredients on hand and ready to go for a cold day. Cheesy croutons turn this rustic soup into something special.

▲▽▲▽▲▽▲▽▲

Tip

Soup will stay hot much longer in a heated bowl.

Serves 4 to 6

1 lb	fresh chorizo sausage (bulk or with casings removed)	500 g
6	cloves garlic, minced	6
1	red bell pepper, chopped	1
1 cup	chopped onion	250 mL
2 tbsp	chili powder	25 mL
1 tsp	ground cumin	5 mL
½ tsp	cayenne pepper	2 mL
4	cans (each 14 to 19 oz/398 to 540 mL) red kidney beans, drained and rinsed	4
1	can (14 oz/398 mL) crushed tomatoes	1
4 cups	beef stock	1 L
1	bay leaf	1
	Salt and freshly ground black pepper	
	Sour cream	
	Chile Cheddar Croutons (see recipe, page 370)	

1. In a large, heavy pot, over medium heat, sauté chorizo, breaking up with the back of a wooden spoon, until no longer pink, about 5 minutes. Add garlic, red pepper and onion; sauté until lightly browned, about 8 minutes. Add chili powder, cumin and cayenne; sauté for 1 minute.
2. Add beans, tomatoes, stock and bay leaf; bring to a boil. Reduce heat and simmer for 20 minutes. Discard bay leaf. Season with salt and black pepper to taste.
3. Ladle into heated bowls and garnish with sour cream and croutons.

Half-Time Chili Soup with Lamb

▲▽▲▽▲▽▲▽▲▽▲▽▲▽▲▽▲▽▲▽▲▽▲▽▲▽▲▽▲▽▲▽▲▽▲▽

The red and black beans make for an interesting color combo in this warming classic, perfect for the big game. Poblano chiles give the soup a delicious fruity, peppery flavor that is too good to pass up, so be sure to look for them at your local grocery. Topping this soup with rich cheese and avocado is really gilding the lily, but we couldn't resist.

▲▽▲▽▲▽▲▽▲▽

Tip

We can't overstate how important it is to brown meat properly before slow-cooking it. The flavor that develops during the browning process is critical to the overall flavor of the soup. If you overcrowd your pot, the meat will only steam and become gray and never brown. It may be necessary for you to work in batches if your pot isn't very large.

Serves 6

¼ cup	olive oil	50 mL
1 cup	chopped onion	250 mL
1 lb	boneless lamb shoulder or leg, cut into 1-inch (2.5 cm) pieces	500 g
4	cloves garlic, minced	4
1 cup	chopped red bell pepper	250 mL
1 cup	chopped seeded poblano chile peppers	250 mL
1	can (14 to 19 oz/398 to 540 mL) red kidney beans, drained and rinsed	1
1	can (14 to 19 oz/398 to 540 mL) black beans, drained and rinsed	1
1	can (14 oz/398 mL) diced tomatoes, with juice	1
6 cups	beef stock	1.5 L
2 tbsp	chili powder (or to taste)	25 mL
1 tsp	dried oregano	5 mL
1 tsp	salt	5 mL
½ tsp	freshly ground black pepper	2 mL
1 tbsp	Worcestershire sauce	15 mL
2 tsp	balsamic vinegar	10 mL
1 cup	shredded Cheddar cheese (optional)	250 mL
1	avocado, diced (optional)	1

1. In a large pot, heat oil over medium heat. Add onion and sauté until softened, about 6 minutes. Add lamb, garlic, red pepper and poblano chiles; sauté until lamb is browned on all sides, about 10 minutes.

2. Add red and black beans, tomatoes with juice, stock, chili powder, oregano, salt, pepper, Worcestershire sauce and vinegar; bring to a boil. Cover, reduce heat to medium-low, and simmer for 1 hour or until lamb is tender. Taste and adjust seasoning with vinegar, salt and pepper, if necessary.

3. Ladle into heated bowls and garnish with cheese and avocado, if desired.

Spicy Black Bean Soup

▲▼▲▼▲▼▲▼▲▼▲▼▲▼▲▼▲▼▲▼▲▼▲▼▲▼▲▼▲▼▲▼▲▼▲

Black beans are a Cuban staple, and there is no end to their versatility. Here, we've kept it simple, but feel to garnish with your favorite salsa.

▲▼▲▼▲▼▲▼▲

Tips

Chipotle chiles are smoked jalapeños, often found canned in a vinegary tomato sauce called adobo. Look for them in the Mexican aisle of your grocery store. They tend to be fiery, so we often use only 1 or 2 at a time.

If not using homemade chicken stock, be sure to purchase a low-sodium brand.

Serves 4

3	slices bacon, chopped	3
1	onion, chopped	1
3	cloves garlic, minced	3
1	large carrot, chopped	1
2	chipotle chile peppers in adobo sauce, chopped (see tip, at left)	2
5 cups	water	1.25 L
2 cups	chicken stock	500 mL
2 cups	dried black beans, soaked overnight or quick-soaked (see tip, page 110) and drained	500 mL
2	bay leaves	2
1¼ tsp	ground cumin	6 mL
¼ cup	chopped fresh cilantro	50 mL
	Salt and freshly ground black pepper	
	Sour cream	
	Additional chopped fresh cilantro	

1. In a large pot, sauté bacon over medium heat until browned and crispy, about 5 minutes. Remove with a slotted spoon to a plate lined with paper towels. Set aside.
2. Pour off all but 1 tbsp (15 mL) fat in the pot. Add onion and sauté until softened, about 6 minutes. Add garlic and carrot; sauté for 2 minutes. Add chipotle chiles, water, stock, beans, bay leaves and cumin; bring to a boil. Reduce heat and simmer until beans are tender, about 1½ hours. Stir in cilantro and salt and pepper to taste.
3. Ladle into heated bowls and garnish with sour cream, cilantro and reserved bacon.

Caribbean Black Bean Soup

▲▽▲

Natives of the Caribbean love to combine sweet and savory elements in a dish. We love it as well. That's why, for this soup, we paired the smoky flavors of black beans and bacon with the bright notes of a tropical fruit salsa.

▲▽▲▽▲▽▲▽▲▽▲

Tip

For a thicker consistency, after Step 2, mash some of the beans with a potato masher or process 2 cups (500 mL) of the soup in a blender or food processor.

Serves 6 to 8

2 tbsp	unsalted butter	25 mL
8	slices bacon, chopped	8
1	onion, chopped	1
3	cloves garlic, minced	3
1	carrot, chopped	1
1	stalk celery, chopped	1
1 tsp	dried thyme	5 mL
1 tsp	ground cumin	5 mL
6 cups	beef stock	1.5 L
2 cups	water	500 mL
2 cups	dried black beans, soaked overnight or quick-soaked (see tip, page 110) and drained	500 mL
1	bay leaf	1
1 tsp	salt	5 mL
½ tsp	freshly ground black pepper	2 mL
1	lime, cut into 6 to 8 wedges	1

Fruit Salsa

2	oranges, sectioned	2
1	banana, diced	1
½ cup	finely chopped red onion	125 mL
¼ cup	chopped fresh cilantro	50 mL
2 tbsp	freshly squeezed lime juice	25 mL

1. In a large pot, melt butter over medium heat. Add bacon and sauté until it renders its fat but is still soft, about 2 minutes. Add onion and sauté until softened, about 6 minutes. Add garlic, carrot, celery, thyme and cumin; sauté until vegetables are softened, about 5 minutes.
2. Add stock, water, beans and bay leaf; bring to a boil. Reduce heat and simmer for 1 hour. Add salt and pepper; simmer until beans are tender, about 30 minutes. Taste and adjust seasoning with salt and pepper, if necessary. Discard bay leaf.
3. *Prepare the fruit salsa:* In a small bowl, combine oranges, banana, red onion, cilantro and lime juice.
4. Ladle soup into heated bowls and garnish each with a heaping tablespoon (15 mL) of fruit salsa and a lime wedge. Diners may squeeze the lime over their soup, if they desire.

Black Bean, Butternut Squash and Poblano Chile Soup

▲▽▲▽▲▽▲▽▲▽▲▽▲▽▲▽▲▽▲▽▲▽▲▽▲▽▲▽▲▽▲▽▲

The savory combination of earthy black beans, smoky chipotle chiles and sweet butternut squash is absolutely irresistible.

▲▽▲▽▲▽▲▽▲▽▲

Tips

You can often find butternut squash already peeled and diced in your grocer's produce aisles, which makes this already easy soup even easier.

Serves 6 to 8

1 tbsp	olive oil	15 mL
2	cloves garlic, minced	2
2	large poblano chile peppers, seeded and chopped	2
1	onion, chopped	1
1 tbsp	cumin seeds	15 mL
2	cans (each 14 to 19 oz/398 to 540 mL) black beans, drained and rinsed	2
1	butternut squash (about 1½ lbs/750 g), peeled and cut into ½-inch (1 cm) dice	1
1	can (14 oz/398 mL) diced tomatoes, with juice	1
6 cups	chicken or vegetable stock	1.5 L
1 tbsp	minced drained chipotle chile peppers in adobo sauce (see tip, at left)	15 mL
1 tsp	salt	5 mL
	Sour cream	

1. In a large, heavy pot, heat oil over medium heat. Add garlic, poblano chiles, onion and cumin seeds; sauté until onion is softened, about 6 minutes.
2. Add beans, squash, tomatoes with juice, stock, chipotle chiles and salt; bring to a boil. Reduce heat and simmer, stirring occasionally, until squash is tender, about 30 minutes.
3. Ladle into heated bowls and garnish each with a dollop of sour cream.

Black Bean and Rice Soup with Chorizo

▲▽▲▽▲▽▲▽▲▽▲▽▲▽▲▽▲▽▲▽▲▽▲▽▲▽▲▽▲▽▲▽▲▽▲▽▲▽▲

Black beans make some of the best soups. They are flavorful enough on their own, but when combined with spicy chorizo sausage, chile powder and a smoked ham hock, they really come into their own. As with many legume-based soups, holding them over for a few days only intensifies their flavor. They tend to thicken to a porridge-like consistency on sitting, but can be thinned with a bit of stock or water, whatever is at hand, before reheating.

▲▽▲▽▲▽▲▽▲▽▲

Tip

Here's how to quick-soak dried beans: In a colander, rinse beans under cold water and discard any discolored ones. In a saucepan, combine beans with enough cold water to cover them by 2 inches (5 cm). Bring to a boil over medium heat and boil for 2 minutes. Remove from heat and let soak, covered, or 1 hour.

Serves 8

3 tbsp	olive oil	45 mL
2 cups	chopped onions	500 mL
2	carrots, chopped	2
1	stalk celery, chopped	1
4	cloves garlic, minced	4
1 cup	dry red wine	250 mL
1	can (14 oz/398 mL) diced tomatoes, with juice	1
1	smoked ham hock (about 8 oz/250 g) or 1 cup (250 mL) chopped ham	1
2 cups	dried black beans, soaked overnight or quick-soaked (see tip, at left) and drained	500 mL
5 cups	chicken stock	1.25 L
2 cups	water	500 mL
1 tsp	dried oregano	5 mL
½ tsp	hot pepper flakes	2 mL
½ tsp	ground cumin	2 mL
½ tsp	chili powder or chipotle chile powder	2 mL
Pinch	ground cloves	Pinch
1 lb	smoked chorizo sausage, cut into 1-inch (2.5 cm) pieces or crumbled	500 g
2 tsp	salt	10 mL
	Freshly ground black pepper	
4 cups	hot cooked white rice	1 L
½ cup	plain yogurt	125 mL
¼ cup	finely chopped red bell pepper	50 mL
¼ cup	minced fresh cilantro	50 mL
1	lime, cut into 8 wedges	1

1. In a large pot, heat oil over medium heat. Add onions and sauté until softened, about 6 minutes. Add carrots and celery; sauté until starting to soften, about 5 minutes. Add garlic and sauté for 1 minute. Add wine and tomatoes with juice; cook until liquid is reduced by half, about 5 minutes.

▲▽▲▽▲▽▲▽▲▽▲▽▲▽▲▽▲▽▲▽▲▽▲▽▲▽▲▽▲▽▲▽▲▽▲

Tip

If you like your soup thicker, mash some of the beans in the pot with a potato masher. This will break up the beans and thicken the soup.

2. Add ham, beans, stock, water, oregano, hot pepper flakes, cumin, chili powder and cloves; bring to a boil. Partially cover, reduce heat to low and simmer gently until beans are almost tender, about 1 hour. Add chorizo and salt; cover and simmer until beans are tender and sausage has flavored the soup, 30 to 45 minutes. Season with salt and black pepper to taste.

3. If using a ham hock, remove from the soup and let cool slightly. Pick the meat from the bone and shred into bite-size pieces. Discard bone, fat and skin. Return meat to the soup and simmer until heated through.

4. Divide rice among heated bowls and top with soup. Garnish with yogurt, red pepper, cilantro and lime wedges. Diners may squeeze the lime over their soup, if they desire.

Broccoli Rabe, Spelt and Bean Soup with Chorizo

▲▽▲▽▲▽▲▽▲▽▲▽▲▽▲▽▲▽▲▽▲▽▲▽▲▽▲▽▲▽▲▽▲▽▲▽▲▽▲

Broccoli rabe looks like leggy broccoli. It has a bitter quality we enjoy in this spicy, meaty soup. Spelt is an ancient grain that is showing up more frequently on our grocery shelves. If you can't find it, wheat berries or barley are good substitutes.

▲▽▲▽▲▽▲▽▲▽▲

Tip

Spelt is an ancient relative of wheat. Thousands of years ago, other grains proved more adaptable, with higher yields, so spelt was relegated to small production. Spelt is a firm grain with a nutty taste. Because it is low on the glycemic index and palatable for some who suffer from wheat allergies, spelt has seen a resurgence in popularity.

Serves 6 to 8

2 cups	water	500 mL
1 cup	spelt (see tip, at left), soaked overnight	250 mL
1 tsp	salt, divided	5 mL
¼ cup	extra-virgin olive oil	50 mL
3	cloves garlic, minced	3
1	large onion, chopped	1
1	stalk celery, chopped	1
1 lb	fresh chorizo sausage (bulk or with casings removed)	500 g
1 tsp	dried oregano	5 mL
1 cup	dry white wine (Sauvignon Blanc or Chardonnay)	250 mL
1	can (14 to 19 oz/398 to 540 mL) cannellini, white kidney or great Northern beans, drained and rinsed	1
1	can (14 to 19 oz/398 to 540 mL) black beans or red kidney beans, drained and rinsed	1
1	can (14 oz/398 mL) diced tomatoes, with juice	1
6 cups	chicken or vegetable stock	1.5 L
1	bunch broccoli rabe, chopped	1
¼ cup	minced fresh flat-leaf (Italian) parsley	50 mL
½ tsp	hot pepper flakes (optional)	2 mL
	Freshly ground black pepper	
	Freshly grated Parmesan cheese (optional)	

1. In a saucepan, bring water, spelt and ½ tsp (2 mL) of the salt to a boil over medium heat. Reduce heat and simmer until spelt is tender, about 45 minutes. Drain and set aside.

2. In a large pot, heat oil over medium heat. Add garlic, onion and celery; sauté until softened, about 6 minutes. Add chorizo, oregano and the remaining salt; sauté, breaking up chorizo with the back of a wooden spoon, until no longer pink, about 5 minutes. Add wine and cook until reduced by half, about 5 minutes.

Tip

San Marzano tomatoes, imported from Italy, are thought by many to be the best canned tomatoes in the world. They hail from a small town of the same name near Naples, whose volcanic soil is thought to filter impurities from the water and render tomatoes with a thick flesh, fewer seeds and a stronger taste. Look for the words "San Marzano" on the label to be sure you're getting the best.

3. Add beans, tomatoes with juice, stock and reserved spelt; bring to a boil. Cover, reduce heat to low and simmer gently for about 30 minutes to blend the flavors. Add broccoli rabe, parsley and hot pepper flakes (if using); simmer until broccoli rabe is tender, about 5 minutes. Season with salt and black pepper to taste.

4. Ladle into heated bowls and garnish with cheese, if desired.

Wild Mushroom and Navy Bean Soup

Wild mushrooms are so easy to find in grocery stores nowadays that it is a crime not to use them. They add big flavor to soups, and we love the colors and shapes for the visual interest they add.

Tip

To clean mushrooms, you can either rinse them quickly in water or wipe them with a damp paper towel. Mushrooms will be much happier in your refrigerator if you store them in a paper bag.

Serves 6

¼ cup	unsalted butter	50 mL
1½ lbs	wild (exotic) mushrooms, sliced	750 g
3	cloves garlic, minced	3
1 cup	thinly sliced green onions	250 mL
½ tsp	salt	2 mL
2 tbsp	all-purpose flour	25 mL
6 cups	beef or mushroom stock	1.5 L
½ cup	dry white wine	125 mL
2	cans (each 14 to 19 oz/398 to 540 mL) navy beans, drained and rinsed	2
1 cup	whipping (35%) cream	250 mL
Pinch	cayenne pepper	Pinch
	Freshly ground black pepper	
¼ cup	minced fresh chives	50 mL

1. In a large pot, melt butter over medium heat. Add mushrooms, garlic, green onions and salt; sauté until mushrooms have released their liquid and are browned, about 10 minutes. Sprinkle with flour and sauté for 2 minutes.
2. Gradually whisk in stock and wine. Add beans and bring to a boil, stirring often. Reduce heat and simmer for about 20 minutes to blend the flavors. Stir in cream, cayenne and salt and black pepper to taste; reheat over medium heat until steaming, stirring often.
3. Ladle into heated bowls and garnish with chives.

Navy Bean and Ham Soup

We return to this soup time and time again when we're looking for the simple flavors of ham and beans.

Tip

Here's how to quick-soak dried beans: In a colander, rinse beans under cold water and discard any discolored ones. In a saucepan, combine beans with enough cold water to cover them by 2 inches (5 cm). Bring to a boil over medium heat and boil for 2 minutes. Remove from heat and let soak, covered, or 1 hour.

Serves 6 to 8

8 cups	cold water	2 L
2 cups	dried navy beans, soaked overnight or quick-soaked (see tip, at left) and drained	500 mL
2	large smoked ham hocks (about 1¾ lbs/875 g total)	2
1	onion, coarsely chopped	1
1	carrot, coarsely chopped	1
1	clove garlic, coarsely chopped	1
2	sprigs fresh thyme	2
1	bay leaf	1
	Salt and freshly ground black pepper	
2 tbsp	chopped fresh parsley	25 mL

1. In a large pot, bring water, beans, ham hocks, onion, carrot, garlic, thyme and bay leaf to a boil over medium heat. Reduce heat and simmer until beans are tender, about 1½ hours. Discard thyme sprigs and bay leaf.
2. Remove ham hocks from the soup and let cool slightly. Pick the meat from the bones and shred into bite-size pieces. Discard bones, fat and skin. Return meat to the soup and simmer until heated through. Season with salt and pepper to taste.
3. Ladle into heated bowls and garnish with parsley.

Red Bean and Rice Soup

▲▼▲▼▲▼▲▼▲▼▲▼▲▼▲▼▲▼▲▼▲▼▲▼▲▼▲▼▲▼▲▼▲▼▲

This New Orleans classic is soul food at its finest. Be sure to pass plenty of extra hot sauce around the table for those spicy personalities in your family.

▲▼▲▼▲▼▲▼▲▼

Tip

It's important not to salt dried beans at the beginning of the cooking process. Sodium prevents the beans from becoming tender. Add salt during the last half of the cooking process (at least 30 minutes before the beans are done) so they can absorb the flavor. If you wait until the end to season with salt, the soup will only taste salty.

Serves 6 to 8

3	slices bacon, cut into ½-inch (1 cm) pieces	3
2	cloves garlic, chopped	2
1	onion, finely chopped	1
1½ cups	chopped celery	375 mL
1½ cups	chopped carrots	375 mL
1	small ham hock (about 8 oz/250 g)	1
2 cups	dried red kidney beans, soaked overnight or quick-soaked (see tip, page 115) and drained	500 mL
6 cups	chicken stock (approx.)	1.5 L
1	bay leaf	1
½ tsp	dried oregano	2 mL
½ tsp	dried thyme	2 mL
1 tsp	salt	5 mL
3 tbsp	dry sherry	45 mL
2 tsp	Louisiana-style hot pepper sauce (such as Tabasco)	10 mL
	Freshly ground black pepper	
2 cups	hot cooked white rice	500 mL
	Chopped green onions	

1. In a large, heavy pot, sauté bacon over medium heat until it renders its fat, about 3 minutes. Add garlic, onion, celery and carrots; sauté until softened, about 6 minutes. Add ham hock, beans, stock, bay leaf, oregano and thyme; bring to a boil. Reduce heat and simmer for 1 hour. Add salt and simmer until beans are tender, about 30 minutes. Discard bay leaf.
2. Remove ham hock from the soup and let cool slightly. Pick the meat from the bone and shred into bite-size pieces. Discard bone, fat and skin. Return meat to the soup and add sherry, hot pepper sauce and salt and pepper to taste. Thin with a little more stock, if necessary, and simmer for 5 minutes, or until hot.
3. Divide rice among heated bowls and top with soup. Garnish with green onions.

White Bean Soup with Pancetta and Sage

▲▼▲▼▲▼▲▼▲▼▲▼▲▼▲▼▲▼▲▼▲▼▲▼▲▼▲▼▲▼▲▼▲▼▲▼▲

While we typically advocate the use of canned beans as a time-saving, quality product, in this soup we like the slightly firmer texture you get when using dried beans.

▲▼▲▼▲▼▲▼

Tip

Pancetta is the Italian version of bacon. If you can't find it, feel free to substitute regular bacon.

Serves 6 to 8

1 tbsp	olive oil	15 mL
3 oz	pancetta, minced	90 g
8	cloves garlic, chopped	8
1	large onion, chopped	1
½ cup	chopped carrot	125 mL
½ cup	chopped celery	125 mL
1½ cups	dried great Northern beans, soaked overnight or quick-soaked (see tip, page 115) and drained	375 mL
1	can (14 oz/398 mL) diced tomatoes, with juice	1
8 cups	chicken stock	2 L
2 tbsp	chopped fresh sage	25 mL
1½ tsp	salt	7 mL
½ tsp	freshly ground black pepper	2 mL
	Extra-virgin olive oil	

1. In a large pot, heat oil over medium heat. Add pancetta and sauté until golden brown and crispy, about 5 minutes. Remove with a slotted spoon to a plate lined with paper towels. Set aside.
2. Add garlic, onion, carrot and celery to the pot; sauté until softened, about 6 minutes. Add beans, tomatoes with juice, stock, sage, salt and pepper; bring to a boil. Reduce heat and simmer, stirring occasionally and thinning with hot water if necessary, until beans are tender, about 1½ hours. Taste and adjust seasoning with salt and pepper, if necessary.
3. Ladle into heated bowls, garnish with reserved pancetta and drizzle with olive oil.

Butternut Squash, White Bean and Pancetta Soup

▲▽▲

The Italians have been combining white beans with butternut squash forever, and once you taste this wonderful partnership, you will too.

▲▽▲▽▲▽▲▽▲▽▲

Tip

Parmesan's rich, nutty flavor is a welcome addition to many soups. By far the best Parmesan is Parmigiano-Reggiano, made in Italy. While it's not cheap, the flavor is well worth the price. You should always buy your cheese in a large chunk and grate it yourself.

Serves 6 to 8

1 tbsp	olive oil	15 mL
3 oz	pancetta, chopped	90 g
1	onion, minced	1
1	large clove garlic, minced	1
2	cans (each 14 to 19 oz/398 to 540 mL) cannellini or white kidney beans, drained and rinsed	2
5 cups	chicken stock	1.25 L
4 cups	diced peeled butternut squash	1 L
1 tsp	finely chopped fresh sage	5 mL
¼ tsp	ground nutmeg	1 mL
⅔ cup	finely grated Parmigiano-Reggiano cheese	150 mL
¼ tsp	freshly ground black pepper	1 mL
	Salt	
	Additional finely grated Parmigiano-Reggiano cheese	
	Extra-virgin olive oil	

1. In a large, heavy pot, heat oil over medium heat. Add pancetta and sauté until golden brown and crispy, about 5 minutes. Remove with a slotted spoon to a plate lined with paper towels. Set aside.
2. Add onion to the pot and sauté until golden, about 8 minutes. Add garlic and sauté for 1 minute. Add beans, stock, squash, sage and nutmeg; bring to a boil. Cover, reduce heat to low and simmer gently, stirring occasionally, until squash is tender, about 30 minutes. Using a potato masher or the back of a wooden spoon, mash some of the squash and beans to thicken the soup. Remove from heat and stir in cheese, pepper and salt to taste. Thin with more stock if necessary.
3. Ladle into heated bowls and garnish with cheese and reserved pancetta. Drizzle with olive oil.

Chunky Bean and Vegetable Soup

▲▽▲

We can't say enough about how nice it is to open a can of beans when making a quick soup. Otherwise, we would be cooking for hours, and sometimes that is simply not in the cards. This weeknight favorite has always been a hit at our homes — for both the diners and the cooks!

▲▽▲▽▲▽▲▽▲▽

Tip
If you can't find canned butter beans, you can substitute navy beans, cannellini beans or white kidney beans.

Serves 6

¼ cup	olive oil	50 mL
1	large onion, chopped	1
3	carrots, chopped	3
2	stalks celery, chopped	2
1	parsnip, chopped	1
1	small bulb fennel, sliced	1
½	celery root (celeriac), diced	½
1 tsp	dried basil	5 mL
1 tsp	dried oregano	5 mL
1 cup	dry white wine	250 mL
6 cups	chicken or vegetable stock	1.5 L
2	cans (each 14 to 19 oz/398 to 540 mL) butter beans (lima beans), drained and rinsed	2
	Salt and freshly ground black pepper	
	Buttery Croutons (optional, see recipe, page 368)	
	Cilantro Swirl (optional, see variation, page 363)	

1. In a large pot, heat oil over medium heat. Add onion and sauté until softened, about 6 minutes. Add carrots, celery, parsnip, fennel and celery root; sauté until vegetables start to soften, about 10 minutes. Add basil and oregano; sauté until fragrant, about 2 minutes. Add wine and cook until reduced by half, about 5 minutes.
2. Add stock and bring to a boil. Reduce heat and simmer until vegetables are tender, about 30 minutes. Add beans and simmer until heated through, about 5 minutes. Season with salt and pepper to taste.
3. Ladle into heated bowls and garnish with croutons or drizzle Cilantro Swirl into the center of the soup and draw a chopstick or knife through the center to create a marbling effect.

Cranberry Bean and Lentil Soup with Cranberry Sauce

The unusual addition of cranberry sauce gives a nice fruity zip to this bean and lentil soup. Though ham and bacon are delicious, we sometimes want a meatless bean soup, and this rendition satisfies in every way.

Variation

This soup is tasty with the addition of grilled or roasted onions, zucchini, yellow squash and red bell peppers.

Serves 6 to 8

2 tbsp	olive oil	25 mL
2 tbsp	unsalted butter	25 mL
1	onion, chopped	1
1	carrot, chopped	1
1	stalk celery, chopped	1
½ tsp	dried thyme	2 mL
6 cups	chicken or vegetable stock (approx.)	1.5 L
2 cups	dried cranberry or pinto beans, soaked overnight or quick-soaked (see tip, page 115) and drained	500 mL
1 cup	dried lentils, rinsed	250 mL
1 tsp	salt	5 mL
1 cup	whole-berry cranberry sauce	250 mL
2 tsp	balsamic vinegar	10 mL
	Freshly ground black pepper	
¼ cup	minced fresh flat-leaf (Italian) parsley	50 mL

1. In a large pot, heat oil and butter over medium heat. Add onion and cook until softened, about 6 minutes. Add carrot and celery; sauté until starting to soften, about 5 minutes. Add thyme and sauté until fragrant, about 1 minute.
2. Add stock and bring to a boil. Add beans, reduce heat and simmer until beans are almost tender, about 1 hour. Add lentils and salt; simmer until lentils are tender, about 45 minutes. Whisk in cranberry sauce and vinegar. Season with salt and pepper to taste.
3. Ladle into heated bowls and garnish with parsley.

Tuscan Bean and Barley Soup

▲▽▲▽▲▽▲▽▲▽▲▽▲▽▲▽▲▽▲▽▲▽▲▽▲▽▲▽▲▽▲▽▲▽▲▽▲▽▲

Meredith had this soup in Lucca, Italy, and fell in love. The contrast of the boldly flavored beans and chewy barley is delightful.

▲▽▲▽▲▽▲▽▲▽▲

Tips

An immersion blender is one of our favorite kitchen tools. Because it can be immersed in the soup, it saves you from transferring hot liquids from the pot to a blender or food processor. Look for one that has a detachable blade unit for easy cleaning.

To make cheese curls, run a vegetable peeler down the side of a chunk of Parmigiano-Reggiano cheese until you have enough curls to garnish 6 to 8 bowls.

Serves 6 to 8

2 tbsp	olive oil	25 mL
3 oz	pancetta, finely chopped	90 g
1	onion, chopped	1
1	carrot, chopped	1
1	stalk celery, chopped	1
½	bulb fennel, diced	½
2 cups	dried cranberry, cannellini, white kidney or great Northern beans, soaked overnight or quick-soaked (see tip, page 115) and drained	500 mL
4	cloves garlic, minced	4
5	sprigs fresh rosemary	5
5	sprigs fresh sage	5
2	sprigs fresh thyme	2
½ cup	pearl barley	125 mL
	Salt and freshly ground black pepper	
	Extra-virgin olive oil	
	Parmesan curls (see tip, at left)	

1. In a large pot, heat oil over medium heat. Add pancetta and sauté until golden brown and crispy, about 5 minutes. Remove with a slotted spoon to a plate lined with paper towels. Set aside.
2. Add onion, carrot, celery and fennel to the pot; sauté until softened, about 6 minutes. Add beans, garlic, rosemary, sage, thyme and about 6 cups (1.5 L) water, or as much as is needed to cover the beans by about 2 inches (5 cm); bring to a boil. Reduce heat and simmer until beans are tender, about 1½ hours. Discard rosemary, sage and thyme sprigs.
3. Meanwhile, cook barley according to package directions and set aside.
4. Using an immersion blender, or in a food processor or blender in batches, purée soup until smooth. Return to the pot, if necessary. Add barley and pancetta; bring to a simmer over medium heat. Season with salt and pepper to taste.
5. Ladle into heated bowls, drizzle with olive oil and garnish with Parmesan curls.

Chickpea Soup with Spinach

▲▼▲▼▲▼▲▼▲▼▲▼▲▼▲▼▲▼▲▼▲▼▲▼▲▼▲▼▲▼▲▼▲▼▲▼

When you're looking for a fast and easy dish that can be made with pantry items you have on hand on a regular basis, look no further than this fresh-tasting soup. If you can't find harissa and don't feel up to making your own, just use ½ tsp (2 mL) cayenne pepper (or more, if you like!) to add a little heat.

▲▼▲▼▲▼▲▼▲

Tip

Harissa is a spicy North African condiment made from oil, chiles, garlic, cumin, coriander and sometimes cinnamon and dried mint. It can be found in a can or a jar at Middle Eastern grocers and at some large grocery stores. If you can't find it, make your own (see page 364).

Serves 6

3 tbsp	unsalted butter	45 mL
1	onion, minced	1
1 lb	spinach (about 10 cups/2.5 L), trimmed	500 g
3	cloves garlic, minced	3
2 tsp	dried basil	10 mL
½ tsp	hot pepper flakes	2 mL
1 tsp	harissa (optional, see tip, at left)	5 mL
2	cans (each 14 to 19 oz/398 to 540 mL) chickpeas, drained and rinsed	2
1	can (14 oz/398 mL) diced tomatoes, with juice	1
6 cups	vegetable or chicken stock	1.5 L
	Salt and freshly ground black pepper	
¼ cup	fresh basil, cut into ribbons	50 mL
	Parmesan curls (see tip, page 121)	

1. In a large pot, melt butter over medium heat until sizzling. Add onion and sauté until softened, about 6 minutes. Add 3 handfuls of spinach and sauté until wilted. Keep adding spinach, a few handfuls at a time, sautéing until all of the spinach is wilted. Add garlic, dried basil, hot pepper flakes and harissa (if using); sauté for 3 minutes.
2. Add chickpeas, tomatoes with juice and stock; bring to a boil. Reduce heat and simmer for at least 30 minutes to blend the flavors. Season with salt and black pepper to taste.
3. Ladle into heated bowls and garnish with fresh basil and Parmesan curls.

Chickpea Soup with Chorizo and Garlic

▲▽▲▽▲▽▲▽▲▽▲▽▲▽▲▽▲▽▲▽▲▽▲▽▲▽▲▽▲▽▲▽▲▽▲

We love the spicy sausage and the tender, meaty beans in this soup. Best of all, it comes together fast enough for Tuesday night dinner before the soccer game.

▲▽▲▽▲▽▲▽▲▽▲

Tip

For a thicker soup, mash some of the beans in the pot with a potato masher.

Variation

If you prefer smoked chorizo sausage instead of fresh, cut it into 1-inch (2.5 cm) pieces, or crumble, and reduce the sautéing time to 2 minutes.

Serves 6

¼ cup	olive oil	50 mL
1	onion, chopped	1
1	carrot, chopped	1
1	stalk celery, chopped	1
1	zucchini, chopped	1
1 lb	fresh chorizo sausage (bulk or with casings removed)	500 g
3 tbsp	finely chopped garlic	45 mL
1 tsp	dried thyme	5 mL
6 cups	chicken or vegetable stock	1.5 L
2 tbsp	tomato paste	25 mL
1 tsp	paprika	5 mL
2	cans (each 14 to 19 oz/398 to 540 mL) chickpeas, drained and rinsed	2
½ tsp	salt	2 mL
¼ tsp	freshly ground black pepper	1 mL
2 tbsp	minced fresh flat-leaf (Italian) parsley	25 mL

1. In a large pot, heat oil over medium heat. Add onion, carrot, celery and zucchini; sauté until softened, about 6 minutes. Add chorizo, garlic and thyme; sauté, breaking chorizo up with the back of a wooden spoon, until no longer pink, about 5 minutes.
2. Add stock, tomato paste and paprika; bring to a simmer. Add chickpeas and simmer until heated through, about 10 minutes. Season with salt and pepper.
3. Ladle into heated bowls and garnish with parsley.

Coconut Curried Chickpea Soup

▲▽▲▽▲▽▲▽▲▽▲▽▲▽▲▽▲▽▲▽▲▽▲▽▲▽▲▽▲▽▲▽▲▽▲▽▲▽▲

Fragrant and hearty, this vegetarian soup is sure to satisfy. Coconut milk adds flavor and richness, while the curry powder gives it a unique complexity found only in Indian-inspired dishes. If you like it hot, add a pinch or two of cayenne pepper.

▲▽▲▽▲▽▲▽▲▽▲

Tip

To toast coconut, add it to a dry skillet and cook over medium heat, stirring constantly, until golden brown. Transfer to a heatproof plate to cool.

Serves 6

2 tbsp	olive oil	25 mL
1	onion, finely chopped	1
2	cloves garlic, minced	2
1 tbsp	curry powder	15 mL
1 lb	small red-skinned potatoes, cut into ½-inch (1 cm) dice	500 g
4 cups	vegetable stock	1 L
1 cup	unsweetened coconut milk	250 mL
½ tsp	salt	2 mL
2	cans (each 14 to 19 oz/398 to 540 mL) chickpeas, drained and rinsed	2
1	zucchini, cut into ½-inch (1 cm) dice	1
1 tbsp	packed light brown sugar	15 mL
1 tbsp	freshly squeezed lime juice	15 mL
2 cups	packed baby spinach (about 3 oz/90 g)	500 mL
	Salt and freshly ground black pepper	
	Toasted sweetened shredded coconut (see tip, at left)	

1. In a large pot, heat oil over medium heat. Add onion and sauté until softened, about 6 minutes. Add garlic and sauté for 1 minute. Add curry powder and sauté for 10 seconds. Add potatoes and stir to coat.
2. Add stock and coconut milk; cook for 10 minutes. Add chickpeas and zucchini; cook for 10 minutes, or until potatoes and zucchini are tender. Stir in brown sugar and lime juice. Add spinach and stir until wilted. Season with salt and pepper to taste.
3. Ladle into heated bowls and garnish with coconut.

Green Lentil Soup

▲▼▲▼▲▼▲▼▲▼▲▼▲▼▲▼▲▼▲▼▲▼▲▼▲▼▲▼▲▼▲▼▲▼▲▼▲

Small green lentils, also known as Puy lentils, are common in France and are now easy to get everywhere else. They are slightly smaller and more delicate than the typical brown lentil, and are a nice change of pace, but brown lentils will work well in this soup too.

▲▼▲▼▲▼▲▼▲▼

Tip

San Marzano tomatoes, imported from Italy, are thought by many to be the best canned tomatoes in the world. They hail from a small town of the same name near Naples, whose volcanic soil is thought to filter impurities from the water and render tomatoes with a thick flesh, fewer seeds and a stronger taste. Look for the words "San Marzano" on the label to be sure you're getting the best.

Serves 6 to 8

4	slices bacon, chopped	4
4	cloves garlic, minced	4
2	stalks celery, chopped	2
1	onion, chopped	1
1	carrot, chopped	1
2	small bay leaves	2
1 tsp	dried thyme	5 mL
2¼ cups	dried green lentils, rinsed	550 mL
10 cups	chicken stock (approx.)	2.5 L
1	can (14 oz/398 mL) diced tomatoes, with juice	1
	Salt and freshly ground black pepper	

1. In a large pot, sauté bacon over medium heat until browned and crispy, about 5 minutes. Remove with a slotted spoon to a plate lined with paper towels. Set aside.
2. Add garlic, celery, onion, carrot, bay leaves and thyme to the pot; sauté until vegetables are softened, about 6 minutes. Add lentils, stock and tomatoes with juice; bring to a boil. Reduce heat and simmer until lentils are tender, about 45 minutes. Thin with a little more stock, if necessary, and simmer for 5 minutes, or until hot. Discard bay leaves. Season with salt and pepper to taste.
3. Ladle into heated bowls and garnish with reserved bacon.

Lentil Soup with Spring Greens

▲▼

Spring greens, usually thought of only as a salad ingredient, make a lovely addition to this earthy lentil soup.

▲▼▲▼▲▼▲▼

Tip
Seasoning with a little bit of lemon juice at the end of cooking heightens the flavor of the soup. Although most home cooks think only in terms of salt and pepper when it comes to adjusting the seasoning in their dishes, we've found that a little acid goes a long way toward making a soup taste just right.

Serves 6

2 tbsp	olive oil	25 mL
1 cup	chopped onion	250 mL
3	cloves garlic, minced	3
8 oz	spicy fresh sausage (such as chorizo or Italian), crumbled	250 g
1	smoked ham hock (about 8 oz/250 g)	1
2	carrots, sliced	2
1	parsnip, sliced	1
6 cups	chicken stock	1.5 L
1 cup	dried brown lentils, rinsed	250 mL
½ tsp	salt	2 mL
Pinch	freshly ground black pepper	Pinch
2 cups	mixed spring greens	500 mL
½ cup	chopped fresh cilantro	125 mL
2 tbsp	freshly squeezed lemon juice	25 mL
	Bacon Croutons (see recipe, page 369)	

1. In a large pot, heat oil over medium heat. Add onion and sauté until softened, about 6 minutes. Add garlic and sauté for 1 minute. Add sausage and sauté, breaking up with the back of a wooden spoon, until no longer pink, about 5 minutes.
2. Add ham hock, carrots, parsnip, stock, lentils, salt and pepper; increase heat to medium-high and bring to a boil. Reduce heat and simmer until lentils are tender, about 45 minutes.
3. Remove ham hock from the soup and let cool slightly. Pick the meat from the bone and shred into bite-size pieces. Discard bone, fat and skin. Return meat to the soup. Bring to a simmer and add spring greens, cilantro and lemon juice; stir until greens have wilted, about 5 minutes. Taste and adjust seasoning with salt and pepper, if necessary.
4. Ladle into heated bowls and garnish with croutons.

Lentil Soup with Roasted Vegetables and Sausage

▲▼▲▼▲▼▲▼▲▼▲▼▲▼▲▼▲▼▲▼▲▼▲▼▲▼▲▼▲▼▲▼▲▼▲▼▲

Roasted butternut squash and red peppers give the hearty lentils a nice sweetness.

▲▼▲▼▲▼▲▼▲▼

Tip

To trim leeks, cut off and discard the root end and the dark green tops (or save the tops for stock). Cut leeks lengthwise and wash under running water to remove any grit or dirt. Then cut as directed in the recipe.

Serves 6

- Preheat oven to 450°F (230°C)
- Large rimmed baking sheet

4 cups	diced peeled butternut squash (½-inch/1 cm dice)	1 L
1	red bell pepper, cut into 1-inch (2.5 cm) pieces	1
2 tbsp	olive oil, divided	25 mL
	Salt and freshly ground black pepper	
2½ cups	chopped leeks, white and light green parts only	625 mL
1 tsp	ground cumin	5 mL
1 tsp	salt	5 mL
½ tsp	freshly ground black pepper	2 mL
½ tsp	dried thyme	2 mL
1¾ cups	dried brown lentils, rinsed	425 mL
6 cups	chicken stock	1.5 L
12 oz	kielbasa or andouille sausage, cut into ½-inch (1 cm) half-moons	375 mL
2 tbsp	minced fresh parsley	25 mL

1. On baking sheet, combine squash, red pepper, 1 tbsp (15 mL) of the oil and salt and pepper to taste; toss to coat evenly and spread into a single layer. Roast in preheated oven, stirring once, until squash is lightly browned, about 45 minutes.
2. Meanwhile, in a large pot, heat the remaining oil over medium heat. Add leeks and sauté until softened, about 12 minutes. Add cumin, salt, pepper and thyme; sauté for 5 minutes. Add lentils and stock; bring to a boil. Reduce heat and simmer until lentils are tender, about 45 minutes. Add sausage and roasted vegetables; simmer until sausage is heated through, about 5 minutes. Taste and adjust seasoning with salt and pepper, if necessary.
3. Ladle into heated bowls and garnish with parsley.

Curried Indian Dal Soup

▲▽▲▽▲▽▲▽▲▽▲▽▲▽▲▽▲▽▲▽▲▽▲▽▲▽▲▽▲▽▲▽▲▽▲▽▲▽▲

Simply cooked lentils, beans and split peas (legumes) are called dal *in Indian cuisine. Legumes are the backbone of Indian meals and supply much-needed protein in what is often a vegetarian diet. This soup comes together quickly and, when served with white or brown rice, is a nutritionally complete meal.*

▲▽▲▽▲▽▲▽▲▽

Tip

Serve with white or brown rice, chapati (Indian flatbread) or flour tortillas.

Serves 6 to 8

1	stick cinnamon, about 1 inch (2.5 cm) long	1
2	whole cloves	2
½ tsp	cardamom seeds	2 mL
½ tsp	cumin seeds	2 mL
½ tsp	coriander seeds	2 mL
2 tbsp	vegetable oil	25 mL
1 tsp	salt	5 mL
½ tsp	ground turmeric	2 mL
1¼ cups	dried yellow lentils, rinsed	300 mL
6 cups	chicken, vegetable or miso stock	1.5 L
	Freshly ground black pepper	
¼ cup	unsalted butter	50 mL
½ cup	chopped onion	125 mL
2	cloves garlic, minced	2
1 tbsp	minced gingerroot	15 mL
¼ tsp	cayenne pepper	1 mL
2 tbsp	chopped fresh cilantro	25 mL
2 tbsp	freshly squeezed lemon juice	25 mL

1. In a small skillet, over medium heat, toast cinnamon, cloves, cardamom seeds, cumin seeds and coriander seeds, shaking the pan or stirring constantly, until fragrant, about 3 minutes, being careful not to burn them. Remove from heat and let cool. Grind to a fine powder in a spice mill or with a mortar and pestle.

2. In a large pot, heat oil over medium heat. Add ground spices, salt and turmeric; sauté until toasty and fragrant, about 1 minute. Add lentils and stock; bring to a boil. Reduce heat and simmer until lentils are tender, about 45 minutes. Using a potato masher, mash some of the lentils to thicken the soup. Thin with a little water, if necessary. Season with salt and black pepper to taste.

3. In a skillet, melt butter over medium heat. Add onion and sauté until starting to brown, about 8 minutes. Add garlic, ginger and cayenne; reduce heat to medium-low and sauté until garlic and ginger are softened, about 3 minutes.

4. Ladle soup into heated bowls and top with onion mixture. Sprinkle with cilantro and lemon juice.

Caribbean Black Bean Soup (page 108)

Overleaf: Wild Mushroom and Navy Bean Soup (page 114)

Spring Pea, Fava Bean and Asparagus Soup with Barley and Lemon

▲▽▲

This soup highlights the best of the spring harvest. Fresh sweet peas and the often misunderstood fava bean join forces with that harbinger of spring we all look forward to: asparagus. This soup is best eaten when just cooked, so that the fresh crispness of the vegetables is in full force.

▲▽▲▽▲▽▲▽▲▽

Tip

Fava beans come in a pod, much like peas. Peel the pod open and dislodge the beans. Blanch the beans in boiling salted water for about 2 minutes. Refresh them under cold running water to cool them off. The pale outer covering will slip right off if you pinch through the covering on the bottom of the bean and then squeeze from the closed end, popping the bean from the rubbery coating. The beans will be bright green and still a little raw. It is a bit of work, but it goes quickly with help from friends and family.

Fontina and Asparagus Soup (page 133)

Overleaf: Coconut Curried Chickpea Soup (page 124)

Serves 6

2 tbsp	unsalted butter	25 mL
1	onion, chopped	1
1	carrot, chopped	1
1	stalk celery, chopped	1
½ tsp	dried thyme	2 mL
6 cups	vegetable stock (or a combination of vegetable and chicken)	1.5 L
¾ cup	pearl barley, rinsed	175 mL
1 cup	shelled and peeled fresh fava beans (about 1 lb/500 g)	250 mL
1 cup	shelled fresh spring peas (about 1 lb/500 g)	250 mL
1	bunch asparagus, trimmed and cut into 1-inch (2.5 cm) pieces	1
¼ cup	minced fresh flat-leaf (Italian) parsley	50 mL
	Salt and freshly ground black pepper	
1 tbsp	grated lemon zest	15 mL
1	lemon, cut into 6 wedges	1

1. In a large pot, melt butter over medium heat until sizzling. Add onion and sauté until softened, about 6 minutes. Add carrot and celery; sauté until starting to soften, 2 to 3 minutes. Add thyme and sauté for 1 minute.
2. Add stock and bring to a boil. Add barley, reduce heat and simmer until barley is almost tender, about 20 minutes. Add beans, peas and asparagus; simmer until vegetables and barley are tender, about 7 minutes. Season with salt and pepper to taste.
3. Ladle into heated bowls and garnish with lemon zest and lemon wedges. Diners may squeeze the lemon over their soup, if they desire.

Split Pea Soup with Pumpernickel Croutons

▲▽▲

▲▽▲▽▲▽▲▽▲▽

Tip

Although we like this soup garnished with Pumpernickel Croutons, feel free to look through the toppings and garnishes chapter (pages 361–374) and mix and match to your heart's delight.

Serves 6 to 8

2 tbsp	olive oil	25 mL
2	stalks celery, finely chopped	2
2	carrots, finely chopped	2
1	onion, finely chopped	1
2	large smoked ham hocks (about 1¾ lbs/875 g total)	2
1 lb	green split peas, rinsed	500 g
8 cups	chicken or vegetable stock	2 L
2	sprigs fresh thyme	2
1	bay leaf	1
	Salt and freshly ground black pepper	
	Pumpernickel Croutons (see variation, page 368)	

1. In a large pot, heat oil over medium heat. Add celery, carrots and onion; sauté until softened, about 6 minutes. Add ham hocks, peas, stock, thyme and bay leaf; bring to a boil. Reduce heat and simmer until soup is thick and peas have broken down slightly, about 1 hour. Discard thyme sprigs and bay leaf.
2. Remove ham hocks from the soup and let cool slightly. Pick the meat from the bones and shred into bite-size pieces. Discard bones, fat and skin. Return meat to the soup and simmer until heated through. Season with salt and pepper to taste.
3. Ladle into heated bowls and garnish with croutons.

Cheese Please Soups

▲▽▲▽▲▽▲▽▲▽▲▽▲▽▲▽▲▽▲▽▲▽▲▽▲▽▲

Pear and Cambozola Soup

▲▽▲▽▲▽▲▽▲▽▲▽▲▽▲▽▲▽▲▽▲▽▲▽▲▽▲▽▲▽▲▽▲▽▲

Surprisingly easy and delicious, this light, elegant soup can be made in minutes and would make a sophisticated starter to any meal. The earthy saltiness of the cheese is the perfect contrast to the sweetness of the pears.

▲▽▲▽▲▽▲▽▲▽

Tips

Be sure to use pears that are ripe and flavorful to get the best flavor in this soup. We used Bartletts because they are easiest to find.

When preparing the pears, add the pieces directly to the lemon juice to prevent browning while you work.

Serves 4

4	large pears, peeled and cut into large chunks	4
1 tbsp	freshly squeezed lemon juice	15 mL
3 cups	chicken stock	750 mL
1 tbsp	chopped fresh sage	15 mL
8 oz	Cambozola cheese, cut into small pieces	250 g
8	Fried Sage Leaves (see recipe, page 367)	8

1. In a large pot, toss pears with lemon juice. Add stock and sage; bring to a simmer over medium heat. Simmer until pears are very soft, 10 to 15 minutes.

2. Using an immersion blender, or in a food processor or blender in batches, purée soup until smooth. Return to the pot, if necessary, and bring to a simmer over medium heat. Add cheese, a few pieces at a time, stirring with a wooden spoon after each addition, until cheese is melted and soup is creamy and smooth.

3. Ladle into heated bowls and garnish each with 2 fried sage leaves.

Fontina and Asparagus Soup

▲▽▲▽▲▽▲▽▲▽▲▽▲▽▲▽▲▽▲▽▲▽▲▽▲▽▲▽▲▽▲▽▲

We love to cook with fontina cheese. It's creamy, it melts beautifully, and it doesn't overpower the other ingredients in a dish. Here, we've paired it with asparagus, and the two bring out the best in each other.

▲▽▲▽▲▽▲▽▲▽▲

Tip

We like to add small amounts of cayenne and nutmeg to many of our soups because they add immeasurably to the flavor without announcing their presence.

Serves 4 to 6

¼ cup	unsalted butter	50 mL
¼ cup	all-purpose flour	50 mL
4 cups	milk	1 L
2 cups	chicken or vegetable stock	500 mL
1 tsp	salt	5 mL
Pinch	cayenne pepper	Pinch
Pinch	ground nutmeg	Pinch
1	bunch asparagus, trimmed and cut into 1-inch (2.5 cm) pieces	1
2 cups	shredded fontina cheese, tossed with 1 tbsp (15 mL) all-purpose flour	500 mL
	Freshly ground black pepper	
	Cheesy Croutons (see recipe, page 369)	

1. In a large soup pot, melt butter over medium-high heat. Sprinkle with flour and sauté until foamy, about 2 minutes.
2. Gradually whisk in milk, stock, salt, cayenne and nutmeg; reduce heat and simmer, whisking, until smooth and creamy, about 3 minutes. Add asparagus and simmer, stirring occasionally, until tender, about 5 minutes.
3. Using an immersion blender, or in a food processor or blender in batches, purée soup until smooth. Return to the pot, if necessary. Add cheese, ½ cup (125 mL) at a time, stirring with a wooden spoon after each addition until cheese is melted. Return pot to low heat, if necessary, to keep soup hot and melt cheese. Do not let boil. Season with salt and black pepper to taste.
4. Ladle into heated bowls and garnish with croutons.

Broccoli and Cheddar Soup

▲▽▲▽▲▽▲▽▲▽▲▽▲▽▲▽▲▽▲▽▲▽▲▽▲▽▲▽▲▽▲▽▲▽▲▽▲▽▲

If you're having trouble getting your children to eat their vegetables, set out bowls of this creamy, cheesy soup. The broccoli adds lovely flavor without yelling, "You're eating a veggie!"

▲▽▲▽▲▽▲▽▲▽▲

Tip

If you prefer, you can substitute 2½ cups (625 mL) chopped cooked fresh broccoli (about 2 large stalks).

Serves 4 to 6

¼ cup	unsalted butter	50 mL
1	onion, finely chopped	1
¼ cup	all-purpose flour	50 mL
3 cups	milk	750 mL
2 cups	chicken or vegetable stock	500 mL
1 tsp	salt	5 mL
Pinch	cayenne pepper	Pinch
Pinch	ground nutmeg	Pinch
2 cups	shredded Cheddar cheese, tossed with 1 tbsp (15 mL) all-purpose flour	500 mL
1 tsp	hot pepper sauce (optional)	5 mL
1	package (10 oz/300 g) frozen chopped broccoli, thawed and drained	1
	Buttery Croutons (see recipe, page 368) or Cornbread Croutons (see recipe, page 369)	

1. In a large pot, melt butter over medium-high heat. Add onion and cook until softened, about 3 minutes. Sprinkle with flour and sauté for 2 minutes.
2. Gradually whisk in milk, stock, salt, cayenne pepper and nutmeg; reduce heat and simmer, whisking, until smooth and creamy, about 3 minutes. Add cheese, ½ cup (125 mL) at a time, stirring with a wooden spoon after each addition until cheese is melted. Do not let boil. Stir in hot pepper sauce (if using). Add broccoli and cook, stirring, until heated through.
3. Ladle into heated bowls and garnish with croutons.

Cheesy Cream of Cauliflower Soup

▲▽▲▽▲▽▲▽▲▽▲▽▲▽▲▽▲▽▲▽▲▽▲▽▲▽▲▽▲▽▲▽▲▽▲▽▲▽▲

If big cauliflower flavor isn't enough, how about adding Cheddar cheese and half-and-half cream into the bargain? This soup is so rich and creamy it makes even a Tuesday night feel like the weekend.

▲▽▲▽▲▽▲▽▲▽▲

Tip

An immersion blender is one of our favorite kitchen tools. Because it can be immersed in the soup, it saves you from transferring hot liquids from the pot to a blender or food processor. Look for one that has a detachable blade unit for easy cleaning.

Serves 6 to 8

- Preheat oven to 400°F (200°F)
- Rimmed baking sheet

1	large head cauliflower, cut into florets (about 4 cups/1 L)	1
2 tbsp	olive oil	25 mL
½ tsp	salt	2 mL
	Freshly ground black pepper	
3 tbsp	unsalted butter	45 mL
1	large onion, chopped	1
3 tbsp	all-purpose flour	45 mL
1 tsp	ground fennel seeds	5 mL
6 cups	chicken or vegetable stock	1.5 L
1½ cups	shredded Cheddar cheese, divided	375 mL
1 cup	half-and-half (10%) cream	250 mL
1 tsp	freshly squeezed lemon juice	5 mL
Pinch	cayenne pepper	Pinch
Pinch	ground nutmeg	Pinch

1. On baking sheet, combine cauliflower, oil, salt and black pepper to taste; toss to coat evenly and spread into a single layer. Roast in preheated oven for 20 minutes or until starting to brown around the edges and is tender. Set aside 6 to 8 nicely browned florets to use as a garnish.
2. In a large pot, melt butter over medium-high heat. Add onion and sauté until softened and starting to brown, about 3 minutes. Sprinkle with flour and fennel seeds; sauté for 2 minutes.
3. Gradually whisk in stock. Add roasted cauliflower and bring to a boil. Reduce heat and simmer, stirring often, until soup has thickened, about 10 minutes.
4. Using an immersion blender, pulse the soup in 3 or 4 quick spurts to partially blend it, leaving it chunky (or process half the soup in a food processor or blender, then return to the pot). Add ½ cup (125 mL) of the cheese, cream, lemon juice, cayenne and nutmeg; reduce heat to low and stir until cheese is melted. Do not let boil. Taste and adjust seasoning with salt and black pepper, if necessary.
5. Ladle into heated bowls and garnish with reserved cauliflower and the remaining cheese.

Roasted Cauliflower, Cheddar and Ham Soup

▲▼▲

When you roast cauliflower, it morphs into a completely different vegetable. Mellow and sweet, roasted cauliflower provides a savory background flavor that pairs beautifully with Cheddar cheese. We couldn't resist adding parsnips, as they add a round, even sweeter note to this new cold weather favorite.

▲▼▲▼▲▼▲▼▲▼

Tip

Use caution when blending hot liquids. It's best to cover the top of the food processor or blender with a towel to prevent any hot soup from splattering out.

Serves 6

- Preheat oven to 400°F (200°C)
- Rimmed baking sheet

1	head cauliflower, separated into 2-inch (5 cm) florets	1
2	parsnips, cut into 1-inch (2.5 cm) pieces	2
2 tbsp	olive oil	25 mL
1 tsp	salt	5 mL
¼ tsp	freshly ground black pepper	1 mL
2 tbsp	unsalted butter	25 mL
2	leeks, white and light green parts only, sliced	2
1	potato, peeled and cut into 1-inch (2.5 cm) cubes	1
5 cups	chicken stock (approx.)	1.25 L
2 cups	diced ham	500 mL
2 cups	milk	500 mL
1 tsp	white wine vinegar	5 mL
Pinch	ground nutmeg	Pinch
Pinch	cayenne pepper	Pinch
1 cup	shredded Cheddar cheese, tossed with 1 tbsp (15 mL) all-purpose flour	250 mL
2 tbsp	minced fresh chives	25 mL

1. On baking sheet, combine cauliflower, parsnips, oil, salt and black pepper; toss to coat evenly and spread in a single layer. Roast in preheated oven until crispy and brown around the edges, 20 to 25 minutes.
2. In a large pot, melt butter over medium heat. Add leeks and sauté until softened, about 6 minutes. Add cauliflower, parsnips, potatoes and stock; bring to a boil. Reduce heat and simmer until vegetables are tender and flavors have blended, about 20 minutes.

Variation

Try nutty Gruyère cheese in place of the Cheddar. If you can't find it, try Swiss or Emmentaler.

3. Using an immersion blender, pulse the soup in 3 or 4 quick spurts to partially blend it, leaving it chunky (or process half the soup in a food processor or blender, then return to the pot.) Stir in ham, milk, vinegar, nutmeg and cayenne. Thin with a little more stock, if necessary, and bring to a simmer. Add cheese, $\frac{1}{2}$ cup (125 mL) at a time, stirring with a wooden spoon after each addition until cheese is melted. Do not let boil. Taste and adjust seasoning with salt and black pepper, if necessary.

4. Ladle into heated bowls and garnish with chives.

Baked Potato Soup with Crispy Potato Skins

▲▼▲

Creamy, rich and comforting, this cheesy potato soup is garnished with crispy potato skins, more cheese, sour cream and bacon, replicating — but improving on — a pub grub favorite.

▲▼▲▼▲▼▲▼▲▼

Tip

Russet baking potatoes will give you the nice crispy skins you expect from real baked potatoes. Though we love them, Yukon gold and red-skinned potatoes won't give the best results in this particular recipe.

▲▼▲▼▲▼▲▼▲▼

Variations

Try using Gruyère instead of Cheddar cheese.

To cut back on fat, try topping the soup with yogurt instead of sour cream.

Serves 6

- Preheat oven to 400°F (200°C)
- Baking sheet

2 lbs	baking potatoes	1 kg
2 tbsp	unsalted butter, melted	25 mL
	Coarse salt	
6	slices bacon, cut into ½-inch (1 cm) pieces	6
1½ cups	diced onions	375 mL
5 cups	chicken stock	1.25 L
5	sprigs fresh thyme	5
1 cup	whipping (35%) cream	250 mL
1 tbsp	Dijon mustard	15 mL
1½ cups	shredded sharp (old) Cheddar cheese, tossed with 1 tbsp (15 mL) all-purpose flour	375 mL
	Salt and freshly ground black pepper	
	Additional shredded Cheddar cheese	
6 tbsp	sour cream	90 mL
6 tbsp	chopped green onions	90 mL

1. Bake potatoes directly on the rack in the center of the preheated oven for 30 minutes. Pierce each potato with a fork in a couple of spots and bake until tender, about 30 minutes. Remove from the oven and increase oven temperature to 450°F (230°C).

2. When potatoes are cool enough to handle, cut each one in half and scrape out the flesh, leaving a ¼-inch (0.5 cm) thick shell. Place potato flesh in a bowl and mash with a fork; set aside. Brush insides of shells lightly with melted butter and season lightly with coarse salt. Cut each shell in half lengthwise, then into ½-inch (1 cm) strips crosswise. Place on baking sheet and bake until golden and crispy, 10 to 15 minutes. Set aside.

3. Meanwhile, in a large, heavy pot, sauté bacon over medium heat until crispy, about 5 minutes. Remove with a slotted spoon to a plate lined with paper towels. Set aside.

Tip

Be careful not to let the soup boil after adding the cheese, or it will curdle.

4. Add onions to the pot and sauté until softened, about 6 minutes. Add stock, thyme and mashed potato, stirring until blended; bring to a boil. Reduce heat and simmer for 30 minutes. Discard thyme sprigs.

5. Gradually whisk in cream and mustard; bring to a simmer. Add cheese, $\frac{1}{2}$ cup (125 mL) at a time, stirring with a wooden spoon after each addition until cheese is melted and soup is smooth. Do not let boil. Season with salt and pepper to taste.

6. Ladle into heated bowls and garnish with potato skins, cheese, sour cream, green onions and reserved bacon.

Mac and Cheese Soup
with Bacon Croutons

Everyone likes mac and cheese, and trust us, bacon croutons only make it better!

Serves 6

¼ cup	unsalted butter	50 mL
1	large onion, finely chopped	1
1	red bell pepper, finely chopped	1
2	cloves garlic, minced	2
⅓ cup	all-purpose flour	75 mL
4 cups	chicken stock	1 L
2 cups	milk	500 mL
1 cup	whipping (35%) cream	250 mL
8 oz	elbow macaroni (about 2 cups/500 mL)	250 g
4 cups	shredded sharp (old) Cheddar cheese, tossed with 1 tbsp (15 mL) all-purpose flour	1 L
¼ tsp	cayenne pepper	1 mL
	Salt and freshly ground black pepper	
	Bacon Croutons (see recipe, page 369)	

1. In a large, heavy pot, melt butter over medium heat. Add onion and red pepper; sauté until softened, about 6 minutes. Add garlic and sauté for 2 minutes. Sprinkle with flour and sauté for 2 minutes.
2. Gradually whisk in stock, milk and cream; bring to a simmer, stirring often. Reduce heat and simmer, stirring often, until soup thickens slightly and flavors have blended, about 20 minutes.
3. Meanwhile, cook macaroni according to package directions. Drain, rinse and set aside.
4. Add cheese to the soup, ½ cup (125 mL) at a time, stirring with a wooden spoon after each addition until cheese is melted and soup is smooth. Do not let boil. Season with cayenne and salt and black pepper to taste.
5. Divide macaroni among heated bowls and top with soup. Garnish with croutons.

Southwest Monterey Jack Soup

▲▽▲

Poblano chiles may be on the mild side, but they are a flavor powerhouse. Here, we combine them with the mild creaminess of Monterey Jack, and just because we can, we've added a serrano chile for a little extra zing.

▲▽▲▽▲▽▲▽▲

Tip

Chile peppers contain oils that can cause chemical burns on your skin. When seeding and chopping them, always wear latex, plastic or rubber gloves.

Serves 6

¼ cup	unsalted butter	50 mL
1	large onion, finely chopped	1
1	serrano or other hot green chile pepper, seeded and minced	1
1	poblano chile pepper, seeded and finely chopped	1
2	cloves garlic, minced	2
⅓ cup	all-purpose flour	75 mL
4 cups	chicken stock	1 L
2 cups	milk	500 mL
1 cup	whipping (35%) cream	250 mL
4 cups	shredded Monterey Jack cheese, tossed with 1 tbsp (15 mL) all-purpose flour	1 L
	Salt and freshly ground black pepper	
	Crispy Tortilla Strips (see recipe, page 372)	

1. In a large, heavy pot, melt butter over medium heat. Add onion, serrano chile and poblano chile; sauté until softened, about 6 minutes. Add garlic and sauté for 2 minutes. Sprinkle with flour and sauté for 2 minutes.
2. Gradually whisk in stock, milk and cream; bring to a simmer, stirring often. Reduce heat and simmer, stirring often, until soup thickens slightly and flavors have blended, about 20 minutes. Add cheese, ½ cup (125 mL) at a time, stirring with a wooden spoon after each addition until cheese is melted and soup is smooth. Do not let boil. Season with salt and pepper to taste.
3. Ladle into heated bowls and garnish with tortilla strips.

Nacho Cheese and Chicken Soup

▲▼▲

Spicy, cheesy chicken soup is garnished with all the familiar flavors of nachos to make a family-friendly treat your loved ones will ask for again and again.

▲▼▲▼▲▼▲▼▲

Tip

When making this recipe, we take advantage of the precooked rotisserie chicken found at almost any grocery store. One chicken usually yields about 3 cups (750 mL) meat.

Serves 6

¼ cup	unsalted butter	50 mL
1	large onion, finely chopped	1
1	serrano or other hot green chile pepper, seeded and minced	1
2	cloves garlic, minced	2
⅓ cup	all-purpose flour	75 mL
2 tbsp	chili powder	25 mL
½ tsp	ground cumin	2 mL
¼ tsp	cayenne pepper	1 mL
4 cups	chicken stock	1 L
2 cups	milk	500 mL
1 cup	whipping (35%) cream	250 mL
3 cups	diced cooked chicken	750 mL
2	tomatoes, seeded and diced	2
4 cups	shredded mild Cheddar cheese, tossed with 1 tbsp (15 mL) all-purpose flour	1 L
	Salt and freshly ground black pepper	
	Crispy Tortilla Strips (see recipe, page 372)	
	Sour cream	
	Chopped fresh cilantro	
	Pickled jalapeño slices	

1. In a large, heavy saucepan, melt butter over medium heat. Add onion and serrano chile; sauté until softened, about 6 minutes. Add garlic and sauté for 2 minutes. Sprinkle with flour, chili powder, cumin and cayenne; sauté until fragrant, about 2 minutes.

2. Gradually whisk in stock, milk and cream; bring to a simmer, stirring often. Reduce heat and simmer, stirring often, until soup thickens slightly and flavors have blended, about 20 minutes. Stir in chicken and tomatoes. Add cheese, ½ cup (125 mL) at a time, stirring with a wooden spoon after each addition until cheese is melted. Do not let boil. Season with salt and black pepper to taste.

3. Ladle into heated bowls and garnish with Crispy Tortilla Strips, sour cream, cilantro and jalapeño slices.

Asparagus, Ham and Gruyère Soup

▲▽▲▽▲▽▲▽▲▽▲▽▲▽▲▽▲▽▲▽▲▽▲▽▲▽▲▽▲▽▲▽▲▽▲▽▲

Gruyère is a lovely nutty cheese that is most often found in Swiss cheese fondue. Because it melts beautifully, we thought it would be delicious in this springtime fresh soup.

▲▽▲▽▲▽▲▽▲▽▲

Tip
We've made some suggestions for garnishes, but feel free to look through the toppings and garnishes chapter (pages 361–374) and mix and match to your heart's delight.

Variation
If you feel like gilding the lily, don't hesitate to add ½ cup (125 mL) whipping (35%) cream with the milk for extra richness.

Serves 6

3 tbsp	unsalted butter	45 mL
1	onion, finely chopped	1
1	clove garlic, finely chopped	1
3 tbsp	all-purpose flour	45 mL
4 cups	chicken stock	1 L
1 lb	asparagus, trimmed and cut into ½-inch (1 cm) pieces	500 g
12 oz	ham, cut into ¼-inch (0.5 cm) dice	375 g
2 cups	milk	500 mL
4 cups	shredded Gruyère cheese, tossed with 2 tbsp (25 mL) all-purpose flour	1 L
Pinch	ground nutmeg	Pinch
	Salt and freshly ground black pepper	
	Cornbread Croutons (see recipe, page 369) or Spicy Mustard Croutons (see recipe, page 370)	

1. In a large pot, melt butter over medium heat. Add onion and sauté until softened, about 6 minutes. Add garlic and sauté for 1 minute. Sprinkle with flour and sauté for 1 minute.
2. Gradually whisk in stock. Add asparagus and ham; cook, stirring often, until asparagus is just tender, about 8 minutes.
3. Gradually whisk in milk and bring to a simmer. Add cheese, ½ cup (125 mL) at a time, stirring with a wooden spoon after each addition until cheese is melted and blended. Do not let boil. Season with nutmeg and salt and pepper to taste.
4. Ladle into heated bowls and garnish with croutons.

Zucchini, Cheese and Sausage Soup

▲▽▲▽▲▽▲▽▲▽▲▽▲▽▲▽▲▽▲▽▲▽▲▽▲▽▲▽▲▽▲▽▲▽▲▽▲▽

It's always a good idea to have another use for zucchini, aside from zucchini bread. This hearty soup makes a wonderful vehicle for an overabundance of zucchini and will be a great way to get veggies into the kids.

▲▽▲▽▲▽▲▽▲▽

Tip
If not using homemade chicken stock, be sure to purchase a low-sodium brand.

Variation
For an Oktoberfest twist, replace some of the chicken stock with a bottle of beer and the sausage with diced smoked kielbasa.

Serves 6

2 tbsp	unsalted butter	25 mL
1 lb	Italian sausage (bulk or with casings removed)	500 g
2	cloves garlic, minced	2
1	onion, chopped	1
3 tbsp	all-purpose flour	45 mL
6 cups	chicken stock	1.5 L
3	zucchini, diced	3
½ cup	whipping (35%) cream	125 mL
2 cups	shredded extra-sharp (extra-old) Cheddar cheese, tossed with 1 tbsp (15 mL) cornstarch	500 mL
1 tbsp	freshly squeezed lemon juice	15 mL
	Freshly ground black pepper	
	Buttery Croutons (see recipe, page 368)	

1. In a large, heavy pot, melt butter over medium-high heat. Add sausage and sauté, breaking up with the back of a wooden spoon, until no longer pink, about 5 minutes. Add garlic and onion; sauté for 1 minute. Sprinkle with flour and sauté for 2 minutes.
2. Gradually whisk in stock and bring to a boil. Add zucchini, reduce heat and simmer until tender, about 15 minutes.
3. Gradually whisk in cream and bring to a simmer. Add cheese, ½ cup (125 mL) at a time, stirring with a wooden spoon after each addition until cheese is melted. Do not let boil. Add lemon juice and pepper to taste. Taste and adjust seasoning with lemon juice and pepper, if necessary.
4. Ladle into heated bowls and garnish with croutons.

Cheddar, Beer and Kielbasa Soup

▲▼▲▼▲▼▲▼▲▼▲▼▲▼▲▼▲▼▲▼▲▼▲▼▲▼▲▼▲▼▲▼▲▼▲

Want to get your oompahpah on? One batch of this soup will have you polkaing around the kitchen.

▲▼▲▼▲▼▲▼▲▼

Tip

Soup will stay hot much longer in a heated bowl.

Serves 4 to 6

2 tbsp	olive oil	25 mL
1 lb	kielbasa sausage, cut into ½-inch (1 cm) half-moons	500 g
2 tbsp	unsalted butter	25 mL
2	onions, chopped	2
¼ tsp	freshly ground black pepper	1 mL
4	cloves garlic, minced	4
¼ cup	all-purpose flour	50 mL
4 cups	chicken stock	1 L
1	bottle (12 oz/341 mL) lager beer	1
4	sprigs fresh thyme	4
3 cups	shredded Cheddar cheese, tossed with 1 tbsp (15 mL) all-purpose flour	750 mL
	Salt	
2 tbsp	minced fresh flat-leaf (Italian) parsley	25 mL
	Spicy Mustard Croutons (see recipe, page 370)	

1. In a large pot, heat oil over medium heat. Add sausage and sauté until lightly browned, 3 to 4 minutes. Remove with a slotted spoon to a plate lined with paper towels. Set aside.
2. Add butter to the pot and heat until melted. Add onions and pepper; sauté until onions are slightly caramelized, about 10 minutes. Add garlic and sauté for 1 minute. Sprinkle with flour and sauté for 2 minutes.
3. Gradually whisk in stock, beer and thyme; bring to a boil, stirring often. Reduce heat and simmer, stirring occasionally, for 30 minutes. Discard thyme sprigs. Add cheese, ½ cup (125 mL) at a time, stirring with a wooden spoon after each addition until cheese is melted and soup is smooth. Do not let boil. Add reserved sausage. Remove from heat, taste and adjust seasoning with salt and pepper, if necessary.
4. Ladle into heated bowls and garnish with parsley and croutons.

Lasagna Soup

▲▽▲

Sometimes genius comes in the form of a soup, and this is one of those times. It was inspired by Meredith's son Kyle, who, on a trip to the grocery store with Mom, thought up the clever idea of putting all the elements of one of his favorite dishes into a soup bowl. A creamy mixture of ricotta, Parmesan and mozzarella cheeses melts underneath a flavorful sausage, tomato and pasta soup. The hot soup melts the cheese, giving the diner a delightful lasagna-like experience in every spoonful.

▲▽▲▽▲▽▲▽▲▽

Tip

San Marzano tomatoes, imported from Italy, are thought by many to be the best canned tomatoes in the world. Look for the words "San Marzano" on the label to be sure you're getting the best.

Serves 6

2 tsp	olive oil	10 mL
1½ lbs	Italian sausage (bulk or with casings removed)	750 g
2	onions, finely chopped	2
4	cloves garlic, minced	4
2 tsp	dried oregano	10 mL
½ tsp	hot pepper flakes	2 mL
2 tbsp	tomato paste	25 mL
1	can (28 oz/796 mL) diced tomatoes, with juice	1
6 cups	chicken stock	1.5 L
2	bay leaves	2
8 oz	fusilli pasta	250 g
½ cup	finely chopped fresh basil	125 mL
	Salt and freshly ground black pepper	
8 oz	ricotta cheese	250 g
½ cup	freshly grated Parmesan cheese	125 mL
¼ tsp	salt	1 mL
Pinch	freshly ground black pepper	Pinch
2 cups	shredded mozzarella cheese	500 mL

1. In a large pot, heat oil over medium heat. Add sausage and sauté, breaking up with the back of a wooden spoon, until no longer pink, about 5 minutes. Drain any excess fat. Add onions and sauté until softened, about 6 minutes. Add garlic, oregano and hot pepper flakes; sauté for 1 minute. Add tomato paste and sauté until paste turns a rusty brown, about 5 minutes.

2. Add tomatoes with juice, stock and bay leaves; bring to a boil. Reduce heat and simmer for about 30 minutes to blend the flavors. Add pasta, increase heat to medium-high and boil until tender to the bite, about 8 minutes. Discard bay leaves. Stir in basil and season with salt and black pepper to taste.

3. In a small bowl, combine ricotta, Parmesan, salt and black pepper.

4. Divide ricotta cheese mixture evenly among heated bowls. Sprinkle with mozzarella and top with soup.

Hearty Soups for Meat Lovers

▲▽▲▽▲▽▲▽▲▽▲▽▲▽▲▽▲▽▲▽▲▽▲▽▲▽▲▽▲▽

Steak and Potato Soup

▲▽▲▽▲▽▲▽▲▽▲▽▲▽▲▽▲▽▲▽▲▽▲▽▲▽▲▽▲▽▲▽▲▽▲▽▲

All your favorite steakhouse flavors can be found in this soup. Sautéed mushrooms, potatoes, crispy shallots and, of course, tender cubes of steak are brought together in a creamy, beefy soup with just a hint of steak sauce.

▲▽▲▽▲▽▲▽▲

Tips

When browning the beef, make sure you add only enough at one time to make a single layer. Do not overcrowd the pan, or the beef will not brown properly.

Other types of potatoes will work, but we preferred the texture of baking potatoes in this recipe.

Serves 6

1 lb	boneless beef top sirloin steak, cut into ½-inch (1 cm) cubes	500 g
	Salt and freshly ground black pepper	
2 tbsp	olive oil, divided	25 mL
2 tbsp	unsalted butter	25 mL
1	large onion, chopped	1
12 oz	mushrooms, sliced	375 g
2	cloves garlic, minced	2
1 tsp	salt	5 mL
½ tsp	freshly ground black pepper	2 mL
½ tsp	dried thyme	2 mL
2 tbsp	all-purpose flour	25 mL
5 cups	beef stock	1.25 L
1 lb	baking potatoes, peeled and cut into ½-inch (1 cm) dice	500 g
½ cup	whipping (35%) cream	125 mL
1 tbsp	Dijon mustard	15 mL
2 tsp	steak sauce (A1 or your favorite brand)	10 mL
	Crispy Shallots (see recipe, page 367)	

1. Season steak lightly with salt and pepper. In a large pot, heat half the oil over medium-high heat. Add steak, in two batches, and sauté until just browned but still medium-rare inside, about 2 minutes, adding the remaining oil between batches. Remove with a slotted spoon to a warm plate. Set aside and keep warm.
2. Reduce heat to medium, add butter to the pot and heat until melted. Add onion and sauté until softened, about 6 minutes. Add mushrooms and sauté until they have released their liquid and are starting to brown, about 5 minutes. Add garlic, salt, pepper and thyme; sauté for 1 minute. Sprinkle with flour and sauté for 2 minutes.
3. Gradually whisk in stock and bring to a boil, stirring often. Add potatoes, reduce heat and simmer, stirring often, until tender, about 20 minutes. Gradually whisk in cream, mustard and steak sauce; simmer for 5 minutes. Do not let boil.
4. Divide steak among heated bowls and top with soup. Garnish with Crispy Shallots.

Beef Stroganoff and Noodle Soup

▲▽

For this spin on a classic dish, creamy, beefy soup, loaded with mushrooms and gilded with a touch of Cognac, is ladled onto tender bites of steak and silky egg noodles. Make sure you don't skimp on the cut of meat — tough steak will ruin the luxurious effect. If you really want to make a splash, try using beef tenderloin.

▲▽▲▽▲▽▲▽▲▽

Tip

To clean mushrooms, you can either rinse them quickly in water or wipe them with a damp paper towel. Mushrooms will be much happier in your refrigerator if you store them in a paper bag.

Serves 4 to 6

1½ lbs	boneless beef top sirloin or other grilling steak, halved lengthwise, then cut crosswise into ¼-inch (0.5 cm) thick slices	750 g
	Salt and freshly ground black pepper	
2 tbsp	vegetable oil (approx.)	25 mL
¼ cup	unsalted butter, divided	50 mL
¼ cup	finely chopped shallots	50 mL
1½ lbs	mushrooms, thickly sliced	750 g
3 tbsp	all-purpose flour	45 mL
4 cups	beef stock	1 L
2 tbsp	cognac	25 mL
½ cup	whipping (35%) cream	125 mL
1 tbsp	Dijon mustard	15 mL
4 oz	wide egg noodles	125 g
1 cup	sour cream	250 mL
1 tbsp	chopped fresh dill	15 mL

1. Season steak with salt and pepper to taste. In a large pot, heat 1 tbsp (15 mL) of the oil over high heat. Add steak, in two or three batches, and sauté until just browned but still rare inside, about 1 minute per side, adding oil as needed between batches. Remove with a slotted spoon to a warm plate. Set aside and keep warm.
2. Reduce heat to medium, add 3 tbsp (45 mL) of the butter to the pot and heat until melted. Add shallots and sauté until softened, about 3 minutes. Add mushrooms and sauté until they have released their liquid and are browned, about 10 minutes. Sprinkle with flour and sauté for 2 minutes.
3. Gradually whisk in stock, then Cognac; bring to a boil. Reduce heat and simmer, stirring often, until soup is slightly thickened and flavors have blended, about 15 minutes. Gradually whisk in cream and mustard; simmer for 5 minutes. Do not let boil.
4. Meanwhile, in a large pot of boiling salted water, cook noodles until tender to the bite, 6 to 8 minutes. Drain, transfer to a bowl, add the remaining butter and toss to coat. Season with salt and pepper to taste. Keep warm.
5. In a bowl, whisk together sour cream and dill.
6. Divide beef and noodles among heated bowls and top with soup. Top each with a dollop of dilled sour cream.

Amish Beef and Noodle Soup

▲▼▲▼▲▼▲▼▲▼▲▼▲▼▲▼▲▼▲▼▲▼▲▼▲▼▲▼▲▼▲▼▲▼▲▼▲

Amish dishes are typically basic, wholesome fare and this soup is no different. Tender, slow-cooked beef, vegetables and noodles make it dinner.

▲▼▲▼▲▼▲▼▲

Tip

When we instruct you to cut vegetables to a certain size, it's because we think size really does matter in the recipe. In some recipes, we like disciplined dice because the vegetables cook more evenly, and we think the uniformly chopped vegetables make for a nice texture and a more attractive soup.

Serves 6 to 8

2 lbs	boneless beef chuck roast, trimmed and cut into 2-inch (5 cm) chunks	1 kg
	Salt and freshly ground black pepper	
2 tbsp	vegetable oil, divided	25 mL
1	onion, chopped	1
5 cups	beef stock	1.25 L
4	boiling potatoes (about 1¼ lbs/625 g), cut into ½-inch (1 cm) dice	4
3	carrots, cut into ½-inch (1 cm) dice	3
2	stalks celery, cut into ½-inch (1 cm) slices	2
3 cups	water	750 mL
	Hearty Noodles (see recipe, page 368)	

1. Season beef with salt and pepper to taste. In a large pot, heat half the oil over medium-high heat. Add beef, in two batches, and sauté until browned on all sides, about 5 minutes per batch, adding the remaining oil between batches. Remove with a slotted spoon to a warm plate.
2. Reduce heat to medium and add onion; sauté until softened, 3 to 4 minutes. Return beef and any accumulated juices to the pot and add stock; bring to a boil. Cover, reduce heat to low and simmer gently until beef is tender and easily pulled apart, 1½ to 2 hours.
3. Remove beef from the pot with a slotted spoon and, using two forks, pull apart into bite-size shreds. Discard any fat and gristle. Return beef to the pot and add potatoes, carrots, celery and water; increase heat and simmer until vegetables are tender, about 25 minutes. Taste and adjust seasoning with salt and pepper, if necessary.
4. Divide noodles among heated bowls and top with soup.

South of the Border Beef Soup

▲▽▲

A touch of cinnamon, cumin and oregano gives this soup an unexpected, but authentic, Mexican flavor. If you like it hot, feel free to add another serrano chile.

▲▽▲▽▲▽▲▽▲▽

Tip

We can't overstate how important it is to brown meat properly before slow-cooking it. The flavor that develops during the browning process is critical to the overall flavor of the soup. If you overcrowd your pot, the meat will only steam and become gray and will never brown.

Serves 6

2 lbs	boneless beef chuck roast, trimmed and cut into ½-inch (1 cm) pieces	1 kg
	Salt and freshly ground black pepper	
2 tbsp	vegetable oil, divided	25 mL
1	onion, finely chopped	1
3	cloves garlic, finely chopped	3
1	poblano chile pepper, seeded and chopped	1
1	serrano or other hot green chile pepper, seeded and chopped	1
1½ tsp	ground cumin	7 mL
1 tsp	dried oregano	5 mL
½ tsp	ground cinnamon	2 mL
4 cups	beef stock	1 L
1 cup	tomato sauce	250 mL
1	can (14 to 19 oz/398 to 540 mL) pinto beans, drained and rinsed	1
	Pico de Gallo Salsa (see recipe, page 364)	

1. Season beef with salt and pepper to taste. In a large pot, heat half the oil over medium-high heat. Add beef, in two or three batches, and sauté until browned on all sides, about 5 minutes per batch, adding oil as needed between batches. Remove with a slotted spoon to a warm plate.

2. Reduce heat to medium and add onion to the pot; sauté until browned, about 8 minutes. Add garlic, poblano chile and serrano chile; sauté until onion is caramelized, 2 to 3 minutes. Add cumin, oregano and cinnamon; sauté for 1 minute.

3. Return beef and any accumulated juices to the pot and add stock and tomato sauce; bring to a boil. Partially cover, reduce heat to low and simmer gently until beef is tender, 1½ to 2 hours. Add beans and simmer for 10 minutes. Adjust seasoning with salt and pepper, if necessary.

4. Ladle into heated bowls and garnish each with a dollop of salsa.

Burgundy Beef Soup

▲▽

*Wine is a natural
ingredient in soups
because it adds flavor
and its acid tenderizes
meat as it marinates or
cooks. Burgundy is a
French blended wine
of mostly Pinot Noir
grapes. It is a softer,
gentler wine than, say,
Cabernet Sauvignon,
so it is one of our
favorite wines for
cooking. That said,
don't break the bank
on a really fine wine
for this soup. There are
many bottles in the
under-$15 category
that will be just fine
for sipping while the
soup simmers.*

▲▽▲▽▲▽▲▽▲▽

Tip

Soup will stay hot much
longer in a heated bowl.

Serves 6

2 tbsp	olive oil, divided	25 mL
4	slices bacon, chopped	4
2 lbs	boneless beef chuck roast, trimmed and cut into 1-inch (2.5 cm) chunks	1 kg
½ tsp	salt	2 mL
	Freshly ground black pepper	
2 cups	frozen pearl onions, thawed	500 mL
3	carrots, sliced	3
2	stalk celery, sliced	2
2	cloves garlic, minced	2
2	potatoes, peeled and diced	2
1 tsp	dried thyme	5 mL
1 tsp	dried basil	5 mL
1	bay leaf	1
2 cups	dry red wine	500 mL
6 cups	beef stock	1.5 L
1 tsp	balsamic vinegar	5 mL
6	Wild Mushroom Risotto Cakes (optional, see recipe, page 373)	6
¼ cup	minced fresh flat-leaf (Italian) parsley	50 mL

1. In a large pot, heat half the oil over medium heat. Add bacon and sauté until crispy, about 5 minutes. Remove with a slotted spoon to a plate lined with paper towels. Set aside.
2. Season beef with salt and pepper to taste. Add to the pot, in two batches, and sauté until browned on all sides, about 5 minutes per batch, adding the remaining oil between batches. Remove with a slotted spoon to a warm plate.
3. Add onions, carrots and celery to the pot. Reduce heat, if necessary, to keep the bottom from burning. Sauté until vegetables start to soften, about 4 minutes. Add garlic, potatoes, thyme, basil and bay leaf; sauté for 2 minutes.
4. Add wine and scrape up any browned bits on the bottom of the pot. Return beef and any accumulated juices to the pot and add stock; bring to a boil. Cover, reduce heat to low and simmer gently until beef is tender, 1½ to 2 hours. Discard bay leaf and stir in vinegar. Taste and adjust seasoning with salt and pepper, if necessary.
5. Place risotto cakes (if using) in heated bowls and top with soup. Garnish with reserved bacon and parsley.

Beef and Balsamic Roasted Onion Soup

▲▼▲

Combining balsamic vinegar with roasted onions brings out the best elements in both. The sweet but tart vinegar and flavorful onions, made slightly sweet by the roasting process, provide a nice counterpoint to the savory beef.

▲▼▲▼▲▼▲▼▲▼▲

Tip

When browning the beef, make sure you add only enough at one time to make a single layer. Do not overcrowd the pan, or the beef will not brown properly.

Serves 6

• Large rimmed baking sheet

1 lb	boneless beef for stew, trimmed and cut into 2-inch (5 cm) chunks	500 g
	Salt and freshly ground black pepper	
3 tbsp	olive oil, divided	45 mL
1½ cups	dry red wine	375 mL
6 cups	beef stock	1.5 L
½ tsp	dried thyme	2 mL
6	onions, cut into ¼-inch (0.5 cm) slices	6
¼ cup	balsamic vinegar, divided	50 mL
¾ cup	whipping (35%) cream	175 mL
	Garlic Croutons (see Variation, page 368)	

1. Season beef with salt and pepper to taste. In a large pot, heat 1 tbsp (15 mL) of the oil over medium-high heat. Add beef and sauté until browned on all sides, about 5 minutes. Remove with a slotted spoon to a warm plate.
2. Add wine to the pot and scrape up any browned bits on the bottom. Reduce heat to medium, return beef and any accumulated juices to the pot and add stock and thyme; bring to a boil. Reduce heat and simmer until beef is tender and easily pulled apart, 1½ to 2 hours.
3. Meanwhile, preheat oven to 400°F (200°C). On baking sheet, combine onions, the remaining oil and salt and pepper to taste; toss to coat evenly and spread in a single layer. Roast, stirring once or twice, until deeply browned, 45 to 50 minutes. Drizzle with 3 tbsp (45 mL) of the vinegar and roast, stirring occasionally, until onions are dark brown and glazed, 10 to 15 minutes.
4. Remove beef from the pot with a slotted spoon and, using two forks, pull apart into bite-size shreds. Discard any fat and gristle. Return beef to the pot and add roasted onions, cream and the remaining vinegar; simmer for 5 minutes to blend the flavors. Do not let boil. Taste and adjust seasoning with salt and pepper, if necessary.
5. Ladle into heated bowls and garnish with croutons.

Beef, Barley and Mushroom Soup

▲▽▲▽▲▽▲▽▲▽▲▽▲▽▲▽▲▽▲▽▲▽▲▽▲▽▲▽▲▽▲▽▲▽▲▽▲

Deeply beefy, this take on an old classic delivers hearty flavors with a healthy touch. It's the perfect soup for a cold winter day when you want to take the chill off but don't want to overindulge.

▲▽▲▽▲▽▲▽▲▽▲

Tip

We can't overstate how important it is to brown meat properly before slow-cooking it. The flavor that develops during the browning process is critical to the overall flavor of the soup. If you overcrowd your pot, the meat will only steam and become gray and will never brown.

Serves 6

1½ lbs	boneless beef for stew, trimmed and cut into 1-inch (2.5 cm) chunks	750 g
	Salt and freshly ground black pepper	
3 tbsp	olive oil, divided	45 mL
1	large onion, chopped	1
2	bay leaves	2
½ tsp	dried thyme	2 mL
6 cups	beef stock	1.5 L
2	carrots, cut into small dice	2
2	stalks celery, cut into small dice	2
8 oz	shiitake mushrooms, stems removed and caps sliced thinly	250 g
½ cup	pearl barley	125 mL
¼ cup	chopped fresh parsley	50 mL

1. Season beef with salt and pepper to taste. In a large pot, heat 1 tbsp (15 mL) of the oil over medium-high heat. Add beef, in two batches, and sauté until browned on all sides, about 5 minutes per batch, adding oil as needed between batches. Remove with a slotted spoon to a warm plate.
2. Reduce heat to medium and add onion to the pot; sauté until just browned, about 5 minutes. Add bay leaves and thyme; sauté for 1 minute. Return beef and any accumulated juices to the pot and add stock; bring to a boil. Reduce heat and simmer until beef is tender and easily pulled apart, 1½ to 2 hours.
3. In a skillet, heat the remaining oil over medium heat. Add carrots and celery; sauté for 2 minutes. Add mushrooms and sauté until lightly browned, about 5 minutes. Add barley and sauté for 1 minute. Set aside.
4. Remove beef from the pot with a slotted spoon and, using two forks, pull apart into bite-size shreds. Discard any fat and gristle. Return beef to the pot and add sautéed vegetables; bring to a simmer over medium heat. Reduce heat and simmer until barley is tender, about 40 minutes. Discard bay leaves. Taste and adjust seasoning with salt and pepper, if necessary.
5. Ladle into heated serving bowls and garnish with parsley.

Beef and Roasted Butternut Squash Soup

▲▼▲▼▲▼▲▼▲▼▲▼▲▼▲▼▲▼▲▼▲▼▲▼▲▼▲▼▲▼▲▼▲▼▲▼▲

In this soup, the hearty flavors of beef are balanced by the subtly sweet flavors of roasted squash for the perfect answer to a cold fall day.

▲▼▲▼▲▼▲▼

Tip
You can often find butternut squash already peeled and diced in your grocer's produce aisles.

Serves 6

• Large rimmed baking sheet

1½ lbs	boneless beef for stew, trimmed and cut into 1-inch (2.5 cm) chunks	750 g
	Salt and freshly ground black pepper	
4 tbsp	olive oil, divided	60 mL
2	large onions, chopped	2
2	bay leaves	2
½ tsp	dried thyme	2 mL
6 cups	beef stock	1.5 L
1	butternut squash (about 1½ lbs/750 g), peeled and cut into ½-inch (1 cm) dice	1
½ tsp	salt	2 mL
¼ tsp	freshly ground black pepper	1 mL
	Buttery Croutons (see recipe, page 368)	

1. Season beef with salt and pepper to taste. In a large pot, heat 1 tbsp (15 mL) of the oil over medium-high heat. Add beef, in two batches, and sauté until browned on all sides, about 5 minutes per batch, adding oil as needed between batches. Remove with a slotted spoon to a warm plate.
2. Reduce heat to medium and add onions to the pot; sauté until just browned, about 5 minutes. Add bay leaves and thyme; sauté for 1 minute. Reduce heat to medium, return beef and any accumulated juices to the pot and add stock; bring to a boil. Reduce heat and simmer until beef is tender and easily pulled apart, 1½ to 2 hours.
3. Meanwhile, preheat oven to 425°F (220°C). On baking sheet, combine squash, the remaining olive oil, salt and pepper; toss to coat evenly and spread in a single layer. Roast, turning occasionally, until just tender and browned in spots, about 40 minutes.
4. Remove beef from the pot with a slotted spoon and, using two forks, pull apart into bite-size shreds. Discard any fat and gristle. Return beef to the pot and add roasted squash; simmer for 10 minutes to blend the flavors. Discard bay leaves. Taste and adjust seasoning with salt and pepper, if necessary.
5. Ladle into heated bowl and garnish with croutons.

Beef and Bean Soup with Bitter Greens

▲▼▲▼▲▼▲▼▲▼▲▼▲▼▲▼▲▼▲▼▲▼▲▼▲▼▲▼▲▼▲▼▲▼▲

Bitter greens are better-tasting than they sound. They are the tougher greens, such as escarole, endive, frisée, Swiss chard, kale and beet greens, and they abound in the cooler months. When cooked properly, they become tender and delicious. Use whatever looks best at your grocery store for a delicious, earthy dose of vitamins and minerals.

▲▼▲▼▲▼▲▼▲

Tip

To make cheese curls, run a vegetable peeler down the side of a chunk of Parmigiano-Reggiano cheese until you have enough curls to garnish 6 bowls.

Serves 6

1½ lbs	boneless beef for stew, trimmed and cut into 1-inch (2.5 cm) chunks	750 g
	Salt and freshly ground black pepper	
2 tbsp	olive oil, divided	25 mL
3 tbsp	unsalted butter	45 mL
1	onion, minced	1
3	cloves garlic, minced	3
2 tsp	dried oregano	10 mL
1 tsp	salt	5 mL
½ tsp	hot pepper flakes (optional)	2 mL
2	cans (each 14 to 19 oz/398 to 540 mL) kidney beans, drained and rinsed	2
1	can (14 oz/398 mL) diced tomatoes, with juice	1
6 cups	beef stock	1.5 L
2	bunches bitter greens, thinly sliced (6 to 8 cups/1.5 to 2 L)	2
	Parmesan curls (see tip, at left)	

1. Season beef with salt and black pepper to taste. In a large pot, heat half the oil over medium-high heat. Add beef, in two batches, and sauté until browned on all sides, about 5 minutes per batch, adding the remaining oil between batches. Remove with a slotted spoon to a warm plate.
2. Reduce heat to medium, add butter to the pot and heat until melted. Add onion and sauté until softened, 3 to 4 minutes. Add garlic, oregano, salt and hot pepper flakes (if using); sauté for 2 minutes.
3. Return beef and any accumulated juices to the pot and add beans, tomatoes with juice and stock; bring to a boil. Cover, reduce heat to low and simmer gently until meat is tender, 1½ to 2 hours. Add greens one handful at a time, stirring until wilted before adding more. Taste and adjust seasoning with salt and black pepper, if necessary.
4. Ladle into heated bowls and garnish with Parmesan curls.

Beef, Chickpea and Spinach Soup

▲▽▲▽▲▽▲▽▲▽▲▽▲▽▲▽▲▽▲▽▲▽▲▽▲▽▲▽▲▽▲▽▲▽▲▽▲▽▲

Those of us who grew up with Popeye know that it is important to eat your spinach. This soup is so full of goodness, you won't even notice that it is actually good for you.

▲▽▲▽▲▽▲▽▲▽

Tip

Instead of buying precut stew meat, we usually buy a roast and cut it up ourselves. It is cheaper, and we like to cut away some of the sinew and fat that butchers leave on. Also, precut meat is often sold in chunks that are larger than we need or not uniform in size.

Serves 6

1½ lbs	boneless beef for stew, trimmed and cut into 1-inch (2.5 cm) chunks	750 mL
	Salt and freshly ground black pepper	
3 tbsp	unsalted butter, divided	45 mL
1	onion, minced	1
3	cloves garlic, minced	3
2	carrots, sliced	2
1	stalk celery, sliced	1
2 tsp	dried basil	10 mL
1 tsp	dried oregano	5 mL
1 tsp	salt	5 mL
¼ tsp	freshly ground black pepper	1 mL
2	cans (each 14 to 19 oz/398 to 540 mL) chickpeas, drained and rinsed	2
1	can (14 oz/398 mL) diced tomatoes, with juice	1
6 cups	beef stock	1.5 L
8 oz	spinach (about 5 cups/1.25 L), trimmed and roughly chopped	250 g
2 tsp	balsamic vinegar	10 mL
	Spaetzle (see recipe, page 371)	
	Minced fresh flat-leaf (Italian) parsley	

1. Season beef with salt and pepper to taste. In a large pot, melt half the butter over medium-high heat. Add beef, in two batches, and sauté until browned on all sides, about 5 minutes per batch, adding the remaining butter between batches. Remove with a slotted spoon to a warm plate.
2. Reduce heat to medium and add onion to the pot; sauté until softened, 3 to 4 minutes. Add garlic, carrots, celery, basil, oregano, salt and pepper; sauté until vegetables are softened, about 5 minutes.
3. Return beef and any accumulated juices to the pot and add chickpeas, tomatoes with juice and stock; bring to a boil. Cover, reduce heat to low and simmer gently until meat is tender, 1½ to 2 hours. Add spinach one handful at a time, stirring until wilted before adding more. Stir in vinegar. Taste and adjust seasoning with salt and pepper, if necessary.
4. Divide spaetzle among heated bowls and top with soup. Garnish with parsley.

Short-Rib Soup

▲▽▲▽▲▽▲▽▲▽▲▽▲▽▲▽▲▽▲▽▲▽▲▽▲▽▲▽▲▽▲▽▲▽▲▽▲▽▲

Short ribs and shank bones make the most heavenly soups. The bones contain so much gelatin and rich flavor that the meat surrounding the bones is really just an afterthought. You owe it to yourself to make this soup during the cold winter months — you'll be so glad you did!

▲▽▲▽▲▽▲▽▲▽▲

Tip

Seasoning with a little bit of vinegar at the end of cooking heightens the flavor of the soup. Although most home cooks think only in terms of salt and pepper when it comes to adjusting the seasoning in their dishes, we've found that a little acid goes a long way toward making a soup taste just right.

Serves 6

2	cloves garlic, minced	2
2 tsp	each chopped fresh rosemary and thyme	10 mL
1 tsp	each ground coriander, ground cumin, curry powder, salt and freshly ground black pepper	5 mL
3 lbs	beef short ribs	1.5 kg
¼ cup	olive oil, divided	50 mL
6 cups	beef stock	1.5 L
2	stalks celery, chopped	2
2	onions, chopped	2
2	carrots, chopped	2
1	parsnip, chopped	1
1 tsp	balsamic vinegar	5 mL
¼ tsp	cayenne pepper	1 mL
	Barley Risotto (see recipe, page 372)	
¼ cup	minced fresh flat-leaf (Italian) parsley	50 mL

1. In a bowl, combine garlic, rosemary, thyme, coriander, cumin, curry powder, salt and black pepper. Rub over ribs and let stand at room temperature for 30 minutes, or cover and refrigerate overnight.

2. In a large pot, heat half the oil over medium-high heat. Add ribs, in batches, and sauté until browned, about 5 minutes per side, adding oil as needed between batches and reducing the heat if the bottom of the pot begins to blacken. Remove with a slotted spoon to a warm plate.

3. Add stock to the pot and scrape up any browned bits on the bottom; bring to a boil. Return ribs and any accumulated juices to the pot; cover, reduce heat to low and simmer gently for 1½ hours. Add celery, onions, carrots and parsnip; cover and simmer until vegetables are tender and meat is falling off the bones, about 45 minutes.

4. Remove ribs from the pot with a slotted spoon and let cool slightly, then pick the meat from the bones, tearing into bite-size pieces. Discard bones. Skim the fat from the surface of the soup with a large spoon, if desired. Return meat to the pot and add vinegar and cayenne. Taste and adjust seasoning with salt and black pepper, if necessary.

5. Divide risotto among heated bowls and top with soup. Garnish with parsley.

Beef and Ale Soup

▲▽▲▽▲▽▲▽▲▽▲▽▲▽▲▽▲▽▲▽▲▽▲▽▲▽▲▽▲▽▲▽▲▽▲

Ales and beers make great additions to soups. Try using a full-bodied ale or a wheat beer for the best flavor, but if you don't have any on the basement steps or in the refrigerator, even a Bud Light (Carla's beer of choice) will make a good soup better.

▲▽▲▽▲▽▲▽▲▽

Variation
Replace the noodles with Barley Risotto (page 372) or Wild Mushroom Risotto Cakes (page 373).

Serves 6

2	cloves garlic, minced	2
2 tsp	each chopped fresh rosemary and thyme	10 mL
1 tsp	each salt and freshly ground black pepper	5 mL
3 lbs	beef short ribs	1.5 kg
¼ cup	olive oil, divided	50 mL
4 cups	beef stock	1 L
2 cups	ale, lager or wheat beer	500 mL
1	bay leaf	1
2	stalks celery, chopped	2
2	onions, chopped	2
2	carrots, chopped	2
2 cups	diced celery root (celeriac) (½-inch/1 cm dice)	500 mL
1 tsp	balsamic vinegar	5 mL
¼ tsp	cayenne pepper	1 mL
	Hearty Noodles (see recipe, page 368)	
¼ cup	minced fresh flat-leaf (Italian) parsley	50 mL

1. In a bowl, combine garlic, rosemary, thyme, salt and black pepper. Rub over ribs and let stand at room temperature for 30 minutes, or cover and refrigerate overnight.

2. In a large pot, heat half the oil over medium-high heat. Add ribs, in batches, and sauté until browned, about 5 minutes per side, adding oil as needed between batches and reducing the heat if the bottom of the pot begins to blacken. Remove with a slotted spoon to a warm plate.

3. Add stock, ale and bay leaf to the pot and scrape up any browned bits on the bottom; bring to a boil. Return ribs and any accumulated juices to the pot; cover, reduce heat to low and simmer gently for 1½ hours. Add celery, onions, carrots and celery root; cover and simmer until vegetables are tender and meat is falling off the bones, about 45 minutes.

4. Remove ribs from the pot with a slotted spoon and let cool slightly, then pick the meat from the bones, tearing into bite-size pieces. Discard bones. Skim the fat from the surface of the soup with a large spoon, if desired. Return meat to the pot and add vinegar and cayenne. Discard bay leaf. Taste and adjust seasoning with salt and black pepper, if necessary.

5. Divide noodles among heated bowls and top with soup. Garnish with parsley.

Taco Soup

▲▽▲▽▲▽▲▽▲▽▲▽▲▽▲▽▲▽▲▽▲▽▲▽▲▽▲▽▲▽▲▽▲▽▲▽▲▽▲

This simple but fun soup lets diners garnish to suit their own tastes. Try setting all the garnishes in a line on your kitchen counter so your guests can pick and choose as they like.

▲▽▲▽▲▽▲▽▲▽

Tip

San Marzano tomatoes, imported from Italy, are thought by many to be the best canned tomatoes in the world. They hail from a small town of the same name near Naples, whose volcanic soil is thought to filter impurities from the water and render tomatoes with a thick flesh, fewer seeds and a stronger taste. Look for the words "San Marzano" on the label to be sure you're getting the best.

Serves 6

1 tbsp	olive oil	15 mL
2	cloves garlic, minced	2
1	onion, finely chopped	1
2 tbsp	chili powder	25 mL
2 tsp	ground cumin	10 mL
1 tsp	dried oregano	5 mL
1½ lbs	lean ground beef	750 g
2	cans (each 14 to 19 oz/398 to 540 mL) pinto beans, drained and rinsed	2
1	can (28 oz/796 mL) diced tomatoes, with juice	1
4 cups	beef stock	1 L
½ tsp	salt	2 mL
	Freshly ground black pepper	
	Crispy Tortilla Strips (see recipe, page 372)	
	Shredded Cheddar cheese	
	Sour cream	
	Diced fresh tomatoes	
	Chopped green onions	

1. In a large pot, heat oil over medium heat. Add garlic and onion; sauté until softened, about 6 minutes. Add chili powder, cumin and oregano; sauté for 1 minute. Add ground beef and sauté, breaking up with the back of a wooden spoon, until no longer pink, about 5 minutes.
2. Add beans, canned tomatoes with juice, stock, salt and pepper; bring to a boil. Reduce heat and simmer for 20 minutes to blend the flavors. Taste and adjust seasoning with salt and pepper, if necessary.
3. Ladle into heated bowls and garnish as desired with tortilla strips, cheese, sour cream, fresh tomatoes and green onions.

Beef Stroganoff and Noodle Soup (page 149)

Overleaf: Texas Cowboy Soup (page 162)

Ground Beef Soup with Chili and Cornmeal Dumplings

▲▽▲

Everyone in your family will look forward to this one-pot dinner, full of meat and beans and topped with tender cornbread.

▲▽▲▽▲▽▲▽▲▽

Tip

Make sure the soup is simmering in Step 4 to cook the dumplings properly. Don't lift the lid right off though, just lift it a little to peek in so you don't release all of the heat.

Serves 6

¼ cup	olive oil	50 mL
1	onion, chopped	1
1	red or green bell pepper, chopped	1
1½ lbs	lean ground beef	750 g
3	cloves garlic, minced	3
2 tbsp	chili powder	25 mL
2	cans (each 14 to 19 oz/398 to 540 mL) kidney beans, drained and rinsed	2
1	can (14 oz/398 mL) diced tomatoes, with juice	1
4 cups	beef stock	1 L
2 tsp	salt	10 mL
	Freshly ground black pepper	
2	green onions, thinly sliced	2

Cornmeal Dumplings

½ cup	all-purpose flour	125 mL
½ cup	yellow cornmeal	125 mL
1 tsp	baking powder	5 mL
¼ tsp	salt	1 mL
1	egg	1
½ cup	milk	125 mL
2 tbsp	vegetable oil	25 mL

1. In a large pot, heat olive oil over medium heat. Add onion and red pepper; sauté until starting to soften, about 2 minutes. Add ground beef and sauté, breaking up with the back of a wooden spoon, until only a trace of pink remains, about 2 minutes. Add garlic and chile powder; sauté for 2 minutes to blend the flavors. Add beans, tomatoes with juice, stock, salt and pepper to taste; bring to a boil. Reduce heat and simmer while you assemble the dumplings.

2. *Prepare the dumplings:* In a large bowl, combine flour, cornmeal, baking powder and salt.

3. In a measuring cup, whisk together egg, milk and vegetable oil; pour into dry ingredients and mix just until combined.

4. Dot cornmeal mixture over top of soup; cover and simmer until dumplings are cooked through, about 25 minutes.

5. Ladle into heated bowls and garnish with green onions.

Garlic Soup and Pork Rolls (page 168)

Overleaf: Wild Mushroom and Orzo Soup with Italian Meatballs (page 164)

Texas Cowboy Soup

▲▽▲

When you're cooking out of a chuckwagon, necessity is the mother of invention, especially when you're feeding armed, hungry cowhands. Many a meal has been made of beef, beans and whatever else was available, and a soup similar to this was surely on the menu for many nights around the campfire.

▲▽▲▽▲▽▲▽▲▽▲

Tips

If you can't find canned tomatoes with green chiles, just use canned diced tomatoes and add a small can of chopped green chiles.

Instead of canned corn, you can use 3 cups (750 mL) frozen corn kernels. Thaw and drain before adding to soup.

Serves 8 to 10

6	slices bacon, chopped	6
1½ lbs	lean ground beef	750 g
4	cloves garlic, chopped	4
1	onion, chopped	1
2 tbsp	chili powder	25 mL
1 tsp	ground cumin	5 mL
½ tsp	salt	2 mL
¼ tsp	freshly ground black pepper	1 mL
2	baking potatoes, peeled and diced	2
2	cans (each 14 to 19 oz/398 to 540 mL) pinto beans, drained and rinsed	2
1	can (14 oz/398 mL) diced tomatoes, drained	1
1	can (14 oz/398 mL) diced tomatoes with green chile peppers, with juice	1
4 cups	beef stock	1 L
1	can (14 oz/398 mL) corn kernels, drained	1
	Cornbread Croutons (see recipe, page 369)	

1. In a large pot, sauté bacon over medium heat until starting to brown. Add ground beef and sauté, breaking up with the back of a wooden spoon, until no longer pink, about 5 minutes. Add garlic, onion, chili powder, cumin, salt and pepper; sauté until onion starts to soften, about 3 minutes.
2. Add potatoes, beans, both cans of tomatoes and stock; bring to a boil. Reduce heat and simmer until potatoes are just tender, about 20 minutes. Add corn and simmer for 10 minutes.
3. Ladle into heated bowls and garnish with croutons.

Meatball Soup

▲▽▲▽▲▽▲▽▲▽▲▽▲▽▲▽▲▽▲▽▲▽▲▽▲▽▲▽▲▽▲▽▲▽▲▽▲

This soup reminds us of pasta with meatballs, and nothing tastes finer on a blustery fall day.

▲▽▲▽▲▽▲▽▲▽

Tip

Parmesan's rich, nutty flavor is a welcome addition to many soups. By far the best Parmesan is Parmigiano-Reggiano, made in Italy. While it's not cheap, the flavor is well worth the price. You should always buy your cheese in a large chunk and grate it yourself.

Serves 8

3 tbsp	olive oil	45 mL
2	onions, finely chopped	2
2	cloves garlic, minced	2
1	carrot, cut into small dice	1
1	stalk celery, cut into small dice	1
1 tsp	dried basil	5 mL
1 tsp	dried oregano	5 mL
1	can (28 oz/796 mL) crushed tomatoes	1
1 cup	dry red wine	250 mL
8 cups	beef stock	2 L
1 tbsp	balsamic vinegar	15 mL
1 tbsp	packed brown sugar	15 mL
1 tsp	salt	5 mL
	Italian Meatballs (see recipe, page 368, or tip, page 164)	
1 cup	orzo	250 mL
	Freshly ground black pepper	
	Freshly grated Parmesan cheese	
¼ cup	minced fresh flat-leaf (Italian) parsley	50 mL

1. In a large pot, heat oil over medium heat. Add onions and sauté until softened, about 6 minutes. Add garlic, carrot, celery, basil and oregano; sauté until vegetables are almost soft, about 5 minutes.
2. Add tomatoes and wine; cook until liquid is slightly reduced, about 5 minutes. Add stock, vinegar, brown sugar and salt; bring to a boil. Carefully add meatballs and bring back to a boil. Cover, reduce heat to low and simmer gently for 10 minutes. Increase heat to medium-high and bring soup to a boil. Stir in orzo and boil, uncovered, until meatballs are cooked through and orzo is tender, about 10 minutes. Season with salt and pepper to taste.
3. Divide meatballs among heated bowls and top with soup. Garnish with cheese and parsley.

Wild Mushroom and Orzo Soup with Italian Meatballs

▲▽▲▽▲▽▲▽▲▽▲▽▲▽▲▽▲▽▲▽▲▽▲▽▲▽▲▽▲▽▲▽▲▽▲▽▲▽▲

Wild mushrooms have a big, beefy flavor that partners well with meatballs. This soup's gutsy Italian flavors are sure to make it one of your favorites.

▲▽▲▽▲▽▲▽▲▽

Tip

Grocery stores sometimes carry uncooked meatballs, packaged in the meat case, that they have made up themselves. We think it makes good sense to take advantage of this step-saving bonus, especially when the meatballs are of good quality. One caveat, though, is that store-bought meatballs are usually on the large side. We cut them in half and then reroll them into a ball. It only takes a minute, and they are a more "attackable" size in your soup bowl.

Serves 6 to 8

2 tbsp	unsalted butter	25 mL
2 tbsp	olive oil	25 mL
1	large onion, minced	1
1½ lbs	wild (exotic) mushrooms, sliced	750 g
1	stalk celery, chopped	1
1 tsp	salt	5 mL
1 tsp	dried basil	5 mL
1 tsp	dried oregano	5 mL
6 cups	beef or chicken stock	1.5 L
	Italian Meatballs (see recipe, page 368)	
1 cup	orzo	250 mL
¼ cup	minced fresh flat-leaf (Italian) parsley	50 mL
2 tsp	freshly squeezed lemon juice	10 mL
¼ cup	freshly grated Parmigiano-Reggiano cheese	50 mL
	Freshly ground black pepper	
	Additional freshly grated Parmigiano-Reggiano cheese	

1. In a large pot, heat butter and oil over medium-high heat. Add onion and sauté until starting to soften, about 2 minutes. Add mushrooms, celery, salt, basil and oregano; sauté until vegetables begin to soften and mushrooms have released their liquid, about 5 minutes.
2. Add stock and bring to a boil. Carefully add meatballs and bring back to a boil. Reduce heat and simmer until meatballs are cooked through and vegetables are tender, about 25 minutes. Increase heat to medium-high and bring soup to a boil. Stir in orzo and boil until tender, about 8 minutes. Add parsley, lemon juice, cheese and salt and pepper to taste.
3. Ladle into heated bowls and pass additional cheese at the table.

Lamb and Lentil Soup

▲▽▲

This Indian-inspired soup is redolent with the flavors of the East: curry powder, cumin, mint and yogurt.

▲▽▲▽▲▽▲▽▲

Tip

Although we like this soup garnished with Yogurt Mint Cream, feel free to look through the toppings and garnishes chapter (pages 361–374) and mix and match to your heart's delight.

Serves 6

2 tbsp	olive oil	25 mL
1 lb	ground lamb	500 g
4	cloves garlic, chopped	4
2	stalks celery, chopped	2
2	carrots, chopped	2
1	onion, chopped	1
1 tbsp	curry powder	15 mL
1 tsp	ground cumin	5 mL
1 tsp	salt	5 mL
¼ tsp	freshly ground black pepper	1 mL
1½ cups	dried brown lentils, rinsed	375 mL
1	can (14 oz/398 mL) diced tomatoes, with juice	1
7 cups	beef stock (approx.)	1.75 L
	Mint Yogurt Swirl (see variation, page 364)	

1. In a large pot, heat oil over medium heat. Add ground lamb and sauté, breaking up with the back of a wooden spoon, until no longer pink, about 5 minutes. Add garlic, celery, carrots and onion; sauté until softened, about 6 minutes. Add curry powder, cumin, salt and pepper; sauté for 1 minute.

2. Add lentils, tomatoes with juice and stock; bring to a boil. Reduce heat and simmer until lentils are just tender, but not mushy, about 45 minutes. Thin with a little more stock, if necessary. Taste and adjust seasoning with salt and pepper, if necessary.

3. Ladle into heated bowls and top each with a dollop of Yogurt Mint Cream.

Oxtail and Barley Soup

▲▽▲▽▲▽▲▽▲▽▲▽▲▽▲▽▲▽▲▽▲▽▲▽▲▽▲▽▲▽▲▽▲▽▲▽▲▽▲

Oxtail soup is one of those oldie-but-goodie soups that is making a huge comeback in upscale restaurants. It gets its rich, deep flavor from browning the oxtail pieces to a deep golden brown before adding the wine and stock. It takes a bit of time, but this step is crucial to obtain the necessary depth of flavor. We like to give this soup a good long cook to tenderize the delicious meat that surrounds the bone and to get all that velvety collagen out of the bones and into the soup.

▲▽▲▽▲▽▲▽▲▽▲

Tip

Five-spice powder is a blend of ground cloves, fennel seeds, cinnamon, star anise and Szechwan peppercorns. Most large grocery stores stock it, but if you can't find it, just use a mixture of the individual spices. It will still taste delicious.

Serves 4 to 6

3 tbsp	olive oil	45 mL
3	slices bacon, chopped	3
4 lbs	oxtails, cut into 3-inch (7.5 cm) segments	2 kg
2	carrots, chopped	2
1	stalk celery, chopped	1
1	onion, chopped	1
2	cloves garlic, chopped	2
1	can (14 oz/398 mL) diced tomatoes, with juice	1
4 cups	beef stock	1 L
1 cup	dry white wine	250 mL
1 tsp	salt	5 mL
1 tsp	dried marjoram	5 mL
½ tsp	five-spice powder (optional)	2 mL
¼ tsp	freshly ground black pepper	1 mL
2 cups	water	500 mL
1 cup	pearl barley	250 mL
¼ cup	minced fresh flat-leaf (Italian) parsley	50 mL
	Garlic Croutons (see variation, page 368)	

1. In a large pot, heat oil over medium heat. Add bacon and sauté until browned and crispy, about 5 minutes. Remove with a slotted spoon to a plate lined with paper towels. Set aside.

2. Increase heat to medium-high and add half the oxtails, cut ends down, to the pot; let cook, undisturbed, until browned, about 8 minutes. Turn to brown the other end, then brown the sides. Remove with a slotted spoon to a warm plate. Repeat with remaining oxtails.

3. Reduce heat to medium and add carrots, celery and onion to the pot; sauté until softened, 3 to 4 minutes. Return the oxtails and any accumulated juices to the pot and add garlic, tomatoes with juice, stock, wine, salt, marjoram, five-spice powder (if using) and pepper; bring to a boil. Cover, reduce heat to low and simmer gently until meat is falling off the bones, about 2 hours.

Tip

We can't overstate how important it is to brown meat properly before slow-cooking it. The flavor that develops during the browning process is critical to the overall flavor of the soup. If you overcrowd your pot, the meat will only steam and become gray and will never brown.

4. Meanwhile, in a saucepan, bring water to a boil over medium heat. Add barley and a pinch of salt; cover, reduce heat to low and simmer until tender, about 20 minutes.

5. Remove oxtails from the pot with a slotted spoon and let cool slightly, then pick the meat from the bones. Discard bones. Skim the fat from the surface of the soup with a large spoon. Return meat to the pot and add reserved bacon; reheat, if necessary. Taste and adjust seasoning with salt and pepper, if necessary.

6. Divide barley among heated bowls and top with soup. Garnish with parsley and croutons.

Garlic Soup and Pork Rolls

▲▽▲▽▲▽▲▽▲▽▲▽▲▽▲▽▲▽▲▽▲▽▲▽▲▽▲▽▲▽▲▽▲▽▲▽▲▽▲

Our families loved this hearty soup, which has lots of stick-to-your-ribs meat to fill up even the hungriest man. The pork rolls, adapted from a recipe in Italian Slow and Savory *by Joyce Goldstein, give this soup its earthy, rich flavor. This is truly a meal in a bowl.*

▲▽▲▽▲▽▲▽▲

Tip

If you can't find boneless pork chops for this dish, don't despair! Just buy bone-in chops, cut the bone away with a sharp knife and use the cutlets as directed. You now have a bonus — you can add the bones to the soup (with the stock) for extra flavor. Remove the bones from the soup before serving.

Serves 6

4	slices bacon, finely chopped	4
4	cloves garlic, minced	4
¼ cup	minced fresh flat-leaf (Italian) parsley	50 mL
¼ tsp	freshly ground black pepper	1 mL
6	boneless center-cut pork chops, ¼-inch (0.5 cm) thick	6
3	slices prosciutto	3
⅓ cup	pine nuts	75 mL
⅓ cup	dried currants, plumped in warm water	75 mL
⅓ cup	olive oil	75 mL
3	cloves garlic, finely chopped	3
1	onion, chopped	1
2	cans (each 14 to 19 oz/398 to 540 mL) chickpeas or white kidney beans, drained and rinsed	2
1	can (14 oz/398 mL) diced tomatoes, with juice	1
4 cups	chicken or vegetable stock	1 L
1 tsp	paprika	5 mL
½ tsp	salt	2 mL
¼ tsp	freshly ground black pepper	1 mL
2 tbsp	minced fresh flat-leaf (Italian) parsley	25 mL
2 tbsp	torn fresh basil	25 mL
	Parmesan curls (optional, see tip, page 156)	

1. In a bowl, combine bacon, garlic, parsley and pepper. Place a sheet of plastic wrap on top of pork chops. Using a meat mallet, pound chops to make them thinner and longer, so they can be easily stuffed and rolled. Cut prosciutto into 6 pieces to fit the pounded pork chops. Spread bacon mixture over each slice of pork and top with a sprinkling of pine nuts and currants and a piece of prosciutto. Starting at one short side, roll up jellyroll-style and secure with a wooden toothpick.
2. In a large, heavy pot, heat oil over medium heat. Add pork rolls, garlic and onion; sauté until pork rolls are lightly browned, about 5 minutes. Add chickpeas, tomatoes with juice, stock and paprika; bring to a boil. Reduce heat and simmer until pork is cooked through, about 20 minutes.
3. Remove pork rolls from the pot with a slotted spoon and slice crosswise into bite-sized pieces. Season with salt and pepper.
4. Divide pork roll slices among heated bowls and top with soup. Garnish with parsley, basil and Parmesan curls (if using).

Cuban Pork and Black Bean Soup

▲▼▲▼▲▼▲▼▲▼▲▼▲▼▲▼▲▼▲▼▲▼▲▼▲▼▲▼▲▼▲▼▲▼▲

When slow-cooked, pork becomes meltingly tender, almost shredding itself as you stir the pot. In this soup, we've paired it with traditional Cuban flavors, such as black beans and cumin, with just a touch of heat.

▲▼▲▼▲▼▲▼▲

Tip

When browning the pork, make sure you add only enough at one time to make a single layer. Do not overcrowd the pan, or the pork will not brown properly.

Serves 6

2 lbs	boneless pork shoulder blade (butt), trimmed and cut into ½-inch (1 cm) pieces	1 kg
	Salt and freshly ground black pepper	
2 tbsp	vegetable oil, divided	25 mL
1	onion, finely chopped	1
6	cloves garlic, finely chopped	6
1 cup	diced ham	250 mL
1½ tsp	ground cumin	7 mL
½ tsp	cayenne pepper	2 mL
1	can (14 oz/398 mL) diced tomatoes, with juice	1
4 cups	chicken stock	1 L
1	can (14 to 19 oz/398 to 540 mL) black beans, drained and rinsed	1
2 cups	fresh or frozen corn kernels, thawed if frozen	500 mL
1	lime, cut into 6 wedges	1

1. Season pork with salt and pepper to taste. In a large, heavy pot, heat half the oil over medium-high heat. Add pork, in two or three batches, and sauté until browned on all sides, about 5 minutes per batch, adding oil as needed between batches. Remove with a slotted spoon to a warm plate.
2. Reduce heat to medium and add onion to the pot; sauté until softened, 3 to 4 minutes. Add garlic and sauté for 1 minute. Add ham and cumin; sauté for 1 minute. Return pork and any accumulated juices to the pot and add tomatoes with juice and stock; bring to a boil. Partially cover, reduce heat to low and simmer gently until pork is tender, 1½ to 2 hours. Add beans and corn; simmer for 10 minutes. Adjust seasoning with salt and pepper, if necessary.
3. Ladle into heated bowls and garnish with lime wedges. Diners may squeeze the lime over their soup, if they desire.

Potato and Ham Soup

Easy, satisfying and simple, this soup delivers it all. It's the kind of soup your grandmother would have made for you on a cold, gray day. We love you, Grandma!

Tip
Soup will stay hot much longer in a heated bowl.

Serves 6

3 tbsp	unsalted butter	45 mL
1	onion, chopped	1
1 tsp	salt	5 mL
3 tbsp	all-purpose flour	45 mL
5 cups	chicken stock	1.25 L
1½ lbs	Yukon gold potatoes, peeled and cut into small dice	750 g
12 oz	ham, cut into small dice	375 g
½ cup	whipping (35%) cream	125 mL
½ tsp	freshly ground black pepper	2 mL
¼ cup	finely chopped fresh chives	50 mL

1. In a large pot, melt butter over medium heat. Add onion and salt; sauté until onion is softened, about 6 minutes. Sprinkle with flour and sauté for 2 minutes.
2. Gradually whisk in stock. Add potatoes and ham; bring to a boil, stirring often. Cover, reduce heat to low and simmer gently, stirring occasionally, until potatoes are tender, about 20 minutes. Stir in cream and pepper. Taste and adjust seasoning with salt and pepper, if necessary. Reheat until steaming, stirring often. Do not let boil.
3. Ladle into heated bowls and garnish with chives.

Pumpkin Soup with Ham and Swiss Chard

▲▼▲

This is a soup you can make with ingredients that you usually have in the pantry or refrigerator. We can't resist making soup out of canned pumpkin. The flavor is great and it is so, so easy.

▲▼▲▼▲▼▲▼▲▼▲

Tip

We like to add small amounts of cayenne and nutmeg to many of our soups because they add immeasurably to the flavor without announcing their presence.

Serves 6

2 tbsp	unsalted butter	25 mL
2	onions, chopped	2
1	clove garlic, minced	1
1	bunch Swiss chard, roughly chopped (about 4 cups/1 L)	
1 tsp	salt	5 mL
½ cup	dry white wine	125 mL
1	can (28 oz/796 mL) pumpkin purée (not pie filling)	1
6 cups	chicken or vegetable stock	1 L
1½ cups	diced ham	375 mL
1½ cups	half-and-half (10%) cream	375 mL
1 tsp	white wine vinegar	5 mL
Pinch	ground nutmeg	Pinch
Pinch	cayenne pepper	Pinch
	Freshly ground black pepper	
	Minced fresh flat-leaf (Italian) parsley	

1. In a large pot, melt butter over medium heat. Add onions and sauté until softened, about 6 minutes. Add garlic, Swiss chard and salt; sauté until garlic and chard are tender, about 4 minutes. Add wine and cook until reduced by half, about 5 minutes.

2. Add pumpkin purée, stock and ham; bring to a boil. Reduce heat and simmer for about 20 minutes to blend the flavors. Stir in cream, vinegar, nutmeg, cayenne and salt and black pepper to taste; reheat until steaming, stirring often. Do not let boil

3. Ladle into heated bowls and garnish with parsley.

Sausage Soup with Butter Beans

▲▼▲

If you're looking for a quick soup with stick-to-your-ribs status, this is the one. It comes together in the blink of an eye. Thick with sausage and butter beans, this is one soup you will make again and again.

▲▼▲▼▲▼▲▼▲▼▲

Tip

If you can't find canned butter beans, you can substitute navy beans, cannellini beans or white kidney beans.

Serves 6 to 8

¼ cup	olive oil	50 mL
2	carrots, chopped	2
2	stalks celery, chopped	2
1	onion, chopped	1
2	potatoes, peeled and cut into ½-inch (1 cm) dice	2
2	cans (each 14 to 19 oz/398 to 540 mL) butter beans (lima beans), drained and rinsed	2
1	bag (1 lb/500 g) frozen Italian-cut green beans, thawed	1
1	can (14 oz/398 mL) diced tomatoes, with juice	1
2 lbs	kielbasa sausage, cut into ½-inch (1 cm) slices	1 kg
6 cups	beef stock	1.5 L
1 tsp	dried basil	5 mL
¼ tsp	cayenne pepper	1 mL
	Salt and freshly ground black pepper	
¼ cup	minced fresh flat-leaf (Italian) parsley	50 mL
	Shaved Parmigiano-Reggiano cheese (optional)	

1. In a large pot, heat oil over medium heat. Add carrots, celery and onion; sauté until softened, about 6 minutes.
2. Add potatoes, butter beans, green beans, tomatoes with juice, kielbasa, stock, basil and cayenne; bring to a boil. Reduce heat and simmer for 20 minutes to blend the flavors. Season with salt and black pepper to taste. Stir in parsley.
3. Ladle into heated bowls and garnish with cheese, if desired.

Succotash Sausage Soup

▲▽▲▽▲▽▲▽▲▽▲▽▲▽▲▽▲▽▲▽▲▽▲▽▲▽▲▽▲▽▲▽▲▽▲▽▲

Succotash is a favorite late-summer side dish. In this creamy soup, we've made it a meal by adding hearty kielbasa sausage.

▲▽▲▽▲▽▲▽▲▽

Tip

To trim leeks, cut off and discard the root end and the dark green tops (or save the tops for stock). Cut leeks lengthwise and wash under running water to remove any grit or dirt. Then cut as directed in the recipe.

Serves 6 to 8

¼ cup	unsalted butter	50 mL
1 lb	kielbasa sausage, cut into thin half-moons	500 g
2 cups	chopped leeks, white and light green parts only	500 mL
3	garlic cloves, chopped	3
1	large red bell pepper, finely chopped	1
3 tbsp	all-purpose flour	45 mL
1 tbsp	chopped fresh thyme	15 mL
6 cups	chicken stock	1.5 L
2 cups	frozen baby lima beans, thawed	500 mL
½ tsp	salt	2 mL
¼ tsp	freshly ground black pepper	1 mL
1	can (14 oz/398 mL) cream-style corn	1
1½ cups	fresh or frozen white corn kernels, thawed if frozen	375 mL
½ cup	whipping (35%) cream	125 mL
	Fresh thyme leaves	

1. In a large, heavy pot, melt butter over medium heat. Add sausage, leeks, garlic and red pepper; sauté until vegetables are softened and sausage is browned, about 6 minutes. Sprinkle with flour and thyme; sauté for 2 minutes.

2. Gradually whisk in stock. Add lima beans, salt and pepper; bring to a boil, stirring often. Reduce heat and simmer, stirring occasionally, until lima beans are tender, about 10 minutes. Add cream-style corn and corn kernels; simmer for 10 minutes. Stir in cream. Taste and adjust seasoning with salt and pepper, if necessary. Reheat until steaming, stirring often. Do not let boil.

3. Ladle into heated bowls and garnish each with a few thyme leaves.

Italian Tomato and Sausage Soup with Crispy Ravioli

▲▼▲▼▲▼▲▼▲▼▲▼▲▼▲▼▲▼▲▼▲▼▲▼▲▼▲▼▲▼▲▼▲▼▲▼▲▼▲

Crispy fried ravioli make a delightful garnish to this tomatoey sausage soup.

▲▼▲▼▲▼▲▼▲▼▲

Tips

For an extra-crispy coating, be sure to use panko bread crumbs for the ravioli. These Japanese bread crumbs can be found in the Asian section of most grocery stores.

San Marzano tomatoes, imported from Italy, are thought by many to be the best canned tomatoes in the world. They hail from a small town of the same name near Naples, whose volcanic soil is thought to filter impurities from the water and render tomatoes with a thick flesh, fewer seeds and a stronger taste. Look for the words "San Marzano" on the label to be sure you're getting the best.

Serves 6

- Preheat oven to 400°F (200°C)
- Rimmed baking sheet

6 cups	cherry or grape tomatoes	1.5 L
3 tbsp	olive oil, divided	45 mL
1 tsp	salt	5 mL
½ tsp	freshly ground black pepper	2 mL
1	can (14 oz/398 mL) diced tomatoes, with juice	1
1 lb	Italian sausage (bulk or with casings removed)	500 g
6	cloves garlic, minced	6
1 cup	chopped onion	250 mL
1 tsp	dried oregano	5 mL
¼ tsp	hot pepper flakes	1 mL
4 cups	beef stock	1 L
1 tbsp	red wine vinegar	15 mL

Crispy Ravioli

	Vegetable oil	
2	eggs	2
2 tbsp	water	25 mL
1 cup	panko bread crumbs	125 mL
1	package (9 oz/275 g) cheese ravioli (preferably miniature)	1
	Freshly grated Parmesan cheese	

1. On baking sheet, combine cherry tomatoes, 2 tbsp (25 mL) of the olive oil, salt and black pepper; toss to coat evenly and spread in a single layer. Roast in preheated oven until tomatoes are shriveled and have brown spots, 35 to 45 minutes.

2. Transfer to a food processor or blender, including any accumulated liquid in the pan, and add canned tomatoes; process until smooth. Set aside.

Tip

Use shallow soup bowls (soup plates) so the ravioli don't sink to the bottom.

3. In a large pot, heat the remaining olive oil over medium heat. Add sausage and sauté, breaking up with the back of a wooden spoon, until no longer pink, about 5 minutes. Add garlic, onion, oregano and hot pepper flakes; sauté until onion is softened, about 6 minutes. Add reserved tomatoes and stock; bring to a boil. Reduce heat and simmer for 40 minutes to blend the flavors. Taste and adjust seasoning with salt and pepper, if necessary.

4. *Prepare the ravioli:* In a straight-sided skillet, heat 1 inch (2.5 cm) of vegetable oil over medium-high heat to 350°F (180°C).

5. Meanwhile, in a shallow bowl, whisk together eggs and water. Place panko crumbs in a separate shallow bowl. Working in batches, dip ravioli in egg wash to coat completely, letting excess liquid drip back into the bowl. Dredge ravioli in crumbs. Place on a baking sheet and repeat until all the ravioli are coated. Discard any excess egg wash and crumbs. Carefully add ravioli to hot oil and fry, turning once, until golden brown, about 1 minute per side. Remove with a slotted spoon to a plate lined with paper towels.

6. Ladle soup into heated bowls and top each with 3 to 4 ravioli and a sprinkling of cheese.

Sausage-Stuffed Pepper Soup

▲▽

We like to take advantage of the summertime, when vegetables are, if not cheap, then at least better priced. Beautiful red peppers get star treatment here as they are stuffed with flavorful sausage stuffing.

▲▽▲▽▲▽▲▽▲▽▲▽

Tip

For a colorful take on this spicy dish, use multicolored peppers. Most grocers stock red, yellow, green and orange bell peppers, so use a variety. If you like a lot of heat, try stuffing poblano chile peppers.

Serves 6

1½ cups	water	375 mL
¾ cup	long-grain white rice	175 mL
1 tbsp	salt, divided	15 mL
3 tbsp	olive oil, divided	45 mL
3	cloves garlic, minced, divided	3
2	onions, chopped, divided	2
1½ lbs	spicy or mild sausage (bulk or with casings removed)	750 g
1	egg	1
½ cup	chopped fresh parsley, divided	125 mL
½ tsp	freshly ground black pepper	2 mL
6	red bell peppers	6
2	carrots, sliced	2
1	stalk celery, sliced	1
1	can (28 oz/796 mL) crushed tomatoes	1
1 cup	dry white wine	250 mL
6 cups	beef stock	1.5 L
1 tbsp	balsamic vinegar	15 mL
1 tbsp	packed brown sugar	15 mL

1. In a small saucepan, bring water to a boil over medium heat. Add rice and a pinch of salt; cover, reduce heat to low and simmer gently until water is almost absorbed, about 15 minutes. Remove from heat and let stand until water is absorbed and rice is tender, 2 to 3 minutes. Uncover, fluff with a fork and let cool.
2. In a skillet, heat 1 tbsp (15 mL) of the oil over medium heat. Add one-third of the garlic and half the onion; sauté until softened, about 6 minutes. Transfer to a large bowl and add ¾ cup (175 mL) of the rice, sausage, egg, half the parsley, 2 tsp (10 mL) of the salt and pepper. Use your hands to mix the filling together.
3. Cut the tops from the red peppers and hollow out the ribs and seeds. Fill peppers with sausage mixture.
4. In a large pot, heat the remaining oil over medium heat. Add the remaining onion and sauté until softened, about 6 minutes. Add carrots, celery and the remaining garlic; sauté until vegetables are softened, about 6 minutes.

Tip

The stuffed peppers can be prepared through Step 3 up to 1 day ahead. Place in an airtight container and refrigerate until you're ready to make the soup.

5. Add tomatoes and wine; bring to a boil. Cook until sauce has thickened, about 5 minutes. Add stock, vinegar, brown sugar and the remaining salt; bring to a boil. Carefully add stuffed peppers, cut side up, and bring back to a boil. Cover, reduce heat to low and simmer gently until stuffed peppers are cooked through, about 45 minutes. Add the remaining rice to thicken the soup, if desired. Taste and adjust seasoning with salt and pepper, if necessary.

6. Place stuffed peppers in heated bowls and top with soup. Garnish with the remaining parsley.

Stuffed Cabbage Soup

▲▽▲▽▲▽▲▽▲▽▲▽▲▽▲▽▲▽▲▽▲▽▲▽▲▽▲▽▲▽▲▽▲▽▲▽▲▽▲

We remembered stuffed cabbage rolls — or pigs in a blanket, as they call them in West Virginia — that Grandma used to make and thought they would make a pretty good soup . . . and we were right! Thank you, Grandma Gray, for the inspiration for this recipe.

▲▽▲▽▲▽▲▽▲▽

Tip

Napa cabbage is also sometimes called Chinese cabbage. The long leaves are easy to roll up, but if you're a purist (and we respect that), go ahead and use regular round cabbage leaves for these tasty meat-filled bundles.

Serves 8

1½ cups	water	375 mL
¾ cup	long-grain white rice	175 mL
1 tbsp	salt, divided	15 mL
3 tbsp	olive oil, divided	45 mL
3 cups	chopped onion, divided	750 mL
3	cloves garlic, minced, divided	3
8 oz	lean ground beef	250 g
8 oz	regular or lean ground pork	250 g
8 oz	lean ground veal	250 g
1	egg	1
½ cup	chopped fresh parsley, divided	125 mL
2 tsp	paprika	10 mL
½ tsp	freshly ground black pepper	2 mL
8	large napa cabbage leaves	8
3 cups	chopped napa cabbage	750 mL
2	carrots, sliced	2
1	stalk celery, sliced	1
1	can (28 oz/796 mL) crushed tomatoes	1
1 cup	dry white wine	250 mL
8 cups	beef stock	2 L
1 tbsp	white wine vinegar	15 mL
1 tbsp	packed brown sugar	15 mL

1. In a small saucepan, bring water to a boil over medium heat. Add rice and a pinch of salt; cover, reduce heat to low and simmer gently until water is almost absorbed, about 15 minutes. Remove from heat and let stand until water is absorbed and rice is tender, 2 or 3 minutes. Uncover, fluff with a fork and let cool.
2. In a skillet, heat 1 tbsp (15 mL) of the oil over medium heat. Add 1 cup (250 mL) of the onion and one-third of the garlic; sauté until starting to soften, about 3 minutes. Transfer to a large bowl and add ¾ cup (175 mL) of the rice, beef, pork, veal, egg, half the parsley, paprika, 2 tsp (10 mL) of the salt and pepper. Use your hands to mix the filling together. Set aside.
3. Bring a large pot of salted water to a boil over medium heat. Add the whole cabbage leaves and cook until tender, 2 to 3 minutes. Drain and refresh under cold running water. Blot dry.

Tip

The cabbage rolls can be prepared through Step 4 up to 1 day ahead. Place in an airtight container and refrigerate until you're ready to make the soup.

4. Place about ⅓ cup (75 mL) of the filling in the center of each cabbage leaf and, starting at the thick end, fold the sides in and roll up the cabbage to enclose the filling.

5. In a large pot, heat the remaining oil over medium heat. Add the remaining onion and sauté until starting to soften, about 2 minutes. Add chopped cabbage, carrots, celery and the remaining garlic; sauté until vegetables are almost softened, about 5 minutes.

6. Add tomatoes and wine; bring to a boil. Cook until sauce has thickened, about 5 minutes. Add stock, vinegar, brown sugar and the remaining salt; bring to a boil. Carefully add cabbage rolls and bring back to a boil. Cover, reduce heat to low and simmer gently until cabbage rolls are cooked through, about 30 minutes. Add the remaining rice to thicken the soup, if desired. Taste and adjust seasoning with salt and pepper, if necessary.

7. Place cabbage rolls in heated bowls and top with soup. Garnish with the remaining parsley.

Creamy Sausage, Chickpea and Rosemary Soup

▲▼▲▼▲▼▲▼▲▼▲▼▲▼▲▼▲▼▲▼▲▼▲▼▲▼▲▼▲▼▲▼▲▼▲▼▲▼▲

Chickpeas are a surprisingly wonderful addition to this Italian-inspired soup. They work beautifully with the woodsy rosemary and fennel–spiced Italian sausage.

▲▼▲▼▲▼▲▼▲▼▲

Tip

Be careful not to let the soup boil after adding the cream, or it will curdle.

Serves 6

1 tbsp	olive oil	15 mL
12 oz	Italian sausage (bulk or with casings removed)	375 g
1	onion, finely chopped	1
2	cloves garlic, minced	2
1	zucchini, cut into small dice	1
½ tsp	salt	2 mL
¼ tsp	freshly ground black pepper	1 mL
6 cups	chicken stock	1.5 L
2 cups	finely diced red-skinned potatoes	500 mL
1 tbsp	finely chopped fresh rosemary	15 mL
1	can (14 to 19 oz/398 to 540 mL) chickpeas, drained and rinsed	1
½ cup	whipping (35%) cream	125 mL
	Garlic Croutons (see variation, page 368)	

1. In a large pot, heat oil over medium heat. Add sausage and sauté, breaking up with the back of a wooden spoon, until no longer pink, about 5 minutes. Add onion and sauté until softened, about 6 minutes. Add garlic, zucchini, salt and pepper; sauté for 5 minutes.
2. Add stock, potatoes and rosemary; bring to a boil. Reduce heat and simmer until potatoes are tender, about 15 minutes. Using a potato masher or the back of a wooden spoon, mash some of the potatoes to thicken the soup slightly. Stir in chickpeas and cream; simmer, stirring often, until heated through, about 10 minutes. Do not let boil. Taste and adjust seasoning with salt and pepper, if necessary.
3. Ladle into heated bowls and garnish with croutons.

Hunter's Soup

▲▽▲

Hunter's soup is kind of a catch-all soup. Just insert whatever game you managed to snag into this soup of vegetables and seasonings. Since we no longer hunt for our dinner (most of us, anyway), we've taken advantage of easily procured beef chuck and pork shoulder blade (butt). The long, slow cook makes these tough cuts tender and oh so good. We like to serve this soup over Hearty Noodles (see recipe, page 368).

▲▽▲▽▲▽▲▽▲▽▲

Tip

When browning the meat, make sure you add only enough at one time to make a single layer. Do not overcrowd the pan, or the meat will not brown properly.

Serves 6

⅓ cup	all-purpose flour	75 mL
2 tsp	dried oregano	10 mL
1 tsp	salt	5 mL
½ tsp	freshly ground black pepper	2 mL
1 lb	boneless beef chuck roast, trimmed and cut into 1-inch (2.5 cm) chunks	500 g
1 lb	boneless pork shoulder blade (butt), trimmed and cut into 1-inch (2.5 cm) chunks	500 g
¼ cup	olive oil, divided	50 mL
2 cups	dry red wine	500 mL
2	carrots, chopped	2
1	each onion and parsnip, chopped	1
1	stalk celery, chopped	1
1	small celery root (celeriac), chopped	1
1	potato, peeled and diced	1
1	can (14 oz/398 mL) diced tomatoes, with juice	1
8 oz	mushrooms, sliced	250 g
6 cups	beef stock (approx.)	1.5 L
1	bay leaf	1
1 tbsp	balsamic vinegar	15 mL
¼ cup	minced fresh flat-leaf (Italian) parsley	50 mL

1. In a large bowl, combine flour, oregano, salt, and pepper. Add beef and pork; toss to coat.
2. In a large pot, heat one-third of the oil over medium-high heat. Add meat, in three batches, and sauté until browned, about 5 minutes per batch, adding oil as needed between batches. Reduce heat if the bottom of the pan becomes too brown. Remove with a slotted spoon to a warm plate.
3. Add wine to the pot and scrape up any brown bits on the bottom. Cook until reduced by half, about 5 minutes. Return the meat and any accumulated juices to the pot and add carrots, onion, parsnip, celery, celery root, potato, tomatoes with juice, mushrooms, stock and bay leaf; bring to a boil, adding more stock if necessary to submerge the vegetables. Cover, reduce heat to low and simmer gently until meat is tender, about 1 hour. Discard bay leaf and stir in vinegar. Taste and adjust seasoning with salt and pepper, if necessary.
4. Ladle into heated bowls and garnish with parsley.

Burgoo

▲▽▲▽▲▽▲▽▲▽▲▽▲▽▲▽▲▽▲▽▲▽▲▽▲▽▲▽▲▽▲▽▲

A regional soup from Kentucky and Indiana, burgoo in its heyday was likely to include squirrel, venison, rabbit and any other four-legged critter that could be found in your backyard and considered vittles. Due to the lack of squirrel and opossum meat at the local supermarket, we substituted ground beef, chicken, pork and veal for the wildlife and threw in just about anything else we could find lying around in the way of vegetables. Chock full of meats, beans and vegetables, this soup is a party waiting to happen. Feel free to make it a big party, because this soup feeds an army.

▲▽▲▽▲▽▲▽▲▽▲

Tips

This soup can be made ahead and stored in an airtight container in the refrigerator for up to 2 days or in the freezer for up to 2 months.

Soak beans overnight or quick-soak them (see page 115). Drain before using.

Serves 12

2 cups	soaked dried white kidney beans	500 mL
⅓ cup	vegetable oil	75 mL
1 lb	lean ground beef	500 g
1 lb	lean ground chicken	500 g
8 oz	regular or lean ground pork	250 g
8 oz	lean ground veal	250 g
2 tsp	salt	10 mL
4	cloves garlic, minced	4
4	carrots, sliced	4
3	stalks celery, sliced	3
2	onions, chopped	2
2	cans (each 14 oz/398 mL) diced tomatoes, with juice	2
8 cups	beef stock (approx.)	2 L
1 cup	dry red wine	250 mL
¼ cup	Worcestershire sauce	50 mL
2	bay leaves	2
2 tsp	dried thyme	10 mL
1 tsp	freshly ground black pepper	5 mL
¼ tsp	cayenne pepper	1 mL
2 cups	fresh or frozen corn kernels	500 mL
1 tbsp	balsamic vinegar	15 mL
⅓ cup	minced fresh flat-leaf (Italian) parsley	75 mL

1. Place beans in a large saucepan and cover with water; bring to a simmer over medium heat. Reduce heat and simmer for 30 minutes (the beans won't be tender yet). Drain and set aside.
2. In an extra-large pot, heat oil over medium heat. Add ground beef and sauté, breaking up with the back of a wooden spoon, until sizzling, about 3 minutes. Add chicken and sauté, breaking up, until sizzling, about 3 minutes. Add pork, veal and salt; sauté, breaking up, until no longer pink. Drain fat, if desired.
3. Add garlic, carrots, celery and onions; sauté until vegetables start to soften, about 10 minutes. Add reserved beans, tomatoes with juice, stock, wine, Worcestershire sauce, bay leaves, thyme, black pepper and cayenne; bring to a boil. Reduce heat and simmer for 45 minutes. Add corn and simmer for 10 minutes. Discard bay leaves and stir in vinegar. Taste and adjust seasoning with salt and black pepper, if necessary.
4. Ladle into heated bowls and garnish with parsley.

Chicken and Turkey Soups to Comfort the Soul

▲▽▲▽▲▽▲▽▲▽▲▽▲▽▲▽▲▽▲▽▲▽▲▽▲▽▲▽▲

Old-Fashioned Chicken Noodle Soup

▲▽▲▽▲▽▲▽▲▽▲▽▲▽▲▽▲▽▲▽▲▽▲▽▲▽▲▽▲▽▲▽▲▽▲▽▲

There's no better way for a mother to show her kids how much she loves them than to make them a steaming bowl of chicken noodle soup. If you want to share your love, make this recipe and you'll be sure to have enough for all your family and friends. When making this soup, we like to make lots and keep individual portions in the freezer for those times when someone we love needs it most.

▲▽▲▽▲▽▲▽▲▽

Tip

Seasoning with a little bit of lemon juice at the end of cooking heightens the flavor of the soup. Although most home cooks think only in terms of salt and pepper when it comes to adjusting the seasoning in their dishes, we've found that a little acid goes a long way toward making a soup taste just right.

Serves 10

1	whole chicken (about 3 lbs/1.5 kg), rinsed, or 3 lbs (1.5 kg) skinless chicken thighs	1
16 cups	chicken stock	4 L
2	carrots, thinly sliced	2
2	stalks celery, sliced	2
½ cup	chopped onion	125 mL
2	sprigs fresh thyme	2
12 oz	wide egg noodles	375 g
½ cup	finely chopped fresh parsley	125 mL
1 tbsp	freshly squeezed lemon juice	15 mL
	Salt and freshly ground black pepper	
	Additional finely chopped fresh parsley	

1. In a large pot, bring chicken and stock to a boil over medium-high heat. Partially cover, reduce heat to low and simmer gently until a thermometer inserted into the thickest part of a breast registers 170°F (75°C), about 45 minutes. Skim the soup if any scum develops on the surface.
2. Using tongs, transfer chicken to a large plate and let cool slightly. Remove skin and bones and discard. Shred meat into bite-size pieces.
3. Skim the fat from the surface of the stock with a large spoon and return to a simmer over medium heat. Add carrots, celery, onion and thyme; simmer until vegetables are softened, about 15 minutes. Remove thyme sprigs. Return chicken to the pot and stir in noodles, parsley and lemon juice; increase heat to medium-high and bring to a boil. Boil until noodles are tender, about 5 minutes. Season with salt and pepper to taste.
4. Ladle into heated bowls and garnish with parsley.

Creamy Chicken Noodle Soup

We like to use fine egg noodles for this rendition of chicken noodle soup, but if you like big, thick noodles, feel free to make the substitution.

Tip

When adding noodles to soups, we don't always have the time or the inclination to cook them separately. Often we toss them directly into the stock to cook. However, when we have the time or when we're making the soup ahead of time, we cook the noodles in salted boiling water and add them to the bowls separately, pouring the stock on top. When noodles are left in soup for any length of time, they become soggy, flabby and absorb a great deal of the stock.

Serves 6

1	whole chicken (about 3 lbs/1.5 kg), rinsed, or 3 lbs (1.5 kg) skinless chicken thighs	1
2	stalks celery, including leafy tops, cut into large chunks	2
1	large onion (unpeeled), halved	1
1	large carrot, cut into large chunks	1
8 cups	chicken stock	2 L
4	sprigs fresh thyme	4
1	bay leaf	1
2 tbsp	unsalted butter	25 mL
1	onion, finely chopped	1
1 tsp	salt	5 mL
1½ tsp	chopped fresh thyme	2 mL
¼ tsp	freshly ground black pepper	1 mL
6 oz	fine egg noodles	175 g
1 cup	whipping (35%) cream	250 mL
½ cup	finely chopped fresh parsley, divided	125 mL
2 tsp	freshly squeezed lemon juice	10 mL

1. In a large pot, combine chicken, celery, halved onion, carrot, stock, thyme sprigs and bay leaf. If chicken isn't immersed, add water or stock to cover. Bring to a boil over medium-high heat. Partially cover, reduce heat to low and simmer gently until a thermometer inserted into the thickest part of a breast registers 170°F (75°C), about 45 minutes. Skim the soup if any scum develops on the surface.
2. Using tongs, transfer chicken to a large plate and let cool slightly. Remove skin and bones and discard. Shred the meat into bite-size pieces. Set aside.
3. Strain the stock (see page 8) and discard all solids. Skim the surface of the stock and remove fat, if desired. Set aside.
4. Add butter to the pot and melt over medium heat. Add chopped onion and sauté until softened, about 6 minutes. Pour in stock and add salt, chopped thyme and pepper; bring to a boil. Add noodles, reduce heat and boil gently until noodles are almost tender, about 4 minutes. Return chicken to the pot and stir in cream and half the parsley; heat until steaming, about 5 minutes. Do not let boil. Stir in lemon juice. Taste and adjust seasoning with salt and pepper, if necessary.
5. Ladle into heated bowls and garnish with remaining parsley.

Winter Chicken Pot Pie Soup

▲▽▲

We've taken the best of chicken pot pie and turned it into a satisfying soup for a fall or winter day. It's thickened only slightly, which means the crust will sometimes fall into the soup. When that happens, never fear — the crust then becomes a rich dumpling. Why didn't we think of using pastry dough as dumplings before? It tastes terrific.

▲▽▲▽▲▽▲▽▲

Tip

If your bowls are wide, you might need a double recipe of the pastry. If you find that too daunting a task, go ahead and use store-bought puff pastry. The soup will be delicious either way.

Serves 6

- 6 individual ovenproof 2-cup (500 mL) bowls
- Baking sheet

1	whole chicken (about 3 lbs/1.5 kg), rinsed, or 3 lbs (1.5 kg) skinless chicken thighs	1
1	small onion, quartered	1
1	carrot, quartered	1
1	stalk celery, quartered	1
6 cups	chicken stock	1.5 L
10	whole black peppercorns	10
1	bay leaf	1
1 tsp	dried thyme	5 mL
½ tsp	salt	2 mL
¼ cup	unsalted butter	50 mL
1	large onion, finely chopped	1
2	carrots, sliced	2
2	parsnips, sliced	2
1	small bulb fennel (or ½ large), sliced	1
¼ cup	all-purpose flour	50 mL
1	boiling potato or sweet potato, peeled and diced	1
2 tbsp	freshly squeezed lemon juice	25 mL
Pinch	cayenne pepper	Pinch
	Freshly ground black pepper	
¼ cup	minced fresh flat-leaf (Italian) parsley	50 mL
	Flaky Pastry (see recipe, page 370)	
1	egg, beaten	1

1. In a large pot, combine chicken, quartered onion and carrot, celery, stock, peppercorns, bay leaf, thyme and salt. If chicken isn't immersed, add water or stock to cover. Bring to a boil over medium-high heat. Partially cover, reduce heat to low and simmer gently until a thermometer inserted into the thickest part of a breast registers 170°F (75°C), about 45 minutes. Skim the soup if any scum develops on the surface.

2. Using tongs, transfer chicken to a large plate and let cool slightly. Remove skin and bones and discard. Shred the meat into bite-size pieces. Set aside.

Tip

The soup can be prepared through Step 5 up to 2 days ahead. Store in an airtight container in the refrigerator until ready to use, then reheat over low heat. Top with pastry just before baking.

3. Strain the stock (see page 8), reserving the vegetables. Skim the surface of the stock and remove fat, if desired. Cut up the vegetables to add later to the soup; set liquid and vegetables aside separately. Discard bay leaf and peppercorns.

4. Add butter to the pot and melt over medium-high heat. Add chopped onion and sauté until softened, about 6 minutes. Add sliced carrots, parsnips and fennel; sauté until starting to brown, about 10 minutes. Add flour and sauté for 2 minutes.

5. Gradually whisk in reserved stock and bring to a boil, stirring often. Cook until slightly thickened, about 5 minutes. Return chicken and reserved vegetables to the pot and add potato; bring to a boil. Reduce heat and simmer until vegetables are tender, about 30 minutes. Add lemon juice, cayenne and salt and black pepper to taste. Stir in parsley.

6. Ladle soup into ovenproof bowls. Roll out pastry to $\frac{1}{8}$-inch (3 mm) and cut rounds to fit over the bowls. Brush the edges of the bowls with the beaten egg and fit the pastry rounds on top, pinching around the edges to seal. Brush the pastry with the egg and refrigerate the soups for 20 minutes to firm up the pastry. Meanwhile, preheat oven to 400°F (200°C).

7. Place bowls on baking sheet and bake until pastry is browned and crispy, about 20 minutes. Carefully transfer the bowls to serving plates and serve.

Chicken and Dumpling Soup

▲▼▲▼▲▼▲▼▲▼▲▼▲▼▲▼▲▼▲▼▲▼▲▼▲▼▲▼▲▼▲▼▲▼▲▼▲▼▲

Two types of dumplings exist in the world of chicken and dumplings. One is the drop biscuit kind that floats on top of a chicken stew. The other is a thick, soft, noodle-like dumpling that works best for soups. We use the latter in our favorite version.

▲▼▲▼▲▼▲▼▲▼

Tip

When we're trying to eat healthy and lower the amount of fat in a soup, we take the skin off the breast and thighs before cooking. Other times, we leave it on and enjoy the extra richness and flavor the fat imparts.

When we instruct you to cut vegetables to a certain size, it's because we think size really does matter in the recipe. In some recipes, we like disciplined dice because the vegetables cook more evenly, and we think the uniformly chopped vegetables make for a nice texture and a more attractive soup.

Serves 6 to 8

1	whole chicken (about 3 lbs/1.5 kg), rinsed, or 3 lbs (1.5 kg) skinless chicken thighs	1
2	stalks celery, including leafy tops, cut into large chunks	2
1	large onion (unpeeled), halved	1
1	large whole carrot, quartered	1
8 cups	chicken stock	2 L
4	sprigs fresh thyme	4
1	bay leaf	1
2	carrots, cut diagonally into ½-inch (1 cm) thick slices	2
2	stalks celery, halved lengthwise and cut into ½-inch (1 cm) thick slices	2
2 tsp	salt	10 mL
¼ tsp	freshly ground black pepper	1 mL
¼ cup	finely chopped fresh parsley	50 mL
	Additional finely chopped fresh parsley	

Dumplings

1½ cups	all-purpose flour	375 mL
2 tsp	baking powder	10 mL
½ tsp	salt	2 mL
½ cup + 1 tbsp	milk	140 mL
2 tbsp	unsalted butter	25 mL

1. In a large pot, combine chicken, celery, halved onion, quartered carrot, stock, thyme and bay leaf. If chicken isn't immersed, add water or stock to cover. Bring to a boil over medium-high heat. Partially cover, reduce heat to low and simmer gently until a thermometer inserted into the thickest part of a breast registers 170°F (75°C), about 45 minutes. Skim the soup if any scum develops on the surface.
2. Using tongs, transfer chicken to a large plate and let cool slightly. Remove skin and bones and discard. Shred the meat into bite-size pieces. Set aside.
3. Strain the stock (see page 8) and discard all solids. Skim the surface of the stock and remove fat, if desired. Pour stock back into pot. Bring to a simmer over medium heat and add sliced carrots, celery, salt and pepper. Simmer until vegetables are almost tender, about 10 minutes.

Tip

Soup will stay hot much longer in a heated bowl.

4. *Meanwhile, prepare the dumplings:* In a bowl, combine flour, baking powder and salt. In a saucepan, heat milk and butter over medium heat until butter is melted. Add to the flour mixture and stir until just combined. Transfer to a floured work surface and knead lightly once or twice until dough holds together. Using a floured rolling pin, roll out dough to $\frac{1}{8}$-inch (3 mm) thickness. Using a knife, cut dough into $1\frac{1}{2}$- by 1-inch (4 by 2.5 cm) strips.

5. Add dumplings to the soup and simmer until dumplings are cooked through but not mushy, 7 to 8 minutes. Stir in reserved chicken and parsley. Taste and adjust seasoning with salt and pepper, if necessary.

6. Ladle into heated bowls and garnish with parsley.

Chicken and Cabbage Soup with Dumplings

▲▽▲▽▲▽▲▽▲▽▲▽▲▽▲▽▲▽▲▽▲▽▲▽▲▽▲▽▲▽▲▽▲▽▲▽▲▽▲

Who can resist the combination of tender chicken, cabbage and dumplings in a rich stock? If soup is healing, then this is a recipe for health, bar none.

▲▽▲▽▲▽▲▽▲▽

Tip

Savoy cabbage is a more tender variety. It has lots of texture, is a brighter green and looks kind of wrinkly, but because it is not as dense as a regular head of cabbage, it cooks a little more quickly. If you can't find it, go ahead and use napa cabbage or the usual standby. If using regular cabbage, increase the cooking time in Step 4 by 10 minutes.

Serves 6

¼ cup	unsalted butter	50 mL
1	large onion, finely chopped	1
2	carrots, sliced	2
2	stalks celery, sliced	2
2	cloves garlic, minced	2
1 tsp	dried thyme	5 mL
1	bay leaf	1
1	whole chicken (about 3 lbs/1.5 kg), rinsed, or 3 lbs (1.5 kg) skinless chicken thighs	1
8 cups	chicken stock (approx.)	2 L
½ tsp	salt	2 mL
½	head savoy cabbage, cored and thinly sliced	½
½ tsp	cayenne pepper	2 mL
	Freshly ground black pepper	
	Fluffy Dumpling Batter (see recipe, page 371)	
¼ cup	minced fresh flat-leaf (Italian) parsley	50 mL

1. In a large pot, melt butter over medium heat until sizzling. Add onion and sauté until softened, about 6 minutes. Add carrots, celery, garlic, thyme and bay leaf; sauté until vegetables start to soften, about 5 minutes.
2. Add chicken, stock and salt. If chicken isn't immersed, add water or stock to cover. Bring to a boil over medium-high heat. Partially cover, reduce heat to low and simmer gently until a thermometer inserted into the thickest part of a breast registers 170°F (75°C), about 45 minutes. Skim the soup if any scum develops on the surface.
3. Using tongs, transfer chicken to a large plate and let cool slightly. Remove skin and bones and discard. Shred the meat into bite-size pieces.

Tip

We sometimes poach chicken in chicken stock and vegetables to make the stock richer and fuller tasting.

4. Bring soup to a simmer over medium heat and add cabbage. Cover, reduce heat to low and simmer gently until cabbage is tender, about 20 minutes. Add reserved chicken, cayenne and salt and black pepper to taste; increase heat to medium and bring to a simmer. Discard bay leaf.

5. Drop heaping tablespoons (15 mL) of the batter into the simmering liquid. It should make about 12 dumplings. Cover, reduce heat to low and simmer gently until a toothpick inserted in the center of the dumplings comes out clean, 12 to 15 minutes.

6. Ladle dumplings and soup into heated bowls and garnish with parsley.

Pennsylvania Dutch Chicken-Corn Soup with Tiny Dumplings

▲▼▲

Tiny dumplings (called "rivels" by the Pennsylvania Dutch) are easy to make. The dry dough is simply rubbed between the palms of your hands, creating little lumps that make this delightful soup an extra hearty bowlful.

▲▼▲▼▲▼▲▼▲▼

Tip

When we're trying to eat healthy and lower the amount of fat in a soup, we take the skin off the breast and thighs before cooking. Other times, we leave it on and enjoy the extra richness and flavor the fat imparts.

Serves 6 to 8

1	whole chicken (about 3 lbs/1.5 kg), rinsed, or 3 lbs (1.5 kg) skinless chicken thighs	1
9 cups	chicken stock	2.25 L
3 tbsp	unsalted butter	45 mL
2 cups	chopped onions	500 mL
1 cup	diced carrots	250 mL
¾ cup	diced celery	175 mL
½ tsp	dried thyme	2 mL
1 cup	frozen corn kernels	250 mL
2	cans (each 14 oz/398 mL) creamed corn	2
2 tbsp	minced fresh parsley	25 mL
	Salt and freshly ground black pepper	
	Additional minced fresh parsley	

Dumplings

2	eggs	2
2 cups	all-purpose flour	500 mL
½ tsp	salt	2 mL
	Water (if necessary)	

1. In a large pot, combine chicken and stock. If chicken isn't immersed, add water or stock to cover. Bring to a boil over medium-high heat. Partially cover, reduce heat to low and simmer gently until a thermometer inserted into the thickest part of a breast registers 170°F (75°C), about 45 minutes. Skim the soup if any scum develops on the surface.

2. Using tongs, transfer chicken to a large plate and let cool slightly. Remove skin and bones and discard. Shred the meat into bite-size pieces. Set aside.

3. Strain stock (see page 8) into a large bowl. Skim the fat from the surface of the stock with a large spoon and set stock aside.

4. Add butter to the pot and melt over medium heat. Add onions, carrots, celery and thyme; cover and sauté until vegetables are softened, about 6 minutes. Add stock and bring to a boil. Reduce heat and simmer until vegetables are almost tender, about 15 minutes.

Tip

All-purpose flour can vary in protein content and moisture level, and therefore in its ability to absorb added liquid. As a result, you may or may not need to add water to the dumpling dough. The dough should be quite dry, but you do want small clumps to form.

5. *Meanwhile, prepare the dumplings:* In a bowl, using a fork, combine eggs, flour and salt until moistened and starting to clump together but still slightly crumbly, gradually adding up to 3 tbsp (45 mL) water as necessary if dough is too dry.

6. Working with a handful of dough at a time, over the pot, rub dough gently between your hands, letting small lumps fall into the soup. Stir gently and simmer for 5 minutes. Add reserved chicken, corn kernels and creamed corn; simmer until heated through and dumplings are tender, about 5 minutes. Add parsley and season with salt and pepper to taste.

7. Ladle into heated bowls and garnish with parsley.

Amish Chicken and Corn Soup

▲▽▲

The Amish are known to be frugal and wise guardians of their resources, so we put together a soup that uses even the corn cobs, for added flavor. You'll love the extra corniness and will feel righteous when serving this delectable meal in a bowl.

▲▽▲▽▲▽▲▽▲▽▲▽

Tip

If you won't be able to finish this soup in one sitting, we recommend adding the noodles to the serving bowls instead of the soup. When a soup with noodles sits overnight, the noodles absorb lots of the stock and become mushy. Just divide the noodles among the serving bowls and ladle the soup on top. Store the soup and noodles separately in the refrigerator.

Serves 6 to 8

¼ cup	unsalted butter	50 mL
1	onion, chopped	1
2	carrots, chopped	2
2	parsnips, chopped	2
1	stalk celery, chopped	1
1 tsp	dried thyme	5 mL
1 tsp	salt	5 mL
¼ tsp	freshly ground black pepper	1 mL
1	bay leaf	1
3	cobs corn, corn kernels cut from cob and cobs reserved	3
1	whole chicken (about 3 lbs/1.5 kg), rinsed, or 3 lbs (1.5 kg) skinless chicken thighs	1
8 cups	chicken stock	2 L
8 oz	wide dried egg noodles	250 g
3 tbsp	all-purpose flour	45 mL
2 tbsp	unsalted butter, softened	25 mL
¼ cup	minced fresh flat-leaf (Italian) parsley	50 mL
	Additional minced fresh flat-leaf (Italian) parsley	

1. In a large pot, heat butter over medium heat. Add onion and sauté until softened, about 6 minutes. Add carrots, parsnips, celery, thyme, salt, pepper and bay leaf; sauté until vegetables start to soften, about 5 minutes.

2. Add corn cobs, chicken and stock. If chicken isn't immersed, add water or stock to cover. Bring to a boil over medium-high heat. Partially cover, reduce heat to low and simmer gently until a thermometer inserted into the thickest part of a breast registers 170°F (75°C), about 45 minutes. Skim the soup if any scum develops on the surface.

3. Meanwhile, in a large pot of boiling salted water, cook egg noodles according to package directions until tender to the bite. Drain and rinse under cold water to stop the cooking; drain well. Set aside.

4. Using tongs, transfer chicken to a large plate and let cool slightly. Remove corn cobs from the soup and discard. Remove skin and bones from chicken and discard. Shred the meat into bite-size pieces.

Tip

The addition of the flour and butter mixture thickens the soup and enriches the flavor.

5. Return chicken to the pot and add corn kernels; bring to a simmer over medium heat. Simmer until corn is tender, about 5 minutes.

6. In a small bowl, combine flour and butter until a paste forms. Stir into soup and simmer, stirring often, until soup is thickened, about 3 minutes. Stir in noodles and parsley. Taste and adjust seasoning with salt and pepper, if necessary. Discard bay leaf.

7. Ladle into heated bowls and garnish with parsley.

Spicy Chicken and Mushroom Soup

▲▽▲

Dried and fresh mushrooms combine to make this soup extra hearty. We use a full teaspoon of cayenne pepper to give this soup a kick-in-the-pants quality. If you don't like your pants kicked, use less.

▲▽▲▽▲▽▲▽▲▽

Tip

Filtering the mushroom liquid removes any dirt that may have been loosened from the mushrooms as they soaked.

Serves 6

½ oz	dried porcini mushrooms	15 g
1 cup	boiling water	250 mL
¼ cup	unsalted butter	50 mL
1	onion, finely chopped	1
2	carrots, sliced	2
1	stalk celery, sliced	1
1	clove garlic, minced	1
12 oz	mushrooms, sliced	375 g
8 oz	mixed wild (exotic) mushrooms (such as shiitake, oyster and cremini), stemmed and sliced	250 g
1 tsp	cayenne pepper	5 mL
1 tsp	dried thyme	5 mL
½ tsp	salt	2 mL
	Freshly ground black pepper	
1	whole chicken (about 3 lbs/1.5 kg), rinsed, or 3 lbs (1.5 kg) skinless chicken thighs	1
6 cups	chicken stock	1.5 L
1	bay leaf	1
1 tsp	freshly squeezed lemon juice	5 mL
2 tbsp	minced fresh chives or parsley	25 mL

1. In a small bowl, soak dried mushrooms in boiling water until softened, about 30 minutes. Using a slotted spoon, gently lift mushrooms from liquid and swish in a bowl of cold water to remove any clinging sand or dirt. Coarsely chop and set aside. Pour mushroom liquid through a sieve lined with a coffee filter into a small bowl and set aside.

2. In a large pot, melt butter over medium heat until sizzling. Add onion and sauté until softened, about 6 minutes. Add carrots and celery; sauté until starting to soften, about 3 minutes. Add garlic, porcini mushrooms, regular mushrooms, wild mushrooms, cayenne, thyme, salt and black pepper to taste; sauté until mushrooms start to release their liquid, about 5 minutes.

Tip

Seasoning with a little bit of lemon juice at the end of cooking heightens the flavor of the soup. Although most home cooks think only in terms of salt and pepper when it comes to adjusting the seasoning in their dishes, we've found that a little acid goes a long way toward making a soup taste just right.

3. Add chicken, stock and bay leaf. If chicken isn't immersed, add water or stock to cover. Bring to a boil over medium-high heat. Partially cover, reduce heat to low and simmer gently until a thermometer inserted into the thickest part of a breast registers 170°F (75°C), about 45 minutes. Skim the soup if any scum develops on the surface.

4. Using tongs, transfer chicken to a large plate and let cool slightly. Remove skin and bones and discard. Shred the meat into bite-size pieces.

5. Return chicken to the pot and stir in lemon juice. Taste and adjust seasoning with lemon juice, cayenne, salt and black pepper, if necessary. Discard bay leaf.

6. Ladle into heated bowls and garnish with chives.

Chicken Chimichurri Soup

▲▽▲

Chimichurri is a lusty sauce for grilled meats that hails from sunny Argentina. It is usually made with finely chopped parsley, red wine vinegar, olive oil and garlic, with a little heat from chile peppers. Since we're crazy for the taste of cilantro, we added some to the recipe and loved the results. We thought our chimichurri would add a little somethin'-somethin' to chicken soup, and liked it so much that you will now find the ingredients for chimichurri in our refrigerators 24/7.

Serves 6 to 8

Chimichurri

2	cloves garlic	2
1 cup	fresh flat-leaf (Italian) parsley	250 mL
¼ cup	fresh cilantro	50 mL
2 tbsp	dried oregano	25 mL
2 tbsp	dried basil	25 mL
1 tbsp	paprika	15 mL
½ tsp	hot pepper flakes	2 mL
½ tsp	salt	2 mL
¼ tsp	freshly ground black pepper	1 mL
2 tbsp	olive oil	25 mL
2 tbsp	red wine vinegar	25 mL

Soup

¼ cup	olive oil	50 mL
1	large onion, finely chopped	1
2	large carrots, sliced	2
2	stalks celery, sliced	2
½ tsp	dried thyme	2 mL
½ tsp	salt	2 mL
1	whole chicken (about 3 lbs/1.5 kg), rinsed, or 3 lbs (1.5 kg) skinless chicken thighs	1
1	bay leaf	1
1	can (14 oz/398 mL) diced tomatoes, with juice	1
6 cups	chicken stock	1.5 L
1 cup	dry white wine	250 mL
	Freshly ground black pepper	
1 cup	cooked long-grain white rice	250 mL

1. *Prepare the chimichurri:* In a food processor fitted with a metal blade, combine garlic, parsley, cilantro, oregano, basil, paprika, hot pepper flakes, salt, black pepper, olive oil and vinegar. Process until a smooth paste forms, about 30 seconds. Transfer to a bowl and let stand at room temperature for 1 hour to blend the flavors.

2. *Prepare the soup:* In a large pot, heat oil over medium heat. Add onion and sauté until starting to soften, about 2 minutes. Add carrots, celery, thyme and salt; sauté until vegetables are softened, about 5 minutes.

Tip

The chimichurri can be refrigerated in an airtight container for up to 2 weeks. Let warm to room temperature before using.

3. Add chicken, bay leaf, tomatoes with juice, stock and wine. If chicken isn't immersed, add water or stock to cover. Bring to a boil over medium-high heat. Partially cover, reduce heat to low and simmer gently until a thermometer inserted into the thickest part of a breast registers 170°F (75°C), about 45 minutes. Skim the soup if any scum develops on the surface.

4. Using tongs, transfer chicken to a large plate and let cool slightly. Remove skin and bones and discard. Shred the meat into bite-size pieces.

5. Return chicken to the pot and bring to a simmer over medium heat. Stir in ¼ cup (50 mL) chimichurri. Taste and adjust seasoning with salt, black pepper and chimichurri, if necessary. Discard bay leaf.

6. Divide rice among heated bowls and top with soup. Garnish with a dollop of chimichurri.

Chicken Soup with Tomatoes, Wine and Orange

▲▽▲

You'll love the fresh flavor from the orange zest and the rich stock that comes from the chicken in this Provençal-style soup.

▲▽▲▽▲▽▲▽▲▽▲

Tip
We like to use a Microplane grater to grate citrus zest.

Serves 6

¼ cup	olive oil	50 mL
1	large onion, finely chopped	1
2	large carrots, sliced	2
2	stalks celery, sliced	2
½ tsp	dried thyme	2 mL
1	whole chicken (about 3 lbs/1.5 kg), rinsed and cut into 8 pieces, or 3 lbs (1.5 kg) skinless chicken thighs	1
1	bay leaf	1
1	can (14 oz/398 mL) diced tomatoes, with juice	1
4 cups	chicken stock	1 L
1 cup	dry white wine	250 mL
1 tbsp	balsamic vinegar	15 mL
Pinch	cayenne pepper	Pinch
	Grated zest of 1 orange	
	Salt and freshly ground black pepper	
1 cup	hot cooked long-grain white rice	250 mL
¼ cup	minced fresh flat-leaf (Italian) parsley	50 mL

1. In a large pot, heat oil over medium heat. Add onion and sauté until softened, about 6 minutes. Add carrots, celery and thyme; sauté until vegetables start to soften, about 3 minutes. Add chicken and cook until starting to brown, about 3 minutes.

2. Add bay leaf, tomatoes with juice, stock and wine; bring to a simmer. Partially cover, reduce heat to low and simmer gently until juices run clear when chicken is pierced, about 45 minutes. Skim the soup if any scum develops on the surface.

3. Using tongs, transfer chicken to a large plate and let cool slightly. Remove skin and bones and discard. Shred the meat into bite-size pieces.

4. Return chicken to the pot and bring to a simmer. Stir in vinegar, cayenne, orange zest and salt and black pepper to taste. Discard bay leaf.

5. Divide rice among heated bowls and top with soup. Garnish with parsley.

Chicken, Squash and Sausage Soup

▲▽▲

Sweet butternut squash and apples alongside salty, savory sausage make a great team and an interesting departure from the standard chicken soup.

▲▽▲▽▲▽▲▽▲

Tips

We like to use Granny Smith apples in this recipe because they hold up well to the rigors of roasting and keep their shape.

For the best appearance and texture, cut the apples and squash into ½-inch (1 cm) dice and cut the kielbasa into ½-inch (1 cm) thick half-moons.

Serves 6

- Preheat oven to 425°F (220°C)
- 2 large rimmed baking sheets

1	whole chicken (about 3 lbs/1.5 kg), rinsed, or 3 lbs (1.5 kg) skinless chicken thighs	1
2	stalks celery, including leafy tops, cut into large chunks	2
1	large onion (unpeeled), halved	1
1	large carrot, quartered	1
8 cups	chicken stock	2 L
4	sprigs fresh thyme	4
1	bay leaf	1
3	Granny Smith apples, peeled and diced	3
1½ lb	butternut squash, peeled and diced	750 g
3 tbsp	olive oil	45 mL
½ tsp	salt	2 mL
¼ tsp	freshly ground black pepper	1 mL
1 lb	kielbasa sausage, cut into half-moons	500 g
2 tbsp	minced fresh flat-leaf (Italian) parsley	25 mL

1. In a large pot, combine chicken, celery, onion, carrot, stock, thyme and bay leaf. If chicken isn't immersed, add water or stock to cover. Bring to a boil over medium-high heat. Partially cover, reduce heat to low and simmer gently until a thermometer inserted into the thickest part of a breast registers 170°F (75°C), about 45 minutes. Skim the soup if any scum develops on the surface.

2. Meanwhile, drizzle baking sheets evenly with oil. Divide squash and apples between the two sheets. Season with salt and pepper; toss to coat and spread in a single layer. Roast in preheated oven, turning occasionally, until just tender and brown in spots, about 40 minutes.

3. Using tongs, transfer chicken to a large plate and let cool slightly. Remove skin and bones and discard. Shred the meat into bite-size pieces. Set aside.

4. Strain the stock (see page 8) and discard all solids. Skim the surface of the stock and remove fat, if desired. Return stock to pot and bring to a simmer over medium heat. Add sausage and roasted squash and apples; simmer for 10 minutes to blend the flavors. Add chicken and heat until steaming, about 5 minutes.

5. Ladle into heated bowls and garnish with parsley.

Chicken Soup with Roasted Vegetables

▲▼▲

Roasted root vegetables are sweet and hearty and make this soup the perfect ending to a cold fall or winter day.

▲▼▲▼▲▼▲▼▲▼

Tips

We sometimes poach chicken in chicken stock and vegetables to make the stock richer and fuller tasting.

When we instruct you to cut vegetables to a certain size, it's because we think size really does matter in the recipe. In some recipes, we like disciplined dice because the vegetables cook more evenly, and we think the uniformly chopped vegetables make for a nice texture and a more attractive soup.

Serves 6

- Preheat oven to 450°F (230°C)
- 2 large rimmed baking sheets

1	whole chicken (about 3 lbs/1.5 kg), rinsed, or 3 lbs (1.5 kg) skinless chicken thighs	1
2	stalks celery, including leafy tops, cut into large chunks	2
1	large onion (unpeeled), halved	1
1	large carrot, quartered	1
8 cups	chicken stock	2 L
4	sprigs fresh thyme	4
1	bay leaf	1
1/3 cup	olive oil	75 mL
2	parsnips, cut into 1/2-inch (1 cm) dice	2
2	carrots, cut into 1/2-inch (1 cm) dice	2
2	onions, cut into 1/2-inch (1 cm) thick wedges	2
1	large sweet potato, cut into 1/2-inch (1 cm) dice	1
1	large bulb fennel, cut into 1/2-inch (1 cm) thick wedges	1
1 tsp	salt	5 mL
1/2 tsp	freshly ground black pepper	2 mL
1/2 cup	chopped fresh parsley	125 mL
	Garlic Croutons (see variation, page 368)	

1. In a large pot, combine chicken, celery, halved onion, quartered carrot, stock, thyme and bay leaf. If chicken isn't immersed, add water or stock to cover. Bring to a boil over medium-high heat. Partially cover, reduce heat to low and simmer gently until a thermometer inserted into the thickest part of a breast registers 170°F (75°C), about 45 minutes. Skim the soup if any scum develops on the surface.

2. Meanwhile, drizzle baking sheets evenly with oil. Divide parsnips, carrots, onion wedges, sweet potato and fennel between the two sheets. Season with salt and pepper; toss to coat and spread in a single layer. Roast in preheated oven, turning occasionally, until just tender and brown in spots, about 40 minutes.

Tip

Soup will stay hot much longer in a heated bowl.

3. Using tongs, transfer chicken to a large plate and let cool slightly. Remove skin and bones and discard. Shred the meat into bite-size pieces. Set aside.

4. Strain the stock (see page 8) and discard all solids. Skim the surface of the stock and remove fat, if desired. Return stock to pot and bring to a simmer over medium heat. Add roasted vegetables and simmer until tender, about 10 minutes. Add reserved chicken and parsley; heat until steaming, about 5 minutes.

5. Ladle into heated bowls and garnish with croutons.

Creamy Chicken and Wild Rice Soup

△▽△▽△▽△▽△▽△▽△▽△▽△▽△▽△▽△▽△▽△▽△▽△▽△▽△▽△

Somehow, the addition of wild rice makes this homey soup feel like fall. Wild rice is high in protein and dietary fiber and low in fat, but we must admit that what we really love about it is its chewy texture and nutty flavor.

△▽△▽△▽△▽△▽

Tip

Although we like this soup garnished with Buttery Croutons, feel free to look through the toppings and garnishes chapter (pages 361–374) and mix and match to your heart's delight.

Serves 6

1	whole chicken (about 3 lbs/1.5 kg), rinsed, or 3 lbs (1.5 kg) skinless chicken thighs	1
2	stalks celery, including leafy tops, cut into large chunks	2
1	large onion (unpeeled), halved	1
1	large carrot, quartered	1
8 cups	chicken stock	2 L
4	sprigs fresh thyme	4
1	bay leaf	1
½ cup	wild rice	125 mL
3 tbsp	unsalted butter	45 mL
2	carrots, diced	2
2	stalks celery, diced	2
1	onion, finely chopped	1
3 tbsp	all-purpose flour	45 mL
1 tsp	salt	5 mL
¼ tsp	freshly ground black pepper	1 mL
1½ cups	half-and-half (10%) cream	375 mL
¼ cup	finely chopped fresh parsley	50 mL
2 tsp	freshly squeezed lemon juice	10 mL
	Buttery Croutons (see recipe, page 368)	

1. In a large pot, combine chicken, celery chunks, halved onion, quartered carrot, stock, thyme and bay leaf. If chicken isn't immersed, add water or stock to cover. Bring to a boil over medium-high heat. Partially cover, reduce heat to low and simmer gently until a thermometer inserted into the thickest part of a breast registers 170°F (75°C), about 45 minutes. Skim the soup if any scum develops on the surface.
2. Using tongs, transfer chicken to a large bowl and let cool slightly.
3. Meanwhile, strain the stock (see page 8) and discard all solids. Skim the surface of the stock and remove fat, if desired. Transfer 2 cups (500 mL) of the stock to a saucepan. Set the remaining stock aside.
4. Add wild rice to the stock in saucepan and bring to a boil over medium-high heat. Reduce heat to medium-low, cover and simmer until rice is tender and liquid is absorbed, about 50 minutes.

Tip

Be careful not to let the soup boil after adding the cream, or it will curdle.

5. While the rice is cooking, remove skin and bones from chicken and discard. Shred the meat into bite-size pieces. Set aside.

6. In a large pot, melt butter over medium heat. Add diced carrots, diced celery and chopped onion; sauté until softened, about 6 minutes. Add flour and sauté for 2 minutes. Gradually whisk in the remaining stock, salt and pepper; bring to a simmer, stirring often. Add cream, parsley and reserved chicken; heat, stirring often, until steaming, about 5 minutes. Do not let boil. Stir in lemon juice. Taste and adjust seasoning with salt and pepper, if necessary.

7. Ladle into heated bowls and garnish with croutons.

Barley Soup with Chicken and Fennel

▲▽▲▽▲▽▲▽▲▽▲▽▲▽▲▽▲▽▲▽▲▽▲▽▲▽▲▽▲▽▲▽▲▽▲▽▲▽

Fennel is an Italian, lightly licorice-flavored bulb. It is used raw in salads, where it's nice and crispy, or cooked in a variety of dishes. Its personality shines in this healthy, fresh-tasting soup.

▲▽▲▽▲▽▲▽▲▽▲

Tip

When we're trying to eat healthy and lower the amount of fat in a soup, we take the skin off the breast and thighs before cooking. Other times, we leave it on and enjoy the extra richness and flavor the fat imparts.

Serves 6

1	whole chicken (about 3 lbs/1.5 kg), rinsed, or 3 lbs (1.5 kg) skinless chicken thighs	1
1	onion, quartered	1
1	carrot, quartered	1
1	stalk celery, quartered	1
6	whole black peppercorns	6
1	bay leaf	1
1 tsp	dried thyme	5 mL
1 tsp	salt	5 mL
5 tbsp	unsalted butter, divided	75 mL
1	onion, chopped	1
3	carrots, diced	3
2	stalks celery, diced	2
2	small bulbs fennel, thinly sliced	2
1 cup	pearl barley	250 mL
2 tbsp	all-purpose flour	25 mL
¼ cup	minced fresh flat-leaf (Italian) parsley	50 mL
2 tbsp	freshly squeezed lemon juice	25 mL
Pinch	cayenne pepper (optional)	Pinch
Pinch	ground nutmeg (optional)	Pinch
	Freshly ground black pepper	
	Garlic Croutons (see variation, page 368)	

1. In a large pot, combine chicken, quartered onion, carrot and celery, peppercorns, bay leaf, thyme and salt. Add enough water to cover by 2 inches (5 cm). Bring to a boil over medium-high heat. Partially cover, reduce heat to low and simmer gently until a thermometer inserted into the thickest part of a breast registers 170°F (75°C), about 45 minutes. Skim the soup if any scum develops on the surface.

2. Using tongs, transfer chicken to a large bowl and let cool slightly.

3. Meanwhile, strain the stock (see page 8) and discard all solids. Skim the surface of the stock and remove fat, if desired. Set aside.

Tip

We like to add small amounts of cayenne and nutmeg to many of our soups because they add immeasurably to the flavor without announcing their presence.

4. In a large pot, melt 3 tbsp (45 mL) of the butter over medium-high heat. Add chopped onion and sauté until starting to soften, about 3 minutes. Add diced carrots, diced celery and fennel; sauté until starting to soften, about 5 minutes. Add reserved stock and barley; bring to a boil. Reduce heat and simmer until barley is tender, about 25 minutes.

5. While the soup is cooking, remove skin and bones from chicken and discard. Shred meat into bite-sized pieces. Set aside.

6. In a small bowl, combine the remaining butter and flour, mashing until a paste forms. Add to the soup, whisking until it dissolves. Add chicken and parsley; bring to a simmer. Stir in lemon juice, cayenne (if using) and nutmeg (if using). Taste and adjust seasoning with salt and black pepper, if necessary.

7. Ladle into heated bowls and garnish with croutons.

Chicken and Barley Soup
with Dried Mushrooms and Dill

▲▼▲▼▲▼▲▼▲▼▲▼▲▼▲▼▲▼▲▼▲▼▲▼▲▼▲▼▲▼▲▼▲▼▲▼▲▼▲

Barley is one of the healthiest grains, as it is low on the glycemic index and a good source of fiber. The dried mushrooms add a smoky flavor that we love, and the dill gives a little spike of flavor. Try this soup out on a cold December day.

▲▼▲▼▲▼▲▼▲▼

Tip
Filtering the mushroom liquid removes any dirt that may have been loosened from the mushrooms as they soaked.

Serves 6

½ oz	dried porcini, chanterelle or shiitake mushrooms	15 g
1 cup	boiling water	250 mL
¼ cup	olive oil	50 mL
1	onion, finely chopped	1
2	carrots, sliced	2
2	cloves garlic, minced	2
1	stalk celery, diced	1
½ tsp	salt	2 mL
¼ tsp	freshly ground black pepper	1 mL
1	whole chicken (about 3 lbs/1.5 kg), rinsed, or 3 lbs (1.5 kg) skinless chicken thighs	1
8 cups	chicken stock	2 L
1½ cups	pearl barley	375 mL
2 tbsp	minced fresh dill	25 mL
2 tbsp	freshly squeezed lemon juice	25 mL
	Buttery Croutons (optional, see recipe, page 368)	

1. In a small bowl, soak dried mushrooms in boiling water until softened, about 30 minutes. Using a slotted spoon, gently lift mushrooms from liquid and swish in a bowl of cold water to remove any clinging sand or dirt. Coarsely chop and set aside. Pour mushroom liquid through a sieve lined with a coffee filter into a small bowl and set aside.
2. In a large pot, heat oil over medium heat. Add onion and sauté until starting to soften, about 3 minutes. Add carrots, garlic, celery, salt and pepper; sauté until vegetables are softened, about 6 minutes.
3. Add chicken and stock. If chicken isn't immersed, add water or stock to cover. Bring to a boil over medium-high heat. Partially cover, reduce heat to low and simmer gently until a thermometer inserted into the thickest part of a breast registers 170°F (75°C), about 45 minutes. Skim the soup if any scum develops on the surface.

Tip

Seasoning with a little bit of lemon juice at the end of cooking heightens the flavor of the soup. Although most home cooks think only in terms of salt and pepper when it comes to adjusting the seasoning in their dishes, we've found that a little acid goes a long way toward making a soup taste just right.

4. Using tongs, transfer chicken to a large plate and let cool slightly.
5. If desired, skim the fat from the surface of the soup with a large spoon. Add reserved mushrooms, mushroom liquid and barley. Bring to a simmer over medium-high heat. Reduce heat and simmer until barley is tender, about 25 minutes.
6. While the soup is cooking, remove skin and bones from chicken and discard. Shred meat into bite-size pieces.
7. Add chicken to the pot, along with dill and lemon juice; heat until steaming, about 5 minutes. Taste and adjust seasoning with salt and pepper, if necessary.
8. Ladle into heated bowls and garnish with croutons, if desired.

Curried Chicken Soup with Three Grains

▲▽

In this soup, we've combined the glory of grains with the zip of Southeast Asia. We love the chewy goodness of the barley and spelt, but couldn't resist adding a kick by way of rich coconut milk, lime and curry powder.

▲▽▲▽▲▽▲▽▲▽

Tip

Spelt is an ancient relative of wheat. Thousands of years ago, other grains proved more adaptable, with higher yields, so spelt was relegated to small production. Spelt is a firm grain with a nutty taste. Because it is low on the glycemic index and palatable for some who suffer from wheat allergies, spelt has seen a resurgence in popularity.

Serves 6

¼ cup	unsalted butter	50 mL
1	large onion, finely chopped	1
2 tbsp	curry powder	25 mL
2	carrots, sliced	2
2	stalks celery, sliced	2
2	cloves garlic, minced	2
1 tsp	dried thyme	5 mL
1	whole chicken (about 3 lbs/1.5 kg), rinsed, or 3 lbs (1.5 kg) skinless chicken thighs	1
1	can (14 oz/398 mL) diced tomatoes, with juice	1
8 cups	chicken stock, approx.	2 L
1 tsp	salt	5 mL
½ cup	spelt (see tip, at left)	125 mL
½ cup	pearl barley	125 mL
½ cup	long-grain white rice	125 mL
1	can (14 oz/400 mL) unsweetened coconut milk	1
	Juice of 1 lime	
½ tsp	cayenne pepper	2 mL
	Freshly ground black pepper	
¼ cup	minced fresh cilantro	50 mL
1	lime, cut into 6 wedges (optional)	1

1. In a large pot, melt butter over medium heat until sizzling. Add onion and sauté until softened, about 6 minutes. Add curry powder and sauté for 1 minute. Add carrots, celery, garlic and thyme; sauté until vegetables start to soften and curry is fragrant, about 3 minutes.
2. Add chicken, tomatoes with juice, stock and salt. If chicken isn't immersed, add water or stock to cover. Bring to a boil over medium-high heat. Partially cover, reduce heat to low and simmer gently until a thermometer inserted into the thickest part of a breast registers 170°F (75°C), about 45 minutes. Skim the soup if any scum develops on the surface.
3. Using tongs, transfer chicken to a large plate and let cool slightly.

Tip

Making your own curry powder guarantees a fresh, lively character in your dishes. Purchased curry powder may have been sitting on your grocer's shelf for a long time, which reduces its flavor. You'll find a recipe for curry powder on page 27.

4. Meanwhile, return soup to medium heat and bring to a simmer. Add spelt; cover, reduce heat to low and simmer gently until starting to soften, about 30 minutes. Add barley and simmer for 10 minutes. Add rice and simmer until grains are tender, about 15 minutes.

5. While soup is cooking, remove skin and bones from chicken and discard. Shred meat into bite-size pieces.

6. Add chicken to the pot, along with coconut milk, lime juice, cayenne and salt and black pepper to taste; heat until steaming, about 5 minutes.

7. Ladle into heated bowls and garnish with cilantro and lime wedges (if using). Diners may squeeze the lime over their soup, if they desire.

Chicken Andouille Soup

▲▼▲▼▲▼▲▼▲▼▲▼▲▼▲▼▲▼▲▼▲▼▲▼▲▼▲▼▲▼▲▼▲▼▲▼▲

Andouille (pronounced "ond-doo-wee") is a spicy sausage with Cajun roots, so be careful because it can be hot. Much like chorizo sausage, it can be found cooked or smoked and sometimes fresh. Either way, it's sure to be full of flavor and will make a great addition to your soup, turning it into more of a meal.

▲▼▲▼▲▼▲▼▲

Tip

We sometimes poach chicken in chicken stock and vegetables to make the stock richer and fuller tasting.

Serves 6

½ cup	unsalted butter, divided	125 mL
1	onion, finely chopped	1
2	carrots, sliced	2
1	stalk celery, sliced	1
1	clove garlic, minced	1
1	whole chicken (about 3 lbs/1.5 kg), rinsed and cut into 8 pieces, or 3 lbs (1.5 kg) skinless chicken thighs	1
1 tsp	dried thyme	5 mL
½ tsp	salt	2 mL
	Freshly ground black pepper	
6 cups	chicken stock	1.5 L
1	bay leaf	1
1	green bell pepper, coarsely chopped	1
1	red bell pepper, coarsely chopped	1
¼ cup	all-purpose flour	50 mL
¼ cup	tomato paste	50 mL
½ tsp	cayenne pepper	2 mL
2 tbsp	olive oil	25 mL
1 lb	andouille sausage, sliced	500 g
¼ cup	minced fresh flat-leaf (Italian) parsley	50 mL

1. In a large pot, melt half the butter over medium heat until sizzling. Add onion and sauté until starting to soften, about 2 minutes. Add carrots and celery; sauté until starting to soften, about 2 minutes. Add garlic, chicken, thyme, salt and pepper to taste; cook until chicken begins to color slightly, about 5 minutes.
2. Add stock and bay leaf; bring to a simmer. Partially cover, reduce heat to low and simmer gently until juices run clear when chicken is pierced, about 45 minutes. Skim the soup if any scum develops on the surface.
3. Using tongs, transfer chicken to a large plate and let cool slightly. Remove skin and bones and discard. Shred meat into bite-size pieces, cover and refrigerate.

Tip

If you prefer, rather than using sliced andouille sausage, you could use bulk sausage or remove it from its casings. Sauté, breaking up with the back of a wooden spoon, until no longer pink, about 5 minutes, before adding it to the soup.

4. Meanwhile, in another large pot, melt the remaining butter over medium heat until sizzling. Add green and red peppers; sauté until starting to soften, about 3 minutes. Add flour and sauté until starting to brown, about 10 minutes, reducing heat as necessary if roux starts to get too brown. Add tomato paste and cayenne; sauté until peppers are tender, about 5 minutes.

5. Gradually whisk a few ladles of the soup into the roux. Cook, stirring, until thickened, about 3 minutes. Pour into the soup and cook over low heat, stirring occasionally, for 30 to 60 minutes to let the flavors develop.

6. While the soup is cooking, in a skillet, heat oil over medium-high heat. Add sausage and sauté until no longer pink. Add to the soup, along with reserved chicken; reheat until steaming. Skim the fat from the surface of the soup with a large spoon and discard. Taste and adjust seasoning with salt, black pepper and cayenne, if necessary.

7. Ladle into heated bowls and garnish with parsley.

Spring Chicken Soup with Herbed Crust

▲▼

Everyone loves pastry-topped soups, and why not? The pastry is delicious in and of itself, and by pairing it with soup you have a meal in a bowl. No need for accompaniments.

▲▼▲▼▲▼▲▼▲▼

Tip

If your bowls are wide, you might need a double recipe of the pastry. If you find that too daunting a task, go ahead and use store-bought puff pastry. The soup will be delicious either way.

Serves 6

- 4-quart (4 L) ovenproof bowl (such as a soufflé dish) or 6 individual 2-cup (500 mL) ovenproof bowls
- Baking sheet

¼ cup	unsalted butter	50 mL
1	onion, finely chopped	1
2	carrots, sliced	2
1	stalk celery, sliced	1
1	clove garlic, minced	1
3 lbs	skinless chicken thighs	1.5 kg
1 tsp	dried thyme	5 mL
½ tsp	salt	2 mL
	Freshly ground black pepper	
6 cups	chicken stock	1.5 L
1	bay leaf	1
1	potato, peeled and diced	1
1 cup	frozen peas, thawed	250 mL
1	bunch asparagus, trimmed and cut into 1-inch (2.5 cm) pieces	1
¼ cup	minced fresh flat-leaf (Italian) parsley	50 mL
Pinch	cayenne pepper	Pinch
	Grated zest and juice of ½ lemon	
	Herbed Flaky Pastry (see variation, page 371)	
1	egg, beaten	1

1. In a large pot, melt butter over medium heat until sizzling. Add onion and sauté until starting to soften, about 2 minutes. Add carrots and celery; sauté until starting to soften, about 2 minutes. Add garlic, chicken, thyme, salt and pepper to taste; sauté until chicken starts to color slightly, about 5 minutes.

2. Add stock and bay leaf; bring to a simmer. Partially cover, reduce heat to low and simmer until juices run clear when chicken is pierced, about 40 minutes.

3. Using tongs, transfer chicken to a large plate and let cool slightly. Remove bones and discard. Shred the meat into bite-size pieces.

Tip

The soup can be prepared through Step 4 up to 2 days ahead. Store in an airtight container in the refrigerator until ready to use, then reheat over low heat. Top with pastry just before baking.

4. Return chicken to the pot and add potato; simmer until potato is almost tender, about 10 minutes. Add peas and asparagus; simmer until tender, about 5 minutes. Add parsley, cayenne, lemon zest and lemon juice. Taste and adjust seasoning with salt and pepper, if necessary. Preheat oven to 400°F (200°C).

5. Ladle soup into ovenproof bowl or bowls. Roll out pastry to ⅛-inch (3 mm) thickness and cut rounds to fit over the bowl(s). Brush the edges of the bowl(s) with the beaten egg and fit the pastry rounds on top, pinching around the edges to seal. Brush the pastry with the egg.

6. Place bowl(s) on baking sheet and bake until pastry is browned and crispy, about 20 minutes. Carefully transfer the bowls to serving plates and serve.

Farmhouse-Fresh Chicken Soup

▲▼▲▼▲▼▲▼▲▼▲▼▲▼▲▼▲▼▲▼▲▼▲▼▲▼▲▼▲▼▲▼▲▼▲▼▲▼▲

Fresh from the farm ingredients showcase springtime vegetables in this hearty and quick soup. Feel free to substitute other vegetables that may have shown up on your doorstep, such as fresh tomatoes, parsnips, radicchio, escarole or fresh mushrooms.

▲▼▲▼▲▼▲▼▲

Tip

To trim leeks, cut off and discard the root end and the dark green tops (or save the tops for stock). Cut leeks lengthwise and wash under running water to remove any grit or dirt. Then cut as directed in the recipe.

Serves 6 to 8

2 tbsp	olive oil	25 mL
1	onion, chopped	1
2	carrots, chopped	2
2	leeks, white and light green parts only, thinly sliced	2
2	summer squash or zucchini, chopped	2
2	cloves garlic, minced	2
1	stalk celery, chopped	1
2 tsp	minced fresh thyme	10 mL
1 tsp	salt	5 mL
	Freshly ground black pepper	
1 cup	dry white wine	250 mL
6 cups	chicken or vegetable stock	1.5 L
10	small new potatoes, quartered	10
10	spears asparagus, trimmed and sliced	10
2 cups	chopped baby spinach	500 mL
1 cup	frozen peas, thawed	250 mL
2	boneless skinless chicken breasts, thinly sliced	2
2 tsp	freshly squeezed lemon juice	10 mL
Pinch	cayenne pepper	Pinch
2 tbsp	minced fresh Italian (flat-leaf) parsley	25 mL

1. In a large pot, heat oil over medium heat. Add onion and sauté until softened, about 6 minutes. Add carrots, leeks, squash, garlic, celery, thyme, salt and black pepper to taste; sauté until softened, about 5 minutes.

2. Add wine and cook until almost evaporated, about 5 minutes. Add stock and potatoes; bring to a boil. Cover, reduce heat to low and simmer gently until potatoes are almost tender, about 15 minutes.

3. Add asparagus, spinach, peas and chicken; simmer until vegetables are tender and chicken is no longer pink inside, about 5 minutes. Add lemon juice and cayenne. Taste and adjust seasoning with salt and black pepper, if necessary.

4. Ladle into heated bowls and garnish with parsley.

Chicken Potage with Leeks, Apples and Potato

▲▼▲▼▲▼▲▼▲▼▲▼▲▼▲▼▲▼▲▼▲▼▲▼▲▼▲▼▲▼▲▼▲▼▲▼▲

Make this soup when you have leftover mashed potatoes. We use chicken breasts so the soup cooks in a jiffy, and we love the addition of tart, tangy apples.

▲▼▲▼▲▼▲▼▲▼

Tip
Soup will stay hot much longer in a heated bowl.

Serves 6

¼ cup	unsalted butter	50 mL
1	leek, white and light green parts only, sliced	1
2	carrots, sliced	2
1	stalk celery, sliced	1
1	clove garlic, minced	1
2 lbs	boneless skinless chicken breasts, cut into small chunks	1 kg
1 tsp	dried thyme	5 mL
½ tsp	salt	2 mL
	Freshly ground black pepper	
6 cups	chicken stock	1.5 L
3	crisp sweet-tart apples (such as Braeburn, Jazz or Mutsu), peeled and diced	3
1	bay leaf	1
2 cups	mashed potatoes	500 mL
¼ cup	minced fresh flat-leaf (Italian) parsley	50 mL
	Grated zest and juice of ½ lemon	
Pinch	cayenne pepper	Pinch
	Buttery Croutons (see recipe, page 368)	

1. In a large pot, melt butter over medium heat until sizzling. Add leek and sauté until starting to soften, about 2 minutes. Add carrots and celery; sauté until starting to soften, about 2 minutes. Add garlic, chicken, thyme, salt and black pepper to taste; sauté until chicken starts to brown slightly, about 5 minutes.
2. Add stock, apples and bay leaf; bring to a simmer. Partially cover, reduce heat to low and simmer gently until chicken is no longer pink inside and vegetables are tender, about 25 minutes.
3. Stir in mashed potatoes until blended and soup is creamy. Simmer until steaming, about 10 minutes. Add parsley, lemon zest, lemon juice and cayenne. Taste and adjust seasoning with salt and black pepper, if necessary.
4. Ladle into heated bowls and garnish with croutons.

Chicken, Barley and Spring Vegetable Soup

▲▽▲

We love barley not only for its health benefits but also for its agreeable chewiness. The fresh vegetables in this recipe add to the simple, clean flavors we look for in a springtime soup.

▲▽▲▽▲▽▲▽▲▽▲

Tip

This fresh soup doesn't fare well made ahead of time. The vegetables are delicate and tend to gray and lose their crisp texture during storage.

Serves 6 to 8

8 cups	chicken stock	2 L
1½ lbs	boneless skinless chicken breasts	750 g
½ cup	pearl barley	125 mL
2	carrots, cut diagonally into ¼-inch (0.5 cm) thick slices	2
8 oz	snow peas, trimmed and halved diagonally	250 g
1 cup	frozen baby peas, thawed	250 mL
¼ cup	finely chopped fresh parsley	50 mL
1 tsp	salt	5 mL
¼ tsp	freshly ground black pepper	1 mL
1 tsp	freshly squeezed lemon juice	5 mL
	Buttery Croutons (see recipe, page 368)	

1. In a large pot, bring stock to a simmer over medium-high heat. Add chicken, reduce heat and simmer for 10 minutes. Remove from heat, cover and let stand until chicken is no longer pink inside, about 5 minutes. Using tongs, transfer chicken to a plate and let cool slightly. Shred into bite-size pieces. Set aside.

2. Meanwhile, return stock to a simmer over medium heat and add barley. Reduce heat and simmer for 20 minutes. Add carrots and simmer until barley is just tender, about 15 minutes. Add snow peas and simmer for 2 minutes. Add baby peas and reserved chicken; heat until steaming. Add parsley, salt, pepper and lemon juice. Taste and adjust seasoning with salt and pepper, if necessary.

3. Ladle into heated bowls and garnish with croutons.

Creamy Pesto Chicken Soup with Potato Gnocchi

▲▽▲

Potato gnocchi and pesto team up often in Italian cuisine and work just as well in this creamy chicken soup. Making gnocchi is not difficult, but if time is of the essence, store-bought gnocchi works well too.

▲▽▲▽▲▽▲▽▲▽▲▽

Tip

When making this recipe, we take advantage of the precooked rotisserie chicken found at almost any grocery store. One chicken usually yields about 3 cups (750 mL) meat.

Serves 6

2 tbsp	unsalted butter	25 mL
1	onion, finely chopped	1
8 cups	chicken stock	2 L
1 tsp	salt	5 mL
¼ tsp	freshly ground black pepper	1 mL
1 cup	whipping (35%) cream	250 mL
¼ cup	pesto (store-bought or see recipe, page 363)	50 mL
1	package (1 lb/500 g) fresh potato gnocchi	1
3 cups	shredded cooked chicken	750 mL
¼ cup	finely chopped fresh parsley	50 mL
2 tsp	freshly squeezed lemon juice	10 mL
	Additional finely chopped fresh parsley	

1. In a large pot, melt butter over medium heat. Add onion and sauté until softened, about 6 minutes. Add stock, salt and pepper; bring to a boil.
2. Stir in cream and pesto; bring to a simmer, stirring often. Do not let boil. Add gnocchi and simmer for 3 minutes. Add chicken, parsley and lemon juice. Taste and adjust seasoning with salt and pepper, if necessary.
3. Ladle into heated bowls and garnish with parsley.

Easy Chipotle Chicken Soup

▲▽▲▽▲▽▲▽▲▽▲▽▲▽▲▽▲▽▲▽▲▽▲▽▲▽▲▽▲▽▲▽▲▽▲

Perfect for a busy weeknight, this fast and easy soup will be warming you up in less than 20 minutes. We use store-bought rotisserie chicken and tortilla chips when time is short and tummies are growling.

▲▽▲▽▲▽▲▽▲

Tip

Chipotle chiles are smoked jalapeños, often found canned in a vinegary tomato sauce called adobo. Look for them in the Mexican aisle of your grocery store. They tend to be fiery, so we often use only 1 or 2 at a time. You can freeze any leftovers by dropping them by spoonfuls onto parchment-lined baking sheets and freezing until solid. Then transfer to freezer bags.

Serves 6

6 cups	chicken stock	1.5 L
4	cloves garlic, thinly sliced	4
1 to 2	chipotle chile peppers in adobo sauce, minced (see tip, at left)	1 to 2
½ tsp	freshly ground black pepper	2 mL
2	cans (each 14 to 19 oz/398 to 540 mL) chickpeas, drained and rinsed	2
3 cups	shredded cooked chicken	750 mL
	Salt	
¼ cup	chopped fresh cilantro	50 mL
1	avocado, diced	1
	Crispy Tortilla Strips (see recipe, page 372)	
1	lime, cut into 6 wedges	1

1. In a large pot, bring stock, garlic, chipotles to taste and pepper to a boil over medium-high heat. Reduce heat and simmer for 15 minutes to blend the flavors. Add chickpeas, chicken and salt to taste.
2. Ladle into heated bowls and garnish with cilantro, avocado, tortilla strips and lime wedges. Diners may squeeze the lime over their soup, if they desire.

Creamy Roasted Garlic, Chicken and Mushroom Soup

▲▽▲▽▲▽▲▽▲▽▲▽▲▽▲▽▲▽▲▽▲▽▲▽▲▽▲▽▲▽▲▽▲▽▲▽

Garlic's intense flavor is softened and sweetened by the roasting process. In this soup, it lends a lovely flavor, which is brought out even more by the addition of a bit of fresh garlic.

▲▽▲▽▲▽▲▽▲▽

Tip

To clean mushrooms, you can either rinse them quickly in water or wipe them with a damp paper towel. Mushrooms will be much happier in your refrigerator if you store them in a paper bag.

Serves 6

- Preheat oven to 350°F (180°C)
- Small baking dish

3	heads garlic	3
2 tbsp	olive oil	25 mL
	Salt and freshly ground black pepper	
3 tbsp	unsalted butter	45 mL
2	onions, finely chopped	2
2	cloves garlic, minced	2
1 lb	mushrooms, sliced	500 g
3 tbsp	all-purpose flour	45 mL
4 cups	chicken stock	1 L
3 cups	shredded cooked chicken	750 mL
1 cup	whipping (35%) cream	250 mL
¼ cup	chopped fresh parsley	50 mL
	Crispy Shallots (see recipe, page 367)	

1. Slice the top ½ inch (1 cm) off each head of garlic. Place in baking dish, drizzle with oil and sprinkle with salt and pepper to taste. Cover dish tightly with foil and bake in preheated oven until garlic is golden brown and tender, about 45 minutes. Let cool completely. Squeeze garlic between fingertips to release cloves. Transfer cloves to small bowl and mash into a paste with a fork. Set aside.

2. In a large pot, melt butter over medium heat. Add onion and sauté until softened, about 6 minutes. Add minced garlic and mushrooms; sauté until mushrooms release their liquid and start to brown, about 10 minutes. Sprinkle with flour and sauté for 2 minutes.

3. Gradually whisk in stock and reserved roasted garlic paste; simmer for 20 minutes to blend the flavors. Stir in chicken and cream; heat until steaming, about 5 minutes, stirring often. Do not let boil. Stir in parsley. Taste and adjust seasoning with salt and pepper, if necessary.

4. Ladle into heated bowls and garnish with crispy shallots.

Chicken, Pinto Beans and Green Chile Soup

▲▽▲▽▲▽▲▽▲▽▲▽▲▽▲▽▲▽▲▽▲▽▲▽▲▽▲▽▲▽▲▽▲▽▲▽▲

Who doesn't love a 30-minute meal? We know we do, especially on a hectic weeknight when we want something good but don't have time to put together anything too involved. This is the perfect soup on those busy nights.

▲▽▲▽▲▽▲▽▲▽▲

Tip

San Marzano tomatoes, imported from Italy, are thought by many to be the best canned tomatoes in the world. They hail from a small town of the same name near Naples, whose volcanic soil is thought to filter impurities from the water and render tomatoes with a thick flesh, fewer seeds and a stronger taste. Look for the words "San Marzano" on the label to be sure you're getting the best.

Serves 8

1 tbsp	olive oil	15 mL
2	poblano chile peppers, seeded and chopped	2
1	onion, chopped	1
3	cloves garlic, minced	3
2 tsp	ground cumin	10 mL
1 tsp	dried oregano	5 mL
1 tsp	ground coriander	5 mL
¼ tsp	cayenne pepper	1 mL
1	can (14 oz/398 mL) diced tomatoes, with juice	1
5 cups	chicken stock	1.25 L
1 tsp	salt	5 mL
¼ tsp	freshly ground black pepper	1 mL
2	cans (each 14 to 19 oz/398 to 540 mL) pinto beans, drained and rinsed	2
3 cups	shredded cooked chicken	750 mL
½ cup	shredded Monterey Jack or Cheddar cheese	125 mL
½ cup	sour cream	125 mL

1. In a large pot, heat oil over medium heat. Add poblano chiles and onion; sauté until softened, about 6 minutes. Add garlic, cumin, oregano, coriander and cayenne; sauté for 2 minutes.
2. Stir in tomatoes with juice, stock, salt and black pepper; bring to a boil. Reduce heat and simmer for 20 minutes to blend the flavors. Add beans and chicken; heat until steaming, about 5 minutes. Taste and adjust seasoning with salt, if necessary.
3. Ladle into heated bowls and garnish with cheese and sour cream.

White Bean, Chicken and Pesto Soup

▲▽▲▽▲▽▲▽▲▽▲▽▲▽▲▽▲▽▲▽▲▽▲▽▲▽▲▽▲▽▲▽▲▽▲▽▲▽▲

This is another of those "from the pantry" soups that we love to make when dinner — even takeout — seems like too much of a hassle. Feel free to substitute any kind of canned bean or even leftover ham, pork or beef.

▲▽▲▽▲▽▲▽▲▽

Tip

Seasoning with a little bit of vinegar at the end of cooking heightens the flavor of the soup. Although most home cooks think only in terms of salt and pepper when it comes to adjusting the seasoning in their dishes, we've found that a little acid goes a long way toward making a soup taste just right.

Serves 8

1 tbsp	olive oil	15 mL
1	onion, chopped	1
3	cloves garlic, minced	3
1	stalk celery, chopped	1
1	carrot, chopped	1
1 tsp	dried oregano	5 mL
¼ tsp	cayenne pepper	1 mL
6 cups	chicken stock	1.5 L
1 tsp	salt	5 mL
¼ tsp	freshly ground black pepper	1 mL
2	cans (each 14 to 19 oz/398 to 540 mL) cannellini or white kidney beans, drained and rinsed	2
3 cups	shredded cooked chicken	750 mL
¼ cup	pesto (store-bought or see recipe, page 363), divided	50 mL
2 tsp	white wine vinegar	10 mL
	Extra-virgin olive oil	

1. In a large pot, heat oil over medium heat. Add onion and sauté until softened, about 6 minutes. Add garlic, celery, carrot, oregano and cayenne; sauté for 2 minutes.
2. Stir in stock, salt and black pepper; bring to a boil. Reduce heat and simmer until vegetables are softened, about 20 minutes. Add beans, chicken, 2 tbsp (25 mL) of the pesto and vinegar; heat until steaming, about 5 minutes. Taste and adjust seasoning with salt and black pepper, if necessary.
3. Ladle into heated bowls and garnish each with a small dollop of the remaining pesto and a drizzle of olive oil.

Smoky Peanut and Chicken Soup

▲▽▲▽▲▽▲▽▲▽▲▽▲▽▲▽▲▽▲▽▲▽▲▽▲▽▲▽▲▽▲▽▲▽▲▽▲▽▲

Award-winning chef Rick Bayless's delightful peanut mole sauce was the inspiration for this unique, mouth-watering soup. We love the interplay between the smoky, spicy chipotle chiles and the peanut butter. A touch of cinnamon and allspice rounds out the flavors, and the addition of chicken makes it a meal.

▲▽▲▽▲▽▲▽▲▽▲

Tip

We don't like to use the natural-style peanut butters in soups, because they don't tend to blend as well into the other liquids.

Serves 4 to 6

2 tbsp	unsalted butter	25 mL
1	onion, finely chopped	1
2	cloves garlic, minced	2
2	chipotle chile peppers in adobo sauce, minced (see tip, page 220)	2
½ tsp	ground cinnamon	2 mL
½ tsp	salt	2 mL
¼ tsp	freshly ground black pepper	1 mL
¼ tsp	ground allspice	1 mL
2 tbsp	all-purpose flour	25 mL
5 cups	chicken stock	1.25 L
1 cup	whipping (35%) cream	250 mL
¾ cup	creamy peanut butter	175 mL
3 cups	shredded cooked chicken	750 mL
1 tbsp	packed brown sugar	15 mL
1 tbsp	freshly squeezed lime juice	15 mL
2 tbsp	chopped roasted peanuts	25 mL
¼ cup	chopped green onions	50 mL

1. In a large pot, melt butter over medium heat. Add onion and sauté until softened, about 6 minutes. Add garlic, chipotles, cinnamon, salt, pepper and allspice; sauté for 1 minute. Add flour and sauté for 2 minutes.

2. Gradually whisk in stock and bring to a simmer, stirring often. Reduce heat to low and simmer for 15 minutes to blend the flavors. Whisk in cream and peanut butter until blended. Heat until steaming, about 5 minutes, stirring often. Do not let boil. Stir in chicken, brown sugar and lime juice; heat until steaming. Taste and adjust seasoning with salt and pepper, if necessary.

3. Ladle into heated bowls and garnish with peanuts and green onions.

Succotash Sausage Soup (page 173)

Overleaf: Chicken Soup with Tomatoes, Wine and Orange (page 200)

Chicken Paprikash Soup with Spaetzle

▲▽▲▽▲▽▲▽▲▽▲▽▲▽▲▽▲▽▲▽▲▽▲▽▲▽▲▽▲▽▲▽▲▽▲▽

In Hungary, paprika is more than just red dust sprinkled over potato salad. It's a savory spice used to give soups, stews and a variety of other dishes a distinctive and delicious flavor. This soup uses that flavor to its fullest. Chicken, red peppers and onions, along with tender spaetzle dumplings, swim in a creamy, crimson soup, topped generously with a dollop of sour cream.

▲▽▲▽▲▽▲▽▲

Tip

When making this recipe, we take advantage of the precooked rotisserie chicken found at almost any grocery store. One chicken usually yields about 3 cups (750 mL) meat.

Serves 6

2 tbsp	olive oil	25 mL
2 tbsp	unsalted butter	25 mL
2	red bell peppers, diced	2
1	onion, chopped	1
¼ cup	all-purpose flour	50 mL
2 tbsp	Hungarian sweet paprika	25 mL
6 cups	chicken stock	1.5 L
3 cups	shredded cooked chicken	750 mL
½ cup	whipping (35%) cream	125 mL
1½ cups	sour cream	375 mL
2 tbsp	finely chopped fresh parsley	25 mL
	Spaetzle (see recipe, page 371)	

1. In a large pot, heat oil and butter over medium heat. Add red peppers and onion; sauté until softened, about 6 minutes. Add flour and sauté for 2 minutes. Add paprika and sauté for 1 minute.
2. Gradually whisk in stock and bring to a simmer, stirring often. Partially cover, reduce heat and simmer for 40 minutes to blend the flavors. Stir in chicken and cream; heat until steaming, about 5 minutes, stirring often. Do not let boil.
3. In a small bowl, whisk together sour cream and parsley.
4. Divide spaetzle among heated bowls and top with soup. Garnish each with a generous dollop of sour cream mixture.

Easy Chipotle Chicken Soup
(page 220)

Overleaf: Creamy Chicken and
Wild Rice Soup (page 204)

Chicken and Sausage Gumbo

▲▽▲

If you want a good gumbo, you have to start with a good roux. Roux is a combination of fat and flour, cooked together and used to thicken soups, stews and sauces. For a proper gumbo, the roux must be cooked long enough to develop a deep reddish brown color. When it gets to this point, in addition to being a thickening agent, it lends a unique flavor that is critical to authentic gumbo.

▲▽▲▽▲▽▲▽▲

Tip

Creole or Cajun seasoning is a combination of many things, but mostly cayenne pepper, dried thyme, dried oregano, black pepper and paprika in equal proportions.

Serves 6

¼ cup	unsalted butter	50 mL
¼ cup	all-purpose flour	50 mL
1 cup	chopped onion	250 mL
½ cup	diced celery	125 mL
½ cup	finely chopped red bell pepper	125 mL
½ cup	finely chopped green bell pepper	125 mL
3	cloves garlic, chopped	3
1	bay leaf	1
1 tsp	dried thyme	2 mL
1	can (14 oz/398 mL) diced tomatoes, with juice	1
1	package (10 oz/300 g) frozen okra, thawed and cut into ½-inch (1 cm) slices	1
1 lb	smoked andouille sausage, cut into ½-inch (1 cm) thick slices	500 g
3 cups	chicken stock	750 mL
2 tsp	Creole or Cajun seasoning	10 mL
3 cups	shredded cooked chicken	750 mL
	Salt and freshly ground black pepper	
3 cups	hot cooked long-grain white rice	750 mL

1. In a large pot, melt butter over medium-high heat. Add flour and sauté until mixture is a dark reddish brown, about 5 minutes. Add onion, celery and red and green peppers; sauté until tender, about 6 minutes. Add garlic, bay leaf and thyme; sauté for 1 minute.
2. Add tomatoes with juice, okra, sausage, stock and Creole seasoning; bring to a boil. Cover, reduce heat to low and simmer gently, stirring often, for 20 minutes to blend the flavors. Add chicken and heat until steaming, about 5 minutes. Season with salt and pepper to taste. Discard bay leaf.
3. Divide rice among heated bowls and top with soup.

Day-after-Thanksgiving Turkey Soup

▲▼▲

What's for dinner the day after Thanksgiving? How about a nice, comforting, yet light soup to calm overly full tummies? You'll feel great using the last flavor from your turkey and, heck, if you want you can throw in some of your other leftovers, such as mashed potatoes, green beans and gravy, for extra flavor.

▲▼▲▼▲▼▲▼▲

Tip

Soup will stay hot much longer in a heated bowl.

Serves 12

1	cooked turkey carcass, skin and fat removed	1
4	carrots, sliced	4
3	large onions, finely chopped	3
2	parsnips, sliced	2
2	potatoes, peeled and diced (optional)	2
12 cups	chicken stock	3 L
2	bay leaves	2
2 tsp	dried thyme	10 mL
4 cups	diced cooked turkey	1 L
1 cup	frozen peas, thawed	250 mL
	Salt and freshly ground black pepper	
¼ cup	minced fresh flat-leaf (Italian) parsley	50 mL

1. In a large pot, combine turkey, carrots, onions, parsnips, potatoes (if using), stock, bay leaves and thyme. If the turkey isn't immersed, add more water to cover. Bring to a simmer over medium heat; reduce heat and simmer for 2 hours.
2. Using tongs, transfer turkey bones to a large plate and let cool. Pick any meat from bones and discard bones. Return meat to the pot and add diced turkey and peas; heat until steaming, about 5 minutes. Season with salt and pepper to taste. Discard bay leaves.
3. Ladle into heated bowls and garnish with parsley.

Turkey Green Chile Soup

▲▽▲

Roasted poblano chiles give this soup a smoky character that goes so well with the pinto beans and turkey. These fruity peppers are sometimes a bit on the spicy side, so be sure to taste before adding all of them to the soup.

▲▽▲▽▲▽▲▽▲▽

Tip

To roast peppers, lay halved and seeded peppers on a baking sheet and broil until the skins blacken. (Or, on a gas stove, turn a few burners to high and lay peppers directly over the flames. Turn with tongs until blackened on all sides.) Transfer to a heatproof bowl and cover with plastic wrap. When cool enough to handle, scrape the skins from the peppers with the back of a knife. Don't worry about a little bit of black remaining on the peppers.

Serves 6

3 tbsp	olive oil	45 mL
3	roasted poblano chile peppers (see tip, at left), cut into thin strips	3
3	cloves garlic, minced	3
1	onion, chopped	1
1½ lbs	lean ground turkey	750 g
2 tsp	ground cumin	10 mL
1 tsp	salt	5 mL
½ tsp	ground cinnamon	2 mL
¼ tsp	freshly ground black pepper	1 mL
¼ tsp	chipotle chile powder (optional)	1 mL
2	cans (each 14 to 19 oz/398 to 540 mL) pinto beans, drained and rinsed	2
1 cup	dry white wine	250 mL
6 cups	chicken or vegetable stock	1.5 L
1 cup	shredded Monterey Jack cheese	250 mL
¼ cup	minced fresh cilantro	50 mL

1. In a large pot, heat oil over medium heat. Add poblano chiles, garlic and onion; sauté until softened, about 6 minutes. Add turkey, cumin, salt, cinnamon, pepper and chipotle powder (if using); sauté, breaking up turkey with the back of a wooden spoon, until no longer pink, about 5 minutes.
2. Add beans and wine; cook until wine is reduced by half, about 5 minutes. Add stock and bring to a simmer. Partially cover, reduce heat to low and simmer gently for about 20 minutes to blend the flavors. Taste and adjust seasoning with salt and pepper, if necessary.
3. Ladle into heated bowls and garnish with cheese and cilantro.

Go Fish: Fish and Shellfish Soups

▲▽▲▽▲▽▲▽▲▽▲▽▲▽▲▽▲▽▲▽▲▽▲▽▲▽▲▽

Bouillabaisse

▲▽▲▽▲▽▲▽▲▽▲▽▲▽▲▽▲▽▲▽▲▽▲▽▲▽▲▽▲▽▲▽▲▽▲

Perhaps one of the most famous of fish soups, bouillabaisse hails from the sunny Mediterranean, where a huge variety of seafood abounds. Purists lament that, to be bouillabaisse, the soup must contain rascasse, a fish rarely found outside of the Med. But we know better and have made lovely bouillabaisse with fish found at our local fishmongers. Just use whatever comes in on the truck that day, and your fish soup will be delicious.

▲▽▲▽▲▽▲▽▲

Tip

Before preparing this soup, be sure to read page 7 for information on preparing fish bones and heads.

Serves 4

3 tbsp	olive oil	45 mL
2 lbs	fish bones and heads, fins and gills discarded, soaked (see page 7)	1 kg
8 oz	medium shrimp, peeled and deveined, shells reserved	250 g
5	cloves garlic, crushed	5
2	onions, quartered	2
5	whole black peppercorns	5
3	parsley stems	3
1	bay leaf	1
1	small bulb fennel, quartered	1
6 cups	fish stock	1.5 L
1 cup	dry white wine	250 mL
½ cup	diced canned tomato, with juice	125 mL
½ tsp	salt	2 mL
½ tsp	saffron threads	2 mL
1 lb	mussels, scrubbed and debearded (see tips, page 237)	500 g
	Grated zest of ½ orange	
½ cup	Rouille (see recipe, page 362), divided	125 mL
1 lb	rockfish, snapper or sea bass fillets, skin removed and cut into 4 portions	500 g
	Freshly ground black pepper	
	Crusty bread	

1. In a large pot, heat oil over medium heat. Add fish bones and heads and shrimp shells; sauté until shells turn pink, about 4 minutes. Add garlic and onions; sauté until garlic is fragrant, about 2 minutes. Add peppercorns, parsley stems, bay leaf, fennel, stock, wine, tomato and salt; bring to a boil. Reduce heat and simmer for 40 minutes.

2. Strain the stock (see page 8) and discard all solids. Add saffron and let stand until saffron blooms and softens, about 5 minutes.

3. In another large pot, bring 2 cups (500 mL) of the stock to a simmer over medium heat. Add mussels, cover and cook until mussels have opened, 5 to 8 minutes. Discard any mussels that do not open. Using a slotted spoon, transfer mussels to a bowl and let cool slightly. Remove the top shells, leaving the mussels attached to the bottom shells. Cover and keep warm.

Tip

The quality of this dish is dependent on the availability of the freshest fish and fish bones and heads. Though it might sound gross, the heads give body and texture to the dish. Avoid oily or strong-tasting fish, such as salmon or tuna, and focus on firm-fleshed white fish, such as snapper, sea bass or rockfish.

4. Add the mussel cooking liquid to the rest of the fish stock and bring to a simmer over medium heat. Stir in orange zest and half the rouille.

5. Season fish with salt and pepper to taste and slide into the stock. Simmer until fish is opaque and flakes easily with a fork, about 4 minutes. Using a slotted spoon, transfer fish to a plate and keep warm.

6. Add shrimp to the stock and simmer until pink and opaque, about 2 minutes. Using a slotted spoon, transfer shrimp to the plate with the fish.

7. Divide fish, shrimp and mussels among heated shallow bowls. Ladle stock over the seafood and top each with a dollop of rouille. Serve with crusty bread.

Sicilian Fish Soup

▲▽▲

Fresh tomatoes, olives, capers, mint and pine nuts give this fish soup a distinctly Sicilian flair. We like to serve this Mediterranean bowl-from-the-sea with toasts smeared with a garlicky mayonnaise. Use the freshest firm-fleshed, mild fish you can find.

▲▽▲▽▲▽▲▽▲▽

Tip

Before shopping for fish, check fish sustainability/endangered lists (such as www. montereybayaquarium.org/cr/seafoodwatch.asp) or with your fishmonger to be sure that you're not purchasing fish species that are being overfished or fished illegally.

Serves 6

2 tbsp	olive oil	25 mL
1	onion, chopped	1
3	cloves garlic, chopped	3
18	green olives, quartered	18
3	tomatoes, seeded and finely chopped, with their juices	3
3 cups	fish or chicken stock	750 mL
½ cup	dry white wine	125 mL
¾ cup	chopped fresh flat-leaf (Italian) parsley	175 mL
2 tbsp	drained capers	25 mL
¼ tsp	hot pepper flakes	1 mL
2 lbs	mixed fresh fish fillets (such as snapper, cod, sea bass, swordfish, shark and halibut), skin removed and cut into large pieces	1 kg
	Salt and freshly ground black pepper	
12	toasted baguette slices	12
	Aïoli (see recipe, page 362)	
½ cup	chopped fresh mint	125 mL
½ cup	toasted pine nuts	125 mL

1. In a large pot, heat oil over medium heat. Add onion and sauté until softened, about 6 minutes. Add garlic and sauté for 1 minute. Add olives, tomatoes, stock, wine, parsley, capers and hot pepper flakes; bring to a boil. Partially cover, reduce heat and simmer for 10 minutes. Add fish, cover and simmer until fish is opaque and flakes easily with a fork, 12 to 15 minutes. Season with salt and pepper to taste. Using a fork, break fish into large bite-size pieces.
2. Spread baguette slices with some of the aïoli.
3. Ladle soup into heated bowls. Garnish with mint and pine nuts and serve with baguette slices on the side. Pass the remaining aïoli for guests to dollop on their soup as desired.

Arugula Soup with Salmon and Roasted Grape Tomatoes

▲▽▲▽▲▽▲▽▲▽▲▽▲▽▲▽▲▽▲▽▲▽▲▽▲▽▲▽▲▽▲▽▲▽▲▽▲▽▲

We love the big chunk of salmon, topped with salty cheese and tart roasted tomatoes, in a soup that acts somewhat like a sauce. It's almost like a salad, soup and entrée all at once.

▲▽▲▽▲▽▲▽▲▽▲

Tip

Seasoning with a little bit of lemon juice at the end of cooking heightens the flavor of the soup. Although most home cooks think only in terms of salt and pepper when it comes to adjusting the seasoning in their dishes, we've found that a little acid goes a long way toward making a soup taste just right.

Serves 6

- Preheat oven to 425°F (220°C)
- Rimmed baking sheet, lined with parchment paper

2 cups	grape or cherry tomatoes	500 mL
3 tbsp	olive oil, divided	45 mL
	Salt and freshly ground black pepper	
6	skinless salmon fillets (about 2 lbs/1 kg total)	6
1	onion, minced	1
2	cloves garlic, minced	2
6 cups	chicken or vegetable stock	1.5 L
10 oz	baby arugula (about 10 cups/2.5 L), chopped	300 g
2 tsp	freshly squeezed lemon juice	10 mL
1 tsp	salt	5 mL
Pinch	cayenne pepper	Pinch
Pinch	ground nutmeg	Pinch
½ cup	crumbled feta cheese	125 mL
¼ cup	minced fresh flat-leaf (Italian) parsley	50 mL

1. On prepared baking sheet, combine tomatoes, 1 tbsp (15 mL) of the oil and salt and black pepper to taste; toss to coat evenly and spread in a single layer. Roast in preheated oven for 10 minutes.
2. Season salmon with salt and black pepper to taste. Add to baking sheet and roast until fish is opaque and flakes easily with a fork and tomatoes are soft, about 10 minutes.
3. Meanwhile, in a large pot, heat the remaining oil over medium heat. Add onion and sauté until softened, about 6 minutes. Add garlic and sauté for 1 minute. Add stock and bring to a simmer. Add arugula and simmer, stirring occasionally, until wilted, about 2 minutes. Stir in lemon juice, salt, cayenne and nutmeg. Taste and adjust seasoning with salt and black pepper, if necessary.
4. Arrange salmon in heated bowls and top with soup. Garnish with roasted tomatoes, feta and parsley.

Curried Salmon Soup in Coconut Stock

▲▽▲▽▲▽▲▽▲▽▲▽▲▽▲▽▲▽▲▽▲▽▲▽▲▽▲▽▲▽▲▽▲▽▲

This soup sings when you can find really fresh wild salmon. If you live in an area where you don't have access to quality fresh seafood, look in the freezer section of your grocery store, where you can often find frozen salmon that was caught and then frozen directly on the boat. These frozen fillets are often of higher quality than what can be found fresh or thawed in the fish case. Look for brightly colored fish packed in 1-lb (500 g) clear plastic parcels, and thaw in the refrigerator overnight or in a bowl of cold water.

▲▽▲▽▲▽▲▽

Tip

Garam masala is an Indian spice blend containing black pepper, cinnamon, cloves, coriander, cardamom and other spices.

Serves 6

3 tbsp	olive oil	45 mL
4	green onions, thinly sliced	4
2	cloves garlic, minced	2
1	onion, minced	1
1	knob gingerroot (about 1 inch/2.5 cm), minced	1
1 tbsp	garam masala or curry powder	15 mL
1	sweet potato, peeled and cut into ½-inch (1 cm) dice	1
4 cups	chicken stock	1 L
1 tsp	salt	5 mL
1	can (14 oz/400 mL) unsweetened coconut milk	1
1	can (14 oz/398 mL) baby corn, drained	1
1 lb	skinless salmon fillet, cut into 1-inch (2.5 cm) cubes	500 g
	Freshly ground black pepper	
¼ cup	minced fresh cilantro	50 mL
1	lime, cut into 6 wedges	1

1. In a large pot, heat oil over medium heat. Add green onions, garlic, onion and ginger; sauté for 1 minute. Add garam masala and sauté until fragrant, about 1 minute.
2. Add sweet potato, stock and salt; bring to a boil. Reduce heat and simmer for 5 minutes. Add coconut milk and baby corn; simmer until heated through, about 5 minutes. Add salmon and simmer, stirring occasionally, until fish is opaque and flakes easily with a fork, about 4 minutes. Season with salt and pepper to taste.
3. Ladle into heated bowls and garnish with cilantro and lime wedges. Diners may squeeze the lime over their soup, if they desire.

Snapper in Chinese Stock with Habanero

▲▼▲▼▲▼▲▼▲▼▲▼▲▼▲▼▲▼▲▼▲▼▲▼▲▼▲▼▲▼▲▼▲▼

This soup contains nice large pieces of fish swimming in a lovely, spicy, vegetable-studded stock. Habaneros are the hottest of the hot chiles, so if you are sensitive go ahead and switch to a milder chile, such as a serrano.

▲▼▲▼▲▼▲▼▲

Tip
Tilapia, rockfish, cod or even salmon would be delicious in this dish.

Serves 6

2 tbsp	vegetable oil	25 mL
¼ cup	minced shallots	50 mL
2 cups	thinly sliced snow peas	500 mL
1 cup	thinly sliced red bell pepper	250 mL
6 cups	Chinese Chicken Stock (see recipe, page 12)	1.5 L
	Salt and freshly ground black pepper	
6	pieces skinless red snapper or other light white fish (each about 6 oz/175 g)	6
½	habanero pepper, finely diced	½
¼ cup	minced fresh cilantro	50 mL
1	lime, cut into 6 wedges	1

1. In a large pot, heat oil over medium heat. Add shallots and sauté until starting to soften, about 1 minute. Add snow peas and red pepper; sauté until starting to soften, about 5 minutes.
2. Add stock and bring to a boil. Season with salt and pepper to taste. Add fish, reduce heat to low and simmer gently until fish is opaque and flakes easily with a fork, about 4 minutes.
3. Carefully transfer fish to heated bowls and top with stock. Garnish each bowl with a light sprinkle of habanero, cilantro and a lime wedge. Diners may squeeze the lime over their soup, if they desire.

Clam Soup with Orzo and Tiny Meatballs

▲▼▲▼▲▼▲▼▲▼▲▼▲▼▲▼▲▼▲▼▲▼▲▼▲▼▲▼▲▼▲▼▲▼▲▼▲▼▲

Clams, pasta and tiny meatballs in a savory stock make an appealing combination, and this soup comes together quickly enough for a weeknight meal.

▲▼▲▼▲▼▲▼▲▼▲

Tips

Grocery stores sometimes carry uncooked meatballs, packaged in the meat case, that they have made up themselves. We think it makes good sense to take advantage of this step-saving bonus, especially when the meatballs are of good quality. One caveat, though, is that store-bought meatballs are usually on the large side. We cut them in half and then reroll them into a ball. It only takes a minute, and they are a more "attackable" size in your soup bowl.

Have the fishmonger tap each clam individually to make sure it is alive and check again just before cooking. Live clams will close when tapped. Any clams that do not open while cooking were dead before they were cooked and should be discarded.

Serves 6 to 8

2 tbsp	unsalted butter	25 mL
2 tbsp	olive oil	25 mL
1	large onion, minced	1
1	stalk celery, chopped	1
1 cup	dry white wine (such as Sauvignon Blanc or Chardonnay)	250 mL
1 tsp	salt	5 mL
1 tsp	dried basil	5 mL
1 tsp	dried oregano	5 mL
6 cups	beef or chicken stock	1.5 L
	Italian Meatballs (see recipe, page 368), rolled into 1-inch (2.5 cm) balls	
1 cup	orzo	250 mL
40	clams (see tip, at left), scrubbed	40
¼ cup	minced fresh flat-leaf (Italian) parsley	50 mL
¼ cup	freshly grated Parmigiano-Reggiano cheese	50 mL
2 tsp	freshly squeezed lemon juice	10 mL
	Freshly ground black pepper	
	Additional grated Parmigiano-Reggiano cheese	

1. In a large pot, heat butter and oil over medium heat. Add onion and sauté until softened, about 6 minutes. Add celery, wine, salt, basil and oregano; cook until wine is reduced by half, about 5 minutes.

2. Add stock and bring to a boil. Add meatballs and return to a boil. Reduce heat and simmer until meatballs are cooked through, about 25 minutes. Increase heat to medium and bring to a boil. Add orzo and clams; boil until orzo is tender and clams have opened, about 8 minutes. Discard any clams that do not open. Stir in parsley, cheese and lemon juice. Season with salt and pepper to taste.

3. Ladle into heated bowls and pass additional cheese at the table.

Mussels in Wine, Garlic and Tomato Stock

▲▼▲▼▲▼▲▼▲▼▲▼▲▼▲▼▲▼▲▼▲▼▲▼▲▼▲▼▲▼▲▼▲▼▲

A glass of dry white wine, a large loaf of crusty bread and this buttery, garlic-laced soup, packed with sweet, fresh mussels, make up the perfect meal.

▲▼▲▼▲▼▲▼▲

Tips

Have the fishmonger tap each mussel individually to make sure it is alive and check again just before cooking. Live mussels will close when tapped. Any mussels that do not open while cooking were dead before they were cooked and should be discarded.

To scrub and debeard mussels, hold each mussel under cool running water and scrub the shell with a stiff-bristled brush. Next, grab the fibers of the "beard" with your fingers and pull them out, tugging toward the hinged point of the shell.

Serves 8 to 10

¼ cup	olive oil	50 mL
3 tbsp	unsalted butter	45 mL
⅓ cup	finely chopped shallots	75 mL
6	cloves garlic, minced	6
1	can (28 oz/796 mL) diced tomatoes, with juice	1
3 cups	fish or chicken stock	750 mL
1 cup	dry white wine	250 mL
½ tsp	salt	2 mL
	Freshly ground black pepper	
2 lbs	mussels, scrubbed and debearded (see tips, at left)	1 kg
1 tsp	grated lemon zest	5 mL
2 tbsp	freshly squeezed lemon juice	25 mL
¼ cup	minced fresh flat-leaf parsley	50 mL

1. In a large pot, heat oil and butter over medium heat. Add shallots and sauté until softened, about 3 minutes. Add garlic and sauté for 1 minute. Add tomatoes with juice, stock, wine, salt and pepper to taste; cook for 10 minutes to blend the flavors.
2. Add mussels, cover and cook until mussels have opened, 5 to 8 minutes. Discard any mussels that do not open. Stir in lemon zest and lemon juice. Taste and adjust seasoning with salt and pepper, if necessary.
3. Ladle into heated bowls and garnish with parsley.

Billy Bi (Cream of Mussel Soup)

▲▽▲▽▲▽▲▽▲▽▲▽▲▽▲▽▲▽▲▽▲▽▲▽▲▽▲▽▲▽▲▽▲▽▲▽▲

Billy bi (or billi-bee) soup is an old classic, and once you make it you'll know why. We like the chunky quality provided by the mussels, though many French versions strain them out. There are several stories about the origin of this French soup, one being that a chef at the famed Maxim's in Paris named it after his favorite customer, American tin tycoon William B. (Billy B.) Leeds.

▲▽▲▽▲▽▲▽▲▽

Tip

Because adding delicate eggs to a pot of hot soup would result in scrambled eggs, we use a technique called tempering. By gradually adding hot soup to the eggs, the temperature of the eggs rises slowly, so that when they eventually make it into the soup, they are already hot and stay fluid and velvety.

Serves 6

⅓ cup	unsalted butter, divided	75 mL
1	large shallot, minced	1
1 cup	dry white wine	250 mL
4 lbs	mussels, scrubbed and debearded (see tips, page 237)	2 kg
1	onion, minced	1
¼ cup	all-purpose flour	50 mL
¼ tsp	salt	1 mL
Pinch	freshly ground black pepper	Pinch
1	bay leaf	1
5 cups	fish or shellfish stock	1.25 L
2	egg yolks	2
1 cup	whipping (35%) cream	250 mL
Pinch	ground nutmeg	Pinch
Pinch	cayenne pepper	Pinch
¼ cup	minced fresh flat-leaf (Italian) parsley	50 mL

1. In a large pot, melt 2 tbsp (25 mL) of the butter over medium heat until sizzling. Add shallot and sauté until starting to soften, about 1 minute. Add wine and bring to a boil.

2. Add mussels, cover and cook until mussels have opened, 5 to 8 minutes. Discard any mussels that do not open. Remove from heat. Using a slotted spoon, transfer mussels to a bowl and let cool slightly. Separate the meat from the shells; discard shells and set meat aside. Strain the cooking liquid (see page 8) and discard all solids; set aside.

3. In another large pot, melt the remaining butter over medium heat until sizzling. Add onion and sauté until softened, about 6 minutes. Add flour, salt, black pepper and bay leaf; sauté for 2 minutes. Gradually whisk in stock and reserved mussel liquid; cook, stirring, until slightly thickened, about 3 minutes. Reduce heat and simmer for about 20 minutes to blend the flavors. Discard bay leaf.

4. In a large bowl, whisk together egg yolks, cream, nutmeg and cayenne. Gradually whisk a few ladles full of the soup into the yolk mixture. Slowly pour back into the pot, stirring constantly. Add mussel meat and simmer, stirring constantly, until heated through. Do not let boil, or the eggs will curdle.

5. Ladle into heated bowls and garnish with parsley.

Mussel Soup with White Beans

▲▽▲▽▲▽▲▽▲▽▲▽▲▽▲▽▲▽▲▽▲▽▲▽▲▽▲▽▲▽▲▽▲▽▲▽▲▽

Why don't we cook with mussels more often? Their briny flavor perks up our taste buds and makes us think of sea breezes and salt spray. This soup is so packed with mussels that even a large pot won't generally accommodate them, so we used two pots to cook them.

▲▽▲▽▲▽▲▽▲▽

Tips

Here's how to quick-soak dried beans: In a colander, rinse beans under cold water and discard any discolored ones. In a saucepan, combine beans with enough cold water to cover them by 2 inches (5 cm). Bring to a boil over medium heat and boil for 2 minutes. Remove from heat and let soak, covered, for 1 hour.

For the wine, try Sauvignon Blanc or Chardonnay.

Serves 6

2 cups	dried cannellini, white kidney or great Northern beans, soaked overnight or quick-soaked (see tip, at left) and drained	500 mL
2	cloves garlic, chopped	2
1	onion, sliced	1
1	stalk celery, sliced	1
1	carrot, sliced	1
1	bay leaf	1
1 tsp	salt	5 mL
¼ cup	extra-virgin olive oil	50 mL
1	large onion, finely chopped	1
3	cloves garlic, minced	3
4 lbs	mussels, scrubbed and debearded (see tips, page 237)	2 kg
1 cup	dry white wine	250 mL
1	can (14 oz/398 mL) diced tomatoes, with juice	1
3 cups	fish, chicken or vegetable stock	750 mL
	Freshly ground black pepper	
¼ cup	fresh basil, torn into pieces	50 mL

1. In a large pot, combine beans, garlic, onion, celery, carrot and bay leaf. Add enough cold water to cover the vegetables by 2 inches (5 cm) and bring to a simmer over medium-high heat. Partially cover, reduce heat to low and simmer gently for 1 hour. Add salt, cover and simmer until beans are tender, about 30 minutes. Remove from heat and set aside.

2. In each of two large pots, heat half the oil over medium-high heat. Divide the onion between the pots and sauté until starting to soften, about 3 minutes. Divide the garlic and mussels between the pots and sauté for 1 minute. Divide the wine and tomatoes with juice between the pots, cover and bring to a boil. Cook until mussels have opened, 5 to 8 minutes. Discard any mussels that do not open. Remove from heat. Using a slotted spoon, transfer mussels to a large bowl and let cool slightly. Separate the meat from the shells; discard shells and set meat aside.

3. Reheat the bean mixture, if necessary, over medium heat. Add mussel meat, mussel cooking liquid and stock; bring to a simmer. Season with salt and pepper to taste.

4. Ladle into heated bowls and garnish with basil.

Scallop Wontons in Stock

▲▽▲

It is really easy to make your own wontons, and once you've figured out the technique, you'll be able to make any kind of wonton, using fillings such as shrimp, sausage or even squash purée.

▲▽▲▽▲▽▲▽▲

Tip

Chicken backs and necks can be found in most grocery stores. If you don't see them in the freezer case, ask the meat department where they can be found, or if they can order some for you.

Serves 6

Baking sheet, lined with parchment paper

2 lbs	chicken necks and backs, rinsed	1 kg
10 cups	chicken stock	2.5 L
5	whole black peppercorns	5
4	thin slices gingerroot	4
1	onion, quartered	1
1	carrot, quartered	1
1	stalk celery, quartered	1
1	bay leaf	1
2 tbsp	fish sauce (nam pla)	25 mL
2 tsp	granulated sugar	10 mL
	Salt	
¼ cup	chopped green onions	50 mL

Wontons

8 oz	scallops, trimmed of small white muscle on side, if necessary	250 g
2 tbsp	chopped green onion	25 mL
2 tbsp	dry white wine	25 mL
1 tbsp	soy sauce	15 mL
¼ tsp	five-spice powder	1 mL
¼ tsp	freshly ground black pepper	1 mL
Pinch	ground nutmeg	Pinch
Pinch	cayenne pepper	Pinch
	Salt	
24	wonton wrappers, thawed if frozen	24
1	egg, lightly beaten	1

1. In a large stockpot, bring chicken parts, stock, peppercorns, ginger, onion, carrot, celery and bay leaf to a simmer over medium heat. Reduce heat and simmer for 30 minutes, skimming the scum as it forms on the surface and discarding it.

2. *Meanwhile, prepare the wontons:* In a food processor fitted with a metal blade, combine scallops, green onion, wine, soy sauce, five-spice powder, black pepper, nutmeg and cayenne. Pulse until filling is finely chopped but not a paste. To taste for seasoning, heat a small skillet over medium heat and fry a spoon-sized patty until opaque. Taste and adjust seasoning with salt and black pepper, if necessary.

Tip

Five-spice powder is a blend of ground cloves, fennel seeds, cinnamon, star anise and Szechwan peppercorns. Most large grocery stores stock it, but if you can't find it, just use a mixture of the individual spices. It will still taste delicious.

3. Place a rounded teaspoon (5 mL) of filling in the center of each wonton wrapper. Brush beaten egg around the edges of the wrapper. Lift two opposite corners together to form a triangle and enclose filling, pressing all edges firmly to eliminate air pockets and seal. Place wontons on prepared baking sheet, making sure they don't touch.

4. Strain the stock (see page 8) and discard all solids; return stock to the pot. Skim the surface of the stock and remove fat, if desired. Add fish sauce and sugar; bring to a simmer over medium heat. Simmer for 5 minutes. Add wontons and simmer until wrappers are tender and filling is cooked through, about 8 minutes. Taste stock and season with salt, if necessary.

5. Ladle stock into heated bowls and top each with 4 wontons. Garnish with green onions.

Seared Scallop Minestrone with Lemon and Parsley

▲▽▲▽▲▽▲▽▲▽▲▽▲▽▲▽▲▽▲▽▲▽▲▽▲▽▲▽▲▽▲▽▲▽▲▽▲▽

For the perfect start to a classic dinner party, serve this beautiful soup. Scallops cook so quickly that dropping them into the soup to cook would be a crime. It only takes a minute or two to sear them in a skillet, which also browns and crisps up the outsides for a nice textural contrast.

▲▽▲▽▲▽▲▽▲

Tips

Day boat, or dry, scallops are usually of a higher quality than wet scallops, so expect to pay a little more. Day boat scallops are harvested from smaller boats that return to port each day to unload their catch. Wet scallops can sit out at sea for days and are therefore processed in a solution that helps to preserve them. Unfortunately, the solution also imparts a metallic taste and affects the texture of the cooked scallops, as the scallops absorb the solution, then exude it as they cook, preventing them from searing and forming a nice crust.

Serves 6

¼ cup	olive oil, divided	50 mL
1	leek, white and light green parts only, thinly sliced	1
2	carrots, cut into ½-inch (1 cm) dice	2
1	stalk celery, cut into ½-inch (1 cm) dice	1
1	red bell pepper, cut into ½-inch (1 cm) dice	1
½ tsp	salt	2 mL
½ tsp	minced fresh thyme (or 1 tsp/5 mL dried)	2 mL
1	can (14 to 19 oz/398 to 540 mL) navy beans, drained and rinsed	1
6 cups	shellfish or chicken stock	1.5 L
1	bay leaf	1
Pinch	cayenne pepper	Pinch
	Grated zest of 1 lemon	
	Freshly ground black pepper	
12	large scallops (preferably day boat, or dry, scallops), trimmed of small white muscle on side, if necessary	12
¼ cup	minced fresh flat-leaf (Italian) parsley	50 mL
	Parmesan curls (see tip, page 156)	

1. In a large pot, heat 3 tbsp (45 mL) of the oil over medium heat. Add leek and sauté until softened, about 6 minutes. Add carrots, celery, red pepper, salt and thyme; sauté until vegetables start to soften, about 5 minutes.

2. Add beans, stock and bay leaf; bring to a boil. Reduce heat and simmer until vegetables are tender, about 20 minutes. Season with cayenne, lemon zest and salt and black pepper to taste. Discard bay leaf.

3. Pat scallops dry with paper towels and season with salt and black pepper to taste. In a large skillet, heat the remaining oil over medium-high heat. Add scallops, in two batches, and sear, turning once, until browned on both sides, about 4 minutes per batch. Transfer the first batch to a plate and keep warm while searing the second batch.

4. Ladle soup into heated bowls and top each with 2 scallops. Garnish with parsley and Parmesan curls.

Coconut Curry and Shrimp Soup

▲▽▲▽▲▽▲▽▲▽▲▽▲▽▲▽▲▽▲▽▲▽▲▽▲▽▲▽▲▽▲▽▲▽▲▽▲

Thai red curry paste, which you can find in the Asian section of most grocery stores, is one of our favorite add-ins when we want to kick up the flavor in a soup. Here, we've used it to lend a punch to this rich and creamy coconut milk–based soup. Mushrooms and shrimp make it a meal, but it's the wonderful balance of spicy, sweet and a little sour that keeps us coming back for more.

▲▽▲▽▲▽▲▽▲

Tip

To clean mushrooms, you can either rinse them quickly in water or wipe them with a damp paper towel. Mushrooms will be much happier in your refrigerator if you store them in a paper bag.

Serves 6

4 cups	chicken stock	1 L
2½ tbsp	granulated sugar	32 mL
2½ tbsp	fish sauce (nam pla)	32 mL
1½ tsp	Thai red curry paste	7 mL
2	cans (each 14 oz/400 mL) unsweetened coconut milk	2
8 oz	mushrooms, sliced	250 g
1 lb	medium shrimp, peeled and deveined	500 g
⅓ cup	chopped fresh cilantro	75 mL
3 tbsp	freshly squeezed lime juice	45 mL
	Whole fresh cilantro leaves	

1. In a large pot, bring stock, sugar, fish sauce and curry paste to a boil over medium heat; boil for 1 minute. Add coconut milk and return to a boil. Add mushrooms, reduce heat and simmer until tender, about 4 minutes. Add shrimp and simmer until pink and opaque, about 2 minutes. Remove from heat and stir in chopped cilantro and lime juice.
2. Ladle into heated bowls and garnish with whole cilantro leaves.

Thai Shrimp Wonton Soup

▲▼▲▼▲▼▲▼▲▼▲▼▲▼▲▼▲▼▲▼▲▼▲▼▲▼▲▼▲▼▲▼▲▼▲▼▲

Serve this Thai-inspired wonton soup as a light but flavor-packed starter at your next dinner party.

▲▼▲▼▲▼▲▼▲▼

Tips

Smash lemongrass pieces with the back of a knife to release the essential oils and aroma.

Wild lime leaves are often found in the herb section of fine grocery stores or at Asian markets. You may also find them in the frozen section. Wild lime leaves always come in pairs, with one leaf attached to the end of another.

Serves 8

Baking sheet, lined with parchment paper

8 cups	chicken stock	2 L
6	thin slices gingerroot	6
2	stalks lemongrass, cut into 2-inch (5 cm) sections and bruised	2
8	wild lime leaves	8
4	small serrano or other hot green chile peppers, quartered lengthwise and seeded	4
2 tbsp	fish sauce (nam pla)	25 mL
2 tsp	granulated sugar	10 mL
1/3 cup	freshly squeezed lime juice	75 mL
1/4 cup	fresh cilantro leaves	50 mL
1/4 cup	coarsely chopped Thai or Italian basil	50 mL
	Salt	
1/4 cup	chopped green onions	50 mL

Wontons

8 oz	shrimp, peeled and deveined	250 g
1	can (5 oz/142 mL) water chestnuts, drained	1
2	cloves garlic	2
1/4 cup	chopped green onions	50 mL
2 tbsp	chopped fresh cilantro	25 mL
1 tbsp	minced gingerroot	15 mL
1 1/2 tbsp	fish sauce	22 mL
1/2 tsp	toasted sesame oil	2 mL
	Salt and freshly ground black pepper	
32	wonton wrappers, thawed if frozen	32
1	egg, lightly beaten	1

1. In a large pot, bring stock, ginger, lemongrass, lime leaves and chiles to a simmer over medium heat. Simmer for 30 minutes.

2. *Meanwhile, prepare the wontons:* In a food processor fitted with a metal blade, combine shrimp, water chestnuts, garlic, green onions, cilantro, ginger, fish sauce and sesame oil. Pulse until filling is finely chopped but not a paste. To taste for seasoning, heat a small skillet over medium heat and fry a spoon-sized patty until opaque. Taste and adjust seasoning with salt and pepper, if necessary.

Variation

Let your creative genius emerge by varying the fillings in your wontons. Try pork, chicken or vegetable fillings. Any would work well in this spicy Asian stock.

3. Place a rounded teaspoon (5 mL) of filling in the center of each wonton wrapper. Brush beaten egg around the edges of the wrapper. Lift two opposite corners together to form a triangle and enclose filling, pressing all edges firmly to eliminate air pockets and seal. Place wontons on prepared baking sheet, making sure they don't touch.

4. Strain the soup (see page 8) and discard all solids; return stock to the pot. Add fish sauce and sugar; bring to a simmer over medium heat. Simmer for 5 minutes. Add wontons and simmer until wrappers are tender and filling is cooked through, about 8 minutes. Remove from heat and stir in lime juice, cilantro and basil. Taste stock and season with salt, if necessary.

5. Ladle stock into heated bowls and top each with 4 wontons. Garnish with green onions.

Shrimp Bisque

▲▼▲▼▲▼▲▼▲▼▲▼▲▼▲▼▲▼▲▼▲▼▲▼▲▼▲▼▲▼▲▼▲▼▲▼▲

This bisque is a lighter version of the often too-thick standard. The shrimp flavor is bold because the shells are cooked and then processed with the soup.

▲▼▲▼▲▼▲▼▲

Tip

It may seem odd to cook the shells and then grind them up, but the technique imparts a more pronounced shrimp taste to the bisque. Be sure to use a sieve with a very fine mesh to remove all the shell bits and other solids from the soup.

Serves 4

2 tbsp	unsalted butter	25 mL
½ cup	finely chopped onion	125 mL
2	tomatoes, halved and seeded	2
1	clove garlic, smashed	1
½ cup	diced carrot	125 mL
½ cup	diced parsnip	125 mL
½ cup	diced celery	125 mL
1 tbsp	all-purpose flour	15 mL
¼ tsp	dried thyme	1 mL
Pinch	salt	Pinch
Pinch	freshly ground black pepper	Pinch
1 lb	medium shrimp, peeled and deveined, shells reserved	500 g
5 cups	shellfish stock	1.25 L
½ cup	whipping (35%) cream	125 mL
Pinch	cayenne pepper	Pinch
Pinch	ground nutmeg	Pinch
2 tbsp	minced fresh chives	25 mL

1. In a large pot, melt butter over medium-high heat. Add onion and sauté for 1 minute. Add tomatoes, garlic, carrot, parsnip, celery, flour, thyme, salt and black pepper; sauté until vegetables are starting to soften, about 4 minutes. Add shrimp shells and sauté until shells turn pink, about 3 minutes. Gradually whisk in stock and bring to a boil, stirring often. Reduce heat and simmer, stirring occasionally, for about 20 minutes to blend the flavors.

2. Working in three batches, ladle soup into a food processor or blender, and process until fairly smooth. Strain through a fine-mesh strainer lined with wet cheesecloth and discard all solids.

3. Transfer soup to a clean pot and bring to a simmer over medium heat. Add shrimp and simmer until pink and opaque, about 2 minutes. Stir in cream, cayenne and nutmeg. Taste and adjust seasoning with salt and black pepper, if necessary

4. Ladle into heated bowls and garnish with chives.

Shrimp and Corn Bisque

▲▽▲

There is something irresistible about the marriage of August-sweet corn and fresh shrimp. The only thing that could make this soup better is a glass of Chardonnay and a really good loaf of bread with butter.

▲▽▲▽▲▽▲▽▲▽

Tip
We like to add small amounts of cayenne and nutmeg to many of our soups because they add immeasurably to the flavor without announcing their presence.

Serves 6

5 tbsp	unsalted butter, divided	75 mL
2	onions, finely chopped, divided	2
2	stalks celery, diced, divided	2
1	carrot, diced	1
2 lbs	medium shrimp, peeled, deveined and halved lengthwise, shells reserved	1 kg
1	clove garlic, minced	1
6	whole black peppercorns	6
1	bay leaf	1
½ tsp	dried thyme	2 mL
4	ears corn, kernels removed and reserved and cobs cut into quarters	4
8 cups	shellfish, chicken or vegetable stock	2 L
3 tbsp	all-purpose flour	45 mL
½ tsp	salt	2 mL
1 cup	whipping (35%) cream	250 mL
Pinch	ground nutmeg	Pinch
Pinch	cayenne pepper	Pinch
	Freshly ground black pepper	
3 tbsp	minced fresh chives	45 mL

1. In a large pot, melt 2 tbsp (25 mL) of the butter over medium heat. Add half the onions, half the celery and the carrot; sauté until softened, about 6 minutes. Add shrimp shells, garlic, peppercorns, bay leaf and thyme; sauté until shells turn pink and garlic is fragrant, about 4 minutes. Add corn cobs and stock; bring to a boil. Reduce heat and simmer for 30 minutes.

2. Meanwhile, in a saucepan, melt remaining butter over medium heat. Add remaining onion and celery; sauté until softened, about 6 minutes. Add flour and salt; sauté for 2 minutes. Gradually whisk in cream and cook, stirring, until slightly thickened, about 3 minutes. Remove from heat and set aside.

3. Strain the stock (see page 8) and discard all solids; return stock to the pot and bring to a simmer over medium heat. Add corn kernels and simmer until almost tender, about 5 minutes. Add shrimp and simmer until pink and opaque, about 2 minutes. Add cream mixture and bring to a simmer, stirring often. Stir in nutmeg and cayenne. Season with salt and black pepper to taste.

4. Ladle into heated bowls and garnish with chives.

Crab Soup

▲▽▲

Crab soup is one of life's great indulgences, but for a special occasion, nothing kicks off dinner quite like it. Because it's made with lots of butter, wine and whipping cream, we usually serve it in smaller cups or bowls as a starter. We've given this soup an update by garnishing it with a dollop of lemony, creamy crab salad. We use backfin crabmeat, which is a bit less chunky — and less pricy — than the crab usually found in crab salads.

▲▽▲▽▲▽▲▽▲▽

Tip

The crab salad can be made ahead and stored in an airtight container in the refrigerator for up to 1 day.

Serves 4

Crab Salad

1½ lbs	backfin (lump) crabmeat, shells and cartilage picked out, divided	750 g
2 tbsp	mayonnaise	25 mL
2 tsp	minced fresh chives	10 mL
¼ tsp	salt	1 mL
Pinch	freshly ground black pepper	Pinch
Pinch	cayenne pepper	Pinch
	Grated zest of ½ lemon	
1 tbsp	freshly squeezed lemon juice	15 mL

Soup

½ cup	unsalted butter, divided	125 mL
1	shallot, minced	1
½ tsp	salt	2 mL
1 cup	dry white wine	250 mL
¼ cup	all-purpose flour	50 mL
4 cups	shellfish or chicken stock	1 L
2	egg yolks, beaten	2
1 cup	whipping (35%) cream	250 mL
2 tsp	Worcestershire sauce	10 mL
1¼ lbs	backfin (lump) crabmeat, shells and cartilage picked out	625 g
	Grated zest of ½ lemon	
2 tbsp	freshly squeezed lemon juice	25 mL
Pinch	ground nutmeg	Pinch
Pinch	cayenne pepper	Pinch
	Freshly ground black pepper	
1 tsp	minced fresh chives	5 mL

1. *Prepare the crab salad:* In a large bowl, combine crab, mayonnaise, chives, salt, black pepper, cayenne, lemon zest and lemon juice. Taste and adjust seasoning, if necessary. Cover and refrigerate until ready to use.

2. *Prepare the soup:* In a large pot, melt half the butter over medium-high heat until sizzling. Add shallot and salt; sauté until shallot is tender, about 3 minutes. Add wine and cook until reduced to a few tablespoons, about 5 minutes.

Tip

Because adding delicate eggs to a pot of hot soup would result in scrambled eggs, we use a technique called tempering. By gradually adding hot soup to the eggs, the temperature of the eggs rises slowly, so that when they eventually make it into the soup, they are already hot and stay fluid and velvety.

3. Add the remaining butter to the pot and heat until melted. Sprinkle with flour and sauté for 2 minutes. Gradually whisk in stock and simmer until slightly thickened, about 3 minutes.

4. In a large bowl, whisk together egg yolks, cream and Worcestershire sauce. Gradually whisk a few ladles full of the soup into the yolk mixture. Slowly pour back into the pot, stirring constantly. Add crab, reduce heat and simmer, stirring constantly, until heated through. Do not let boil, or the eggs will curdle. Remove from heat and stir in lemon zest, lemon juice, nutmeg and cayenne. Season with salt and black pepper to taste.

5. In a microwave, warm the crab salad on High for 30 seconds. Stir, taste and, if still cold, heat for another 15 seconds. (It doesn't need to be hot, just warm.)

6. Ladle soup into heated bowls and top each with a dollop of crab salad. Garnish with chives.

Easy Crab Bisque

▲▽▲▽▲▽▲▽▲▽▲▽▲▽▲▽▲▽▲▽▲▽▲▽▲▽▲▽▲▽▲▽▲▽▲▽▲▽

Traditional crab bisque, made from scratch with fresh crabs and homemade crab stock, is a wonderful thing, but quite time-consuming. Our version, using lump crabmeat, is so decadent and mouth-watering your guests will be sure you spent all day making it. We won't tell if you don't!

▲▽▲▽▲▽▲▽▲▽▲

Tip

Be careful not to let the soup boil after adding the cream, or it will curdle.

Serves 6

3 tbsp	unsalted butter	45 mL
1 tbsp	olive oil	15 mL
1	onion, finely chopped	1
½ cup	minced celery	125 mL
½ cup	minced carrot	125 mL
2	cloves garlic, minced	2
3 tbsp	all-purpose flour	45 mL
5 cups	chicken stock	1.25 L
1 cup	clam juice	250 mL
½ cup	dry sherry	125 mL
2 tbsp	tomato paste	25 mL
2	bay leaves	2
½ tsp	salt	2 mL
¼ tsp	freshly ground black pepper	1 mL
1 cup	whipping (35%) cream	250 mL
12 oz	backfin (lump) crabmeat, shells and cartilage picked out	375 g
¼ cup	chopped green onions	50 mL
	Minced fresh chives	
	Hot pepper sauce	

1. In a large pot, heat butter and oil over medium heat. Add onion, celery and carrot; sauté until softened, about 6 minutes. Add garlic and sauté for 1 minute. Sprinkle with flour and sauté for 2 minutes.
2. Gradually whisk in stock, clam juice, sherry, tomato paste, bay leaves, salt and pepper; cook, stirring often, until slightly thickened, about 10 minutes. Add cream and bring to a simmer, stirring often. Add crab and green onions; simmer, stirring often, until heated through. Do not let boil. Discard bay leaves. Taste and adjust seasoning with salt and pepper, if necessary.
3. Ladle into heated bowls and garnish with chives. Pass hot pepper sauce at the table.

San Francisco Cioppino

▲▽

When Meredith was a child, trips to San Francisco always included slices of fresh sourdough bread, slathered in butter, and heaping bowls of cioppino. This tomato-stocked soup, packed with generous amounts of clams, mussels, crab, shrimp and fish, is a special treat that's easy to make any time the spirit moves you.

▲▽▲▽▲▽▲▽▲▽

Tip

Dungeness crab is usually found already cooked at your fishmonger. Ask your fishmonger to clean it for you, or you can clean it yourself. To do this, pull the back of the crab away from the body. Then turn the crab over and pull on the triangular-shaped section to remove it. Turn the crab again and, using your thumb or a spoon, gently scrape away the gills on either side. Remove and discard the intestine, which runs down the center of the back. The "crab butter" (the yellow stuff in the cavity) can be removed or left inside. Some people consider it a delicacy.

Serves 6

2 tbsp	olive oil	25 mL
1	onion, chopped	1
½	bulb fennel, chopped	½
6	cloves garlic, minced	6
½ tsp	hot pepper flakes (or to taste)	2 mL
2 tbsp	tomato paste	25 mL
1 cup	dry white wine	250 mL
1	can (14 oz/398 mL) tomatoes, with juice, puréed	1
5 cups	fish or shellfish stock	1.25 mL
1	bay leaf	1
1 tsp	salt	5 mL
1 lb	small clams, scrubbed	500 g
1 lb	mussels, scrubbed and debearded (see tips, page 252)	500 g
1	whole Dungeness crab (2 to 3 lbs/1 to 1.5 kg), cleaned and quartered (see tip, at left)	1
1 lb	skinless sea bass or red snapper fillets, cut into 2-inch (5 cm) chunks	500 g
1 lb	large shrimp, peeled and deveined	500 g
¼ cup	chopped fresh parsley	50 mL
2 tbsp	unsalted butter	25 mL
	Buttery Croutons (see recipe, page 368), preferably made with sourdough bread	

1. In a large pot, heat oil over medium heat. Add onion and fennel; sauté until softened, about 6 minutes. Add garlic and hot pepper flakes; sauté for 1 minute. Add tomato paste and sauté until paste turns a rusty brown, about 5 minutes. Add wine and cook until reduced by half, about 5 minutes. Add tomatoes with juice, stock, bay leaf and salt; bring to a boil. Reduce heat and simmer for 20 minutes.
2. Add clams, mussels and crab. Cover and simmer until clams and mussels begin to open, 3 to 5 minutes. Add fish, cover and simmer for 3 minutes. Add shrimp, cover and simmer until shrimp is pink and opaque and fish is opaque and flakes easily with a fork, about 2 minutes. Discard any clams and mussels that do not open. Discard bay leaf. Stir in parsley and butter. Taste and adjust seasoning with salt and hot pepper flakes.
3. Ladle into large heated bowls and garnish with croutons.

Saffron Paella Soup

▲▽▲▽▲▽▲▽▲▽▲▽▲▽▲▽▲▽▲▽▲▽▲▽▲▽▲▽▲▽▲▽▲▽▲▽

One whiff of this soup and you will be transported to the sunny shores of Spain. Carla remembers eating a version of this soup in Andalusia many moons ago and can still taste the fresh seafood and subtle spice of saffron. The chicken, sausage, shrimp and mussels make this hearty soup perfect for dinner any night of the week.

▲▽▲▽▲▽▲▽▲

Tips

Have the fishmonger tap each mussel individually to make sure it is alive and check again just before cooking. Live mussels will close when tapped. Any mussels that do not open while cooking were dead before they were cooked and should be discarded.

To scrub and debeard mussels, hold each mussel under cool running water and scrub the shell with a stiff-bristled brush. Next, grab the fibers of the "beard" with your fingers and pull them out, tugging toward the hinged point of the shell.

Serves 6

¼ cup	olive oil, divided	50 mL
1	large onion, chopped, divided	1
1 lb	chicken thighs	500 g
3	cloves garlic, minced	3
8 cups	chicken stock, divided	2 L
1	can (14 oz/398 mL) diced tomatoes, with juice	1
½ cup	long-grain white rice	125 mL
¼ tsp	salt	1 mL
¼ tsp	saffron threads	1 mL
1	red bell pepper, diced	1
1 lb	smoked Spanish chorizo or andouille sausage, diced	500 g
12	mussels, scrubbed and debearded (see tips, at left)	12
1 cup	frozen peas, thawed	250 mL
1 lb	large shrimp, peeled and deveined	500 g
¼ cup	minced fresh flat-leaf (Italian) parsley	50 mL
	Garlic Croutons (see variation, page 368)	

1. In a large pot, heat 3 tbsp (45 mL) of the oil over medium-high heat. Add half the onion and sauté until starting to soften, about 2 minutes. Add chicken, skin side down, and cook until browned, about 4 minutes. (Be careful not to let the onion burn.) Turn chicken over and brown the other side. Add garlic and sauté for 2 minutes. Add 5 cups (1.25 L) of the stock and tomatoes with juice; bring to a boil. Reduce heat and simmer until juices run clear when chicken is pierced, about 30 minutes. Remove from heat.

2. Using tongs, transfer chicken to a large plate and let cool slightly. Remove skin and bones and discard. Shred the meat into bite-size pieces and set aside. Set cooking liquid aside.

3. In a saucepan, bring the remaining stock to a simmer over medium heat. Add rice, salt and saffron; cover, reduce heat and simmer until rice is almost tender, about 15 minutes. Remove from heat and let stand, covered, until ready to use.

Tip

When we're trying to eat healthy and reduce the amount of fat in a soup, we take the skin off chicken thighs before cooking them. Other times, we leave it on and enjoy the extra richness and flavor the fat imparts.

4. In another large pot, heat the remaining oil over medium heat. Add the remaining onion, red pepper and sausage; sauté until vegetables are softened, about 6 minutes. Add reserved cooking liquid and bring to a simmer. Add reserved chicken and rice, mussels and peas; return to a simmer. Cover, reduce heat to low and simmer gently for 5 minutes. Add shrimp, cover and simmer gently until mussels have opened and shrimp is pink and opaque, 2 to 3 minutes. Discard any mussels that do not open.

5. Ladle into heated bowls, making sure each bowl contains a few shrimp and 2 mussels. Garnish with parsley and croutons.

Seafood and Sausage Gumbo Soup

▲▼▲

A thick stew, rich with fish and chicken and thickened with a roux, okra or filé powder, gumbo's roots can be traced to the heart of Africa. We've taken the best qualities of gumbo and made it into a soup that is sure to satisfy even the staunchest defenders of Southern regional cuisine.

▲▼▲▼▲▼▲▼▲▼▲

Tip

While shucking oysters is not an impossible task, it's certainly one we find unpleasant and even slightly dangerous. Oyster knives have a tendency to slip easily in the process and can slice your palm open if you're not careful. For this reason, we ask our fishmonger to shuck our oysters. If you want to shuck your own, hold the oyster firmly in one hand, with the knife in the other. Slip the knife blade between the top and bottom shell, right by the hinge on the back. Run the knife all the way around the oyster until you get to the other side. Using a twisting motion, pry the top and bottom shells apart. Cut the oyster free from its shell.

Serves 6

2 tbsp	unsalted butter	25 mL
8 oz	spicy sausage, crumbled	250 mL
2	cloves garlic, minced	2
2	stalks celery, diced	2
1	onion, finely chopped	1
1	green bell pepper, diced	1
3 tbsp	all-purpose flour	45 mL
1	can (14 oz/398 mL) diced tomatoes, with juice	1
1 cup	dry white wine	250 mL
2 tbsp	Worcestershire sauce	25 mL
2	bay leaves	2
1 tsp	salt	5 mL
¼ tsp	freshly ground black pepper	1 mL
Pinch	cayenne pepper	Pinch
6 cups	chicken stock	1.5 L
4	chicken thighs (or 2 whole legs)	4
1 lb	medium shrimp, peeled and deveined	500 g
8 oz	oysters, shucked (see tip, at left)	250 g
¼ cup	minced fresh flat-leaf (Italian) parsley	50 mL
1 cup	hot cooked white rice	250 mL

1. In a large pot, melt butter over medium heat. Add sausage and sauté, breaking up with a wooden spoon, until no pink remains, about 5 minutes. Add garlic, celery, onion and green pepper; sauté until softened, about 5 minutes. Sprinkle with flour and sauté until vegetables start to brown, about 5 minutes.

2. Gradually whisk in tomatoes with juice, wine, Worcestershire sauce, bay leaves, salt, black pepper and cayenne; cook, stirring often, until liquid is reduced by half, about 5 minutes. Gradually whisk in stock; bring to a boil. Add chicken, reduce heat and simmer, stirring occasionally, until juices run clear when chicken is pierced, about 30 minutes.

3. Using tongs, transfer chicken to a large plate and let cool slightly. Remove skin and bones and discard. Shred the meat into bite-size pieces. Return to the pot and increase heat to medium-high. Add shrimp, oysters and parsley; bring to a simmer. Cover and simmer until shrimp are pink and opaque, about 2 minutes. Discard bay leaves. Taste and adjust seasoning with salt, black pepper and cayenne, if necessary.

4. Ladle into heated bowls and serve with rice.

Chow Down Chowders

▲▽▲▽▲▽▲▽▲▽▲▽▲▽▲▽▲▽▲▽▲▽▲▽▲▽▲▽

Broccoli, Bacon and Cheddar Chowder

▲▽▲▽▲▽▲▽▲▽▲▽▲▽▲▽▲▽▲▽▲▽▲▽▲▽▲▽▲▽▲▽▲▽▲▽▲▽▲

Picture a ski chalet, four feet of fresh powder, brilliant sunshine and lots of hungry skiers. You'll be the hero of the day if you make this soul-warming soup.

▲▽▲▽▲▽▲▽▲▽▲

Tip

If you prefer, you can substitute 5 cups (1.25 L) chopped cooked fresh broccoli (about 3 large stalks).

Serves 6

8	slices bacon, chopped	8
2 tbsp	unsalted butter	25 mL
1	onion, finely chopped	1
2 tbsp	all-purpose flour	25 mL
3 cups	milk	750 mL
2 cups	chicken or vegetable stock	500 mL
½ tsp	salt	2 mL
Pinch	cayenne pepper	Pinch
12 oz	red-skinned potatoes (about 3 medium), cut into ½-inch (1 cm) dice	375 g
2 cups	shredded Cheddar cheese, tossed with 1 tbsp (15 mL) all-purpose flour	500 mL
1 tsp	hot pepper sauce (optional)	5 mL
2	packages (each 10 oz/300 g) frozen chopped broccoli, thawed and drained	2

1. In a large pot, sauté bacon over medium heat until browned and crispy, about 5 minutes. Remove with a slotted spoon to a plate lined with paper towels. Set aside.
2. Pour off all but 2 tbsp (25 mL) of the fat in the pot. Add butter and heat until melted. Add onion and sauté until softened, about 6 minutes. Sprinkle with flour and sauté for 2 minutes.
3. Gradually whisk in milk, stock, salt and cayenne; bring to a simmer, stirring often. Simmer, stirring often, until smooth and creamy, about 3 minutes. Do not let boil. Add potatoes, reduce heat and simmer, stirring often, until tender, about 20 minutes.
4. Add cheese, ½ cup (125 mL) at a time, stirring with a wooden spoon after each addition until cheese is melted. Do not let boil. Add hot pepper sauce (if using). Add broccoli and simmer, stirring, until heated through. Taste and adjust seasoning with salt and cayenne, if necessary.
5. Ladle into heated bowls and garnish with reserved bacon.

Arugula Soup with Salmon and Roasted Grape Tomatoes (page 233)

Overleaf: Saffron Paella Soup (page 252)

Fresh Corn and Zucchini Chowder with Fresh Thyme

For soups that are dependent on corn for their personality, we like to use locally grown corn on the cob when it's in season. Try to make this soup in August, when fresh corn and zucchini are overflowing the produce bins.

▲▽▲▽▲▽▲▽▲▽

Tip

We cook the corn cobs in the soup to give it even richer corny flavor.

Variations

Reduce the butter to 2 tbsp (25 mL) and, before adding the onions, sauté 8 slices of bacon, finely chopped, until browned and crispy. Remove with a slotted spoon to a plate lined with paper towels. Sauté the onions in the fat remaining in the pot and continue with the recipe. Garnish the soup with the reserved bacon as well as the cayenne.

For a heartier dish, add 2 cups (500 mL) diced ham with the stock.

Rich Lobster and Roasted Corn Chowder (page 278)

Overleaf: Spring Chicken Chowder with Asparagus and Peas (page 266)

Serves 6

¼ cup	unsalted butter	50 mL
1	onion, chopped	1
2	cloves garlic, minced	2
3	ears corn, kernels cut from cobs, cobs reserved	3
2	large zucchini, cut into 1-inch (2.5 cm) cubes	2
1	potato, diced	1
1 tbsp	chopped fresh thyme	15 mL
1 tbsp	chopped fresh flat-leaf (Italian) parsley	15 mL
6 cups	chicken or vegetable stock	1.5 L
1 cup	half-and-half (10%) cream	250 mL
	Salt and freshly ground black pepper	
¼ tsp	cayenne pepper	1 mL

1. In a large pot, melt butter over medium heat. Add onion and sauté until softened, about 6 minutes. Add garlic and sauté until fragrant, about 1 minute. Add corn kernels, zucchini, potato, thyme and parsley; sauté until starting to soften, about 3 minutes.

2. Add stock and corn cobs; bring to a boil. Reduce heat and simmer until vegetables are tender, about 15 minutes. Discard cobs.

3. Using an immersion blender, pulse the soup in 3 or 4 quick spurts to partially blend it, leaving it chunky (or process half the soup in a food processor or blender, then return to the pot). Stir in cream and reheat over medium heat until steaming, stirring often. Do not let boil. Season with salt and black pepper to taste.

4. Ladle into heated bowls and garnish with a light dusting of cayenne pepper.

Corn Chowder with Ham

▲▽▲▽▲▽▲▽▲▽▲▽▲▽▲▽▲▽▲▽▲▽▲▽▲▽▲▽▲▽▲▽▲▽▲▽▲

We use corn cobs in this chowder to enrich the stock, giving it a strong corn flavor. Make this soup in the summer, when corn season is at its peak.

▲▽▲▽▲▽▲▽▲▽▲

Tip
Soup will stay hot much longer in a heated bowl.

Serves 6

6	ears of corn	6
4 cups	vegetable stock or White Chicken Stock (see recipe, page 9)	1 L
2 cups	milk	500 mL
3 tbsp	unsalted butter	45 mL
1 cup	finely chopped red onion	250 mL
2 tbsp	all-purpose flour	25 mL
2	potatoes, peeled and diced	2
8 oz	ham, diced (about 1½ cups/375 mL)	250 g
1 tsp	dried basil	5 mL
1 tsp	salt	5 mL
¼ tsp	freshly ground black pepper	1 mL
¼ tsp	hot pepper flakes	1 mL
Pinch	ground nutmeg	Pinch
¼ cup	minced fresh flat-leaf (Italian) parsley	50 mL

1. Cut corn kernels from the cobs into a bowl. Using the back of a knife, scrape down the cobs, releasing the corn milk into the bowl. Set aside.
2. In a large pot, bring stock and corn cobs to a simmer over medium heat. Simmer for about 30 minutes to extract the flavor from the cobs. Discard cobs. Remove stock from heat and stir in milk.
3. In another large pot, melt butter over medium-high heat. Add onion and sauté until softened, about 4 minutes. Sprinkle with flour and sauté for 2 minutes.
4. Gradually whisk in stock mixture. Add reserved corn, potatoes, ham, basil, salt, black pepper, hot pepper flakes and nutmeg; bring to a boil. Reduce heat and simmer, stirring often, until potatoes are tender, about 20 minutes. Taste and adjust seasoning with salt and black pepper, if necessary.
5. Ladle into heated bowls and garnish with parsley.

Lima Bean Chowder with Corn and Ham

We always have a bag of lima beans in the freezer because they make a great add-in to soups, providing a hearty, almost meaty element. This soup is a wonderful addition to your repertoire, as it uses many ingredients you likely already have in your pantry or refrigerator.

Tip

Although we like this soup garnished with Buttery Croutons, feel free to look through the toppings and garnishes chapter (pages 361–374) and mix and match to your heart's delight.

Serves 6

3 tbsp	unsalted butter	45 mL
1	onion, finely chopped	1
2	carrots, diced	2
1	stalk celery, diced	1
¼ cup	all-purpose flour	50 mL
4 cups	chicken stock	1 L
2	potatoes, peeled and diced	2
1 tsp	salt	5 mL
¼ tsp	freshly ground black pepper	1 mL
2 cups	frozen lima beans, thawed	500 mL
2 cups	milk	500 mL
1½ cups	diced ham	375 mL
1 cup	fresh or frozen corn kernels, thawed if frozen	250 mL
	Buttery Croutons (see recipe, page 368)	

1. In a large pot, melt butter over medium heat. Add onion and sauté until softened, about 6 minutes. Add carrots and celery; sauté for 5 minutes. Sprinkle with flour and sauté for 2 minutes.
2. Gradually whisk in stock. Add potatoes, salt and pepper; bring to a boil. Reduce heat and simmer for 15 minutes, stirring occasionally. Add lima beans, milk, ham and corn; return to a simmer, stirring often. Simmer, stirring often, until potatoes are tender, about 5 minutes. Do not let boil. Taste and adjust seasoning with salt and pepper, if necessary.
3. Ladle into heated bowls and garnish with croutons.

Southwest Chorizo and Corn Chowder

▲▼▲▼▲▼▲▼▲▼▲▼▲▼▲▼▲▼▲▼▲▼▲▼▲▼▲▼▲▼▲▼▲▼▲

Chorizo, a spicy sausage found both cured (often from Spain) and fresh, is commonly used in Mexican dishes. Here, we use fresh chorizo as the basis for a boldly flavored chowder. Corn adds a slightly sweet backdrop.

▲▼▲▼▲▼▲▼▲▼▲

Tip

Chile peppers contain oils that can cause chemical burns on your skin. When seeding and chopping them, always wear latex, plastic or rubber gloves.

Serves 6

1 tsp	vegetable oil	5 mL
8 oz	fresh chorizo sausage (bulk or with casings removed)	250 g
1	large onion, minced	1
1	poblano chile pepper, seeded and cut into small dice	1
1	red bell pepper, cut into small dice	1
1	jalapeño pepper, seeded and minced	1
5 cups	chicken stock, divided	1.25 L
3 cups	fresh or frozen corn kernels, thawed if frozen, divided	750 mL
1 lb	baking potatoes, peeled and cut into small dice	500 g
1 tsp	salt	5 mL
¼ tsp	freshly ground black pepper	1 mL
1 cup	whipping (35%) cream	250 mL
	Crispy Tortilla Strips (see recipe, page 372)	

1. In a large pot, heat oil over medium heat. Add chorizo and sauté, breaking up with the back of a wooden spoon, until no longer pink, about 5 minutes. Add onion, poblano, red pepper and jalapeño; sauté until softened, about 6 minutes.
2. In a food processor or blender, purée 1 cup (125 mL) of the stock and 1 cup (125 mL) of the corn. Pour into the pot and add the remaining stock, potatoes, salt and pepper; bring to a boil. Reduce heat and simmer for 15 minutes. Stir in the remaining corn and cream; return to a simmer, stirring often. Simmer, stirring often, until potatoes are tender, about 5 minutes. Do not let boil. Taste and adjust seasoning with salt and pepper, if necessary.
3. Ladle into heated bowls and garnish with tortilla strips.

Cheesy Zucchini, Sausage and Tomato Chowder

▲▽▲▽▲▽▲▽▲▽▲▽▲▽▲▽▲▽▲▽▲▽▲▽▲▽▲▽▲▽▲▽▲▽▲▽▲▽▲

Cheese and zucchini make a surprisingly wonderful duo in this creamy, rich and satisfying chowder.

▲▽▲▽▲▽▲▽▲▽

Tip

San Marzano tomatoes, imported from Italy, are thought by many to be the best canned tomatoes in the world. They hail from a small town of the same name near Naples, whose volcanic soil is thought to filter impurities from the water and render tomatoes with a thick flesh, fewer seeds and a stronger taste. Look for the words "San Marzano" on the label to be sure you're getting the best.

Serves 6

1 tsp	vegetable oil	5 mL
1 lb	mild Italian sausage (bulk or with casings removed)	500 g
1	large onion, minced	1
1	can (14 oz/398 mL) diced tomatoes, with juice	1
1 lb	baking potatoes, peeled and cut into small dice	500 g
4 cups	chicken or vegetable stock	1 L
1 tsp	salt	5 mL
2	zucchini, cut into small dice	2
1 cup	whipping (35%) cream	250 mL
2 cups	shredded sharp (old) Cheddar cheese, tossed with 1 tbsp (15 mL) all-purpose flour	500 mL
	Freshly ground black pepper	
	Cheesy Croutons (see recipe, page 369), made with Cheddar cheese	

1. In a large pot, heat oil over medium heat. Add sausage and sauté, breaking up with the back of a wooden spoon, until no longer pink, about 5 minutes. Add onion and sauté until softened, about 6 minutes.
2. Add tomatoes with juice, potatoes, stock and salt; bring to a boil. Reduce heat and simmer for 10 minutes. Add zucchini and simmer until vegetables are tender, about 10 minutes. Stir in cream and return to a simmer, stirring often. Add cheese, 1/2 cup (125 mL) at a time, stirring with a wooden spoon after each addition until cheese is melted. Do not let boil. Season with salt and pepper to taste.
3. Ladle into heated bowls and garnish with croutons.

Roasted Butternut Squash Chowder with Sage Butter

▲▽▲

When dealing with fall squash, we often prefer to roast them and scoop out the flesh, rather than peel and cut them into dice, because roasting intensifies their sweetness and flavor. For this recipe, we decided to roast half the squash to make a nice purée for the soup, and dice the other half, so that there are chunks of squash to go with the potatoes. Since we love the combination of sage and butternut squash, we've used fresh sage in the soup itself and garnished with crispy fried sage leaves and browned sage butter ... a touch that elevates this recipe from rustic chowder to more sophisticated fare.

Tip

You can use 1½ cups (375 mL) table (18%) cream instead of the half-and-half and whipping creams.

Serves 6

- Preheat oven to 400°F (200°C)
- Rimmed baking sheet, lined with parchment paper

1	butternut squash (3½ to 4 lbs/1.75 to 2 kg), halved lengthwise and seeded	1
¼ cup	olive oil, divided	50 mL
10	sage leaves, thinly sliced	10
1	large onion, finely chopped	1
1	clove garlic, minced	1
1 cup	dry white wine	250 mL
2	large potatoes, peeled and cut into ½-inch (1 cm) dice	2
6 cups	vegetable or chicken stock (or a blend of the two)	1.5 L
1 tsp	salt	5 mL
1 tsp	freshly squeezed lemon juice	5 mL
Pinch	cayenne pepper	Pinch
Pinch	ground nutmeg	Pinch
	Freshly ground black pepper	
1 cup	half-and-half (10%) cream	250 mL
½ cup	whipping (35%) cream	125 mL
¼ cup	unsalted butter	50 mL
12	whole sage leaves	12

1. Rub the cut side of one of the squash halves with 1 tbsp (15 mL) of the oil and place cut side down on prepared baking sheet. Roast in preheated oven until a knife pierces easily into the thick part of the neck, about 40 minutes. Let cool on pan.

2. Meanwhile, peel and cut the remaining squash half into ½-inch (1 cm) dice; set aside.

3. In a large pot, heat the remaining oil over medium-high heat. Add sliced sage leaves and sauté until fragrant, about 1 minute. Add onion and sauté until softened, about 4 minutes. Add garlic and sauté until fragrant, about 1 minute. Add wine and cook until reduced by half, about 5 minutes. Add diced squash, potatoes, stock and salt; bring to a boil. Reduce heat and simmer until vegetables are tender, about 20 minutes.

▲▽▲▽▲▽▲▽▲▽▲▽▲▽▲▽▲▽▲▽▲▽▲▽▲▽▲▽▲▽▲▽

Tip

When we instruct you to cut vegetables to a certain size, it's because we think size really does matter in the recipe. In some recipes, we like disciplined dice because the vegetables cook more evenly, and we think the uniformly chopped vegetables make for a nice texture and a more attractive soup.

4. Scoop roasted squash from its shell, mash it and add it to the soup. Season with lemon juice, cayenne, nutmeg and black pepper to taste. Stir in half-and-half cream and whipping cream; reheat over medium heat until steaming, stirring often. Taste and adjust seasoning with cayenne, nutmeg, salt and black pepper, if necessary.

5. In a skillet, melt butter over medium heat until sizzling. Add whole sage leaves and sauté until crispy and browned, about 2 minutes. Transfer sage to a plate lined with paper towels. Remove pan from heat.

6. Ladle chowder into heated bowls and top each with a drizzle of sage butter and 2 fried sage leaves.

Spicy Sweet Potato Chowder

▲▼▲▼▲▼▲▼▲▼▲▼▲▼▲▼▲▼▲▼▲▼▲▼▲▼▲▼▲▼▲▼▲▼▲▼▲▼▲

The sweetness of the sweet potatoes and smokiness of the bacon and chipotle chiles make a great combination in this mouth-watering but unconventional chowder.

▲▼▲▼▲▼▲▼▲▼

Tip

Chipotle chiles are smoked jalapeños, often found canned in a vinegary tomato sauce called adobo. Look for them in the Mexican aisle of your grocery store. They tend to be fiery, so we often use only 1 or 2 at a time.

Serves 6

4	slices bacon, cut into ½-inch (1 cm) pieces	4
1	onion, finely chopped	1
2	poblano chile peppers, seeded and diced	2
2	large sweet potatoes, peeled and cut into ½-inch (1 cm) dice	2
2	chipotle chile peppers in adobo sauce, minced (see tip, at left)	2
5 cups	chicken stock	1.25 L
1 cup	whipping (35%) cream	250 mL
1 tbsp	packed light brown sugar	15 mL
½ tsp	salt	2 mL
1 tbsp	freshly squeezed lime juice	15 mL

1. In a large pot, sauté bacon over medium heat until browned and crispy, about 5 minutes. Remove with a slotted spoon to a plate lined with paper towels. Set aside.

2. Pour off all but 1 tbsp (15 mL) of the fat in the pot. Add onion and poblano chiles; sauté until softened, about 6 minutes. Add sweet potatoes, chipotle chiles and stock; bring to a boil. Cover, reduce heat and simmer until sweet potatoes are tender, about 15 minutes. Stir in cream, brown sugar, salt and lime juice; reheat over medium heat until steaming, stirring often. Do not let boil.

3. Ladle into heated bowls and garnish with reserved bacon.

Lentil and Chard Chowder

▲▽▲▽▲▽▲▽▲▽▲▽▲▽▲▽▲▽▲▽▲▽▲▽▲▽▲▽▲▽▲▽▲▽▲▽▲

We've substituted lentils for potatoes in this chowder. The addition of cream at the end gives this vegetable soup a rich, creamy personality.

▲▽▲▽▲▽▲▽

Tip

Parsley root looks like little parsnips (which would work as a substitute) and has a clean parsley flavor that goes with almost anything. Try adding parsley root to any vegetable soup for extra flavor and interest.

Serves 6

¼ cup	unsalted butter	50 mL
1	onion, minced	1
1	carrot, sliced	1
1	stalk celery, sliced	1
1	bunch parsley root (about 6 oz/175 g), peeled and sliced	1
1	bunch Swiss chard (about 6 oz/175 g), tough stems discarded, chard cut into thin ribbons	1
2	cloves garlic, minced	2
8 cups	chicken stock	2 L
1 cup	dried lentils (any color), rinsed	250 mL
1	bay leaf	1
½ tsp	salt	2 mL
	Freshly ground black pepper	
1 cup	whipping (35%) cream	250 mL
2 tsp	freshly squeezed lemon juice	10 mL
Pinch	cayenne pepper	Pinch
Pinch	ground nutmeg	Pinch
¼ cup	chopped fresh parsley	50 mL
	Buttery Croutons (see recipe, page 368)	

1. In a large pot, melt butter over medium heat. Add onion, carrot, celery and parsley root; sauté until softened, about 6 minutes. Add chard and sauté until wilted, about 5 minutes. Add garlic and sauté until fragrant, about 1 minute.

2. Add stock, lentils, bay leaf, salt and black pepper to taste; bring to a boil. Reduce heat and simmer until lentils are tender, about 45 minutes. Discard bay leaf. Stir in cream, lemon juice, cayenne and nutmeg; reheat over medium heat until steaming, stirring often. Do not let boil. Taste and adjust seasoning with salt and black pepper, if necessary.

3. Ladle into heated bowls and garnish with parsley and croutons.

Spring Chicken Chowder
with Asparagus and Peas

▲▽▲▽▲▽▲▽▲▽▲▽▲▽▲▽▲▽▲▽▲▽▲▽▲▽▲▽▲▽▲▽▲▽▲▽

"Ode to Spring" came to mind when we were formulating this soup. The green vegetables and orange sweet potato give flavor, balance and color to an otherwise pale concoction. But don't wait for spring to make it! It tastes good in winter, summer and fall as well — just substitute whatever vegetables are in season.

▲▽▲▽▲▽▲▽▲▽

Tips

We sometimes poach chicken in chicken stock and vegetables to make the stock richer and fuller tasting.

We like to use a Microplane grater to grate citrus zest.

Serves 6

¼ cup	unsalted butter	50 mL
1	onion, finely chopped	1
2	cloves garlic, minced	2
1	stalk celery, diced	1
1 tsp	dried thyme	5 mL
3 tbsp	all-purpose flour	45 mL
½ tsp	salt	2 mL
¼ tsp	freshly ground black pepper	1 mL
6 cups	chicken stock	1.5 L
1	whole chicken (about 3 lbs/1.5 kg), rinsed, or 3 lbs (1.5 kg) skinless chicken thighs	1
1	bay leaf	1
2	sweet potatoes (about 1½ lbs/750 g total), peeled and cut into ½-inch (1 cm) dice	2
1	bunch asparagus (about 12 oz/375 g), trimmed and cut into 1-inch (2.5 cm) pieces	1
1 cup	frozen peas	250 mL
1 cup	half-and-half (10%) cream	250 mL
¼ cup	minced fresh flat-leaf (Italian) parsley	50 mL
Pinch	cayenne pepper	Pinch
	Grated zest and juice of 1 lemon, divided	

1. In a large pot, melt butter over medium heat until sizzling. Add onion and sauté until softened, about 6 minutes. Add garlic, celery and thyme; sauté until celery starts to soften, about 3 minutes. Sprinkle with flour, salt and black pepper; sauté for 2 minutes.

2. Gradually whisk in stock. Add chicken and bay leaf. If chicken isn't immersed, add water or stock to cover. Bring to a boil over medium-high heat. Partially cover, reduce heat to low and simmer gently for 25 minutes. Add sweet potatoes and simmer until a thermometer inserted into the thickest part of a chicken breast registers 170°F (75°C), about 20 minutes. Skim the soup if any scum develops on the surface. Remove from heat.

Tip

Be careful not to let the soup boil after adding the cream, or it will curdle.

3. Using tongs, transfer chicken to a large plate and let cool slightly. Remove skin and bones and discard. Shred meat into bite-size pieces and set aside.

4. Skim the fat from the surface of the stock with a large spoon and return to a simmer over medium heat. Add asparagus and peas; simmer until tender, about 10 minutes. Discard bay leaf. Stir in reserved chicken, cream, parsley, cayenne, half the lemon zest and the lemon juice; reheat over medium heat until steaming, stirring often. Do not let boil. Taste and adjust seasoning with salt and black pepper, if necessary.

5. Ladle into heated bowls and garnish with the remaining lemon zest.

Tuscan Bean Chowder

Beans are not typical chowder fare, but they make a wonderful counterpoint to the potatoes and cream. In this soup, we borrow flavors from our Italian friends and use pancetta — which is much like bacon, without the smokiness — and earthy rosemary.

Tip

You can easily substitute bacon for the pancetta. To remove some of the smoke flavor, blanch it for 1 minute in simmering water. Drain and use as directed.

Serves 6 to 8

1 tbsp	olive oil	15 mL
5 oz	pancetta, minced	150 g
2	onions, finely chopped	2
1 tbsp	chopped fresh rosemary	15 mL
3 cups	chicken stock	750 mL
2	large yellow- or white-fleshed potatoes	2
1	can (14 oz/398 mL) diced tomatoes, with juice	1
2	cans (each 14 to 19 oz/398 to 540 mL) cannellini or white kidney beans, drained and rinsed	2
1 tsp	salt	5 mL
½ tsp	freshly ground black pepper	2 mL
2 cups	half-and-half (10%) cream	500 mL
	Garlic Croutons (see variation, page 368)	

1. In a large pot, heat oil over medium heat. Add pancetta and sauté until golden brown and crispy, about 5 minutes. Add onions and sauté until softened, about 6 minutes. Add rosemary and sauté for 1 minute.

2. Add stock, potatoes and tomatoes with juice. If necessary, add enough water to barely cover. Bring to a boil. Reduce heat and simmer for 15 minutes. Add beans, salt and pepper; simmer until potatoes are tender and beans are heated through, about 5 minutes. Stir in cream and reheat over medium heat until steaming, stirring often. Do not let boil. Taste and adjust seasoning with salt and pepper, if necessary.

3. Ladle into heated bowls and garnish with croutons.

Creamy Cod Chowder

▲▼▲

We like cod because its firm flesh and mild flavor win over the pickiest eaters. In this chowder, we cook the fish in whole fillets to help it retain its firmness, then flake it into the soup at the last minute.

▲▼▲▼▲▼▲▼▲▼

Tip
If you don't have fish stock on hand, you can replace it with 4 cups (1 L) chicken stock and 1 cup (250 mL) clam juice.

Variation
Halibut or tilapia would also work beautifully in this soup.

Serves 6 to 8

6	slices bacon, minced	6
2 tbsp	unsalted butter	25 mL
2	onions, finely chopped	2
1 tbsp	chopped fresh thyme	15 mL
1½ lbs	yellow- or white-fleshed potatoes, peeled and cut into ½-inch (1 cm) dice	750 g
5 cups	fish stock	1.25 L
2½ lbs	boneless skinless cod fillets	1.25 kg
1 tsp	salt	5 mL
½ tsp	freshly ground black pepper	2 mL
1½ cups	whipping (35%) cream	375 mL
¼ cup	minced fresh chives	50 mL

1. In a large pot, sauté bacon over medium heat until browned and crispy, about 5 minutes. Remove with a slotted spoon to a plate lined with paper towels. Set aside.

2. Add butter to the pot and heat until melted. Add onions and thyme; sauté until softened, about 6 minutes. Add potatoes and stock. If necessary, add enough water to barely cover. Bring to a boil. Reduce heat and simmer until potatoes are almost tender, about 15 minutes. Add cod, salt and pepper; simmer until fish is opaque and flakes easily with a fork and potatoes are tender, about 5 minutes.

3. Using a slotted spoon, gently transfer fish to a large plate. Using a fork, flake fish apart and set aside.

4. Stir cream into the pot and reheat over medium heat until steaming, stirring often. Do not let boil. Taste and adjust seasoning with salt and pepper, if necessary. Return fish to the pot.

5. Ladle into heated bowls and garnish with reserved bacon and chives.

Salmon Chowder with Chives

▲▼▲▼▲▼▲▼▲▼▲▼▲▼▲▼▲▼▲▼▲▼▲▼▲▼▲▼▲▼▲▼▲▼▲▼▲▼▲

We love how quick and easy this soup is to pull together. You don't even have to peel the potatoes! The red and golden skins give this otherwise pale soup much-needed color.

▲▼▲▼▲▼▲▼▲

Tip

We've used two types of potatoes here because they have different textures and colors and give the soup more interest. If you only want to use one kind of potato, go ahead. No one will tell on you.

Serves 6

¼ cup	unsalted butter	50 mL
1	shallot, minced	1
¼ cup	all-purpose flour	50 mL
½ tsp	salt	2 mL
8 cups	fish, shellfish or chicken stock	2 L
8 oz	red-skinned potatoes, cut into ½-inch (1 cm) dice	250 g
8 oz	Yukon gold potatoes, cut into ½-inch (1 cm) dice	250 g
1	bay leaf	1
1 lb	boneless skinless salmon fillet, cut into 2-inch (5 cm) pieces	500 g
1 cup	whipping (35%) cream	250 mL
¼ cup	minced fresh chives, divided	50 mL
2 tsp	white wine vinegar	10 mL
Pinch	freshly ground black pepper	Pinch
Pinch	ground nutmeg	Pinch
Pinch	cayenne pepper	Pinch

1. In a large pot, melt butter over medium heat. Add shallot and sauté until starting to soften, about 2 minutes. Sprinkle with flour and salt; sauté for 2 minutes.
2. Gradually whisk in stock. Add red-skinned potatoes, Yukon gold potatoes and bay leaf; bring to a boil. Reduce heat and simmer until potatoes are almost tender, about 15 minutes. Add salmon and simmer until fish is opaque and flakes easily with a fork and potatoes are tender, about 5 minutes. Discard bay leaf. Stir in cream, 2 tbsp (25 mL) of the chives, vinegar, black pepper, nutmeg, cayenne and salt to taste; reheat over medium heat until steaming, stirring often. Do not let boil.
3. Ladle into heated bowls and garnish with the remaining chives.

Salmon Chowder with Pernod in Puff Pastry

▲▽▲▽▲▽▲▽▲▽▲▽▲▽▲▽▲▽▲▽▲▽▲▽▲▽▲▽▲▽▲▽▲▽▲▽

We love to serve this festive soup as a starter, or alone as a celebratory luncheon main course. It is très français *as a result of the pastry and Pernod, a licorice-flavored liqueur. Most of the "sauce" is absorbed by the mushrooms and salmon, so it isn't especially soupy, but we love this dish so much we had to include it.*

▲▽▲▽▲▽▲▽▲▽

Tips

If your bowls are wide, you might need a double recipe of the pastry. If you find that too daunting a task, go ahead and use store-bought puff pastry. The soup will be delicious either way.

Shiitake stems are too tough to eat, but they make a wonderful addition to vegetable stock.

Serves 4

- 4 individual ovenproof 2-cup (500 mL) bowls
- Baking sheet

2 tbsp	unsalted butter	25 mL
2	shallots, minced	2
1 cup	dry white wine	250 mL
¼ cup	Pernod	50 mL
1 cup	shellfish, fish or chicken stock	250 mL
1 cup	whipping (35%) cream	250 mL
1 tbsp	minced fresh tarragon	15 mL
	Salt and freshly ground black pepper	
2	potatoes, cut into ½-inch (1 cm) dice	2
1½ lbs	boneless skinless salmon fillets, cut into 1-inch (2.5 cm) pieces	750 g
8 oz	shiitake mushrooms, stems removed and caps thinly sliced	250 g
	Flaky Pastry (see recipe, page 370)	
1	egg, beaten	1

1. In a saucepan, melt butter over medium heat. Add shallots and sauté until softened, about 2 minutes. Add wine and cook until reduced to a few tablespoons, about 5 minutes. Add Pernod and cook until almost evaporated, about 2 minutes. Stir in stock and cream; cook, stirring often, for 5 minutes. Add tarragon and salt and pepper to taste. Remove from heat.

2. Meanwhile, in a vegetable steamer or saucepan of boiling water, steam or boil potatoes until tender, about 15 minutes.

3. Sprinkle salmon with salt and pepper to taste. Divide salmon, potatoes and mushrooms among ovenproof bowls and sprinkle with salt and pepper to taste. Top with soup.

4. Roll out pastry to ⅛-inch (3 mm) thickness and cut rounds to fit over the bowls. Brush the edges of the bowls with the beaten egg and fit the pastry rounds on top, pinching around the edges to seal. Brush the pastry with the egg and refrigerate the soups for 20 minutes to firm up the pastry. Meanwhile, preheat oven to 400°F (200°C).

5. Place bowls on baking sheet and bake until pastry is browned and crispy, about 20 minutes. Carefully transfer the bowls to serving plates and serve.

New England Clam Chowder

▲▽▲▽▲▽▲▽▲▽▲▽▲▽▲▽▲▽▲▽▲▽▲▽▲▽▲▽▲▽▲▽▲▽▲▽▲▽▲

When most people think of chowder, New England clam chowder is what comes to mind. Our easy version of this cold weather classic uses canned clams and juice, making it a quick weeknight meal in a bowl.

▲▽▲▽▲▽▲▽▲▽

Tip

You can sometimes find fresh raw shelled clams in the refrigerator case. These are nice to use. They will need to be chopped, and the soup should be cooked 5 minutes longer once they are added to ensure that they are fully cooked.

Serves 6 to 8

3	slices bacon, cut crosswise into ¼-inch (0.5 cm) strips	3
1 tbsp	unsalted butter	15 mL
1 cup	chopped onions	250 mL
2	cloves garlic, finely chopped	2
2	stalks celery, chopped	2
2	bay leaves	2
2 tsp	chopped fresh thyme	10 mL
2 lbs	boiling potatoes, peeled and cut into ½-inch (1 cm) dice	1 kg
3 cups	clam juice	750 mL
2 cups	water (approx.)	500 mL
1½ cups	whipping (35%) cream	375 mL
3	cans (each 6½ oz/184 g) minced clams, with juice	3
	Salt and freshly ground black pepper	
2 tbsp	minced fresh flat-leaf (Italian) parsley	25 mL

1. In a large pot, sauté bacon over medium heat until browned and crispy, about 5 minutes. Remove with a slotted spoon to a plate lined with paper towels. Set aside.
2. Add butter to the pot and heat until melted. Add onion, garlic, celery, bay leaves and thyme; sauté until onions are softened, about 6 minutes. Add potatoes, clam juice and water. If necessary, add enough water to barely cover. Bring to a boil. Reduce heat and simmer until potatoes are tender, about 20 minutes. Discard bay leaves.
3. Remove from heat and stir in cream and clams with juice. Reheat over medium heat until steaming, stirring often. Do not let boil. Season with salt and pepper to taste.
4. Ladle into heated bowls and garnish with reserved bacon and parsley.

Manhattan Clam Chowder

▲▽▲

There are as many versions of this chowder as there are cooks who make it. To us, Manhattan clam chowder is defined by the inclusion of clams, potatoes and tomatoes. We upped the ante by cooking the vegetables in bacon drippings (definitely something Grandma would approve of), then garnished the finished soup with the crispy bacon bits.

▲▽▲▽▲▽▲▽▲▽▲

Variations

You can easily adapt this recipe to any seafood you may have on hand, whether mussels, oysters, shrimp or even a fillet of your favorite fish. Just be sure to add them near the end of cooking, as creatures of the sea become rubbery and tough when overcooked.

We also liked this soup with the addition of 8 oz (250 g) sausage (bulk or with casings removed). In Step 2, reduce the oil to 1 tbsp (15 mL) and brown the sausage with the vegetables in Step 3.

Serves 6

¼ cup	olive oil, divided	50 mL
2	cloves garlic, minced	2
1 cup	dry white wine	250 mL
4 lbs	clams (see tip, page 274), scrubbed	2 kg
4	slices bacon, finely chopped	4
1	large onion, finely chopped	1
2	carrots, diced	2
1	stalk celery, diced	1
2	large potatoes, peeled and diced	2
1	can (14 oz/398 mL) diced tomatoes, with juice	1
6 cups	fish, shellfish, vegetable or chicken stock	1.5 L
1	bay leaf	1
½ tsp	dried thyme	2 mL
1 tsp	balsamic vinegar	5 mL
¼ tsp	cayenne pepper	1 mL
	Salt and freshly ground black pepper	
¼ cup	minced fresh flat-leaf (Italian) parsley	50 mL
	Oyster crackers or saltines	

1. In a large pot, heat 2 tbsp (25 mL) of the oil over medium heat. Add garlic and sauté until fragrant, about 1 minute. Add wine and clams; bring to a boil. Cover, reduce heat and simmer until clams have opened, 5 to 8 minutes. Using a slotted spoon, transfer clams to a large bowl and let cool slightly. Discard any clams that do not open. Separate the meat from the shells; discard shells and set meat aside. Strain the cooking liquid (see page 8) and discard all solids; set aside.

2. In another large pot, heat the remaining oil over medium heat. Add bacon and sauté until browned and crispy, about 5 minutes. Remove with a slotted spoon to a plate lined with paper towels. Set aside.

3. Add onion to the pot and sauté until softened, about 6 minutes. Add carrots and celery; sauté until softened, about 5 minutes. Add potatoes, tomatoes with juice, stock, bay leaf, thyme and reserved clam liquid; bring to a boil. Reduce heat and simmer until potatoes are tender, about 20 minutes. Add clam meat and any accumulated juices; simmer for 2 minutes. Discard bay leaf. Stir in vinegar, cayenne and salt and black pepper to taste.

4. Ladle into heated bowls and garnish with reserved bacon and parsley. Serve with oyster crackers on the side.

Clam and Corn Chowder

Corn and shellfish go together beautifully, which is why we paired them in this chowder. We use fresh clams and serve them in their shells for a lovely presentation and "fresh from the sea" flavor.

Tips

If you prefer, you can replace the chicken stock and clam juice with 3 cups (750 mL) fish or shellfish stock.

Have the fishmonger tap each clam individually to make sure it is alive and check again just before cooking. Live clams will close when tapped. Any clams that do not open while cooking were dead before they were cooked and should be discarded.

Serves 6

4	slices bacon, chopped	4
1	onion, chopped	1
1	large bay leaf	1
1 tsp	dried thyme	5 mL
1 lb	boiling potatoes, peeled and cut into ½-inch (1 cm) dice	500 g
2 cups	chicken stock	500 mL
1 cup	clam juice	250 mL
2 cups	fresh or frozen corn kernels, thawed if frozen	500 mL
2 lbs	small clams (see tip, at left), scrubbed	1 kg
1½ cups	milk	375 mL
1 cup	whipping (35%) cream	250 mL
	Salt and freshly ground black pepper	

1. In a large pot, sauté bacon over medium heat until browned and crispy, about 5 minutes. Remove with a slotted spoon to a plate lined with paper towels. Set aside.
2. Add onion to the pot and sauté until softened, about 6 minutes. Add bay leaf and thyme; sauté for 30 seconds. Add potatoes, stock and clam juice; bring to a boil. Reduce heat and simmer until potatoes are tender, about 20 minutes. Add corn and clams; increase heat and bring to a boil. Cover, reduce heat to low and simmer gently until clams have opened, 5 to 8 minutes. Discard any clams that do not open.
3. Stir in milk and cream; reheat over medium heat until steaming, stirring often. Do not let boil. Discard bay leaf. Season with salt and pepper to taste.
4. Ladle into heated bowls and garnish with reserved bacon.

Oyster Chowder

We find oyster chowder to be a reviving kind of soup and imagine eating it after a chilly and wet, gray day by the sea. This soup will definitely lift your spirits and comfort your soul.

Tip

We've found 8-oz (250 g) containers of shucked oysters in the cold case near the fish at the grocery store. They are of high quality and work very well in this soup, but freshly shucked oysters will always be best, if you can find them.

Serves 6

2 tbsp	unsalted butter	25 mL
6	slices bacon, finely chopped	6
1	onion, minced	1
¼ cup	all-purpose flour	50 mL
6 cups	milk	1.5 L
2	potatoes (about 12 oz/375 g), peeled and cut into ½-inch (1 cm) dice	2
1	bay leaf	1
2 tsp	salt	10 mL
¼ tsp	freshly ground black pepper	1 mL
Pinch	ground nutmeg	Pinch
Pinch	cayenne pepper	Pinch
1 lb	refrigerated shucked oysters, with their liquor (see tip, at left)	500 g
1 cup	whipping (35%) cream	250 mL
¼ cup	minced fresh flat-leaf (Italian) parsley	50 mL
	Oyster crackers	

1. In a large pot, melt butter over medium heat until sizzling. Add bacon and sauté until browned and crispy, about 5 minutes. Remove with a slotted spoon to a plate lined with paper towels. Set aside.
2. Pour off all but 3 tbsp (45 mL) of the fat in the pot. Add onion and sauté until softened, about 6 minutes. Sprinkle with flour and sauté for 2 minutes.
3. Gradually whisk in milk. Add potatoes, bay leaf, salt and black pepper; bring to a simmer, stirring often. Reduce heat and simmer, stirring often, until soup is thick and creamy and potatoes are tender, about 20 minutes. Do not let boil. Season with nutmeg and cayenne. Taste and adjust seasoning with salt and black pepper, if necessary.
4. Add oysters with their liquor and cream; return to a simmer, stirring often. Simmer, stirring often, until oysters plump and curl at the edges, 3 to 5 minutes. Do not let boil.
5. Ladle into heated bowls and garnish with reserved bacon, parsley and crackers.

Creamy Saffron Mussel Chowder

▲▽▲

In many regions of France, you'll see sidewalk bistros serving beautiful fresh mussels swimming in a creamy white wine sauce, alongside a heaping dish of crispy pommes frites *(french fries, to us). Diners can barely conceal their joy as they pluck the tender, flavorful morsels from their onyx-colored shells. For this chowder, we removed the mussels from their shells and combined them with the potatoes for a bowl of soup you won't soon forget.*

Serves 6

2 tbsp	olive oil	25 mL
1	onion, chopped	1
1 cup	chopped leeks, white parts only	250 mL
2	cloves garlic, minced	2
½ tsp	salt	2 mL
Pinch	cayenne pepper	Pinch
2 lbs	mussels, scrubbed and debearded (see tips, page 252)	1 kg
1½ cups	dry white wine	375 mL
1 cup	clam juice	250 mL
2	baking potatoes, peeled and diced	2
2½ cups	milk	625 mL
1 cup	whipping (35%) cream	250 mL
Pinch	saffron threads	Pinch
2	sprigs fresh thyme	2
¼ cup	minced fresh flat-leaf (Italian) parsley	50 mL
1 tbsp	freshly squeezed lemon juice	15 mL
	Buttery Croutons (see recipe, page 368)	

1. In a large pot, heat oil over medium heat. Add onion and leeks; sauté until softened, about 6 minutes. Add garlic, salt and cayenne; sauté for 1 minute. Add mussels, wine and clam juice; bring to a boil. Cover, reduce heat to low and simmer gently until mussels have opened, 5 to 8 minutes. Remove from heat. Using a slotted spoon, transfer mussels to a bowl and let cool slightly. Discard any mussels that do not open. Separate the meat from the shells; discard shells and set meat aside.

2. Return pot to medium heat. Add potatoes, milk, cream, saffron and thyme; bring to a simmer, stirring often. Reduce heat and simmer, stirring often, until potatoes are tender, about 20 minutes. Do not let boil. Discard thyme sprigs. Add mussel meat and any accumulated juices, half the parsley and the lemon juice. Remove from heat, taste and adjust seasoning with salt and cayenne, if necessary.

3. Ladle into heated bowls and garnish with croutons and the remaining parsley.

Crab and Corn Chowder

Crab and corn are a match made in heaven. Both are sweet and rich and make a fabulous soup. Since corn isn't always in season, we used frozen corn in this recipe, but of course it would be great with fresh corn too.

Tip

When buying frozen corn, look for the white shoepeg variety for even sweeter flavor.

Serves 6

3 cups	frozen corn kernels, thawed, divided	750 mL
2 tbsp	unsalted butter	25 mL
4	slices bacon, finely chopped	4
1	onion, minced	1
1	stalk celery, minced	1
½ tsp	salt	2 mL
2	potatoes, peeled and cut into small dice	2
6 cups	chicken stock	1.5 L
8 oz	backfin (lump) crabmeat, shells and cartilage picked out	250 g
1 cup	whipping (35%) cream	250 mL
1 tsp	white wine vinegar	5 mL
Pinch	cayenne pepper	Pinch
Pinch	ground nutmeg	Pinch
	Freshly ground black pepper	
2 tbsp	minced fresh chives	25 mL

1. In a food processor or blender, process 2 cups (500 mL) of the corn until almost smooth. (You may need to add some of the stock to get a smooth purée.) Set aside.

2. In a large pot, melt butter over medium heat. Add bacon and sauté until browned and crispy, about 5 minutes. Remove with a slotted spoon to a plate lined with paper towels. Set aside.

3. Pour off all but 3 tbsp (45 mL) of the fat in the pot. Add onion, celery and salt; sauté until softened, about 6 minutes. Add puréed corn, whole corn, potatoes and stock; bring to a boil. Reduce heat and simmer until potatoes are tender, about 20 minutes. Stir in crab, cream, vinegar, cayenne, nutmeg and salt and black pepper to taste; reheat over medium heat until steaming, stirring often. Do not let boil.

4. Ladle into heated bowls and garnish with reserved bacon and chives.

Rich Lobster and Roasted Corn Chowder

▲▼▲▼▲▼▲▼▲▼▲▼▲▼▲▼▲▼▲▼▲▼▲▼▲▼▲▼▲▼▲▼▲▼▲▼▲▼▲

"Decadent" is the best word to describe this luxurious chowder. Fresh lobster is paired with sweet and toasty roasted corn for a unique and memorable taste sensation.

▲▼▲▼▲▼▲▼▲

Tips

You can use either fresh or thawed frozen corn kernels.

If you prefer, you can replace the chicken stock and clam juice with 5 cups (1.25 L) fish or shellfish stock.

Serves 6

- Preheat oven to 425°F (220°C)
- Large rimmed baking sheet

3 cups	corn kernels	750 mL
1½ tbsp	olive oil	22 mL
1 tsp	salt, divided	5 mL
½ tsp	freshly ground black pepper, divided	2 mL
4	slices bacon, chopped	4
2 cups	chopped onions	500 mL
Pinch	cayenne pepper	Pinch
1 lb	boiling potatoes, peeled and diced	500 g
3 cups	chicken stock	750 mL
2 cups	clam juice	500 mL
1½ cups	whipping (35%) cream	375 mL
2 tbsp	unsalted butter	25 mL
3	cooked lobster tails (each about 10 oz/300 g), meat removed and cut into bite-sized chunks	3
3 tbsp	chopped fresh chives	45 mL

1. On baking sheet, combine corn, oil, ½ tsp (2 mL) of the salt and ¼ tsp (1 mL) of the black pepper; toss to coat evenly and spread in a single layer. Roast in preheated oven for 10 minutes. Stir and redistribute into an even layer. Roast until corn is lightly but evenly browned, 10 to 15 minutes. Remove from oven and set aside.

2. In a large pot, sauté bacon over medium heat until browned and crispy, about 5 minutes. Remove with a slotted spoon to a plate lined with paper towels. Set aside.

3. Pour off all but 2 tbsp (25 mL) of the fat in the pot. Add onions and sauté until lightly browned, about 10 minutes. Add cayenne and sauté for 1 minute. Add potatoes, stock, clam juice and the remaining salt and pepper; bring to a boil. Reduce heat and simmer for 15 minutes. Stir in roasted corn and cream; return to a simmer, stirring often. Simmer, stirring often, until potatoes are tender, about 5 minutes. Do not let boil.

4. In a large, heavy skillet, melt butter over medium heat. Add lobster meat and sauté until heated through, about 1 minute.

5. Ladle chowder into heated bowls and top with lobster. Garnish with reserved bacon and chives.

A World of Soups

▲▽▲▽▲▽▲▽▲▽▲▽▲ ▽ ▲▽▲▽▲▽▲▽▲▽▲▽▲▽▲

Oaxacan Black Bean Soup

▲▼▲▼▲▼▲▼▲▼▲▼▲▼▲▼▲▼▲▼▲▼▲▼▲▼▲▼▲▼▲▼▲▼▲▼▲▼▲

This creamy version of black bean soup is kept simple with no added spices, ensuring that the flavor of the bean takes center stage.

▲▼▲▼▲▼▲▼▲▼▲

Tip

Here's how to quick-soak dried beans: In a colander, rinse beans under cold water and discard any discolored ones. In a saucepan, combine beans with enough cold water to cover them by 2 inches (5 cm). Bring to a boil over medium heat and boil for 2 minutes. Remove from heat and let soak, covered, for 1 hour.

Serves 6 to 8

1 tbsp	vegetable oil	15 mL
6 oz	fresh chorizo sausage (bulk or with casings removed)	175 g
1	onion, finely chopped	1
2	cloves garlic, minced	2
2	jalapeño peppers, seeded and minced	2
8 cups	chicken stock (approx.)	2 L
2 cups	dried black beans, soaked overnight or quick-soaked (see tip, at left) and drained	500 mL
1 tsp	salt	5 mL
	Crispy Tortilla Strips (see recipe, page 372)	
¾ cup	crumbled queso fresco, salted farmer's cheese or feta cheese	175 mL

1. In a large pot, heat oil over medium heat. Add chorizo and sauté, breaking up with the back of a wooden spoon, until no longer pink, about 5 minutes. Add onion and sauté until softened, about 6 minutes. Add garlic and jalapeños and sauté for 2 minutes. Add stock and beans; bring to a boil. Reduce heat and simmer, adding more stock if necessary to keep the beans covered, until beans are tender, about 1½ hours. Stir in salt.

2. Using an immersion blender, or in a food processor or blender in batches, coarsely purée soup. Return to the pot, if necessary, and add enough water to thin the soup to a medium-thick consistency, if necessary. Taste and adjust seasoning with salt, if necessary.

3. Ladle into heated bowls and garnish with tortilla strips and cheese.

Albondigas Soup
(Mexican Meatball Soup)

▲▽▲▽▲▽▲▽▲▽▲▽▲▽▲▽▲▽▲▽▲▽▲▽▲▽▲▽▲▽▲▽▲▽▲▽

Growing up in San Diego, Meredith ate her fair share of this brothy but rich soup, which is a common sight in Mexican restaurants. The mint adds a subtle but essential flavor to the tender little meatballs swimming in the mildly spicy stock.

▲▽▲▽▲▽▲▽▲▽

Tips

To make fresh bread crumbs, add day-old bread, crusts removed, to the work bowl of a food processor. Pulse to fine crumbs.

Chile peppers contain oils that can cause chemical burns on your skin. When seeding and chopping them, always wear latex, plastic or rubber gloves.

Serves 6

- Baking sheet, lined with parchment paper

1 lb	lean ground beef	500 g
4	cloves garlic, minced	4
1	egg, beaten	1
½ cup	fresh bread crumbs	125 mL
1 tbsp	finely chopped fresh mint	15 mL
1 tsp	salt	5 mL
½ tsp	freshly ground black pepper	2 mL
2 tbsp	olive oil	25 mL
2	carrots, diced	2
1	onion, finely chopped	1
2	tomatoes, seeded and diced	2
2	jalapeño peppers, seeded and julienned	2
3 cups	thinly sliced white cabbage	750 mL
½ tsp	dried oregano	2 mL
8 cups	chicken stock	2 L
1 cup	loosely packed fresh cilantro leaves	250 mL
1 tbsp	white vinegar	15 mL

1. In a large bowl, gently combine ground beef, garlic, egg, bread crumbs, mint, salt and pepper. In a small skillet, sauté a small spoonful of the beef mixture over medium heat until no longer pink. Taste and adjust the seasoning of the beef mixture with salt and pepper, if necessary. Roll beef mixture into walnut-sized balls and place on prepared baking sheet.

2. In a large pot, heat oil over medium heat. Add carrots and onion; sauté until softened, about 6 minutes. Add tomatoes, jalapeños, cabbage and oregano; sauté until tomatoes start to break down, about 3 minutes. Add stock and bring to a boil. Add meatballs, reduce heat and simmer until cooked through, about 30 minutes. Stir in cilantro and vinegar. Taste and adjust seasoning with salt and pepper, if necessary.

3. Ladle into heated bowls.

Green Posole with Pork and Chicken

▲▼▲▼▲▼▲▼▲▼▲▼▲▼▲▼▲▼▲▼▲▼▲▼▲▼▲▼▲▼▲▼▲▼▲▼▲

Posole is a Mexican soup with meltingly tender pieces of shredded pork and chicken and earthy hominy so thick in the spicy tomatillo- and chile-flavored stock that calling it a soup is a stretch. It lands somewhere between soup and stew, making it a wonderful dish for hearty appetites.

▲▼▲▼▲▼▲▼▲▼▲

Tip

We can't overstate how important it is to brown meat properly before slow-cooking it. The flavor that develops during the browning process is critical to the overall flavor of the soup. If you overcrowd your pot, the meat will only steam and become gray and will never brown.

Serves 8

- Small baking dish

2 lbs	boneless pork shoulder blade (butt), trimmed and cut into 2-inch (5 cm) chunks	1 kg
2 lbs	chicken thighs	1 kg
1½ tsp	salt, divided	7 mL
	Freshly ground black pepper	
2 tbsp	olive oil (approx.), divided	25 mL
1	white onion, chopped	1
6	cloves garlic, thinly sliced	6
1 tsp	dried oregano (preferably Mexican), crumbled	5 mL
10 cups	chicken stock	2.5 L
1 lb	tomatillos, husked	500 g
2	serrano or other hot green chile peppers	2
½ cup	green pumpkin seeds (pepitas), toasted	125 mL
½ cup	chopped fresh cilantro	125 mL
2	cans (each 15 oz/425 mL) white hominy, drained and rinsed	2
	Diced avocado	
	Fresh cilantro leaves	
	Chopped sweet onion	
1	lime, cut into 8 wedges	1

1. Season pork and chicken with 1 tsp (5 mL) of the salt and pepper to taste. In a large pot, heat half the oil over medium-high heat. Add pork and chicken, in batches, and sauté until browned on all sides, about 5 minutes per side, adding oil as needed between batches. Remove with a slotted spoon to a warm plate.

2. Pour off all but 1 tbsp (15 mL) of the fat in the pot. Reduce heat to medium, add onion and sauté until softened, 3 to 4 minutes. Add garlic and oregano; sauté for 1 minute. Return pork, chicken and any accumulated juices to the pot and add stock; bring to a boil over medium-high heat. Cover, reduce heat to low and simmer gently until pork is tender and juices run clear when chicken is pierced, 1½ to 2 hours. Skim the fat from the surface with a large spoon.

Tip

When we're trying to eat healthy and lower the amount of fat in a soup, we take the skin off the chicken thighs before cooking. Other times, we leave it on and enjoy the extra richness and flavor the fat imparts.

3. Meanwhile, preheat broiler. Place tomatillos and chiles in baking dish. Broil until blackened in spots, 5 to10 minutes. Turn and broil until blackened in spots on the other side, about 5 minutes. Let cool, then remove and discard the stems from both the tomatillos and chiles. Transfer to a food processor or blender and add $\frac{1}{2}$ cup (125 mL) liquid from the soup, pumpkin seeds and cilantro; purée until smooth. Set aside.

4. Remove pork and chicken from the pot with a slotted spoon and let cool slightly. Remove skin and bones from the chicken and discard. Shred both chicken and pork into bite-size pieces. Set aside.

5. Strain the stock (see page 8) and discard all solids. Return stock to low heat and add the tomatillo mixture and hominy; bring to a gentle simmer. Simmer for about 20 minutes to blend the flavors. Return meat to the pot and add the remaining salt; simmer until heated through, about 5 minutes.

6. Ladle into heated bowls and garnish with avocado, cilantro, onion and lime wedges. Diners may squeeze the lime over their soup, if they desire.

Tortilla Soup

▲▽

A favorite among Mexican food lovers, this chile-infused soup, thickened by toasted tortillas, is served over chicken, avocado and cheese for a light but satisfying bowl.

▲▽▲▽▲▽▲▽▲▽▲

Tips

When making this recipe, we take advantage of the precooked rotisserie chicken found at almost any grocery store. One chicken usually yields about 3 cups (750 mL) meat.

Most avocados found in the grocery store are as hard as rocks. Luckily, they ripen beautifully on your kitchen counter in a few days. Ripe avocados should yield slightly when pressed.

Serves 8

5	dried ancho chile peppers, stems and seeds removed	5
	Hot water	
3 tbsp	olive oil	45 mL
4	6-inch (15 cm) corn tortillas, cut into 1-inch (2.5 cm) squares	4
1	onion, chopped	1
4	cloves garlic, chopped	4
½ tsp	dried oregano (preferably Mexican)	2 mL
½ tsp	salt	2 mL
1	can (28 oz/796 mL) plum (Roma) tomatoes, with juice	1
8 cups	chicken stock	2 L
2 tbsp	freshly squeezed lime juice	25 mL
3 cups	shredded cooked chicken	750 mL
1½ cups	shredded Monterey Jack cheese	375 mL
1	avocado, diced	1
½ cup	sour cream	125 mL
¼ cup	chopped fresh cilantro	50 mL
	Crispy Tortilla Strips (see recipe, page 372)	
1	lime, cut into 8 wedges	1

1. Heat a dry large skillet over medium heat. Open up dried chiles so they are as flat as possible and place them in the skillet. Using a spatula to press down on them, toast the chiles for about 30 seconds on each side, or until pliable. Be careful not to burn them. Transfer to a bowl, cover with hot water and soak until soft, about 20 minutes. Drain, discarding soaking liquid, and roughly chop chiles.

2. Meanwhile, in a large pot, heat oil over medium-high heat. Add tortillas and sauté until golden brown, about 5 minutes. (They may break up a bit in the process, but that's fine.) Remove with a slotted spoon to a plate; set aside.

Tip

Soup will stay hot much longer in a heated bowl.

3. Add onion to the pot and sauté until softened, 3 to 4 minutes. Add garlic, oregano and salt; sauté for 1 minute. Add chiles, browned tortillas, tomatoes with juice and stock; reduce heat to medium and bring to a boil. Reduce heat and simmer for 40 minutes to blend the flavors.

4. Using an immersion blender, or in a food processor or blender in batches, purée soup until smooth. Return to the pot, if necessary, and bring to a simmer. Stir in lime juice. Taste and adjust seasoning with lime juice and salt, if necessary.

5. Divide chicken, cheese and avocado among heated bowls and top with soup. Garnish with sour cream, cilantro, tortilla strips and lime wedges. Diners may squeeze the lime over their soup, if they desire.

Sopa de Poblano
(Cream of Roasted Poblano Soup)

Poblano chiles are one of our favorite chiles to work with because of their bold, distinctive pepper flavor and mild heat, and this soup is one of the best ways to highlight them.

▲▼▲▼▲▼▲▼▲

Tip

An immersion blender is one of our favorite kitchen tools. Because it can be immersed in the soup, it saves you from transferring hot liquids from the pot to a blender or food processor. Look for one that has a detachable blade unit for easy cleaning.

Serves 6

6	large poblano chile peppers	6
2 tbsp	unsalted butter	25 mL
1	onion, chopped	1
1	clove garlic, chopped	1
5 cups	chicken stock	1.25 L
½ cup	whipping (35%) cream	125 mL
¼ cup	chopped fresh cilantro	50 mL
1 tbsp	freshly squeezed lime juice	15 mL
	Salt and freshly ground black pepper	
	Crispy Tortilla Strips (see recipe, page 372)	

1. Char chiles over a gas flame or on a baking sheet under a broiler until blackened on all sides. Place in a bowl and cover with plastic wrap. Let stand for 5 minutes to steam. Peel, seed and chop.
2. In a large pot, melt butter over medium heat. Add onion and sauté until softened, about 6 minutes. Add garlic and sauté for 1 minute. Add chiles and sauté for 1 minute. Add stock and bring to a boil. Reduce heat and simmer until chiles are tender, about 10 minutes.
3. Using an immersion blender, or in a food processor or blender in batches, purée soup until smooth. Return to the pot, if necessary. Stir in cream and reheat over medium heat, stirring often, until steaming. Do not let boil. Stir in cilantro, lime juice and salt and pepper to taste.
4. Ladle into heated bowls and garnish with tortilla strips.

Brazilian Black Bean Soup

▲▽▲

Brazil's national dish is considered by many to be feijoada *(fay-ZHWAH-duh). It consists of an assortment of meats, including pork ribs, pig's feet, sausages and bacon, accompanied by beans, orange slices and other vegetables. For this recipe, we've taken the elements of* feijoada *and turned it into a soup. The dish has tropical flair, so we included the flavors of orange and cumin to brighten the recipe up a bit.*

▲▽▲▽▲▽▲▽▲▽▲

Tip

San Marzano tomatoes, imported from Italy, are thought by many to be the best canned tomatoes in the world. They hail from a small town of the same name near Naples, whose volcanic soil is thought to filter impurities from the water and render tomatoes with a thick flesh, fewer seeds and a stronger taste. Look for the words "San Marzano" on the label to be sure you're getting the best.

Serves 6

¼ cup	olive oil	50 mL
2	onions, chopped	2
3	cloves garlic, minced	3
3	carrots, sliced	3
2	stalks celery, sliced	2
1 tsp	dried oregano	5 mL
1 tsp	ground cumin	5 mL
1 tsp	salt	5 mL
1	can (14 oz/398 mL) diced tomatoes, with juice	1
6	skinless chicken thighs	6
1	smoked ham hock (about 8 oz/250 g)	1
1 lb	smoked spicy sausage, cut into ½-inch (1 cm) half-moons	500 g
8 cups	beef stock	2 L
1 cup	dried black beans, soaked overnight or quick-soaked (see tip, page 280) and drained	250 mL
¼ cup	minced fresh cilantro	50 mL
	Grated zest of 1 orange	
	Freshly ground black pepper	
1	orange, cut into 6 wedges	1

1. In a large pot, heat oil over medium heat. Add onions and sauté until softened, about 6 minutes. Add garlic, carrots, celery, oregano, cumin and salt; sauté until vegetables are starting to soften, about 5 minutes.
2. Add tomatoes with juice, chicken, ham hock, sausage, stock and beans; bring to a boil. Cover, reduce heat to low and simmer gently until juices run clear when chicken is pierced and beans are tender, about 1½ hours.
3. Using tongs, remove chicken and ham hock from the soup and let cool slightly. Remove bones from the chicken and discard. Pick the meat from the ham hock bone and discard bones, fat and skin. Shred both chicken and ham into bite-size pieces. Return meat to the pot and simmer until heated through. Stir in cilantro, orange zest and salt and pepper to taste.
4. Ladle into heated bowls and serve garnished with orange wedges. Diners may squeeze the orange over their soup, if they desire.

Vatapá

▲▼▲▼▲▼▲▼▲▼▲▼▲▼▲▼▲▼▲▼▲▼▲▼▲▼▲▼▲▼▲▼▲▼▲▼▲

Vatapá is a spicy Brazilian stew containing fish, chicken, coconut milk and peanuts. We've taken liberties with this south-of-the-equator favorite and turned it into a rich soup that will have you singing "The Girl from Ipanema" in no time.

▲▼▲▼▲▼▲▼▲

Tip

Vatapá traditionally includes dried shrimp, which can be difficult to find. If you are fortunate enough to have a good Asian market nearby, Asian dried shrimp will give the soup a subtle shrimpy taste. If using dried shrimp, just add about ½ cup (125 mL) with the tomatoes and stock and leave out the fresh shrimp.

Serves 6

4	skinless chicken thighs	4
½ tsp	salt	2 mL
	Freshly ground black pepper	
¼ cup	vegetable oil	50 mL
1	thumb-sized knob gingerroot, minced	1
1	onion, finely chopped	1
3	cloves garlic, minced	3
½ tsp	cayenne pepper	2 mL
1 cup	dry white wine	250 mL
1	can (14 oz/398 mL) diced tomatoes, with juice	1
4 cups	chicken stock	1 L
1	can (14 oz/400 mL) unsweetened coconut milk	1
½ cup	peanut butter	125 mL
1 lb	skinless firm white fish fillets (such as snapper, grouper, sea bass or tilapia)	500 g
8 oz	shrimp, peeled, deveined and split in half lengthwise	250 g
¼ cup	chopped fresh cilantro	50 mL
2 tbsp	freshly squeezed lime juice	25 mL
	Additional chopped fresh cilantro	
1	lime, cut into 6 wedges	1

1. Season chicken with salt and black pepper to taste. In a large pot, heat oil over medium heat. Add chicken and cook until browned on both sides, about 8 minutes per side. Remove with a slotted spoon to a warm plate.

2. Add ginger and onion to the pot and sauté until onion is softened, 3 to 4 minutes. Add garlic and cayenne; sauté for 1 minute. Add wine and cook until reduced by half, about 5 minutes.

3. Return chicken to the pot and add tomatoes with juice and stock; bring to a boil. Cover, reduce heat to low and simmer gently until juices run clear when chicken is pierced, about 20 minutes.

Tip

Before shopping for fish, check fish sustainability/endangered lists (such as www.montereybayaquarium.org/cr/seafoodwatch.asp) or with your fishmonger to be sure that you're not purchasing fish species that are being overfished or fished illegally.

4. Using tongs, transfer chicken to a large plate and let cool slightly. Remove bones and discard. Shred the meat into bite-size pieces. Return chicken to the pot and gently whisk in coconut milk and peanut butter; bring to a simmer over medium heat. Reduce heat to low and add fish. Cover and simmer for 3 minutes. Add shrimp, cover and simmer until shrimp are pink and opaque and fish is opaque and flakes easily with a fork, about 2 minutes. Gently stir in cilantro and lime juice. Taste and adjust seasoning with salt and black pepper, if necessary.

5. Ladle into heated bowls, making sure each bowl contains a large piece of fish and a few shrimp. Garnish with cilantro and lime wedges. Diners may squeeze the lime over their soup, if they desire.

Cock-a-Leekie

▲▽▲

This soup from the Scottish highlands is a familiar port in a storm. The basic leek and potato formula is enhanced by the addition of chicken, for a more filling meal.

▲▽▲▽▲▽▲▽▲▽▲

Tip

To trim leeks, cut off and discard the root end and the dark green tops (or save the tops for stock). Cut leeks lengthwise and wash under running water to remove any grit or dirt. Then cut as directed in the recipe.

Serves 6

1	whole chicken (about 3 lbs/1.5 kg), rinsed and cut into 8 pieces	1
1	onion, quartered	1
1	carrot, quartered	1
1	stalk celery, quartered	1
10	whole black peppercorns	10
1	bay leaf	1
½ tsp	dried thyme	2 mL
6 cups	chicken stock	1.5 L
1 lb	boiling potatoes, peeled and diced	500 g
2	leeks, white and light green parts only, sliced	2
½ cup	half-and-half (10%) cream	125 mL
2 tsp	freshly squeezed lemon juice	10 mL
Pinch	cayenne pepper	Pinch
Pinch	ground nutmeg	Pinch
	Salt and freshly ground black pepper	
2 tbsp	minced fresh chives	25 mL

1. In a large pot, combine chicken, onion, carrot, celery, peppercorns, bay leaf, thyme and stock. If chicken isn't immersed, add water or stock to cover. Bring to a boil over medium-high heat. Partially cover, reduce heat to low and simmer gently until juices run clear when chicken is pierced, about 45 minutes. Skim the soup if any scum develops on the surface.

2. Using tongs, transfer chicken to a large plate and let cool slightly. Remove skin and bones and discard. Shred the meat into bite-size pieces. Set aside.

3. Strain the stock (see page 8) and discard all solids. Skim the surface of the stock and remove fat, if desired. Return stock to the pot and bring to a simmer over medium heat. Add potatoes and leeks; simmer until potatoes are tender, about 20 minutes.

4. Using an immersion blender, pulse the soup in 3 or 4 quick spurts to partially blend it, leaving it chunky (or process half the soup in food processor or blender in batches, then return to the pot). Return chicken to the pot and stir in cream; reheat over medium heat, stirring often, until steaming. Do not let boil. Stir in lemon juice, cayenne, nutmeg and salt and black pepper to taste.

5. Ladle into heated bowls and garnish with chives.

Scotch Broth

▲▽▲

We love this soup because of its simplicity. Browned meat bones are stewed with stock, vegetables and barley, and the result is satisfying and nourishing right down to your toes. We use lamb in this version, but feel free to substitute beef oxtails if you prefer.

▲▽▲▽▲▽▲▽▲▽▲

Tip

Seasoning with a little bit of vinegar at the end of cooking heightens the flavor of the soup. Although most home cooks think only in terms of salt and pepper when it comes to adjusting the seasoning in their dishes, we've found that a little acid goes a long way toward making a soup taste just right.

Serves 6

1 tbsp	vegetable oil	15 mL
2 lbs	lamb neck bones or shanks, trimmed of excess fat	1 kg
1	onion, chopped	1
1	stalk celery, chopped	1
1	carrot, chopped	1
1/2 cup	chopped leeks (white and light green parts only)	125 mL
2	bay leaves	2
6 cups	beef stock	1.5 L
1 cup	chopped turnip	250 mL
1/2 cup	pearl barley	125 mL
1 tsp	salt	5 mL
1/2 tsp	freshly ground black pepper	2 mL
1/4 cup	minced fresh parsley	50 mL
1 tbsp	malt vinegar	15 mL

1. In a large pot, heat oil over medium-high heat. Add lamb bones and cook until well browned on all sides, about 6 minutes. Using tongs, transfer to a plate.
2. Reduce heat to medium, add onion, celery, carrot and leeks to the pot and sauté until softened, 3 to 4 minutes. Return lamb bones to the pot and add bay leaves, stock, turnip, barley, salt and pepper; bring to a boil. Reduce heat and simmer until meat is falling off the bones, 1 to 1 1/2 hours. Skim the fat from the surface with a large spoon. Discard bay leaves.
3. Remove lamb bones from the pot and let cool slightly. Pick the meat from the bones and shred into bite-size pieces. Discard bones. Return meat to the soup and simmer until heated through. Stir in parsley and vinegar. Taste and adjust seasoning with salt and pepper, if necessary.
4. Ladle into heated bowls.

Mulligatawny

▲▽▲▽▲▽▲▽▲▽▲▽▲▽▲▽▲▽▲▽▲▽▲▽▲▽▲▽▲▽▲▽▲▽▲▽▲▽▲

Mulligatawny came about as a British version of an Indian soup. It has been popular in England for generations because of its somewhat exotic, but faintly familiar, flavors and ingredients. Try it on a rainy day — it really will make you feel better.

▲▽▲▽▲▽▲▽▲

Tips

Garam masala is an Indian spice blend of cinnamon, cardamom, cloves, coriander and cumin. The blend can be purchased at larger grocery stores, but if you can't find it, use curry powder or just add a blend of the spices you have in your pantry. It will still taste great.

If you're using a blender or food processor to purée hot soup, make sure not to fill the bowl more than one-third full. The buildup of pressure from the steam will sometimes blow the cover off, sending hot liquid flying.

Serves 4

¼ cup	unsalted butter, divided	50 mL
1	stick cinnamon, about 4 inches (10 cm) long	1
2 tbsp	curry powder	25 mL
3	onions, sliced, divided	3
¼ tsp	salt, divided	1 mL
2	cloves garlic, minced	2
1	carrot, chopped	1
1	stalk celery, chopped	1
6 cups	chicken stock	1.5 L
1 tsp	garam masala (see tip, at left)	5 mL
1	can (14 oz/400 mL) unsweetened coconut milk	1
	Freshly ground black pepper	
¼ cup	minced fresh cilantro	50 mL

1. In a large pot, melt 2 tbsp (25 mL) of the butter over medium heat until sizzling. Add cinnamon stick and curry powder; sauté for 1 minute. Add one-third of the onions and a pinch of salt; sauté until onions are softened, about 6 minutes. Add garlic, carrot and celery; sauté until starting to soften, about 3 minutes.

2. Add stock and bring to a boil. Reduce heat and simmer until vegetables are tender, about 20 minutes. Discard cinnamon stick.

3. Using an immersion blender, or in a food processor or blender in batches, purée soup until smooth. Return to the pot, if necessary, and keep warm.

4. Meanwhile, in a skillet, melt the remaining butter over medium heat. Add the remaining onions and a pinch of salt; sauté until starting to brown, about 8 minutes. Add garam masala, reduce heat and sauté until onions are caramelized to a rich brown, about 20 minutes. Add coconut milk, increase heat to high and boil until reduced by half, about 7 minutes. Add to the soup and season with salt and pepper to taste.

5. Ladle into heated bowls and garnish with cilantro.

Brown Windsor Soup

▲▼▲▼▲▼▲▼▲▼▲▼▲▼▲▼▲▼▲▼▲▼▲▼▲▼▲▼▲▼▲▼▲▼▲▼▲▼

Back in the '50s and '60s, this soup probably helped foster the reputation of the dreary state of British cuisine. But if done right, this classic can be very fine indeed. Traditionalists would make the soup, then purée it to a sludgy mess. We prefer the vegetables and meat left intact.

▲▼▲▼▲▼▲▼▲

Tip

We can't overstate how important it is to brown meat properly before slow-cooking it. The flavor that develops during the browning process is critical to the overall flavor of the soup. If you overcrowd your pot, the meat will only steam and become gray and will never brown.

Serves 6

⅓ cup	all-purpose flour	75 mL
1 tsp	dried marjoram	5 mL
1 tsp	salt	5 mL
¼ tsp	freshly ground black pepper	1 mL
2 lbs	boneless beef chuck roast, trimmed and cut into 1-inch (2.5 cm) chunks	1 kg
¼ cup	unsalted butter, divided	50 mL
2	cloves garlic, chopped	2
2	carrots, chopped	2
1	onion, coarsely chopped	1
1	parsnip, chopped	1
1	stalk celery, chopped	1
6 cups	beef stock	1.5 L
1	can (14 oz/398 mL) diced tomatoes, with juice	1
½ cup	Madeira	125 mL
2 cups	hot cooked pearl barley	500 mL
¼ cup	minced fresh flat-leaf (Italian) parsley	50 mL

1. In a large bowl, combine flour, marjoram, salt and pepper. Add beef and toss to coat.

2. In a large pot, melt half the butter over medium-high heat. Add beef, in two batches, and sauté until browned on all sides, about 5 minutes per batch, melting the remaining butter between batches. Remove with a slotted spoon to a warm plate.

3. Add garlic, carrots, onion, parsnip and celery to the pot; sauté until starting to soften, about 3 minutes. Return beef and any accumulated juices to the pot and add stock and tomatoes with juice; bring to a boil. Cover, reduce heat to low and simmer gently until beef is tender and easily pulled apart, 1½ to 2 hours.

4. Remove beef from the pot with a slotted spoon and, using two forks, pull apart into bite-size shreds. Discard any fat and gristle. Return beef to the pot and stir in Madeira. Taste and adjust seasoning with salt and pepper, if necessary.

5. Divide barley among heated bowls and top with soup. Garnish with parsley.

Matzo Ball Soup

▲▽▲▽▲▽▲▽▲▽▲▽▲▽▲▽▲▽▲▽▲▽▲▽▲▽▲▽▲▽▲▽▲▽▲▽▲▽▲

Whether your mom made it for you when you were a kid or it's your favorite thing to order at a neighborhood Jewish deli, matzo ball soup is comfort food at its best. The gentle soup, lightly sweetened by carrots and parsnips, is ladled over light-as-a-feather matzo balls.

▲▽▲▽▲▽▲▽▲

Tip

Whether you like your matzo ball soup with chicken meat is a matter of taste; you can add it to the stock or save the meat for another use.

Serves 10

1	whole chicken (about 3 lbs/1.5 kg), rinsed, or 3 lbs (1.5 kg) skinless chicken thighs	1
3	large carrots, cut into large chunks	3
2	stalks celery, including leafy tops, cut into large chunks	2
1	onion (unpeeled), halved	1
1	parsnip, cut into large chunks	1
10	sprigs fresh parsley	10
16 cups	chicken stock	4 L
2 tsp	salt	10 mL
¼ tsp	freshly ground black pepper	1 mL
	Matzo Balls (see recipe, page 372)	

1. In a large, heavy pot, combine chicken, carrots, celery, onion, parsnip, parsley, stock, salt and pepper. Bring to a boil over medium-high heat. Partially cover, reduce heat to low and simmer gently until a thermometer inserted into the thickest part of a breast registers 170°F (75°C), about 45 minutes. Skim the soup if any scum develops on the surface.
2. Using tongs, transfer chicken to a large plate and let cool slightly. Remove skin and bones and discard. Shred the meat into bite-size pieces. Set aside if adding to the soup, or cover and refrigerate if saving for another use.
3. Strain the stock (see page 8) and discard all solids except the carrot. Taste and adjust seasoning with salt and pepper, if necessary. Thinly slice the carrot on the diagonal and return to the soup. Add the chicken meat, if desired. Reheat over medium heat until steaming.
4. Divide matzo balls among heated bowls and top with soup.

Goulash Soup

▲▼▲▼▲▼▲▼▲▼▲▼▲▼▲▼▲▼▲▼▲▼▲▼▲▼▲▼▲▼▲▼▲▼▲

Quality paprika, usually from Hungary, has a wonderful flavor all its own and adds a deep earthiness to this goulash. We like to use sweet Hungarian paprika, but if you like your goulash spicy, you can also use hot Hungarian paprika, or a mixture of both.

▲▼▲▼▲▼▲▼▲▼

Tip

When browning the beef, make sure you add only enough at one time to make a single layer. Do not overcrowd the pan, or the beef will not brown properly.

Serves 6

5	slices bacon, chopped	5
2 lbs	boneless beef chuck roast, trimmed and cut into 2-inch (5 cm) chunks	1 kg
	Salt and freshly ground black pepper	
2 tbsp	olive oil	25 mL
2	onions, finely chopped	2
2	cloves garlic, chopped	2
3 tbsp	sweet Hungarian paprika	45 mL
2 tbsp	all-purpose flour	25 mL
2 tbsp	tomato paste	25 mL
6 cups	beef stock	1.5 L
½ tsp	salt	2 mL
2	red bell peppers, finely diced	2
¼ cup	chopped fresh parsley, divided	50 mL
1 tbsp	red wine vinegar	15 mL
	Sour cream	
	Spaetzle (see recipe, page 371)	

1. In a large pot, sauté bacon over medium heat until browned and crispy, about 5 minutes. Remove and set aside.
2. Season beef with salt and pepper to taste. Add half the oil to the pot and heat over medium-high heat. Add beef, in two batches, and sauté until browned on all sides, about 5 minutes per batch, adding the remaining oil between batches. Remove with a slotted spoon to a warm plate.
3. Reduce heat to medium, add onions to the pot and sauté until softened, 3 to 4 minutes. Add garlic, paprika and flour; sauté for 2 minutes. Add tomato paste and sauté for 1 minute.
4. Gradually whisk in stock. Return beef and any accumulated juices to the pot and add salt; bring to a boil. Cover, reduce heat to low and simmer gently until beef is tender and easily pulled apart, 1½ to 2 hours.
5. Remove beef from the pot with a slotted spoon and, using two forks, pull apart into bite-size shreds. Discard any fat and gristle. Return beef to the pot and add red peppers; simmer over medium heat until peppers are tender, about 10 minutes. Stir in half the parsley and the vinegar. Taste and adjust seasoning with salt and pepper, if necessary.
6. Ladle into heated bowls and garnish with sour cream, spaetzle, reserved bacon and the remaining parsley.

Borscht

▲▼▲▼▲▼▲▼▲▼▲▼▲▼▲▼▲▼▲▼▲▼▲▼▲▼▲▼▲▼▲▼▲▼▲▼▲▼▲

For those who love beets, this sweet-sour, jewel-toned soup is a must. Even those who don't might be won over by it!

▲▼▲▼▲▼▲▼▲▼▲

Tip

Borscht can be served hot or cold. If you want to serve it cold, transfer it to a bowl after Step 2, cover and refrigerate for 3 hours. Serve in chilled bowls, garnished with dilled sour cream.

Serves 6 to 8

• Preheat oven to 400°F (200°C)

1 lb	beets, trimmed	500 g
3	slices bacon, finely chopped	3
2	carrots, cut into small dice	2
2	parsnips, cut into small dice	2
1	onion, finely chopped	1
1	clove garlic, minced	1
6 cups	chicken stock	1.5 L
3 cups	shredded savoy cabbage	750 mL
3 tbsp	red wine vinegar	45 mL
1½ tbsp	liquid honey	22 mL
	Salt and freshly ground black pepper	
½ cup	sour cream	125 mL
1 tbsp	chopped fresh dill	15 mL

1. Wrap beets in a large piece of foil and bake in preheated oven until tender, about 1 hour. Let cool slightly, then peel off skins, and cut beets into ¼-inch (0.5 cm) dice.
2. In a large, heavy pot, sauté bacon over medium heat until starting to brown, about 3 minutes. Add carrots, parsnips, onion and garlic; sauté until softened, about 6 minutes. Add stock, cabbage and beets; bring to a boil. Reduce heat and simmer until vegetables are tender, about 20 minutes. Stir in vinegar, honey and salt and pepper to taste.
3. Meanwhile, in a small bowl, combine sour cream and dill.
4. Ladle soup into heated bowls and top each with a dollop of dilled sour cream.

Russian Cabbage Soup

▲▽▲▽▲▽▲▽▲▽▲▽▲▽▲▽▲▽▲▽▲▽▲▽▲▽▲▽▲▽▲▽▲▽▲▽▲▽▲

If you're looking for a hearty soup, this one fits the bill. Lots of beef chunks and vegetables, along with cabbage and sauerkraut, make this soup a lusty dinner that will warm your family and friends from head to toe.

▲▽▲▽▲▽▲▽▲▽

Variation

Substitute 3 lbs (1.5 kg) boneless pork shoulder blade (butt), trimmed and cut into ½-inch (1 cm) chunks, for the beef, and add 8 oz (250 g) cooked sausage of your choice with the cabbage and sauerkraut.

Serves 8

¼ cup	unsalted butter, divided	50 mL
3 lbs	boneless beef chuck roast, trimmed and cut into ½-inch (1 cm) chunks	1.5 kg
1	onion, chopped	1
2	carrots, chopped	2
1	stalk celery, chopped	1
2 cups	diced celery root (celeriac)	500 mL
2	cloves garlic, minced	2
1	bay leaf	1
1 tsp	dried thyme	5 mL
1 tsp	salt	5 mL
½ tsp	freshly ground black pepper	2 mL
8 cups	beef stock	2 L
½	head savoy cabbage, cored and thinly sliced	½
2 cups	sauerkraut, rinsed and water squeezed out	500 mL
½ cup	sour cream	125 mL
2 tbsp	chopped fresh dill	25 mL

1. In a large pot, melt half the butter over medium-high heat until sizzling. Add beef, in batches, and sauté until browned on all sides, about 5 minutes per batch, adding the remaining butter between batches. Remove with a slotted spoon to a warm plate.
2. Reduce heat to medium and add onion to the pot; sauté until starting to soften, about 2 minutes. Add carrots, celery and celery root; sauté until starting to soften, about 5 minutes. Add garlic, bay leaf, thyme, salt and pepper; sauté for 1 minute.
3. Add stock and bring to a boil, scraping up any brown bits from the bottom of the pot. Return beef and any accumulated juices to the pot, cover, reduce heat to low and simmer gently until beef is tender, about 1 hour. Add cabbage and sauerkraut; increase heat to medium and simmer until cabbage is tender, about 10 minutes. Discard bay leaf. Taste and adjust seasoning with salt and pepper, if necessary.
4. Ladle into heated bowls and top each with a dollop of sour cream. Sprinkle with dill.

Sopa de Ajo (Garlic Soup)

▲▽▲

This peasant soup was dinner when no meat could be found. The bread thickens the soup and gives the impression that there is more food than there really is. We like to serve soups like this with a big salad.

▲▽▲▽▲▽▲▽▲▽▲

Tip

Make sure to let the soup cool as directed before adding the eggs. The eggs may curdle if the soup is too hot.

Serves 6

⅓ cup	olive oil	75 mL
5	cloves garlic, roughly chopped	5
3 cups	torn French or Italian bread (crusts removed)	750 mL
6 cups	chicken or vegetable stock	1.5 L
1 tsp	paprika	15 mL
3	eggs, lightly beaten	3
1 tsp	balsamic vinegar	5 mL
½ tsp	salt	2 mL
¼ tsp	freshly ground black pepper	1 mL
¼ cup	minced fresh flat-leaf (Italian) parsley	50 mL

1. In a large pot, heat oil over medium heat. Add garlic and bread; sauté until garlic is softened but not browned and bread has begun to color and crisp, about 4 minutes.
2. Add stock and paprika; bring to a boil. Reduce heat and simmer for 20 minutes to blend the flavors. Remove from heat and let cool for 10 minutes.
3. In a food processor or blender, in batches, purée soup until smooth, gradually adding eggs and vinegar to the last batch through the feed tube or hole in the lid. Return to the pot and season with salt and pepper. Reheat over medium heat until steaming, stirring constantly. Do not let boil, or the eggs will scramble.
4. Ladle into heated bowls and garnish with parsley.

Caldo Gallego

▲▼

Loosely translated as "Galician hot pot," this hearty soup is peasant food at its best. Loaded with salty pork, beans and potatoes, this rich brew from northern Spain is sure to satisfy.

▲▼▲▼▲▼▲▼▲▼

Tip
When browning the beef, make sure you add only enough at one time to make a single layer. Do not overcrowd the pan, lor the beef will not brown properly.

Variation
Replace the spinach with Swiss chard or kale. Add 5 minutes after adding the potato in Step 3.

Serves 6

8	slices bacon, chopped	8
1 lb	boneless beef chuck roast, trimmed and cut into 1-inch (2.5 cm) chunks	500 g
1 tsp	salt	5 mL
	Freshly ground black pepper	
3	cloves garlic, chopped	3
1	onion, finely chopped	1
1	carrot, sliced	1
1	stalk celery, sliced	1
1	bay leaf	1
8 cups	beef stock	2 L
2 cups	dried chickpeas or great Northern beans, soaked overnight or quick-soaked (see tip, page 310) and drained	500 mL
1	large red-skinned potato, cut into 1-inch (2.5 cm) cubes	1
8 oz	spinach, trimmed and chopped	250 g
1 tbsp	balsamic vinegar	15 mL

1. In a large pot, sauté bacon over medium heat until browned and crispy, about 5 minutes. Remove with a slotted spoon to a plate lined with paper towels. Set aside.
2. Season beef with salt and pepper to taste. Add beef to the pot, in two batches if necessary, and sauté until browned on all sides, about 5 minutes per batch. Remove with a slotted spoon to a warm plate.
3. Add garlic, onion, carrot and celery to the pot and sauté until starting to soften, about 3 minutes. Return beef and any accumulated juices to the pot and add bay leaf, stock and beans; bring to a boil. Cover, reduce heat to low and simmer gently until beans and beef are tender, about 1½ hours. Add potato and simmer until tender, about 15 minutes. Add spinach and simmer, stirring, until wilted. Discard bay leaf. Stir in vinegar. Taste and adjust seasoning with salt and pepper, if necessary.
4. Ladle into heated bowls and garnish with reserved bacon.

Cocido

▲▽▲▽▲▽▲▽▲▽▲▽▲▽▲▽▲▽▲▽▲▽▲▽▲▽▲▽▲▽▲▽▲▽▲▽▲▽▲

Cocido, a Spanish dish that includes various meats, vegetables and beans, is similar to the French pot au feu. There are countless variations, so don't be too worried about making it authentic. Just add your favorite sausage and meats and invite the neighbors over to share this hearty favorite.

▲▽▲▽▲▽▲▽▲▽▲

Tip

We can't overstate how important it is to brown meat properly before slow-cooking it. The flavor that develops during the browning process is critical to the overall flavor of the soup. If you overcrowd your pot, the meat will only steam and become gray and will never brown.

Serves 8

1 lb	boneless beef brisket or chuck, cut into 1-inch (2.5 cm) cubes	500 g
1 tsp	salt	5 mL
	Freshly ground black pepper	
¼ cup	olive oil, divided	50 mL
2	onions, finely chopped	2
3	cloves garlic, minced	3
2	carrots, sliced	2
2	stalks celery, sliced	2
2	turnips, peeled and diced	2
1 lb	smoked chorizo, kielbasa or other spicy sausage, cut into ½-inch (1 cm) half-moons	500 g
1	smoked ham hock (about 8 oz/250 g)	1
1	can (14 to 19 oz/398 to 540 mL) chickpeas, drained and rinsed	1
½	head savoy cabbage, cored and chopped	½
8 cups	beef or chicken stock	2 L
1	bay leaf	1
1 tsp	dried marjoram	5 mL
¼ cup	minced fresh flat-leaf (Italian) parsley	50 mL
1 tsp	balsamic vinegar	5 mL

1. Season beef with salt and pepper to taste. In a large pot, heat half the oil over medium heat. Add beef, in two batches if necessary, and sauté until browned on all sides, about 5 minutes per batch, adding more oil between batches as necessary. Remove with a slotted spoon to a warm plate.

2. Add onions to the pot and sauté until starting to soften, 3 to 4 minutes. Add garlic, carrots, celery and turnips; sauté until softened, about 5 minutes. Return beef and any accumulated juices to the pot and add sausage, ham hock, chickpeas, cabbage, stock, bay leaf and marjoram; bring to a boil. Cover, reduce heat to low and simmer gently until beef is tender, about 1½ hours. Discard bay leaf.

3. Remove ham hock from the soup and let cool slightly. Pick the meat from the bone and shred into bite-size pieces. Discard bone, fat and skin. Return meat to the soup and stir in parsley and vinegar. Taste and adjust seasoning with salt and pepper, if necessary.

4. Ladle into heated bowls.

Zarzuela

▲▽▲▽▲▽▲▽▲▽▲▽▲▽▲▽▲▽▲▽▲▽▲▽▲▽▲▽▲▽▲▽▲▽▲▽▲▽▲

Zarzuela is Spain's answer to bouillabaisse and is a hearty fish stew brimming with mussels, squid, shrimp and fish. This party in a pot relies heavily on good fish stock and the freshest of fish, so when shopping for the ingredients, be sure to ask the fishmonger what came in that day and substitute that for any of the ingredients listed at right.

▲▽▲▽▲▽▲▽▲▽

Tips

For the fish fillets, try sea bass, snapper, grouper or tilapia.

If you have squid with tentacles attached, you can use the tentacles too; just separate from the tubes and cut into bite-size pieces, if necessary.

Serves 6

¼ cup	olive oil	50 mL
3	cloves garlic, minced	3
1	onion, chopped	1
½ tsp	salt	2 mL
Pinch	freshly ground black pepper	Pinch
8 oz	medium shrimp, peeled and deveined	250 g
1 tsp	paprika	5 mL
¼ tsp	cayenne pepper	1 mL
2 tbsp	brandy or cognac	25 mL
3	tomatoes, seeded and diced	3
1 cup	dry white wine	250 mL
12	mussels, scrubbed and debearded (see tips, page 252)	12
6 cups	fish or shellfish stock	1.5 L
¼ tsp	saffron threads	1 mL
	Grated zest of ½ orange	
8 oz	skinless fish fillets (see tip, at left)	250 g
¼ cup	minced fresh flat-leaf (Italian) parsley, divided	50 mL
4 oz	small squid (tubes only), cut into rings	125 g

1. In a large pot, heat oil over medium heat. Add garlic, onion, salt and black pepper; sauté until onion is softened, about 6 minutes. Add shrimp, paprika and cayenne; sauté until shrimp are pink and opaque, about 2 minutes. Remove shrimp with a slotted spoon to a warm plate.

2. Add brandy to the pot and cook until reduced by half, about 5 minutes. Add tomatoes and wine; cook until reduced by half, about 5 minutes. Add mussels, cover and cook until mussels have opened, 5 to 8 minutes. Discard any mussels that do not open. Using a slotted spoon, transfer mussels to a bowl.

3. Add stock, saffron and orange zest to the pot and bring to a simmer. Add fish and half the parsley; cover and cook for 5 minutes. Add squid, cover and cook until fish is opaque and flakes easily with a fork and squid is opaque, 2 to 3 minutes. Return shrimp and mussels to the pot and reheat if necessary. Taste and adjust seasoning with salt and black pepper, if necessary.

4. Divide fish and shellfish among heated bowls and top with stock. Garnish with the remaining parsley.

Romesco

▲▼▲▼▲▼▲▼▲▼▲▼▲▼▲▼▲▼▲▼▲▼▲▼▲▼▲▼▲▼▲▼▲▼▲▼▲▼▲

A delicious seafood soup similar to bourride, romesco hails from the coasts of northern Spain. Make friends with your fishmonger so you can obtain the fish heads and bones that are essential to this dish.

▲▼▲▼▲▼▲▼▲▼▲

Tip

The quality of this dish is dependent on the availability of the freshest fish and fish bones and heads. Though it might sound gross, the heads give body and texture to the dish. Avoid oily or strong-tasting fish, such as salmon or tuna, and focus on firm-fleshed white fish, such as snapper or rock fish.

Serves 6

6 lbs	whole fish, filleted and skinned, heads and bones reserved	3 kg
1	leek, white and light green parts only, thinly sliced	1
6 cups	fish stock	1.5 L
1 cup	dry white wine	250 mL
5	whole black peppercorns	5
4	sprigs fresh thyme (or ¼ tsp/1 mL dried)	4
4	parsley stems	4
1	bay leaf	1
½ tsp	salt	2 mL
	Romesco Sauce (see recipe, opposite)	
	Freshly ground black pepper	

1. Place fish fillets in the refrigerator. Cut the gills from the fish heads, and the fins and tails from the frames, and discard. Soak the bones in a large bowl of cold water with about 1 tsp (5 mL) white vinegar until they are blood-free, about 30 minutes (for more details, see page 8). Drain well.

2. In a large pot, combine fish heads and bones, leek, stock, wine, peppercorns, thyme, parsley, bay leaf and salt. Bring to a boil over medium heat. Reduce heat and simmer for 30 minutes.

3. Strain the stock (see page 8) and discard all solids. Return to a simmer over medium heat. Whisk in about ½ cup (125 mL) of the romesco sauce. Taste and adjust seasoning with salt and pepper, if necessary. Add fish fillets and simmer until fish is opaque and flakes easily with a fork, about 5 minutes for thin fish (less than 1 inch/2.5 cm thick) and 8 to 10 minutes for thicker fish.

4. Divide fish fillets among heated bowls and top with stock and the remaining romesco.

"Romesco" means a couple of things in Spain. It is a soup, a sauce and the name of a dried pepper. All romesco is full-flavored and spicy.

▲▼▲▼▲▼▲▼▲

Tip

To roast peppers, lay halved and seeded peppers on a baking sheet and broil until the skins blacken. (Or, on a gas stove, turn a few burners to high and lay peppers directly over the flames. Turn with tongs until blackened on all sides.) Transfer to a heatproof bowl and cover with plastic wrap. When cool enough to handle, scrape the skins from the peppers with the back of a knife. Don't worry about a little bit of black remaining on the peppers.

Romesco Sauce

Makes about 1½ cups (375 mL)

2 tbsp	olive oil	25 mL
¼ cup	onion, minced	50 mL
¼ cup	chopped roasted red bell pepper	50 mL
2	cloves garlic, chopped	2
1	tomato, seeded and diced	1
½ tsp	cayenne pepper	2 mL
¼ tsp	salt	1 mL
	Freshly ground black pepper	
¼ cup	blanched almonds	50 mL
2 tbsp	red wine vinegar	25 mL
¾ cup	olive oil	175 mL

1. In a skillet, heat the 2 tbsp (25 mL) olive oil over medium heat. Add onion, roasted pepper, garlic and tomato; sauté until starting to soften, 3 to 4 minutes. Add cayenne, salt and black pepper to taste; sauté until mixture has dried a bit, about 2 minutes. Remove from heat.

2. In a food processor fitted with a metal blade, process almonds and vinegar until finely ground. Add onion mixture and process until smooth. With the motor running, through the feed tube, add the ¾ cup (175 mL) oil in a steady, thin stream. The mixture should thicken and emulsify to form a thick, rust-colored sauce. Taste and adjust seasoning with salt and black pepper, if necessary.

French Onion Soup

▲▽▲▽▲▽▲▽▲▽▲▽▲▽▲▽▲▽▲▽▲▽▲▽▲▽▲▽▲▽▲▽▲▽▲▽

The secret to making a really great onion soup lies in the browning of the onions. Take your time and brown them until they are meltingly tender, with lots of brown bits on the bottom of the pan. Those brown bits will transform the soup into the flavor you remember so fondly.

▲▽▲▽▲▽▲▽▲▽

Tip

To trim leeks, cut off and discard the root end and the dark green tops (or save the tops for stock). Cut leeks lengthwise and wash under running water to remove any grit or dirt. Then cut as directed in the recipe.

Serves 6

- 6 individual ovenproof 2-cup (500 mL) bowls
- Baking sheet

¼ cup	unsalted butter	50 mL
2 tbsp	vegetable oil	25 mL
4	leeks, white and light green parts only, thinly sliced	4
2	large white onions, thinly sliced	2
2	large yellow onions, thinly sliced	2
Pinch	salt	Pinch
3	cloves garlic, minced	3
⅓ cup	Madeira	75 mL
6 cups	beef stock	1.5 L
1	bay leaf	1
1 tsp	white wine vinegar	5 mL
	Freshly ground black pepper	
6	slices French bread	6
2 cups	shredded Gruyère cheese	500 mL

1. In a large pot, heat butter and oil over medium heat until sizzling. Add leeks, white onions, yellow onions and salt; sauté until onions start to brown, about 10 minutes. Reduce heat and cook, scraping up browned bits from the bottom of the pot and stirring often, until onions are a deep mahogany brown, about 30 minutes. Add garlic and sauté until fragrant, about 2 minutes.

2. Increase heat to medium-high, add Madeira and cook, scraping up brown bits, until liquid is reduced to a few tablespoons, about 5 minutes. Add stock and bay leaf; bring to a boil. Partially cover, reduce heat to low and simmer gently until flavors are blended and onions are very tender, about 30 minutes. Discard bay leaf. Stir in vinegar and salt and pepper to taste.

3. Meanwhile, preheat broiler and toast bread on both sides.

4. Arrange ovenproof bowls on baking sheet and ladle soup into them. Sprinkle with half the cheese and top with toasted bread. Sprinkle the remaining cheese over the bread. Broil until cheese is melted and lightly browned. Serve immediately.

Provençal Vegetable Soup with Pistou

▲▽▲

Fresh from the farm ingredients showcase springtime vegetables in this hearty and quick soup. Feel free to incorporate other vegetables, such as fresh tomatoes, parsnips, radicchio, escarole or mushrooms.

▲▽▲▽▲▽▲▽▲▽

Tip

Seasoning with a little bit of lemon juice at the end of cooking heightens the flavor of the soup. Although most home cooks think only in terms of salt and pepper when it comes to adjusting the seasoning in their dishes, we've found that a little acid goes a long way toward making a soup taste just right.

Serves 6 to 8

¼ cup	olive oil	50 mL
1	onion, chopped	1
2	carrots, chopped	2
2	leeks, white and light green parts only, thinly sliced	2
2	cloves garlic, minced	2
1	stalk celery, chopped	1
1 tsp	dried thyme	5 mL
1 tsp	salt	5 mL
	Freshly ground black pepper	
1 cup	dry white wine	250 mL
6 cups	chicken or vegetable stock	1.5 L
10	small new potatoes, quartered	10
1	can (14 to 19 oz/398 to 540 mL) navy beans, drained and rinsed	1
10	spears asparagus, trimmed and sliced	10
2	summer squash or zucchini, chopped	2
2 cups	chopped baby spinach	500 mL
1 cup	frozen peas, thawed	250 mL
2 tsp	freshly squeezed lemon juice	10 mL
	Pistou (see recipe, page 363)	

1. In a large pot, heat oil over medium heat. Add onion and sauté until softened, about 6 minutes. Add carrots, leeks, garlic, celery, thyme, salt and pepper to taste; sauté until vegetables start to soften, about 5 minutes. Add wine and cook until reduced by half, about 5 minutes.
2. Add stock and potatoes; bring to a boil. Reduce heat and simmer until potatoes are almost tender, about 15 minutes. Add beans, asparagus, squash, spinach and peas; simmer until vegetables are tender, about 5 minutes. Stir in lemon juice. Taste and adjust seasoning with salt and pepper, if necessary.
3. Ladle into heated bowls and garnish each with a dollop of pistou.

French Cabbage Soup

▲▼▲▼▲▼▲▼▲▼▲▼▲▼▲▼▲▼▲▼▲▼▲▼▲▼▲▼▲▼▲▼▲▼▲▼▲

Leave it to the thrifty French to make a meal out of nothing more than a few vegetables freshly picked from just outside the kitchen door. The addition of sausage makes it more of a meal. A bonne femme *could whip up dinner* tout de suite, *and so can you.*

▲▼▲▼▲▼▲▼▲

Tip

Soup will stay hot much longer in a heated bowl.

Serves 6

¼ cup	unsalted butter	50 mL
2	leeks, white part only, sliced	2
2	carrots, sliced	2
2	stalks celery, sliced	2
2	cloves garlic, minced	2
1 tsp	dried thyme	5 mL
3 tbsp	all-purpose flour	45 mL
8 cups	chicken stock	2 L
1 lb	smoked sausage, cut into ½-inch (1 cm) half-moons	500 g
2	potatoes, peeled and diced	2
½	head green cabbage, cored and thinly sliced	½
½ tsp	salt	2 mL
1	bay leaf	1
½ tsp	cayenne pepper	2 mL
	Freshly ground black pepper	
¼ cup	minced fresh flat-leaf (Italian) parsley	50 mL

1. In a large pot, melt butter over medium heat until sizzling. Add leeks and sauté until softened, about 6 minutes. Add carrots, celery, garlic and thyme; sauté until vegetables start to soften, about 5 minutes. Sprinkle with flour and sauté for 2 minutes.
2. Gradually whisk in stock. Add sausage, potatoes, cabbage, salt and bay leaf; bring to a boil. Cover, reduce heat to low and simmer gently until potatoes and cabbage are tender, about 20 minutes. Discard bay leaf. Add cayenne and salt and black pepper to taste.
3. Ladle into heated bowls and garnish with parsley.

Petite Marmite

▲▼▲

A close relative of pot au feu, petite marmite is a delicious soup consisting of a variety of meats and vegetables simmered in stock, then served all together in individual bowls. A petite marmite is a small bowl in France, so the dish is named after the vessel, not what is inside.

▲▼▲▼▲▼▲▼▲▼

Tip

Save the parsley leaves and the green part of the leeks for another recipe.

Serves 8

12 oz	sliced veal shank (3-inch/7.5 cm pieces)	375 g
2 lbs	beef short ribs	1 kg
1 lb	boneless pork shoulder blade (butt), trimmed and cut into 1-inch (2.5 cm) chunks	500 g
2	onions, finely chopped	2
2	cloves garlic, crushed	2
8	whole black peppercorns	8
8	parsley stems	8
1	bay leaf	1
8 cups	beef stock	2 L
1 cup	dry red wine	250 mL
½ tsp	salt	2 mL
½ tsp	dried thyme	2 mL
2 tbsp	unsalted butter	25 mL
2	leeks, white part only, thinly sliced	2
2	carrots, cut into ¼-inch (0.5 cm) slices	2
2	turnips, peeled and cut into small dice	2
1	stalk celery, thinly sliced	1
	Freshly ground black pepper	

1. In a large pot, combine veal, short ribs, pork, onions, garlic, peppercorns, parsley stems, bay leaf, stock, wine, salt and thyme. Bring to a simmer over medium heat. Cover, reduce heat to low and simmer gently until meats are tender, about 2 hours.

2. Using tongs, remove veal, short ribs and pork from the stock and let cool slightly. Pick the meat and marrow from the veal shanks and discard the bones. Pick the meat from the short ribs and discard the bones. Tear veal, beef and pork into bite-size pieces. Strain the stock (see page 8) and discard all solids. Set meats and stock aside.

3. In another large pot, melt butter over medium heat until sizzling. Add leeks, carrots, turnips and celery; sauté until starting to soften, about 5 minutes. Add reserved stock and meats; bring to a boil. Reduce heat and simmer until vegetables are tender, about 30 minutes. Season with salt and pepper to taste.

4. Ladle into heated bowls.

Pot au Feu

▲▽▲

Loosely translated as "fire pot," this French classic is really two courses in one. The first course consists of the flavorful stock, while the second relies on the various slow-cooked meats and vegetables that contributed so generously to the stock. We like to serve the stock garnished with croutons and set out horseradish, mustard and cornichons (little French sour pickles) to accompany the meat and vegetables. A loaf of French bread and a glass of wine will complete the meal.

▲▽▲▽▲▽▲▽▲

Tip

Sometimes we like to give garlic a rough chop when it is going to cook at a high temperature with browning meats. The rough chop allows it to cook a little more aggressively without over-browning or burning.

Serves 6

6	chicken breasts	6
	Salt and freshly ground black pepper	
3 tbsp	olive oil	45 mL
1 lb	bratwurst, cut into 6 pieces	500 g
1½ lbs	beef short ribs	750 g
4	cloves garlic, roughly chopped (see tip, at left)	4
1 tsp	dried thyme	5 mL
2 cups	dry white wine	500 mL
6 cups	chicken stock (approx.), divided	1.5 L
1	bay leaf	1
3	carrots, quartered lengthwise	3
3	onions, quartered	3
3	stalks celery, halved lengthwise, then halved crosswise	3
3	small new potatoes, quartered	3
2	parsnips, quartered lengthwise	2
¼ cup	minced fresh flat-leaf (Italian) parsley	50 mL
	Buttery Croutons (see recipe, page 368)	
	French-style mustard	
	Prepared horseradish	
	Cornichons	

1. Season chicken with salt and pepper to taste. In a large pot, heat oil over medium heat. Add chicken, skin side down, in batches, and cook until browned on both sides, about 8 minutes per side. Remove with a slotted spoon to a plate.
2. Add bratwurst to the pot and cook until browned on all sides, about 5 minutes. Remove with a slotted spoon to the plate with the chicken. Cover and refrigerate until ready to use.
3. Season short ribs with salt and pepper to taste. Add ribs to the pot and cook, adjusting the heat if necessary so that the bottom of the pot doesn't blacken, until browned on all sides, about 10 minutes. Add garlic and thyme; sauté for 2 minutes. Add wine and cook until reduced by half, about 15 minutes.

Tip

We like garnishing this soup with Buttery Croutons, but you can experiment with the other crouton recipes in this book (pages 368–370) until you find the one you like best.

4. Add 4 cups (1 L) of the stock and bay leaf; bring to a boil. Cover, reduce heat to low and simmer gently for 1 hour. Return bratwurst to the pot and add more stock as needed to cover the meat; bring back to a simmer. Cover and simmer for 45 minutes. Return chicken and accumulated juices to the pot and add carrots, onions, celery, potatoes, parsnips and more stock, if needed; simmer until meats and vegetables are very tender, about 45 minutes.

5. Remove meats and vegetables with a slotted spoon and arrange on a platter. If desired, skim the fat from the surface of the stock with a large spoon. Taste and adjust the seasoning with salt and pepper, if necessary.

6. Ladle stock into heated bowls and garnish with some of the parsley and the croutons. Serve meats and vegetables on the side, garnished with the remaining parsley, mustard, horseradish and cornichons.

Garbure

▲▽▲

A hearty soup from the French countryside, garbure can and should be made with fresh seasonal ingredients. This stick-to-your-ribs dish is chock-full of flavorful smoked meats, beans and garden-fresh cabbage, turnips and leeks. Even though it's made with water instead of stock, this soup's deep, rich flavor really satisfies.

▲▽▲▽▲▽▲▽▲

Tip

Here's how to quick-soak dried beans: In a colander, rinse beans under cold water and discard any discolored ones. In a saucepan, combine beans with enough cold water to cover them by 2 inches (5 cm). Bring to a boil over medium heat and boil for 2 minutes. Remove from heat and let soak, covered, for 1 hour.

Serves 6 to 8

8 oz	bacon, finely chopped	250 g
2	leeks, white and light green parts only, thinly sliced	2
½	small head cabbage, cored and shredded	½
8	cloves garlic, minced	8
2	carrots, sliced	2
2	stalks celery, sliced	2
2	potatoes, peeled and sliced	2
2	turnips, peeled and sliced	2
1	smoked ham hock (about 6 oz/175 g) or ¾ cup (175 mL) chopped ham	1
1 lb	kielbasa sausage, cut into 1-inch (2.5 cm) slices	500 g
8 cups	water	2 L
1 cup	dried great Northern beans, soaked overnight or quick-soaked (see tip, at left) and drained	250 mL
2	bay leaves	2
1 tbsp	salt	15 mL
1 tsp	dried thyme	5 mL
1 tsp	dried oregano	5 mL
1 tsp	freshly ground black pepper	5 mL
¼ cup	minced fresh flat-leaf (Italian) parsley	50 mL

1. In a large pot, sauté bacon over medium heat until it renders its fat, about 5 minutes. Add leeks and cabbage; sauté until softened, about 6 minutes. Add garlic, carrots, celery, potatoes, turnips, ham hock, sausage, water, beans, bay leaves, salt, thyme, oregano and pepper; bring to a boil. Partially cover, reduce heat to low and simmer gently until beans are tender, about 1½ hours. Discard bay leaves.
2. Remove ham hock from the soup and let cool slightly. Pick the meat from the bone and shred into bite-size pieces. Discard bone, fat and skin. Return meat to the soup and simmer until heated through. Taste and adjust seasoning with salt and pepper, if necessary.
3. Ladle into heated bowls and garnish with parsley.

Bourride

Yet another Mediterranean fish soup on the order of bouillabaisse, bourride is simpler and easier to make. If you have the fish stock and the aïoli ready ahead of time, this soup comes together in just a few minutes.

▲▽▲▽▲▽▲▽▲▽

Tip
Before shopping for fish, check fish sustainability/endangered lists (such as www. montereybayaquarium.org/ cr/seafoodwatch.asp) or with your fishmonger to be sure that you're not purchasing fish species that are being overfished or fished illegally.

Serves 6

¼ cup	olive oil	50 mL
3	leeks, white part only, thinly sliced	3
½ tsp	salt	2 mL
	Freshly ground black pepper	
1 lb	spinach (about 10 cups/2.5 L), trimmed	500 g
8 cups	fish, shellfish or chicken stock	2 L
2½ to 3 lbs	firm white fish fillets, skin removed	1.25 to 1.5 kg
¾ cup	Aïoli (see recipe, page 362), divided	175 mL
6	slices French or Italian bread, lightly toasted on one side	6

1. In a large pot, heat oil over medium heat. Add leek, salt and pepper to taste; sauté until starting to soften, 2 to 3 minutes. Add spinach and sauté until wilted.
2. Add stock and bring to a simmer. Add fish and simmer until fish is opaque and flakes easily with a fork, about 8 minutes.
3. Divide fish among heated bowls and quickly whisk ½ cup (125 mL) of the aïoli into the soup. Ladle soup over the fish and top with toasted bread and a dollop of aïoli.

Pappa al Pomodoro
(Tomato and Bread Soup)

▲▽▲

Only a frugal cook trying to feed a hungry crowd would dream up this delicious concoction. Because the ingredient list is short, make sure to use the best of what's available. Juicy ripe red tomatoes, hearty peasant bread, good-quality olive oil and real Parmigiano-Reggiano cheese turn a simple soup into a delightful meal.

▲▽▲▽▲▽▲▽▲

Tip

Depending on how absorbent the bread you're using is, this soup can become very thick. Just add more stock to thin as desired.

Serves 4 to 6

¼ cup	extra-virgin olive oil	50 mL
1	onion, chopped	1
3	cloves garlic, thinly sliced	3
2 lbs	tomatoes, seeded and roughly chopped, with juices	1 kg
4	¾-inch (2 cm) slices day-old Italian peasant bread	4
4 cups	chicken or vegetable stock	1 L
1 tsp	salt	5 mL
¼ tsp	freshly ground black pepper	1 mL
1 cup	torn fresh basil leaves	250 mL
	Freshly grated Parmigiano-Reggiano cheese	
	Additional extra-virgin olive oil	

1. In a large pot, heat oil over medium heat. Add onion and sauté until softened, about 6 minutes. Add garlic and sauté for 1 minute. Add tomatoes with their juices and bring to a boil. Reduce heat and simmer until tomatoes start to break down, about 5 minutes.

2. Add bread, stock, salt and pepper; simmer, breaking bread up with the back of a spoon, until bread has absorbed as much liquid as possible and resembles mush, about 15 minutes. Stir in basil.

3. Ladle into heated bowls and garnish with cheese and a drizzle of olive oil.

Minestrone

▲▽▲

Perhaps the most famous of the Italian soups, minestrone is like eating a garden in a bowl. Beans and pasta are added to create a hearty and delicious meal.

▲▽▲▽▲▽▲▽▲▽▲

Tip

By far the best Parmesan is Parmigiano-Reggiano, made in Italy. Because it's so dear in price, we like to use every square inch, even the rind. Parmigiano-Reggiano rind gives wonderful depth of flavor to minestrone — just add it with the stock and discard it before serving.

Serves 6

2	cans (each 14 to 19 oz/398 to 540 mL) great Northern, cannellini or white kidney beans, drained and rinsed	2
7 cups	chicken stock, divided	1.75 L
¼ cup	olive oil	50 mL
1 cup	finely chopped onion	250 mL
3	cloves garlic, minced	3
2	carrots, thinly sliced	2
2	zucchini, thinly sliced	2
1	stalk celery, sliced	1
2 tsp	dried oregano	10 mL
1 tsp	salt	5 mL
½ tsp	freshly ground black pepper	2 mL
1	can (14 oz/398 mL) diced tomatoes, with juice	1
4 oz	prosciutto, finely chopped	125 g
2 cups	thinly sliced napa or savoy cabbage	500 mL
1 cup	elbow macaroni	250 mL
¼ cup	chopped fresh parsley	50 mL
	Juice of 1 lemon	
½ cup	freshly grated Parmesan cheese	125 mL

1. In a saucepan, bring beans and 3 cups (750 mL) of the stock to a simmer over medium heat. Reduce heat and simmer for 5 minutes.
2. Remove from heat and, using an immersion blender, pulse the beans in 3 or 4 quick spurts to partially purée them (or process half the bean mixture in a food processor or blender in batches, then return to the pot). Set aside.
3. In a large pot, heat oil over medium heat. Add onion and sauté until softened, about 6 minutes. Add garlic, carrots, zucchini, celery, oregano, salt and pepper; sauté until starting to soften, about 5 minutes.
4. Add the remaining stock, tomatoes with juice, prosciutto and cabbage; bring to a boil. Reduce heat and simmer for 10 minutes. Add reserved bean mixture; simmer for 10 minutes. Add macaroni and cook until tender to the bite, about 10 minutes. Stir in parsley and lemon juice. Taste and adjust seasoning with salt and pepper, if necessary.
5. Ladle into heated bowls and garnish with cheese.

Pasta e Fagiole
(Pasta and Bean Soup)

▲▽▲▽▲▽▲▽▲▽▲▽▲▽▲▽▲▽▲▽▲▽▲▽▲▽▲▽▲▽▲▽▲▽▲▽▲▽▲

Great with a salad, crusty bread and a glass of wine, this Italian bean and pasta soup, flavored with pancetta and rosemary, makes a lovely meal when time is short. If you don't have pancetta, you can substitute bacon (see tip, page 268).

▲▽▲▽▲▽▲▽▲▽▲

Tip

When adding noodles to soups, we don't always have the time or the inclination to cook them separately. Often we toss them directly into the stock to cook. However, when we have the time or when we're making the soup ahead of time, we cook the noodles in salted boiling water and add them to the bowls separately, pouring the stock on top. When noodles are left in soup for any length of time, they become soggy, flabby and absorb a great deal of the stock.

Serves 6

1 tbsp	olive oil	15 mL
3 oz	pancetta, finely chopped	90 g
1	onion, finely chopped	1
2	cloves garlic, minced	2
2 tbsp	tomato paste	25 mL
2	cans (each 14 to 19 oz/398 to 540 mL) cannellini or white kidney beans, drained and rinsed	2
5 cups	chicken stock	1.25 L
2	sprigs fresh rosemary	2
¾ tsp	salt	3 mL
¼ tsp	freshly ground black pepper	1 mL
¾ cup	tubetti or other small tubular pasta	175 mL
	Good-quality extra-virgin olive oil	
	Freshly grated Parmesan cheese	

1. In a large, heavy pot, heat oil over medium heat. Add pancetta and sauté until golden brown and crispy, about 5 minutes. Add onion and sauté until softened, about 6 minutes. Add garlic and sauté for 1 minute. Add the tomato paste and sauté until paste turns a rusty brown, about 5 minutes.
2. Add beans, stock, rosemary, salt and pepper; bring to a boil. Reduce heat and simmer for 10 minutes to blend the flavors. Discard rosemary sprigs. Add pasta and cook until tender to the bite, about 8 minutes.
3. Ladle into heated bowls, drizzle with olive oil and sprinkle with cheese.

Risi e Bisi (Rice and Pea Soup)

▲▽

This Venetian soup appears in early spring with the first peas of the season, but don't worry if you can't find fresh from the farmers' market peas in their pods — frozen early peas work beautifully. We stay true to the origins of this soup by using Arborio, or risotto, rice.

▲▽▲▽▲▽▲▽▲

Tips

There's no need to thaw the peas before adding them to the soup.

Be careful not to let the soup boil after adding the cream, or it will curdle.

Serves 6

¼ cup	olive oil	50 mL
1	onion, minced	1
1	clove garlic, minced	1
½ tsp	salt	2 mL
1 cup	Arborio rice	250 mL
6 cups	vegetable stock or White Chicken Stock (see recipe, page 9)	1.5 L
1 lb	frozen early peas	500 g
½ cup	freshly grated Parmesan cheese	125 mL
¼ cup	minced fresh flat-leaf (Italian) parsley, divided	50 mL
¼ cup	whipping (35%) cream	50 mL
3 tbsp	unsalted butter	45 mL
Pinch	cayenne pepper	Pinch
	Freshly ground black pepper	

1. In a large pot, heat oil over medium heat. Add onion and sauté until softened, about 6 minutes. Add garlic and salt; sauté for 1 minute. Add rice and sauté for 2 minutes.
2. Add stock and bring to a boil. Reduce heat and simmer until rice is tender, about 20 minutes. Stir in peas, cheese, 2 tbsp (25 mL) of the parsley, cream, butter and cayenne; increase heat to medium and simmer, stirring often, until steaming. Do not let boil. Season with salt and black pepper to taste.
3. Ladle into heated bowls and garnish with the remaining parsley.

Stracciatella

▲▽▲▽▲▽▲▽▲▽▲▽▲▽▲▽▲▽▲▽▲▽▲▽▲▽▲▽▲▽▲▽▲▽▲▽▲▽▲

This Italian favorite is a quick and easy way to let someone know you care. Because the soup is simple, use your best chicken stock and only real Parmigiano-Reggiano cheese.

▲▽▲▽▲▽▲▽▲▽▲

Tip

Although there are many imitators on the market, real Parmigiano-Reggiano can be identified by the dot-matrix pattern on the rind that spells out its name.

Serves 6

6 cups	chicken stock	1.5 L
3	eggs	3
¼ cup	freshly grated Parmigiano-Reggiano cheese	50 mL
2 tbsp	minced fresh flat-leaf (Italian) parsley	25 mL
Pinch	cayenne pepper	Pinch
	Salt and freshly ground black pepper	
	Garlic Croutons (see variation, page 368)	

1. In a large pot, bring stock to a simmer over medium heat.
2. Meanwhile, in a small bowl, beat eggs, cheese, parsley and cayenne.
3. Gently stir egg mixture into the simmering stock. Remove from heat and let eggs set into strands, about 1 minute. Season with salt and pepper to taste.
4. Ladle into heated bowls and garnish with croutons.

Wedding Soup

▲▽▲

In the steel town where Carla grew up, wedding soup — rich stock with tiny meatballs flavored with Parmesan and prosciutto — was the favorite course at the Knights of Columbus Hall.

▲▽▲▽▲▽▲▽▲▽▲▽

Tip

Parmesan's rich, nutty flavor is a welcome addition to many soups. By far the best Parmesan is Parmigiano-Reggiano, made in Italy. While it's not cheap, the flavor is well worth the price. You should always buy your cheese in a large chunk and grate it yourself.

Serves 6

- Baking sheet, lined with parchment paper

2	slices white bread, crusts removed, shredded	2
¼ cup	milk	50 mL
1	egg, beaten	1
4 oz	lean ground beef	125 g
4 oz	regular or lean ground pork	125 g
4 oz	lean ground veal	125 g
⅓ cup	freshly grated Parmesan cheese	75 mL
2 oz	prosciutto, finely chopped	60 g
¼ cup	minced fresh flat-leaf (Italian) parsley	50 mL
2	cloves garlic, minced	2
1	small onion, minced	1
½ tsp	salt	2 mL
Pinch	ground nutmeg	Pinch
	Freshly ground black pepper	
10 cups	chicken stock	2.5 L
1	head escarole, thinly sliced	1
¾ cup	acini di pepe pasta	175 mL
	Additional freshly grated Parmesan cheese (optional)	

1. In a large bowl, combine bread and milk; let soak for 2 minutes. Add egg, beef, pork, veal, cheese, prosciutto, parsley, garlic, onion, salt, nutmeg and pepper to taste; mix with your hands until well combined.
2. In a small skillet, sauté a small spoonful of the meat mixture over medium heat until no longer pink. Taste and adjust the seasoning of the meat mixture with salt and pepper, if necessary. Roll meat mixture into small balls, about 1 inch (2.5 cm) in diameter, and place on prepared baking sheet.
3. In a large pot, bring stock to a simmer over medium heat. Slowly add meatballs, keeping liquid at a simmer so that the meatballs are moving and don't stick together. Add escarole and simmer until meatballs are cooked through and escarole is tender, about 10 minutes. Add pasta and simmer until tender to the bite, about 4 minutes. Taste and adjust seasoning with salt and pepper, if necessary.
4. Ladle into heated bowls and garnish with cheese, if desired.

Avgolemono (Egg and Lemon Soup)

Avgolemono (pronounced ahv-goh-LEH-moh-noh) is Greece's answer to chicken soup, comforting and rich with eggs and bright with lemon juice. As with so many simple soups, the quality of the stock is very important. Bring out your best homemade stock for this soup, and you won't be sorry.

Tip

Because adding delicate eggs to a pot of hot soup would result in scrambled eggs, we use a technique called tempering. By gradually adding hot soup to the eggs, the temperature of the eggs rises slowly, so that when they eventually make it into the soup, they are already hot and stay fluid and velvety.

Serves 4

6 cups	chicken stock	1.5 L
1/3 cup	long-grain white rice	75 mL
3	eggs	3
1/4 cup	freshly squeezed lemon juice	50 mL
	Salt and freshly ground black pepper	

1. In a large pot, bring stock to a simmer over medium heat. Add rice, cover, reduce heat to low and simmer gently until rice is tender, about 20 minutes. Remove from heat, uncover and let cool for 10 minutes.
2. In a large bowl, whisk eggs. Gradually whisk in 2 cups (500 mL) of the stock. Slowly pour back into the pot, stirring constantly. Stir in lemon juice and salt and pepper to taste.
3. Ladle into heated bowls.

Stifado

▲▽▲▽▲▽▲▽▲▽▲▽▲▽▲▽▲▽▲▽▲▽▲▽▲▽▲▽▲▽▲▽▲▽▲

A Greek soup of lamb, onion, wine, cheese and nuts, stifado is a classic example of using what you have lying around to make a delicious meal. We especially love the whisper of cinnamon in this celebratory soup.

▲▽▲▽▲▽▲▽▲

Tip

Toast nuts on a baking sheet in a 350°F (180°C) oven until lightly browned, about 5 minutes.

Serves 6

2 lbs	boneless lamb shoulder or leg, trimmed and cut into ½-inch (1 cm) chunks	1 kg
1 tsp	dried oregano	5 mL
1 tsp	salt	5 mL
½ tsp	freshly ground black pepper	2 mL
¼ cup	olive oil, divided	50 mL
3	cloves garlic, minced	3
1	onion, finely chopped	1
1	carrot, sliced	1
1	stalk celery, sliced	1
1 tbsp	packed brown sugar	15 mL
1	stick cinnamon, about 4 inches (10 cm) long	1
1	can (14 oz/398 mL) diced tomatoes, with juice	1
6 cups	beef stock	1.5 L
1 cup	dry red wine	250 mL
⅓ cup	toasted walnuts, chopped	75 mL
⅓ cup	crumbled feta cheese	75 mL
¼ cup	minced fresh flat-leaf (Italian) parsley	50 mL

1. Season lamb with oregano, salt and pepper. In a large pot, heat half the oil over medium-high heat. Add lamb, in two batches, and sauté until browned on all sides, about 5 minutes per batch, adding the remaining oil between batches. Remove with a slotted spoon to a warm plate.

2. Add garlic, onion, carrot, celery and brown sugar to the pot and sauté until vegetables are softened, 3 to 4 minutes. Return lamb to the pot with any accumulated juices and add cinnamon stick, tomatoes with juice, stock and wine; bring to a simmer. Cover, reduce heat and simmer until lamb is tender, about 1 hour. Discard cinnamon stick. Taste and adjust seasoning with salt and pepper, if necessary (but remember that feta cheese is salty!).

3. Ladle into heated bowls and garnish with walnuts, feta and parsley.

Middle Eastern Lentil Soup with Garlic

▲▼▲▼▲▼▲▼▲▼▲▼▲▼▲▼▲▼▲▼▲▼▲▼▲▼▲▼▲▼▲▼▲▼▲▼▲▼▲

Cumin and garlic give this nourishing lentil soup its Middle Eastern flair. This is a simple vegetarian version, but we often turn it into a hearty meal by adding Merguez, a spicy sausage.

▲▼▲▼▲▼▲▼

Tip

Soup will stay hot much longer in a heated bowl.

Serves 8

1 tbsp	olive oil	15 mL
1	onion, finely chopped	1
4	cloves garlic, finely chopped	4
1 tsp	ground cumin	5 mL
10 cups	chicken or vegetable stock	2.5 L
2 cups	dried lentils (any color), rinsed	500 mL
1 tsp	salt	5 mL
	Freshly ground black pepper	
2 tbsp	freshly squeezed lemon juice	25 mL

1. In a large pot, heat oil over medium heat. Add onion and sauté until softened, about 6 minutes. Add garlic and sauté for 1 minute. Add cumin and sauté for 1 minute.
2. Add stock, lentils, salt and pepper; bring to a boil. Reduce heat and simmer until lentils are tender, about 45 minutes. Stir in lemon juice. Taste and adjust seasoning with salt and pepper, if necessary.
3. Ladle into heated bowls.

Cock-a-Leekie (page 290)
Overleaf: African Peanut Soup (page 323)

Harira

▲▽

Hailing from Morocco, harira is a hearty soup rich with lamb, chickpeas and lentils. Traditionally, harira is eaten during Ramadan, when devout Muslims take no food or water until the sun sets. The spices — cumin, cinnamon and turmeric — create a spicy soup redolent with the aromas of North Africa.

▲▽▲▽▲▽▲▽▲▽

Tip

Instead of buying precut stew meat, we usually buy a roast and cut it up ourselves. It is cheaper, and we like to cut away some of the sinew and fat that butchers leave on. Also, precut meat is often sold in chunks that are larger than we need or not uniform in size.

Serves 6

1½ lbs	boneless lamb or beef for stew, trimmed and cut into 1-inch (2.5 cm) chunks	750 g
1 tsp	salt	5 mL
¼ tsp	freshly ground black pepper	1 mL
¼ cup	vegetable oil, divided	50 mL
2	onions, finely chopped	2
1	carrot, sliced	1
1	stalk celery, sliced	1
1 tsp	ground cumin	5 mL
½ tsp	ground cinnamon	2 mL
½ tsp	ground turmeric	2 mL
¼ tsp	cayenne pepper	1 mL
1	can (14 oz/398 mL) diced tomatoes, with juice	1
6 cups	beef stock	1.5 L
½ cup	dried brown or green lentils, rinsed	125 mL
1	can (14 to 19 oz/398 to 540 mL) chickpeas, drained and rinsed	1
¼ cup	minced fresh flat-leaf (Italian) parsley	50 mL
1 cup	plain yogurt	250 mL
¼ cup	minced fresh cilantro	50 mL

1. Season lamb with salt and black pepper. In a large pot, heat half the oil over medium-high heat. Add lamb, in two batches, and sauté until browned on all sides, about 5 minutes per batch, adding the remaining oil between batches. Remove with a slotted spoon to a warm plate.

2. Add onions, carrot and celery to the pot and sauté until softened, 3 to 4 minutes. Add cumin, cinnamon, turmeric and cayenne; sauté until fragrant, about 2 minutes. Return lamb to the pot with any accumulated juices and add tomatoes with juice, stock and lentils; bring to a boil. Cover, reduce heat to low and simmer gently until lamb is tender, about 1 hour. Add chickpeas and simmer until heated through, about 10 minutes. Stir in parsley. Taste and adjust seasoning with salt, black pepper and cayenne, if necessary.

3. Ladle into heated bowls and garnish each with a dollop of yogurt and a sprinkle of cilantro.

Pork and Scallion Wonton Soup (page 328)

Overleaf: Tom Yum Gung (Thai Hot-and-Sour Shrimp and Lemongrass Soup) (page 326)

Vegetarian Harira

▲▼▲▼▲▼▲▼▲▼▲▼▲▼▲▼▲▼▲▼▲▼▲▼▲▼▲▼▲▼▲▼▲▼▲▼▲▼▲

This vegetarian version of harira is a nice alternative to the previous, heartier recipe. We like to serve this as a starter soup when we are making a Moroccan-themed dinner.

▲▼▲▼▲▼▲▼▲▼▲

Tip

San Marzano tomatoes, imported from Italy, are thought by many to be the best canned tomatoes in the world. They hail from a small town of the same name near Naples, whose volcanic soil is thought to filter impurities from the water and render tomatoes with a thick flesh, fewer seeds and a stronger taste. Look for the words "San Marzano" on the label to be sure you're getting the best.

Serves 8

3 tbsp	olive oil	45 mL
2	onions, chopped	2
2	cloves garlic, minced	2
1 tsp	ground cumin	5 mL
½ tsp	ground cinnamon	2 mL
¼ tsp	ground ginger	1 mL
¼ tsp	ground turmeric	1 mL
1	can (28 oz/796 mL) crushed tomatoes	1
8 cups	vegetable stock or Roasted Vegetable Stock (see recipe, page 21)	2 L
1 cup	dried brown or green lentils, rinsed	250 mL
1 tsp	salt	5 mL
¼ tsp	freshly ground black pepper	1 mL
2	potatoes, peeled and diced	2
1	can (14 to 19 oz/398 to 540 mL) chickpeas, drained and rinsed	1
3 tbsp	chopped fresh cilantro	45 mL
1	lemon, cut into wedges	1

1. In a large pot, heat oil over medium heat. Add onions and sauté until starting to brown, about 10 minutes. Add garlic, cumin, cinnamon, ginger and turmeric; sauté for 1 minute.
2. Add tomatoes with juice, stock, lentils, salt and pepper; bring to a boil. Reduce heat and simmer for 25 minutes. Add potatoes and simmer for 10 minutes. Add chickpeas and simmer until potatoes and lentils are tender, about 10 minutes.
3. Ladle into heated bowls and garnish with cilantro and lemon wedges. Diners may squeeze the lemon over their soup, if they desire.

African Peanut Soup

▲▽▲▽▲▽▲▽▲▽▲▽▲▽▲▽▲▽▲▽▲▽▲▽▲▽▲▽▲▽▲▽▲▽▲▽▲

Peanut butter sounds like a strange ingredient to base a soup on, but believe us, it works. This mouth-watering soup tastes nothing like a PB& J; rather, its blend of curry spices, sweet potato and fresh ginger gives it a unique, complex flavor that will have you making it again and again.

▲▽▲▽▲▽▲▽▲▽▲

Tip

If you want to make your own curry powder, see our recipe on page 27. Making your own curry powder guarantees a fresh, lively character in your dishes. Purchased curry powder may have been sitting on your grocer's shelf for a long time, which reduces its flavor.

Serves 6

1½ tbsp	olive oil, divided	22 mL
1 lb	lean ground turkey	500 g
1 tsp	salt, divided	5 mL
¼ tsp	freshly ground black pepper	1 mL
1	onion, chopped	1
2	cloves garlic, minced	2
2 tsp	minced gingerroot	10 mL
¼ tsp	hot pepper flakes	1 mL
1 tbsp	curry powder	15 mL
1	can (28 oz/796 mL) diced tomatoes, with juice	1
3 cups	diced peeled sweet potatoes	750 mL
2 cups	chicken stock	500 mL
1	can (14 oz/400 mL) unsweetened coconut milk	1
⅔ cup	chunky peanut butter	150 mL
1 tbsp	packed brown sugar	15 mL

1. In a large pot, heat 1½ tsp (7 mL) of the oil over medium heat. Add turkey and sauté, breaking up with the back of a wooden spoon, until no longer pink, about 5 minutes. Season with ½ tsp (2 mL) of the salt and the black pepper. Remove with a slotted spoon to a plate lined with paper towels.
2. Drain the fat from the pot, add the remaining oil and heat over medium heat. Add onion and sauté until softened, about 6 minutes. Add garlic, ginger, hot pepper flakes and curry powder; sauté for 1 minute. Add tomatoes with juice, sweet potatoes and stock; bring to a boil. Cover, reduce heat to low and simmer gently until potatoes are almost tender, about 10 minutes. Whisk in coconut milk and peanut butter. Return turkey to the pot and stir in brown sugar and the remaining salt; simmer until sweet potatoes are tender and flavors are blended, about 20 minutes. Taste and adjust seasoning with salt and black pepper, if necessary.
3. Ladle into heated bowls.

Tom Kha Gai (Thai Chicken, Coconut and Lemongrass Soup)

▲▽▲▽▲▽▲▽▲▽▲▽▲▽▲▽▲▽▲▽▲▽▲▽▲▽▲▽▲▽▲▽▲▽▲▽▲

Rich, spicy and slightly sweet, this Thai soup is a favorite on restaurant menus. Tell your less-experienced friends that the lemongrass, galangal, lime leaves and chiles are only there to flavor the stock, not to be eaten.

▲▽▲▽▲▽▲▽▲

Tips

Wild lime leaves are often found in the herb section of fine grocery stores or at Asian markets. You may also find them in the frozen section. Wild lime leaves always come in pairs, with one leaf attached to the end of another. If you can't find it, substitute the grated zest of 1 lime with the lime juice.

Smash lemongrass pieces with the back of a knife to release the essential oils and aroma.

Serves 6

3 cups	chicken stock	750 mL
12	wild lime leaves (optional)	12
2	large stalks lemongrass, cut into 2-inch (5 cm) sections and bruised	2
1	thumb-sized knob galangal or gingerroot, sliced	1
2	cans (each 14 oz/400 mL) unsweetened coconut milk	2
1½ tbsp	Thai roasted chile paste (see tip, page 325)	22 mL
1 lb	boneless skinless chicken breasts, cut into bite-size pieces	500 g
1	can (14 oz/398 mL) straw mushrooms, drained	1
¼ cup	packed fresh cilantro leaves	50 mL
1½ tbsp	packed light brown sugar	22 mL
⅓ cup	freshly squeezed lime juice	75 mL
2 tbsp	fish sauce (nam pla)	25 mL
6	small hot chile peppers	6

1. In a large pot, bring stock, lime leaves (if using), lemongrass and galangal to a boil over medium heat. Reduce heat and simmer for 10 minutes. Add coconut milk and chile paste; simmer for 5 minutes. Add chicken and simmer until no longer pink inside, about 5 minutes. Stir in mushrooms, cilantro, brown sugar, lime juice and fish sauce.
2. Ladle into heated bowls and float chiles on top.

Spicy Thai Chicken, Coconut, Lemongrass and Noodle Soup

▲▽▲

This Thai version of chicken noodle soup is wonderful when you have a cold, but not because it's "liquid penicillin" like the traditional version. Rather, it is so spicy that it will surely clear your sinuses!

▲▽▲▽▲▽▲▽▲▽▲

Tips

Thai roasted chili paste, often found in soya bean oil (*nahm prik pao*), is made primarily from roasted red chiles and ground dried shrimp. It is often added to soups, stir-fries, noodle dishes and salad dressings. It can be found in Asian markets or the Asian section of your grocery store.

Chile peppers contain oils that can cause chemical burns on your skin. When seeding and chopping them, always wear latex, plastic or rubber gloves.

Serves 6 to 8

6 cups	chicken stock	1.5 L
12	wild lime leaves (optional, see tip, page 324)	12
2	large stalk lemongrass, cut into 2-inch (5 cm) sections and bruised (see tip, page 324)	2
1	thumb-sized knob galangal or gingerroot, sliced	1
1	can (14 oz/400 mL) unsweetened coconut milk	1
3 tbsp	Thai roasted chile paste (see tip, at left)	45 mL
1 lb	boneless skinless chicken breasts, cut into bite-size pieces	500 g
8 oz	mushrooms, thinly sliced	250 g
1	serrano or other hot green chile pepper, seeded and thinly sliced	1
¼ cup	packed fresh basil leaves (preferably purple Thai basil)	50 mL
2 tbsp	packed light brown sugar	25 mL
½ cup	freshly squeezed lime juice	125 mL
2½ tbsp	fish sauce (nam pla)	32 mL
6 oz	flat rice noodles	175 g

1. In a large pot, bring stock, lime leaves (if using), lemongrass and galangal to a boil over medium heat. Reduce heat and simmer for 10 minutes. Add coconut milk and chile paste; simmer for 5 minutes. Strain the stock and discard the lime leaves, lemongrass and galangal.

2. Return stock to a simmer over medium heat. Add chicken and mushrooms; reduce heat and simmer until chicken is no longer pink inside, about 5 minutes. Stir in chile pepper, basil, brown sugar, lime juice and fish sauce.

3. Meanwhile, in a large bowl, cover noodles with boiling water; soak until completely softened, about 15 minutes.

4. Drain noodles and divide among large heated bowls. Top with soup.

Tom Yum Gung (Thai Hot-and-Sour Shrimp and Lemongrass Soup)

▲▼▲

This lovely, light soup reflects perfectly the Thai sense of flavor balance. Sour, spicy, sweet and salty all come together for a soup that's as easy as it is flavorful. Because it's simple, it's even more important to balance the flavors correctly, so make sure you taste the soup before you serve it and adjust the seasonings if necessary.

▲▼▲▼▲▼▲▼▲▼

Tip
The lime leaves, chiles, galangal and lemongrass are present only to flavor the soup, not to be eaten.

Serves 6 to 8

6 cups	chicken stock or Chinese Chicken Stock (see recipe, page 12)	1.5 L
8	wild lime leaves (see tip, page 324)	8
4	small serrano or other hot green chile peppers, seeded and quartered lengthwise	4
1	thumb-sized knob galangal or gingerroot, thinly sliced	1
1	stalk lemongrass, cut into 2-inch (5 cm) sections and bruised (see tip, page 324)	1
1 tbsp	packed light brown sugar	15 mL
1½ tbsp	fish sauce (nam pla)	22 mL
12 oz	medium shrimp, peeled and deveined	375 g
8 oz	mushrooms, thinly sliced	250 g
¼ cup	freshly squeezed lime juice	50 mL
	Salt	

1. In a large pot, bring stock, lime leaves, chiles, galangal and lemongrass to a boil over medium heat. Reduce heat and simmer for 10 minutes. Add brown sugar and fish sauce; simmer for 5 minutes. Add shrimp and mushrooms; simmer until shrimp are pink and opaque, about 2 minutes. Remove from heat and stir in lime juice. Taste and adjust seasoning with sugar, fish sauce, lime juice and salt, if necessary.
2. Ladle into heated bowls.

Egg Drop Soup

▲▽▲

Almost everyone remembers egg drop soup from dinners with their parents at Chinese restaurants. It used to be the only thing we would take a chance on eating amid all the exotic plates displaying mu shu pork and moo goo gai pan. This simple soup, made with a flavorful Chinese chicken stock and enriched with eggs, is still a good choice today, even though we are no longer intimidated by General Tso's chicken.

Serves 6

8 cups	Chinese Chicken Stock (see recipe, page 12)	2 L
2 tbsp	cornstarch, dissolved in 3 tbsp (45 mL) cold water	25 mL
2	eggs, lightly beaten	2
	Salt and freshly ground black pepper	
2	green onions, thinly sliced	2
	Soy sauce (optional)	

1. In a large pot, bring stock to a boil over medium heat. Stir cornstarch mixture and gradually add to the stock, stirring constantly. Cook, stirring, until soup thickens slightly, about 2 minutes. Gradually drizzle in eggs and give the soup one more light stir. Remove from heat and season with salt and pepper to taste.
2. Ladle into heated bowls and garnish with green onions and a drizzle of soy sauce, if desired.

Pork and Scallion Wonton Soup

If you want to please someone, this soup is sure to bring a smile.

Tip

Five-spice powder is a blend of ground cloves, fennel seeds, cinnamon, star anise and Szechwan peppercorns. Most large grocery stores stock it, but if you can't find it, just use a mixture of the individual spices. It will still taste delicious.

Serves 6

- Baking sheet, lined with parchment paper

8 oz	regular or lean ground pork	250 g
4	green onions, minced, divided	4
1 tbsp	soy sauce	15 mL
½ tsp	five-spice powder (see tip, at left)	2 mL
¼ tsp	freshly ground black pepper	1 mL
24	wonton wrappers, thawed if frozen	24
1	egg, lightly beaten	1
8 cups	Chinese Chicken Stock (see recipe, page 12)	2 L

1. In a large bowl, combine pork, half the green onions, soy sauce, five-spice powder and pepper. Mix with your hands until well combined. To taste for seasoning, heat a small skillet over medium heat and fry a spoon-sized patty until no longer pink. Taste and adjust seasoning with soy sauce, five-spice powder and pepper, if necessary.

2. Place a rounded teaspoon (5 mL) of filling in the center of each wonton wrapper. Brush beaten egg around the edges of the wrapper. Lift two opposite corners together to form a triangle and enclose filling, pressing all edges firmly to eliminate air pockets and seal. Place wontons on prepared baking sheet, making sure they don't touch.

3. In a large pot, bring stock to a simmer over medium heat. Add wontons and simmer until wrappers are tender and filling is cooked through, about 8 minutes.

4. Ladle stock into heated bowls and top each with 4 wontons. Garnish with the remaining green onions.

Hot-and-Sour Soup

▲▽▲

When done right, hot-and-sour soup is a wonderful thing, with the perfect balance of spicy and tart. If you have a cold, this soup will set you right again.

▲▽▲▽▲▽▲▽▲▽

Tip

Filtering the mushroom liquid removes any dirt that may have been loosened from the mushrooms as they soaked.

Serves 6

¼ oz	dried shiitake mushrooms	7 g
½ cup	boiling water	125 mL
8 cups	Chinese Chicken Stock (see recipe, page 12)	2 L
1	can (8 oz/227 mL) bamboo shoots, drained and chopped	1
8 oz	boneless skinless chicken breasts, cut into thin strips	250 g
1½ cups	diced firm tofu	375 mL
⅓ cup	rice vinegar	75 mL
3 tbsp	soy sauce (or to taste)	45 mL
2 tsp	Asian sesame oil	10 mL
1 tsp	Chinese garlic chili sauce (or to taste)	5 mL
	Freshly ground black pepper	
3 tbsp	cornstarch, dissolved in 3 tbsp (45 mL) water	45 mL
2	eggs, beaten	2
2	green onions, minced	2

1. In a small bowl, soak mushrooms in boiling water until softened, about 30 minutes. Using a slotted spoon, gently lift mushrooms from liquid and swish in a bowl of cold water to remove any clinging sand or dirt. Remove and discard tough stems, squeeze mushrooms dry and thinly slice. Pour mushroom liquid through a sieve lined with a coffee filter into a small bowl.

2. In a large pot, bring stock, mushroom liquid, mushrooms, bamboo shoots and chicken to a simmer over medium heat. Add tofu, vinegar, soy sauce, sesame oil and chili sauce. Cook until chicken is no longer pink inside, about 5 minutes. Taste and adjust seasoning with soy sauce and pepper, if necessary. Stir cornstarch mixture and gradually add to the soup. Cook, stirring, until soup thickens slightly, about 2 minutes. Reduce heat to low and gradually drizzle in eggs, stirring gently. Do not let boil, or the egg strands will break up into egg curds.

3. Ladle into heated bowls and garnish with green onions.

Pho Bo (Vietnamese Beef and Noodle Soup)

▲▽▲▽▲▽▲▽▲▽▲▽▲▽▲▽▲▽▲▽▲▽▲▽▲▽▲▽▲▽▲▽▲▽▲▽▲

Pho is a traditional Vietnamese noodle soup typically served as a bowl of white rice noodles in clear, spiced beef stock, with thin cuts of meat or fish, bean sprouts, green onions and fresh herbs. In pho bo, *the beef is sliced paper-thin and cooked directly in the diner's bowl as the hot stock, infused with star anise and cinnamon, is poured over top.*

▲▽▲▽▲▽▲▽▲

Tip
Star anise and dried flat rice noodles are available at Asian markets.

Serves 4

8 oz	boneless beef sirloin, trimmed of fat	250 g
3	¼ inch (0.5 cm) thick slices gingerroot	3
1	onion (unpeeled), halved	1
8 cups	beef stock	2 L
2	whole star anise	2
1	stick cinnamon, about 4 inches (10 cm) long	1
4 oz	flat rice noodles	125 g
2 tbsp	fish sauce (nam pla)	25 mL
2 tsp	packed light brown sugar	10 mL
½ tsp	salt	2 mL
Pinch	freshly ground black pepper	Pinch
1	serrano or other hot green chile pepper, seeded and thinly sliced	1
1 cup	bean sprouts, rinsed	250 mL
½ cup	loosely packed fresh basil leaves	125 mL
¼ cup	thinly sliced green onions	50 mL
4	lime wedges	4

1. Place beef in the freezer for 20 minutes.
2. Heat a dry heavy skillet over medium-high heat. Add ginger and onion; sauté until blackened in spots on all sides, about 5 minutes.
3. In a large pot, bring stock, blackened ginger and onion, star anise and cinnamon stick to a boil. Reduce heat and simmer for 15 minutes to blend the flavors. Strain the stock (see page 8) and discard all solids. Return to pot.
4. With a very sharp knife, cut partially frozen beef across the grain into paper-thin slices. Set aside.
5. In a large bowl, cover noodles with boiling water; soak until completely softened, about 15 minutes.
6. Return stock to a boil over medium-high heat. Stir in fish sauce, brown sugar, salt and pepper. Taste and adjust seasoning with salt and pepper, if necessary.
7. Drain noodles and divide among large heated bowls. Top with slices of raw beef. Pour 2 cups (500 mL) stock into each bowl. Garnish with chile pepper, bean sprouts, basil, green onion and lime wedges. Diners may squeeze the lime over their soup, if they desire.

Pho Ga (Vietnamese Chicken and Noodle Soup)

▲▽▲▽▲▽▲▽▲▽▲▽▲▽▲▽▲▽▲▽▲▽▲▽▲▽▲▽▲▽▲▽▲

Don't let the ingredient list fool you: this traditional Vietnamese comfort food is easy to make and wonderfully impressive to serve. We like to serve both the beef and the chicken pho *when we're entertaining and let our guests do their own garnishing with the bean sprouts, green onions, chiles and herbs.*

▲▽▲▽▲▽▲▽▲▽▲

Tip

Chile peppers contain oils that can cause chemical burns on your skin. When seeding and chopping them, always wear latex, plastic or rubber gloves.

Serves 4

1	4-inch (10 cm) piece gingerroot (unpeeled)	1
1	onion (unpeeled), halved	1
8 cups	chicken stock	2 L
1 lb	chicken wings	500 g
2	whole star anise	2
1	stick cinnamon, about 4 inches (10 cm) long	1
4 oz	flat rice noodles	125 g
2 tbsp	fish sauce (nam pla)	25 mL
2 tsp	packed light brown sugar	10 mL
½ tsp	salt	2 mL
Pinch	freshly ground black pepper	Pinch
2	boneless skinless chicken breasts (about 1 lb/500 g total), cooked and thinly sliced	2
1	serrano or other hot green chile pepper, seeded and thinly sliced	1
1 cup	bean sprouts, rinsed	250 mL
¼ cup	thinly sliced green onions	50 mL
¼ cup	loosely packed fresh mint leaves	50 mL
¼ cup	loosely packed fresh cilantro leaves	50 mL
4	lime wedges	4

1. Heat a dry heavy skillet over medium-high heat. Add ginger and onion; sauté until blackened in spots on all sides, about 5 minutes.
2. In a large pot, bring stock, chicken wings, blackened ginger and onion, star anise and cinnamon stick to a boil. Reduce heat and simmer for 45 minutes. Skim the fat with a large spoon. Strain the stock (see page 8) and discard all solids.
3. In a large bowl, cover noodles with boiling water; soak until completely softened, about 15 minutes.
4. Bring stock to a boil over medium-high heat. Stir in fish sauce, brown sugar, salt and pepper. Taste and adjust seasoning with salt and pepper, if necessary.
5. Drain noodles and divide among large heated bowls. Top with slices of cooked chicken. Pour 2 cups (500 mL) stock into each bowl. Garnish with chile pepper, bean sprouts, green onions, mint, cilantro and lime wedges. Diners may squeeze the lime over their soup, if they desire.

Pho Tom (Vietnamese Shrimp and Noodle Soup)

▲▽▲▽▲▽▲▽▲▽▲▽▲▽▲▽▲▽▲▽▲▽▲▽▲▽▲▽▲▽▲▽▲▽▲▽▲

This pho *is light and flavorful with shrimp, garlic and fresh herbs.*

▲▽▲▽▲▽▲▽▲▽▲

Tip

Star anise and dried flat rice noodles are available at Asian markets.

Serves 6

10 cups	shellfish stock	2.5 L
1 lb	medium shrimp, peeled, deveined and halved lengthwise, shells reserved	500 g
2	cloves garlic, crushed	2
1	onion, sliced	1
1	4-inch (10 cm) piece gingerroot (unpeeled), thinly sliced	1
8	whole black peppercorns	8
2	whole star anise	2
1	stick cinnamon, about 4 inches (10 cm) long	1
4 oz	flat rice noodles	125 g
2 tbsp	fish sauce (nam pla)	25 mL
2 tsp	packed light brown sugar	10 mL
½ tsp	salt	2 mL
Pinch	freshly ground black pepper	Pinch
1	serrano or other hot green chile pepper, seeded and thinly sliced	1
1 cup	bean sprouts, rinsed	250 mL
¼ cup	thinly sliced green onions	50 mL
¼ cup	loosely packed fresh mint leaves	50 mL
¼ cup	loosely packed fresh cilantro leaves	50 mL
1	lime, cut into 6 wedges	1

1. In a large pot, bring stock, shrimp shells, garlic, onion, ginger, peppercorns, star anise and cinnamon stick to a simmer over medium heat. Reduce heat and simmer for 20 minutes to blend the flavors. Strain the stock (see page 8) and discard all solids.
2. In a large bowl, cover noodles with boiling water; soak until completely softened, about 15 minutes.
3. Bring stock to a boil over medium-high heat. Stir in fish sauce, brown sugar, salt and pepper. Taste and adjust seasoning with salt and pepper, if necessary. Add shrimp and cook until pink and opaque, about 1 minute. Remove shrimp with a slotted spoon to a plate and keep warm.
4. Drain noodles and divide among large heated bowls. Top with shrimp. Pour 2 cups (500 mL) stock into each bowl. Garnish with chile pepper, bean sprouts, green onions, mint, cilantro and lime wedges. Diners may squeeze the lime over their soup.

Miso Soup

▲▼▲

Miso soup is the cornerstone of many Japanese meals. It finds its way into breakfast, lunch and dinner because its nourishing, comforting stock is easy to make and lovely to eat.

▲▼▲▼▲▼▲▼▲▼▲

Tip

Wakame is available at Asian markets.

Serves 4 to 6

3 tbsp	instant wakame (seaweed)	45 mL
6 cups	Ichiban Dashi stock (see recipe, page 18)	1.5 L
6 tbsp	sweet white miso paste	90 mL
8 oz	firm tofu, cut into ½-inch (1 cm) cubes	250 g
⅓ cup	chopped green onions	75 mL

1. Soak wakame in cold water for 5 minutes; drain.
2. In a large pot, bring stock to a boil over medium heat. Add miso and stir until dissolved. Add tofu and bring to a simmer. Remove from heat and stir in green onions and wakame.
3. Ladle into heated bowls.

Udon or Soba Noodles in Stock

In Japan, these soft noodles, swimming in a stock flavored with soy sauce and ginger, are typically served with an assortment of accompaniments. Try cooked chicken, ham, fried tofu, slices of hard-boiled egg or any kind of cooked vegetable.

Tip

Be careful not to overcook the noodles.

Serves 4

8 oz	dried udon or soba noodles	250 g
6 cups	Ichiban Dashi stock (see recipe, page 18)	1.5 L
1	thumb-sized knob gingerroot, thinly sliced	1
1½ tbsp	granulated sugar	22 mL
¼ cup	soy sauce	50 mL
1 tbsp	sake or sherry	15 mL
4	green onions, thinly sliced	4

1. Cook noodles according to package directions. Drain and rinse under cold water.
2. In a large pot, heat stock, ginger, sugar, soy sauce and sake over medium heat until steaming, about 5 minutes.
3. Divide noodles among heated bowls and top with stock. Garnish with green onions.

Just Dessert Soups

▲▽▲▽▲▽▲▽▲▽▲▽▲▽▲▽▲▽▲▽▲▽▲▽▲▽▲▽▲▽▲▽

Gingered Crème Anglaise Soup with Chocolate Pavé

▲▽▲

Make this sinfully rich dessert soup for an unforgettable ending to a special evening. Typically, chocolate pavé is served with crème anglaise; we are serving crème anglaise with chocolate pavé, making the crème anglaise the main attraction. If you've ever felt like just drinking crème anglaise, this is your chance to spoon it up to your heart's content.

▲▽▲▽▲▽▲▽▲▽

Tips

Whole milk is important for this recipe as fresh ginger can curdle lower-fat milk.

Chocolate pavé (pah-vay) is a classic French concoction made of chocolate and cream. It is usually made into a larger loaf, cut and served on a plate in a shallow pool of crème anglaise. It is sometimes garnished with raspberries to cut the richness.

Serves 6

Miniature loaf pan, lined with plastic wrap (see tip, opposite)

Soup

3 cups	whole milk	750 mL
2	thumb-sized knobs gingerroot, cut into quarter-sized pieces	2
1	vanilla bean, split lengthwise	1
6	egg yolks	6
⅓ cup	granulated sugar	75 mL
¼ tsp	salt	1 mL
1 cup	whipping (35%) cream	250 mL
	Raspberry Coulis (optional, see recipe, page 366)	
	Chopped candied ginger	

Chocolate Pavé

½ cup	whipping (35%) cream	125 mL
4 oz	bittersweet chocolate, chopped	125 g
¼ cup	chopped candied ginger	50 mL

1. *Prepare the soup:* In a large saucepan, heat milk, ginger and vanilla bean over medium-high heat until a skin forms on top of the milk, about 3 minutes. Remove from heat, cover and let steep for 30 minutes to blend the flavors.

2. Carefully remove the vanilla bean and let cool slightly. Using the flat side of a knife, scrape out seeds. Strain milk and discard ginger. Add vanilla seeds to milk and stir. Discard scraped bean.

3. In a large bowl, whisk together egg yolks, sugar and salt. Gradually whisk in milk mixture, in a steady stream. Return to the pan and cook over medium heat, stirring constantly, until slightly thickened, about 4 minutes. Do not let boil or the mixture will curdle. Remove from heat and stir in cream. Transfer to a large bowl, cover and refrigerate until chilled, about 3 hours.

Tips

The idea here is to create a loaf-shaped pavé. We pulled up the plastic wrap on one side of a 4½- by 2¾-inch (11 by 7 cm) loaf pan to make the shape narrower but taller. If you have the lid of a narrow butter dish, use that; it will give you a more neatly shaped pavé.

The soup can be prepared through Step 3 up to 1 day ahead. The pavé can be prepared through Step 4 up to 2 days ahead.

4. *Prepare the pavé:* In a saucepan, bring cream to a simmer over medium-high heat. Remove from heat and add chocolate. Let stand for 2 minutes, then whisk until melted and smooth. Stir in candied ginger. Pour into prepared loaf pan and refrigerate until firm, about 3 hours.

5. Using the plastic wrap, pull the pavé from the pan and peel off the plastic. Cut into ½-inch (1 cm) slices.

6. Ladle soup into chilled bowls. If using raspberry coulis, pour it into a squeeze bottle with a narrow tip. Squeeze dots of coulis around the edge of the bowls and drag a skewer or toothpick through the center of the dots, in a circular motion, to create a ring of hearts in the soup. Place a slice of pavé in the middle of each bowl. Garnish with candied ginger.

Blueberry Soup with Yogurt Swirl

▲▽▲

Because blueberries aren't always in season, we wanted to try using frozen blueberries to make a dessert soup. We couldn't believe that frozen fruit could compete with the season's best, but we were thrilled with the outcome.

▲▽▲▽▲▽▲▽▲▽▲

Tip

The soup can be prepared through Step 2 up to 1 day ahead.

Serves 6

2 tbsp	water	25 mL
1 tsp	powdered unflavored gelatin	5 mL
3	packages (each 12 oz/375 g) frozen blueberries (5 cups/1.25 L)	3
2 cups	white grape juice	500 mL
2 tbsp	freshly squeezed lemon juice	25 mL
¼ tsp	ground cinnamon	1 mL
Pinch	salt	Pinch
	Yogurt Swirl (see recipe, page 364)	
	Fresh mint leaves (optional)	

1. In a microwave-safe dish, combine water and gelatin and let soften for 5 minutes. Microwave on High for 20 seconds, stir and then microwave on High for another 20 seconds to melt the gelatin.

2. In a food processor or blender, purée gelatin mixture, blueberries, grape juice, lemon juice, cinnamon and salt until smooth and creamy. Strain into a large bowl, cover and refrigerate until chilled, about 2 hours.

3. Ladle into chilled bowls and top with yogurt swirl. Draw a chopstick or knife through the yogurt to create a decorative swirl. Garnish with mint leaves, if desired.

Blueberry Soup with Lemon Verbena in Cantaloupe Bowl

We just had to include this recipe, which incorporates one of our favorite herbs, lemon verbena.

Tips

The soup can be prepared through Step 1 up to 1 day ahead.

Lemon verbena is light green with narrow pointed leaves and lilac-colored blossoms. We usually grow it in our summer herb patch. We love to use verbena in soups, muffins, biscuits and scones, or just add a sprig to a glass of iced tea. If you can't find it, just add 1 tbsp (15 mL) grated lemon zest in its place.

Serves 6

4 cups	blueberries	1 L
2 cups	seedless red grapes	500 mL
1 cup	white grape juice	250 mL
1/3 cup	granulated sugar	75 mL
1/4 cup	packed lemon verbena leaves	50 mL
2 tbsp	freshly squeezed lemon juice	25 mL
Pinch	salt	Pinch
Pinch	ground nutmeg	Pinch
3	small cantaloupes, halved and seeded	3
	Vanilla ice cream	
	Lemon verbena leaves (optional)	

1. In a food processor or blender, purée blueberries, grapes, grape juice, sugar, lemon verbena, lemon juice, salt and nutmeg until smooth. Strain into a large bowl, cover and refrigerate until chilled, about 3 hours.
2. Cut a small slice from the rounded bottom of each cantaloupe so that it sits securely. Place on a tray, cover and refrigerate until ready to serve.
3. Ladle soup into cantaloupe bowls and top each with a small scoop of ice cream. Garnish with lemon verbena, if desired.

Blackberry and White Chocolate Soup

▲▽▲▽▲▽▲▽▲▽▲▽▲▽▲▽▲▽▲▽▲▽▲▽▲▽▲▽▲▽▲▽▲▽▲▽▲▽▲

Tart blackberries pair wonderfully with rich, creamy white chocolate crème anglaise. The real beauty of this soup lies in the yin/yang presentation. It's a dramatic dessert worthy of the most elegant dinner party.

▲▽▲▽▲▽▲▽▲▽

Tip

The soup can be prepared through Step 1 up to 1 day ahead.

Serves 6

6 cups	blackberries	1.5 L
1 cup	white grape juice	250 mL
½ cup	granulated sugar	125 mL
1 tbsp	grated lemon zest	15 mL
1 tbsp	freshly squeezed lemon juice	15 mL
Pinch	salt	Pinch
	White Chocolate Crème Anglaise Swirl (see variation, page 366), chilled	
	Fresh mint leaves (optional)	

1. In a food processor or blender, purée blackberries, grape juice, sugar, lemon zest, lemon juice and salt until smooth. Strain into a large pitcher, cover and refrigerate until chilled, about 3 hours.
2. Pour crème anglaise into another pitcher or a measuring cup with a spout. Pour blackberry soup and crème anglaise simultaneously into chilled bowls so that the blackberry soup is on one half of the bowl and the crème anglaise is on the other half. Garnish with mint, if desired.

Raspberry and White Chocolate Swirl Soup with Brownie Croutons

▲▽▲

Tart and sweet raspberry soup is matched perfectly with the rich creaminess of white chocolate. Dark, intensely chocolate brownie croutons make the perfect accompaniment.

▲▽▲▽▲▽▲▽▲▽▲

Tip

The soup can be prepared through Step 2 up to 1 day ahead.

Serves 6

2	packages (each 12 oz/375 g) unsweetened frozen raspberries (about 3 cups/750 mL)	2
1¼ cups	water	300 mL
½ cup	granulated sugar	125 mL
½ cup	seedless raspberry jam	125 mL
2 tbsp	Grand Marnier, divided	25 mL
½ cup	whipping (35%) cream	125 mL
4 oz	white chocolate, chopped	125 g
	Brownie Croutons (see recipe, page 374)	

1. In a small saucepan, bring raspberries, water and sugar to a boil over medium heat. Reduce heat and simmer, stirring occasionally, until sugar is dissolved and raspberries have softened or broken down, about 4 minutes.
2. In a food processor or blender, purée raspberry mixture, jam and 1 tbsp (15 mL) of the Grand Marnier until smooth. Strain into a large bowl, cover and refrigerate until chilled, about 3 hours.
3. In another saucepan, bring cream to a simmer over medium-high heat. Remove from heat and add white chocolate. Let stand for 2 minutes, then whisk until melted and smooth. Stir in the remaining Grand Marnier. Let cool.
4. Ladle raspberry soup into chilled shallow bowls. Gently drop 5 to 6 spoonfuls of the white chocolate mixture onto the soup. Draw a chopstick or knife through the chocolate mixture to create a marbled effect. Serve with brownie croutons.

Strawberry Soup with Crème Anglaise Swirl

▲▼▲▼▲▼▲▼▲▼▲▼▲▼▲▼▲▼▲▼▲▼▲▼▲▼▲▼▲▼▲▼▲▼▲▼▲▼▲

Nothing could be simpler than this hot weather favorite. It is light, yet sinful with the addition of rich crème anglaise.

▲▼▲▼▲▼▲▼▲▼

Tip

The soup can be prepared through Step 1 up to 1 day ahead.

Serves 6

3	packages (each 10 oz/300 g) frozen strawberries in syrup, thawed	3
1 cup	dry white wine	250 mL
¼ tsp	balsamic vinegar	1 mL
Pinch	salt	Pinch
½ cup	Crème Anglaise Swirl (see recipe, page 366)	125 mL

1. In a food processor or blender, purée strawberries and syrup, wine, vinegar and salt until smooth. Transfer to a large bowl, cover and refrigerate until ready to serve.
2. Pour crème anglaise into a measuring cup with a spout. Ladle soup into chilled bowls. Beginning in the center of the soup, pour in crème anglaise, creating a swirl. If desired, create a cobweb design by drawing a chopstick or knife from the center of the design out to the edge of the bowl, then dragging the chopstick from the outer edge back into the center.

Strawberry Soup
with Rhubarb Compote

▲▼▲▼▲▼▲▼▲▼▲▼▲▼▲▼▲▼▲▼▲▼▲▼▲▼▲▼▲▼▲▼▲▼▲▼▲

*We had great success
using organic
strawberries and find
that they usually have
the best flavor.*

▲▼▲▼▲▼▲▼▲

Tip
Chilled soups will stay
cold for much longer in
chilled bowls.

Serves 6 to 8

1 lb	strawberries, quartered (about 3 cups/750 mL)	500 g
¾ cup	granulated sugar, divided	175 mL
½ cup	freshly squeezed orange juice	125 mL
1 tbsp	balsamic vinegar	15 mL
Pinch	salt	Pinch
2 cups	sliced rhubarb (trimmed, quartered lengthwise and thinly sliced)	500 mL
⅓ cup	water	75 mL
¼ cup	plain yogurt	50 mL
	Fresh mint sprigs (optional)	

1. In a large bowl, combine strawberries, ¼ cup (50 mL) of the sugar, orange juice, vinegar and salt. Cover and refrigerate until chilled, about 2 hours.
2. In a saucepan, bring the remaining sugar, rhubarb and water to a simmer over medium heat. Cover, reduce heat to low and simmer gently until rhubarb is tender, about 10 minutes. Uncover and cook until slightly thickened, about 2 minutes. Let cool.
3. In a food processor or blender, purée strawberry mixture and yogurt until smooth.
4. Ladle soup into chilled bowls, top with rhubarb compote and garnish with mint sprigs, if desired.

Champagne and Strawberry Soup

▲▽▲▽▲▽▲▽▲▽▲▽▲▽▲▽▲▽▲▽▲▽▲▽▲▽▲▽▲▽▲▽▲▽▲▽▲▽▲

Make this refreshing, not too sweet soup when strawberries are at their peak, and you will be rewarded with the summer's best flavor.

▲▽▲▽▲▽▲▽▲

Tips

The soup can be prepared through Step 2 up to 1 day ahead.

No need to break the bank on a fine sparkling wine here. The key is to use a brut sparkling wine; demi-sec will be too sweet. We used Freixenet Cordon Negro Brut with great results. The remaining sparkling wine can be served in champagne flutes along with the soup.

Serves 6

2 lbs	strawberries, thinly sliced (about 6 cups/1.5 L)	1 kg
½ cup	granulated sugar	125 mL
½ cup	cold unsweetened apple juice	125 mL
½ cup	whipping (35%) cream	125 mL
1½ cups	chilled dry Champagne or sparkling wine	375 mL
1 tsp	freshly squeezed lemon juice	5 mL

1. Divide strawberries and sugar between two large bowls and toss to coat. Cover and refrigerate until sugar is melted and mixture is chilled, about 2 hours.
2. In a food processor or blender, purée one bowl of the strawberries, apple juice and whipping cream until smooth. Transfer to a large bowl, cover and refrigerate until chilled, about 2 hours.
3. Gently whisk Champagne and lemon juice into the strawberry purée.
4. Divide the sliced strawberries among 6 chilled bowls and top with strawberry purée.

Chilled Cherry Soup

▲▽▲▽▲▽▲▽▲▽▲▽▲▽▲▽▲▽▲▽▲▽▲▽▲▽▲▽▲▽▲▽▲▽▲▽▲▽▲

To add dimension to this soup, we simmer the apple juice with cinnamon, peppercorns and allspice. Don't forget to remove the spices before serving!

▲▽▲▽▲▽▲▽▲

Tip

The soup can be prepared through Step 3 up to 1 day ahead.

Serves 6

2 cups	unsweetened apple juice	500 mL
¼ cup	liquid honey	50 mL
5	whole black peppercorns	5
5	whole allspice	5
1	stick cinnamon, about 4 inches (10 cm) long	1
1½ lbs	tart cherries, pitted (about 4 cups/1 L)	750 g
2 tsp	freshly squeezed lemon juice	10 mL
1 tbsp	cornstarch, dissolved in 2 tbsp (25 mL) water	15 mL
	Almond Crème Anglaise Swirl (see variation, page 366)	
	Toasted sliced almonds	

1. In a large saucepan, bring apple juice, honey, peppercorns, allspice and cinnamon stick to a simmer over medium heat. Reduce heat and simmer for 5 minutes. Remove from heat, cover and let steep for 30 minutes to blend the flavors.
2. Strain the apple juice mixture and return to the pan. Add cherries and lemon juice; bring to a simmer over medium heat. Stir in cornstarch mixture and simmer, stirring often, until cherries are tender and soup has thickened slightly, about 10 minutes.
3. Transfer to a food processor or blender, in batches, and purée until smooth. Strain into a large bowl, cover and refrigerate until chilled, about 3 hours.
4. Ladle into chilled bowls and top with crème anglaise. Draw a chopstick or knife through the crème to create a decorative swirl. Sprinkle with almonds.

White Grape Gazpacho

▲▽▲▽▲▽▲▽▲▽▲▽▲▽▲▽▲▽▲▽▲▽▲▽▲▽▲▽▲▽▲▽▲

There is nothing we would rather have for dessert on a hot day than this refreshing jellied soup. The spices and wine impart an addictive flavor, while the cold, slightly crisp grapes add just a touch of texture.

▲▽▲▽▲▽▲▽▲▽

Tips

The soup can be prepared through Step 2 up to 1 day ahead.

If you want a sweeter soup, try using a sweeter wine, such as a Muscat or Riesling.

Serves 6

2 cups	white grape juice	500 mL
1 cup	dry white wine	250 mL
¼ cup	granulated sugar	50 mL
Pinch	ground nutmeg	Pinch
5	whole black peppercorns	5
1	whole star anise	1
1	stick cinnamon, about 4 inches (10 cm) long	1
1	envelope (¼ oz/7 g) powdered unflavored gelatin	1
2 tbsp	water	25 mL
1 tsp	grated lemon zest	5 mL
1 tsp	grated orange zest	5 mL
2 cups	mixed seedless grapes, halved	500 mL

1. In a saucepan, bring grape juice, wine, sugar, nutmeg, peppercorns, star anise and cinnamon stick to a simmer over medium heat. Reduce heat and simmer for 5 minutes. Remove from heat, cover and let steep for 10 minutes to blend the flavors.

2. Meanwhile, sprinkle gelatin over water and let soften for 5 minutes. Add to soup and stir until gelatin has dissolved. Strain into a large bowl and stir in lemon and orange zests. Place in a larger bowl filled with ice and water. Stir occasionally until soup begins to thicken slightly, then stir in grapes. Cover and refrigerate until chilled, about 2 hours.

3. Ladle soup into chilled bowls.

Orange Muscat Soup with Mascarpone Cream

▲▼▲▼▲▼▲▼▲▼▲▼▲▼▲▼▲▼▲▼▲▼▲▼▲▼▲▼▲▼▲▼▲▼▲▼▲▼▲

Muscat is a sweet wine with subtle honey and floral notes. Here, we pour it over cold citrus sections to make an easy but delectable soup. The sweetened mascarpone gives it a creaminess that reminds us of the best orange ice pop we ever tasted.

▲▼▲▼▲▼▲▼▲

Tip

To properly section an orange or grapefruit, hold the peeled fruit in the palm of one hand and the knife in the other. Run the knife on the right side of a section next to the right membrane, and then on the left side of the section next to the left membrane. This should free the section. Repeat with the remaining fruit.

Serves 6

6	navel oranges	6
2	ruby red grapefruit	2
2/3 cup	granulated sugar, divided	150 mL
1 tsp	vanilla extract	5 mL
Pinch	salt	Pinch
8 oz	mascarpone cheese, softened	250 g
2 tbsp	Grand Marnier	25 mL
1 tbsp	freshly squeezed lemon juice	15 mL
1½ cups	Muscat wine	375 mL

1. Using a knife, remove peels from oranges and grapefruit, including the white pith, reserving peels. Working with one piece of fruit at a time and holding it over a large bowl, cut into sections (see tip, at left), letting juice run into the bowl. Squeeze reserved peels and membranes over bowl to extract any remaining juice, then discard. Using a slotted spoon, transfer orange and grapefruit sections to another large bowl.

2. Stir ½ cup (125 mL) of the sugar, vanilla and salt into the juice. Pour over fruit, cover and refrigerate until chilled, at least 1 hour or for up to 4 hours.

3. In a small bowl, combine the remaining sugar, mascarpone, Grand Marnier and lemon juice.

4. Divide orange mixture among 6 chilled bowls, pour ¼ cup (50 mL) Muscat over each and top each with a dollop of sweetened mascarpone.

Peach Melba Soup with Raspberry Swirl and Almond Biscotti

▲▽

If you're looking for a dessert that's sure to impress, look no further — this spin on traditional peach melba will no doubt fit the bill. We purée our fabulous wine-poached peaches to make a mouth-watering soup. Then we add a spectacular swirl of raspberry sauce and a scoop of vanilla ice cream. Just for fun, we've used the poaching liquid to create a lovely rose-colored syrup to drizzle on top. Serve with almond biscotti, and you couldn't ask for anything better.

Serves 6

4	peaches	4
2 cups	white dessert wine (or a sweet Riesling)	500 mL
2 cups	water	500 mL
1 cup	granulated sugar	250 mL
	Grated zest of 1 lemon	
2 cups	raspberries	500 mL
1 tbsp	confectioner's (icing) sugar	15 mL
1 tbsp	freshly squeezed lemon juice	15 mL
	Good-quality vanilla ice cream	
	Raspberries	
	Fresh mint sprigs	
	Almond Biscotti (see recipe, page 374)	

1. Using a paring knife, score an X on the bottom of each peach. In a saucepan, combine wine, water, sugar and lemon zest. Add peaches and bring to a boil over medium-high heat. Reduce heat and simmer gently, turning peaches occasionally to ensure even cooking, until skin is slightly loosened, about 5 minutes. Remove peaches from syrup and let cool slightly.

2. Return syrup to high heat and bring to a boil. Boil until reduced by half, about 15 minutes. Remove from heat and set aside.

3. Meanwhile, peel and halve peaches, discarding pits and peels. In a food processor or blender, purée peaches and 1 cup (250 mL) of the syrup until smooth. Transfer to a large bowl, cover and refrigerate until chilled, about 4 hours.

4. In clean food processor or blender, purée raspberries, $\frac{1}{2}$ cup (125 mL) of the syrup, confectioner's sugar and lemon juice until smooth. Strain through a fine-mesh sieve into a large bowl, cover and refrigerate for at least 2 hours or until ready to serve. Refrigerate remaining syrup separately.

Tip

The soup can be prepared through Step 4 up to 1 day ahead.

5. In a saucepan, bring the remaining syrup to a boil over medium heat. Boil until syrup is the consistency of maple syrup, about 10 minutes. (You will have about ¾ cup/175 mL reduced syrup.) Let cool.

6. Ladle peach soup into chilled shallow bowls and top each with a few spoonfuls of raspberry sauce. Draw a chopstick or knife through the raspberry sauce to create a marble effect. Top with ice cream and drizzle with reduced syrup. Garnish with raspberries and mint sprigs. Serve with almond biscotti on the side.

Chilled Minted Melon Soup

▲▼▲▼▲▼▲▼▲▼▲▼▲▼▲▼▲▼▲▼▲▼▲▼▲▼▲▼▲▼▲▼▲▼▲▼▲

Chilled melon soup is very refreshing on a hot summer day when the last thing you want to do is heat up your kitchen. Surprise your guests by serving this instead of sliced melon at your next brunch.

▲▼▲▼▲▼▲▼▲

Tip

The soup can be prepared through Step 2 up to 1 day ahead.

Serves 4

1	large honeydew melon, cut into 1-inch (2.5 cm) pieces	1
½ cup	loosely packed fresh mint leaves, chopped	125 mL
¼ cup	granulated sugar	50 mL
3 tbsp	freshly squeezed lime juice	45 mL
Pinch	salt	Pinch
4	fresh mint sprigs (optional)	4

1. In a large bowl, combine melon, chopped mint, sugar, lime juice and salt. Let stand for 15 minutes.
2. In a food processor or blender, purée soup until smooth. Transfer to a large bowl, cover and refrigerate until chilled, about 3 hours.
3. Ladle into chilled bowls and garnish with mint sprigs.

Champagne Sabayon
with Summer Fruit Compote

▲▽▲▽▲▽▲▽▲▽▲▽▲▽▲▽▲▽▲▽▲▽▲▽▲▽▲▽▲▽▲▽

As far as we're concerned, nothing completes a summer dinner on the patio like this refreshing fruit and sabayon dessert. Use whatever fruit looks best at the market, choosing those with bright, contrasting colors, and you will present your guests with a piece of art in a bowl.

▲▽▲▽▲▽▲▽▲▽

Tips

To prevent sliced nectarines and plums from browning, sprinkle them with lemon juice after slicing. Drain before use.

It may not seem like it, but you will need a large bowl in Step 3 — the contents will triple in volume.

Serves 6

2	nectarines, thinly sliced	2
2	kiwifruit, thinly sliced	2
2	plums or pluots, thinly sliced	2
2 cups	blackberries	500 mL
2 cups	water	500 mL
6	egg yolks	6
⅓ cup	granulated sugar	75 mL
⅔ cup	Champagne	150 mL
¾ cup	whipping (35%) cream	175 mL
	Fresh mint sprigs (optional)	

1. In a large bowl, combine nectarines, kiwis, plums and blackberries. Cover and refrigerate until chilled or for up to 2 hours.
2. In a large saucepan, bring water to a simmer over medium-high heat.
3. Meanwhile, choose a large stainless steel or heatproof glass bowl that will fit over the top of the simmering water without touching the water. Off the heat, add egg yolks and sugar to the bowl and whisk until thickened and pale yellow, about 1 minute. Whisk in Champagne and place bowl over simmering water, adjusting heat as necessary to keep water at a simmer. Whisk quickly and steadily until sabayon gains volume and becomes light and fluffy, 6 to 10 minutes. When sabayon is hot and no longer liquid at the bottom of the bowl, remove saucepan from heat and whisk for 1 minute. Let cool to room temperature.
4. In a chilled bowl, beat cream until stiff peaks form. Fold into sabayon. Serve immediately or cover and refrigerate for up to 4 hours.
5. Divide fruit among 6 chilled shallow bowls and pour sabayon over top. Garnish with mint, if desired.

Chilled Stone Fruit Soup

▲▼▲

Stone fruits such as apricots, nectarines, plums and peaches can be so sweet and flavorful when in season. This simple recipe is designed to highlight their peak flavor. Look for fruit that smells fragrant and yields slightly to pressure. As always, buy locally whenever possible for the best flavor.

▲▼▲▼▲▼▲▼▲

Tip

The soup can be prepared through Step 2 up to 6 hours ahead.

Serves 6

3 lbs	apricots, plums, peaches and/or nectarines, coarsely chopped (about 7½ cups/1.875 L)	1.5 kg
2 cups	unsweetened apple juice	500 mL
¼ cup	granulated sugar (approx.)	50 mL
2 tbsp	liquid honey	25 mL
¼ tsp	ground cinnamon	1 mL
Pinch	salt	Pinch
	Vanilla ice cream or vanilla-flavored yogurt (optional)	

1. In a large saucepan, bring fruit, apple juice, sugar, honey, cinnamon and salt to a simmer over medium-high heat. Cover, reduce heat to low and simmer gently until fruit is tender, 10 to 15 minutes.
2. In a food processor or blender, in batches, purée soup until smooth and creamy. Taste and add up to 2 tbsp (25 mL) sugar if necessary. Strain into a large bowl, cover and refrigerate until chilled, about 3 hours.
3. Ladle into chilled bowls and top with ice cream, if desired.

Pho Tom (Vietnamese Shrimp and Noodle Soup) (page 332)

Overleaf: Raspberry and White Chocolate Swirl Soup with Brownie Croutons (page 341)

Banana Soup with Raspberry and Mint Relish

▲▽▲

Here's the perfect recipe to use up too-ripe bananas that no one wants to eat. If all the ingredients are chilled, this soup takes only minutes to prepare.

▲▽▲▽▲▽▲▽▲▽▲

Tip

The soup can be prepared up to 2 hours ahead; cover and refrigerate until ready to serve.

Variation

For a smoothie-like rendition of this summer cooler, add 1 cup (250 mL) yogurt and reduce the apple juice by half.

Serves 6

4	chilled very ripe bananas, halved	4
2 cups	chilled unsweetened apple juice	500 mL
½ cup	chilled freshly squeezed orange juice	125 mL
2 tbsp	freshly squeezed lemon juice (approx.)	25 mL
Pinch	salt	Pinch
2 tbsp	liquid honey (optional)	25 mL
1	very ripe banana, diced	1
1 cup	raspberries	250 mL
2 tbsp	chopped fresh mint	25 mL

1. In a food processor or blender, purée halved bananas and apple juice until smooth. Transfer to a large bowl and stir in orange juice, lemon juice and salt. Taste and add honey or more lemon juice if necessary.
2. In a small bowl, combine diced banana, raspberries and mint.
3. Ladle soup into chilled bowls and top with raspberry and mint relish.

Crispy Tortilla Strips (page 372), Pistou (page 363), Avocado and Grape Tomato Salsa (page 364) and Aïoli (page 362)

Overleaf: Strawberry Soup with Crème Anglaise Swirl (page 342)

Coconut Soup with Crispy Mango Wontons

▲▼▲▼▲▼▲▼▲▼▲▼▲▼▲▼▲▼▲▼▲▼▲▼▲▼▲▼▲▼▲▼▲▼▲▼▲▼▲

You're going to love this simple dessert soup, redolent with the flavors of the tropics.

▲▼▲▼▲▼▲▼▲▼

Tips

Cream of coconut is a highly sweetened coconut milk that can be found in the section of the grocery store that sells mixers for alcoholic drinks. We like to use Coco López Cream of Coconut.

The soup can be prepared through Step 4 up to 1 day ahead. The wontons can be prepared up to 1 hour ahead and kept warm in a 200°F (100°C) oven.

Serves 8

- Baking sheet, lined with parchment paper
- Candy/deep-fry thermometer

Soup

2 cups	half-and-half (10%) cream	500 mL
1	vanilla bean, split lengthwise	1
¼ tsp	salt, divided	1 mL
4	egg yolks	4
1	can (15 oz/425 mL) cream of coconut (see tip, at left)	1

Crispy Mango Wontons

1	mango, cut into ½-inch (1 cm) dice	1
2 tbsp	liquid honey	25 mL
1 tbsp	freshly squeezed lemon juice	15 mL
Pinch	salt	Pinch
16	wonton wrappers, thawed if frozen	16
	Vegetable oil	

1. *Prepare the soup:* In a saucepan, bring cream and vanilla bean to a simmer over medium-high heat. Remove from heat, cover and let steep for about 10 minutes to blend the flavors.
2. Carefully remove the vanilla bean and let cool slightly. Using the flat side of a knife, scrape out seeds and add to the cream, along with a pinch of salt. Discard scraped bean.
3. In a large heatproof bowl, whisk egg yolks. Gradually whisk in cream mixture, in a steady stream. Return to the pan and cook over medium heat, stirring constantly, until slightly thickened, about 4 minutes. Do not let boil or the mixture will curdle. Cook, stirring constantly, for 1 minute more, then remove from heat.
4. Transfer to a clean heatproof bowl and stir to stop the cooking. Whisk in cream of coconut and the remaining salt. Cover and refrigerate until chilled, about 3 hours.
5. *Prepare the wontons:* In a bowl, combine mango, honey, lemon juice and salt. Taste and adjust seasoning with honey or salt, if necessary.

Tip

Chilled soups will stay cold for much longer in chilled bowls.

6. Lay out wonton wrappers on a work surface and place 1 tbsp (15 mL) mango mixture on 8 of them. Wet your finger or a pastry brush with water and moisten the edges of the wrappers. Top with the remaining wrappers and press to eliminate air pockets. Using the tines of a fork, seal the edges. Place wontons on prepared baking sheet, making sure they don't touch.

7. In a saucepan, heat 2 inches (5 cm) of oil over medium-high heat until it registers 360°F (185°C) on thermometer. Carefully add 4 wontons to the hot oil and fry until browned on the bottom, 20 to 30 seconds. Turn and brown the other side, about 20 seconds. Using a slotted spoon, transfer to a baking sheet lined with paper towels and keep warm. Repeat with the remaining wontons.

8. Ladle soup into chilled bowls and top each with a mango wonton.

Piña Colada Soup with Caramelized Pineapple

▲▽▲

The combination of icy piña colada with warm, vanilla-scented pineapple brings back memories of cruise ships and balmy climes. Nothing tastes better on a hot summer night.

▲▽▲▽▲▽▲▽▲▽▲

Tip

Cream of coconut is a highly sweetened coconut milk that can be found in the section of the grocery store that sells mixers for alcoholic drinks. We like to use Coco López Cream of Coconut.

Serves 6

1	can (15 oz/425 mL) cream of coconut (see tip, at left)	1
2 cups	unsweetened pineapple juice	500 mL
¼ cup	light rum (optional)	50 mL
¼ cup	unsalted butter	50 mL
6	spears fresh pineapple	6
1	vanilla bean, split lengthwise	1
4 cups	crushed ice	1 L
	Fresh mint sprigs (optional)	

1. In a large pitcher, combine cream of coconut, pineapple juice and rum (if using). Cover and refrigerate until chilled, about 2 hours.
2. In a large skillet, melt butter over medium-high heat until sizzling. Add pineapple, in batches if necessary, and vanilla bean; cook, turning once, until pineapple is browned on both sides, about 4 minutes per side. Return pineapple to pan, if necessary. Reduce heat to low and keep warm.
3. Carefully remove the vanilla bean and let cool slightly. Using the flat side of a knife, scrape out seeds and add to the pineapple, gently tossing to evenly distribute the seeds. Discard scraped bean.
4. In a blender, in batches, blend chilled coconut mixture and ice until smooth.
5. Divide warm pineapple among bowls and quickly pour in frozen piña colada soup. Garnish with mint sprigs, if desired.

Frozen Hot Chocolate Soup

▲▽▲▽▲▽▲▽▲▽▲▽▲▽▲▽▲▽▲▽▲▽▲▽▲▽▲▽▲▽▲▽▲▽▲

"Rich" and "easy" are the key words to describe this luscious soup. It's great for dessert, but fast and satisfying enough for a midnight snack.

▲▽▲▽▲▽▲▽▲

Tips

The better the quality of chocolate you use, the better the dessert will be. Some of our favorite brands are Scharffen Berger, Callebaut, Des Alpes, Valrhona and Ghirardelli.

To shave chocolate for the garnish, use a vegetable peeler to shave off curls from a block of chocolate.

Serves 4

½ cup	whipping (35%) cream	125 mL
4 oz	bittersweet chocolate, finely chopped	125 g
3 tbsp	granulated sugar	45 mL
1 tbsp	unsweetened cocoa powder	15 mL
1 cup	milk, divided	250 mL
3 cups	ice cubes	750 mL
	Whipped cream	
	Chocolate shavings	

1. In a small saucepan, bring cream to a simmer over medium-high heat. Remove from heat and add chocolate. Let stand for 2 minutes, then whisk in sugar and cocoa powder until melted and smooth. Gradually add half the milk, stirring until smooth. Let cool to room temperature.
2. In a blender, blend chocolate mixture, the remaining milk and ice on high speed until smooth and the consistency of a frozen daiquiri.
3. Pour into chilled bowls or large goblets and top with whipped cream and chocolate shavings.

Mint Chocolate Chip Soup

▲▽▲▽▲▽▲▽▲▽▲▽▲▽▲▽▲▽▲▽▲▽▲▽▲▽▲▽▲▽▲▽▲▽▲

If you like mint chocolate chip ice cream, then this soup's for you. Drizzling melted chocolate into the cold soup creates delicate strands of solid chocolate, which will fascinate your guests.

▲▽▲▽▲▽▲▽▲

Tips

The soup can be prepared through Step 2 up to 1 day ahead.

To melt chocolate chips, place in a metal or glass heatproof bowl over a pan of simmering water. Stir until melted and smooth.

Serves 6 to 8

3 cups	milk	750 mL
1 cup	whipping (35%) cream	250 mL
1 cup	loosely packed fresh mint leaves	250 mL
6	egg yolks	6
1¼ cups	granulated sugar	300 mL
8 oz	semisweet chocolate chips, melted	250 g
	Fresh mint leaves	

1. In a heavy saucepan, bring milk, cream and mint to a simmer over medium heat. Remove from heat and let steep for 15 minutes to blend the flavors. Strain and discard mint.
2. In a large bowl, whisk together egg yolks and sugar. Gradually whisk in milk mixture, in a steady stream. Return to the pan and cook over medium-low heat, stirring constantly, until custard thickens slightly and coats the back of a spoon, about 12 minutes. Do not boil or the mixture will curdle. Transfer to a large bowl, cover and refrigerate until chilled, about 3 hours.
3. Drizzle melted chocolate into chilled soup, stirring constantly.
4. Ladle into chilled bowls and garnish with mint leaves.

Turtle Soup

▲▼▲▼▲▼▲▼▲▼▲▼▲▼▲▼▲▼▲▼▲▼▲▼▲▼▲▼▲▼▲▼▲▼▲▼▲

Gooey and rich, this dessert can't fail to satisfy. Decadent bittersweet chocolate soup is topped with a scoop of caramel ice cream, drizzled with homemade caramel sauce and sprinkled with toasted pecans, resulting in a candy-like confection on a spoon. Because of its richness, a little bit goes a long way; we've designed it to be served in small portions.

▲▼▲▼▲▼▲▼▲▼

Tip
Toast nuts on a baking sheet in a 350°F (180°C) oven until lightly browned, about 5 minutes.

Serves 8

1 cup	granulated sugar	250 mL
¾ cup	corn syrup, divided	175 mL
½ cup	water	125 mL
1 cup	whipping (35%) cream	250 mL
Pinch	salt	Pinch
2½ cups	half-and-half (10%) cream	625 mL
1 lb	bittersweet chocolate, chopped	500 g
1 tsp	vanilla extract	5 mL
	Caramel or dulce de leche ice cream	
1 cup	chopped pecans, toasted	250 mL

1. In a heavy saucepan, combine sugar, ¼ cup (50 mL) of the corn syrup and water; bring to a boil over medium-high heat, stirring until sugar is dissolved. Cook, without stirring, until mixture is a deep caramel color, 10 to 15 minutes. Remove from heat and stir in whipping cream (it will bubble violently) and salt. Return to high heat and boil, stirring, until sauce is the consistency of a thick syrup, about 2 minutes. Let cool.

2. In another saucepan, bring half-and-half cream to a boil over medium-high heat. Remove from heat and add chocolate. Let stand for 2 minutes, then whisk until melted and smooth. Whisk in the remaining corn syrup and vanilla.

3. Pour warm chocolate soup into shallow bowls and top each with a scoop of ice cream. Drizzle with caramel sauce and sprinkle with pecans.

Coca-Mocha Soup
with Hazelnut Biscotti

▲▼▲

Chocoholics beware! This dessert can be dangerous to your waistline. We had a hard time waiting for it to cool before wolfing it down. The espresso gives this chocolatey soup even more flavor. Once it's topped with a delicious hazelnut cookie and sweetened whipped cream, your guests will swoon with delight — we sure did.

▲▼▲▼▲▼▲▼

Tips

The soup can be prepared through Step 2 up to 1 day ahead.

We used Scharffen Berger bittersweet chocolate with 70% cacao and loved the results. Other brands to try are Callebaut, Des Alpes, Valrhona and Ghirardelli.

Serves 6 to 8

3 cups	milk	750 mL
6	egg yolks	6
⅓ cup	granulated sugar	75 mL
¼ cup	unsweetened cocoa powder	50 mL
2 tbsp	cornstarch	25 mL
¼ tsp	salt	1 mL
6 oz	bittersweet chocolate (see tip, at left), chopped	175 g
1½ cups	whipping (35%) cream, divided	375 mL
½ cup	brewed espresso or strong coffee	125 mL
1¼ tsp	vanilla extract, divided	6 mL
1 tbsp	confectioner's (icing) sugar	15 mL
	Hazelnut Biscotti (see recipe, page 374)	

1. In a saucepan, heat milk over medium heat until steaming.
2. In a large saucepan, whisk together egg yolks, granulated sugar, cocoa powder, cornstarch and salt. Gradually whisk in hot milk. Cook over medium heat, stirring constantly, until thickened and the first bubbles appear, about 2 minutes. Remove from heat and add chocolate, stirring until melted and smooth. Stir in 1 cup (250 mL) of the whipping cream, coffee and 1 tsp (5 mL) of the vanilla. Transfer to a large bowl and let cool. Cover and refrigerate until well chilled, about 4 hours.
3. Just before serving, in a chilled bowl, whip the remaining cream, the remaining vanilla and confectioner's sugar until soft peaks form.
4. Ladle soup into chilled bowls and top with biscotti and a dollop of whipped cream.

Gilding the Lily: Toppings and Garnishes

▲▲▲▲▲▲▲▲▲▲▲▲▲▲▲▲▲▲▲▲▲▲▲▲▲▲▲▲▲

Aïoli

▲▼▲▼▲▼▲▼▲▼▲▼▲▼▲▼▲▼▲▼

Makes about 1 cup (250 mL)
Enough to garnish 8 servings

5	cloves garlic	5
2	egg yolks	2
1 tbsp	freshly squeezed lemon juice	15 mL
1 tbsp	water	15 mL
¼ tsp	salt	1 mL
1 cup	olive oil	250 mL
	Freshly ground black pepper	

1. In a food processor, with the motor running, add garlic through the feed tube and process until finely chopped. Turn the machine off and add egg yolks, lemon juice, water and salt; process until smooth. With the motor running, through the feed tube, gradually add oil in a thin, steady stream; process until thick. Season to taste with salt and pepper.

Tips

This recipe contains raw egg yolks. If the food safety of raw eggs is a concern for you, use pasteurized eggs. Many grocery stores now carry pasteurized eggs in their shells.

When half the oil has been added, the mayonnaise should begin to emulsify and will make a slapping sound as you continue to process.

Cilantro Oil

▲▼▲▼▲▼▲▼▲▼▲▼▲▼▲▼▲▼▲▼

Makes about 1 cup (250 mL)
Enough to garnish 16 servings

2 cups	packed fresh cilantro leaves	500 mL
½ cup	olive oil	125 mL
½ cup	vegetable oil	125 mL

1. Bring a large saucepan of water to a boil. Add cilantro and blanch for 5 seconds. Drain and immediately plunge into a bowl of ice water. Drain well and squeeze out all liquid.

2. In a blender, purée cilantro, olive oil and vegetable oil until smooth. Strain through several layers of cheesecloth or a paper coffee filter into a squeeze bottle, discarding solids.

Tip

Store in an airtight container in the refrigerator for up to 3 days.

Rouille

▲▼▲▼▲▼▲▼▲▼▲▼▲▼▲▼▲▼▲▼

Makes about 1½ cups (375 mL)
Enough to garnish 16 servings

2	slices rustic white bread, crusts removed	2
½ cup	fish stock	125 mL
3	cloves garlic, chopped	3
1	roasted red bell pepper (store-bought or see tip, page 303)	1
⅓ cup	extra-virgin olive oil	75 mL
½ tsp	salt	2 mL
½ tsp	cayenne pepper	2 mL
	Freshly ground black pepper	

1. In a food processor, combine bread and fish stock; let soften for a few minutes. Add garlic, roasted pepper, oil, salt and cayenne; process until emulsified into a sauce. Season to taste with salt and black pepper.

Tip

Store in an airtight container in the refrigerator for up to 2 days.

Pesto

▲▽▲▽▲▽▲▽▲▽▲▽▲▽▲▽▲▽▲▽▲▽▲▽▲▽

Makes about ⅓ cup (75 mL)
Enough to garnish 6 servings

1	clove garlic	1
1 cup	packed fresh basil leaves	250 mL
¼ cup	extra-virgin olive oil	50 mL
½ tsp	salt	2 mL
3 tbsp	freshly grated Parmesan cheese	45 mL
1 tbsp	pine nuts	15 mL

1. In a food processor, pulse garlic, basil, oil and salt until finely chopped. Add cheese and pine nuts; pulse, stopping occasionally to scrape down the bowl, until finely chopped but not puréed.

Tip
To store, transfer to an airtight container and pour a thin layer of olive oil over the top (this will prevent it from browning). Store in the refrigerator for up to 1 week. Stir just before using.

Tarragon Pesto

▲▽▲▽▲▽▲▽▲▽▲▽▲▽▲▽▲▽▲▽▲▽▲▽▲▽

Makes about 1½ cups (375 mL)
Enough to garnish 16 servings

1	clove garlic	1
¾ cup	packed fresh tarragon leaves	175 mL
⅔ cup	packed fresh flat-leaf (Italian) parsley leaves	150 mL
2 tbsp	sliced almonds	25 mL
2 tbsp	shredded Asiago cheese	25 mL
¾ cup	extra-virgin olive oil	175 mL
	Salt and freshly ground black pepper	

1. In a food processor, pulse garlic, tarragon and parsley until finely chopped. Add almonds and cheese; pulse until finely chopped. With the motor running, through the feed tube, gradually add oil in a thin, steady stream; process until combined. Season to taste with salt and pepper.

Tip
To store, transfer to an airtight container and pour a thin layer of olive oil over the top (this will prevent it from browning). Store in the refrigerator for up to 1 week. Stir just before using.

Pistou

▲▽▲▽▲▽▲▽▲▽▲▽▲▽▲▽▲▽▲▽▲▽▲▽▲▽

Pistou, a sauce made of basil, garlic and olive oil, is the Provençal version of pesto.

Makes about ⅓ cup (75 mL)
Enough to garnish 6 servings

1	clove garlic	1
1 cup	packed fresh basil leaves	250 mL
¼ cup	extra-virgin olive oil	50 mL
3 tbsp	freshly grated Parmesan cheese	45 mL
½ tsp	salt	2 mL

1. In a food processor, pulse garlic, basil, oil, cheese and salt, stopping occasionally to scrape down the bowl, until finely chopped.

Tip
To store, transfer to an airtight container and pour a thin layer of olive oil over the top (this will prevent it from browning). Store in the refrigerator for up to 1 week. Stir just before using.

Variation
Cilantro Swirl: Substitute fresh cilantro for the basil.

Avocado and Grape Tomato Salsa

▲▽▲▽▲▽▲▽▲▽▲▽▲▽▲▽▲▽▽

Makes about 2 cups (500 mL)
Enough to garnish 8 servings

1	avocado, diced	1
1½ cups	halved grape tomatoes	375 mL
¼ cup	minced fresh cilantro	50 mL
¼ tsp	salt	1 mL
	Freshly ground black pepper	
	Juice of 1 lime	

1. In a bowl, combine avocado, tomatoes, cilantro, salt, pepper to taste and lime juice. Taste and adjust seasoning with salt and pepper, if necessary. Serve immediately or cover and refrigerate for up to 2 hours.

Pico de Gallo Salsa

▲▽▲▽▲▽▲▽▲▽▲▽▲▽▲▽▲▽▲▽

Makes about 1 cup (250 mL)
Enough to garnish 6 to 8 servings

1	tomato, cut into ½-inch (1 cm) dice	1
½	serrano or other hot green chile pepper, seeded and minced	½
2 tbsp	chopped red onion (½-inch/1 cm pieces)	25 mL
¼ tsp	salt	1 mL
	Freshly ground black pepper	
	Juice of 1 lime	

1. In a bowl, combine tomato, chile, onion, salt, pepper to taste and lime juice. Taste and adjust seasoning with salt and pepper, if necessary. Serve immediately or let stand at room temperature for up to 4 hours.

Harissa

▲▽▲▽▲▽▲▽▲▽▲▽▲▽▲▽▲▽▲▽

Harissa is a Middle Eastern hot sauce. We use it as an ingredient in several recipes, and it also makes a lovely garnish or condiment.

Makes about ½ cup (125 mL)
Enough to garnish 16 servings

2	cloves garlic, crushed	2
1	roasted red bell pepper (store-bought or see tip, page 303)	1
2 tbsp	hot pepper flakes	25 mL
1 tsp	salt	5 mL
½ tsp	ground coriander	2 mL
½ tsp	ground cumin	2 mL
	Extra-virgin olive oil	

1. In a blender or mini food processor, process garlic, roasted pepper, hot pepper flakes, salt, coriander and cumin until a thick paste forms. Pack into a small dry jar and cover with a thin layer of oil. Cover tightly and refrigerate until chilled, about 1 hour. Stir to blend in oil before using.

Tip

Store tightly covered in the refrigerator for up to 1 week. Stir just before using.

Yogurt Swirl

▲▽▲▽▲▽▲▽▲▽▲▽▲▽▲▽▲▽▲▽

Makes about ⅔ cup (150 mL)
Enough to garnish 6 to 8 servings

½ cup	plain yogurt	125 mL
2 tbsp	whipping (35%) cream	25 mL

1. In a small bowl, combine yogurt and cream.

Tip

Store in an airtight container in the refrigerator for up to 1 day.

Variation

Mint Yogurt Swirl: Add 2 tbsp (25 mL) finely chopped fresh mint.

Gingery Whipped Cream

▲▽▲▽▲▽▲▽▲▽▲▽▲▽▲▽▲▽▲▽

Makes about 2¹/₂ cups (625 mL)
Enough to garnish 6 to 8 servings

¹/₂ cup	water	125 mL
¹/₂ cup	granulated sugar	125 mL
1	thumb-sized knob gingerroot, thinly sliced Additional granulated sugar	1
1 cup	cold whipping (35%) cream	250 mL

1. In a small saucepan, bring water and sugar to a boil over medium heat, stirring until sugar dissolves. Add ginger, reduce heat and simmer until ginger is transparent and tender, about 15 minutes.

2. Using a slotted spoon, remove ginger to a plate and roll in sugar. Let dry on a baking rack overnight, then use as a garnish as desired. Transfer ginger syrup to a bowl, cover and refrigerate until chilled, about 2 hours. (You will have more syrup than you need for this recipe. Try adding it to hot tea!)

3. In a chilled bowl, using an electric mixer, beat cream and ¹/₄ cup (50 mL) of the ginger syrup on high speed until fluffy and light.

Tip
Store in an airtight container in the refrigerator for up to 1 day.

Variation
Gingery Crème Fraiche Swirl: Substitute ¹/₂ cup (125 mL) crème fraîche or plain yogurt for the whipping cream. In Step 3, add 2 tbsp (25 mL) ginger syrup to the crème fraiche and mix to blend. Taste and add more ginger syrup, if desired. Finely chop reserved ginger and stir in.

Cilantro Cream

▲▽▲▽▲▽▲▽▲▽▲▽▲▽▲▽▲▽▲▽

Makes about 1¹/₄ cups (300 mL)
Enough to garnish 8 to 12 servings

1	jalapeño pepper, seeded and minced	1
1 cup	packed fresh cilantro, finely chopped	250 mL
1 cup	sour cream	250 mL
1 tbsp	freshly squeezed lime juice	15 mL
Pinch	salt	Pinch

1. In a small bowl, combine jalapeño, cilantro, sour cream, lime juice and salt.

Tip
Store in an airtight container in the refrigerator for up to 2 days.

Maple Cream

▲▽▲▽▲▽▲▽▲▽▲▽▲▽▲▽▲▽▲▽

Makes about 1¹/₂ cups (375 mL)
Enough to garnish 6 to 8 servings

³/₄ cup	whipping (35%) cream	175 mL
3 tbsp	pure maple syrup	45 mL
Pinch	salt	Pinch

1. In a chilled bowl, using an electric mixer, whip cream until soft peaks form. Add maple syrup and salt; whip until well blended.

Tip
Store in an airtight container in the refrigerator for up to 1 day.

Lemon Sour Cream Swirl

▲▽▲▽▲▽▲▽▲▽▲▽▲▽▲▽▲▽▲▽▲▽

Makes about ½ cup (125 mL)
Enough to garnish 6 servings

½ cup	sour cream	125 mL
1 tsp	finely grated lemon zest	5 mL
1 tbsp	freshly squeezed lemon juice	15 mL
Pinch	salt	Pinch

1. In a small bowl, combine sour cream, lemon zest, lemon juice and salt.

Tip
Store in an airtight container in the refrigerator for up to 2 days.

Crème Anglaise Swirl

▲▽▲▽▲▽▲▽▲▽▲▽▲▽▲▽▲▽▲▽▲▽

Makes about 1 cup (250 mL)
Enough to garnish 8 servings

½ cup	milk	125 mL
¼ cup	whipping (35%) cream	50 mL
½	vanilla bean, split lengthwise	½
3 tbsp	granulated sugar	45 mL
Pinch	salt	Pinch
3	egg yolks	3

1. In a saucepan, bring milk, cream, vanilla bean and sugar to a simmer over medium heat, stirring until sugar dissolves. Remove from heat, cover and let steep for 15 minutes to blend the flavors.

2. Carefully remove the vanilla bean and let cool slightly. Using the flat side of a knife, scrape seeds into the milk. Discard scraped bean.

3. In a large heatproof bowl, whisk egg yolks. Gradually whisk in milk mixture, in a steady stream. Return to the pan and cook over medium heat, stirring constantly, until slightly thickened, about

4 minutes. Do not let boil or the mixture will curdle. Cook, stirring constantly, for 1 minute more, then remove from heat.

4. Transfer to a clean heatproof bowl set inside a larger bowl filled with ice and stir custard until cool. Cover and refrigerate until chilled, about 3 hours.

Tip
Store in an airtight container in the refrigerator for up to 3 days.

Variations
Almond Crème Anglaise Swirl: Omit the vanilla bean and add ½ tsp (2 mL) almond extract to the finished crème anglaise.

White Chocolate Crème Anglaise Swirl: Add ½ cup (125 mL) chopped white chocolate to the hot crème anglaise. Stir until melted, then cool in the ice bath.

Raspberry Coulis

▲▽▲▽▲▽▲▽▲▽▲▽▲▽▲▽▲▽▲▽▲▽

Makes about 1 cup (250 mL)
Enough to garnish 6 to 8 servings

1	package (12 oz/375 g) frozen raspberries in syrup, thawed	1
1 tbsp	freshly squeezed lemon juice	15 mL

1. In a food processor or blender, purée raspberries and their syrup until smooth. Strain through a fine-mesh sieve into a bowl and stir in lemon juice.

Tips
Store in an airtight container in the refrigerator for up to 1 week.

For easy garnishing, pour the coulis into a squeeze bottle with a narrow tip.

Lemon and Chive Compound Butter

▲▽▲▽▲▽▲▽▲▽▲▽▲▽▲▽▲▽▲▽▲▽

Makes about ¹⁄₂ cup (125 mL)
Enough to garnish 8 servings

¹⁄₂ cup	unsalted butter, softened	125 mL
2 tsp	minced fresh chives	10 mL
¹⁄₂ tsp	grated lemon zest	2 mL
1 tsp	freshly squeezed lemon juice	5 mL

1. In a bowl, combine butter, chives, lemon zest and lemon juice. Transfer to a sheet of plastic wrap and roll the butter to form a log. Wrap in the plastic wrap.
2. Freeze until firm, at least 1 hour or for up to 1 month. Before using, let thaw at room temperature for 15 minutes, then cut into slices as directed in the recipe. Return the unused portion to the freezer.

Variation

Lemon and Tarragon Compound Butter: Substitute fresh tarragon for the chives.

Crispy Shallots

▲▽▲▽▲▽▲▽▲▽▲▽▲▽▲▽▲▽▲▽

Makes enough to garnish 6 servings

- Candy/deep-fry thermometer

1¹⁄₂ cups	vegetable oil	375 mL
6	shallots, thinly sliced	6
	Salt	

1. In a saucepan, heat oil over medium heat until it registers 350°F (180°C) on thermometer. Add shallots, in two batches, and fry, stirring frequently, until golden brown, 3 to 4 minutes. Using a slotted spoon, remove shallots to a plate lined with paper towels. Season to taste with salt. Serve hot or let cool and use within 3 hours.

Oven-Dried Apple Slices

▲▽▲▽▲▽▲▽▲▽▲▽▲▽▲▽▲▽▲▽

Makes 12 slices
Enough to garnish 6 servings

- Preheat oven to 300°F (150°C)
- Baking sheet, lined with parchment paper or silpat

1	Granny Smith apple	1

1. Thinly slice apple into round slices, so that you have a cross-section of the apple, leaving the core and seeds intact. (You should have at least 12 slices. Don't worry if some of the slices are not whole. They can be patched together.)
2. Arrange slices on prepared baking sheet and patch together any incomplete rounds. Bake in preheated oven until dried, 30 to 45 minutes. Check frequently and, if slices are coloring too much, reduce heat by 25°F (14°C). Let cool on sheet on a wire rack.

Tip

Store in an airtight container for up to 4 days.

Fried Sage Leaves

▲▽▲▽▲▽▲▽▲▽▲▽▲▽▲▽▲▽▲▽

Makes 18 leaves
Enough to garnish 6 to 8 servings

¹⁄₄ cup	unsalted butter	50 mL
18	fresh sage leaves	18

1. In a skillet, melt butter over medium heat. Add sage leaves and cook, turning once, until lightly browned and crispy on both sides, about 2 minutes per side. Using a slotted spoon, remove leaves to a plate lined with paper towels. The butter can be drizzled over the soup or reserved for another use.

Italian Meatballs

Makes about 32 meatballs
Enough for 8 servings of soup

2 tbsp	olive oil	25 mL
1 cup	finely chopped onion	250 mL
2	cloves garlic, minced	2
8 oz	lean ground beef	250 g
8 oz	lean ground veal	250 g
8 oz	regular or lean ground pork	250 g
1	egg	1
1 cup	fresh bread crumbs	250 mL
¼ cup	freshly grated Parmesan cheese	50 mL
¼ cup	minced fresh flat-leaf (Italian) parsley	50 mL
2 tsp	salt	10 mL
1 tsp	dried basil	5 mL
½ tsp	dried oregano	2 mL
¼ tsp	freshly ground black pepper	1 mL

1. In a skillet, heat oil over medium-high heat. Add onion and sauté until starting to soften, about 2 minutes. Add garlic and sauté until onion is softened, about 2 minutes. Let cool for 5 minutes.

2. In a large bowl, using your hands, combine onion mixture, beef, veal, pork, egg, bread crumbs, cheese, parsley, salt, basil, oregano and pepper. To taste for seasoning, heat a small skillet over medium heat and fry a spoon-sized patty until no longer pink. Taste and adjust seasoning with salt and black pepper, if necessary. Roll into small meatballs about 1½ inches (4 cm) in diameter.

Tip

Store in an airtight container in the refrigerator for up to 1 day or in the freezer for up to 1 month. Thaw overnight in the refrigerator.

Hearty Noodles

We've found that the no-cook lasagna pasta sheets make lovely, thick, substantial noodles, with a great texture for soups.

Makes enough for 6 to 8 servings of soup

1	box (9 oz/255 g) no-cook lasagna noodles	1
2 tbsp	unsalted butter	25 mL

1. Bring a large pot of salted water to a boil over medium-high heat. Add noodles and cook until tender and pliable, about 6 minutes. Drain and toss with butter.

Buttery Croutons

Makes about 3 cups (750 mL)
Enough to garnish 6 to 8 servings

- Preheat oven to 400°F (200°C)
- Large rimmed baking sheet

3 cups	cubed rustic white bread (½-inch/1 cm cubes)	750 mL
¼ cup	unsalted butter, melted	50 mL
½ tsp	salt	2 mL

1. On baking sheet, combine bread, butter and salt; toss to coat evenly and spread in a single layer. Bake, stirring once, until crisp, about 10 minutes. Let cool on sheet on a wire rack and use within 3 hours.

Variations

Pumpernickel Croutons: Substitute pumpernickel bread for the white bread and olive oil for the melted butter.

Garlic Croutons: In a small skillet, melt ¼ cup (50 mL) butter over medium heat. Add 3 cloves garlic, minced, and sauté until sizzling, about 2 minutes. Remove from heat. Use garlic butter in place of the melted butter.

Bacon Croutons

▲▽▲▽▲▽▲▽▲▽▲▽▲▽▲▽▲▽▲▽▲▽

Makes about 3½ cups (875 mL)
Enough to garnish 6 to 8 servings

- Preheat oven to 400°F (200°C)
- Large rimmed baking sheet

6	slices bacon, cut into ½-inch (1 cm) pieces	6
3 cups	cubed sourdough bread (½-inch/1 cm cubes)	750 mL
1 tbsp	olive oil	15 mL
¼ tsp	freshly ground black pepper	1 mL

1. Spread bacon on baking sheet and bake for 5 minutes. Add bread cubes, oil and pepper; toss to coat evenly and spread in a single layer. Bake, stirring a few times, until bacon is crisp and bread cubes are golden brown, about 20 minutes. Let cool slightly on sheet on a wire rack and use warm.

Cornbread Croutons

▲▽▲▽▲▽▲▽▲▽▲▽▲▽▲▽▲▽▲▽▲▽

Makes about 5 cups (1.25 L)
Enough to garnish 12 servings

- Preheat oven to 400°F (200°F)
- 9-inch (2.5 L) square baking pan, greased and lined with parchment paper
- Baking sheet

1 cup	yellow cornmeal	250 mL
1 cup	all-purpose flour	250 mL
¼ cup	granulated sugar	50 mL
1 tbsp	baking powder	15 mL
1 tsp	salt	5 mL
1	egg	1
1 cup	milk	250 mL
⅓ cup	vegetable oil	75 mL

1. In a bowl, combine cornmeal, flour, sugar, baking powder and salt.
2. In another bowl, whisk together egg, milk and oil. Add to the cornmeal mixture and stir just until blended. Pour into prepared pan.
3. Bake in preheated oven until a tester inserted in the center comes out clean, about 20 minutes. Let cool completely in pan on a wire rack.
4. Preheat oven to 350°F (180°C). Turn cooled cornbread out of pan and cut into 1-inch (2.5 cm) squares. Transfer to baking sheet and bake until dried and crispy, about 20 minutes. Let cool on sheet on a wire rack and use within 3 hours.

Cheesy Croutons

▲▽▲▽▲▽▲▽▲▽▲▽▲▽▲▽▲▽▲▽▲▽

Makes 18 croutons
Enough to garnish 6 to 9 servings

- Preheat broiler, with rack placed 4 inches (10 cm) from heat
- Large rimmed baking sheet

18	baguette slices (½ inch/1 cm thick) Olive oil	18
½ cup	shredded or grated cheese (any type or a mix) Salt and freshly ground black pepper	125 mL

1. Brush both sides of baguette slices lightly with oil and place on baking sheet. Broil, turning once, until toasted on both sides, about 1 minute per side. Sprinkle with cheese and salt and pepper to taste. Broil until cheese is just melted, about 1 minute. Let cool slightly on sheet on a wire rack and use warm.

Variation

Blue Cheese Croutons: Substitute 6 oz (175 g) blue cheese, crumbled, at room temperature, for the shredded cheese. We like Maytag, Gorgonzola or Saga.

Grilled Cheese Croutons

▲▼▲▼▲▼▲▼▲▼▲▼▲▼▲▼▲▼▲▼

Makes about 3 cups (750 mL)
Enough to garnish 6 servings

¼ cup	unsalted butter, softened	50 mL
¼ tsp	dried thyme	1 mL
6	thin slices bread	6
3 oz	Cheddar cheese, thinly sliced	90 g

1. Heat a large skillet over medium-high heat.
2. Meanwhile, in a small bowl, combine butter and thyme. Spread one side of each bread slice with butter mixture. Place three slices in the pan, buttered side down. Top with cheese, then with the remaining bread slices, buttered side up. Cook, turning once, until toasted on both sides, 2 to 3 minutes per side. Remove from the pan and let cool slightly, then cut into 1-inch (2.5 cm) squares and use warm.

Chile Cheddar Croutons

▲▼▲▼▲▼▲▼▲▼▲▼▲▼▲▼▲▼▲▼

Makes 18 croutons
Enough to garnish 6 to 9 servings

- Preheat broiler
- Large rimmed baking sheet

18	baguette slices (¼ inch/0.5 cm thick)	18
2 tbsp	unsalted butter	25 mL
½ cup	shredded sharp (old) Cheddar cheese	125 mL
1 tbsp	chili powder	15 mL
¼ tsp	cayenne pepper	1 mL
	Salt and freshly ground black pepper	

1. Spread one side of each bread slice with butter. Arrange bread, buttered side up, on baking sheet and broil until golden, about 1 minute. Turn over and sprinkle with cheese, chili powder, cayenne and salt and black pepper to taste. Broil until cheese melts, about 1 minute. Let cool slightly on sheet on a wire rack.

Spicy Mustard Croutons

▲▼▲▼▲▼▲▼▲▼▲▼▲▼▲▼▲▼▲▼

Makes 18 croutons
Enough to garnish 6 to 9 servings

- broiler
- Large rimmed baking sheet

18	baguette slices (¼ inch/0.5 cm thick)	18
2 tbsp	unsalted butter	25 mL
¼ cup	spicy Dijon mustard	50 mL
¼ cup	freshly grated Parmesan cheese	50 mL

1. Spread one side of each bread slice with butter. Arrange bread, buttered side up, on baking sheet and broil until golden, about 1 minute. Turn over and spread with mustard and sprinkle with cheese. Broil until cheese melts, about 1 minute. Let cool slightly on sheet on a wire rack.

Flaky Pastry

▲▼▲▼▲▼▲▼▲▼▲▼▲▼▲▼▲▼▲▼

Makes enough pastry to top 6 small bowls or 1 large casserole dish

1½ cups	all-purpose flour, chilled in freezer for 1 hour	375 mL
9 tbsp	unsalted butter, cut into ½-inch (1 cm) pieces and chilled in freezer for 1 hour	135 mL
¼ tsp	salt	1 mL
⅓ cup	ice water	75 mL

1. In a food processor, pulse flour, butter and salt until butter is the size of peas. While pulsing, quickly pour in water through the feed tube, pulsing no more than 6 or 7 times, until dough looks shaggy and dry.
2. Turn out onto a work surface and, with the heel of your hand, smear dough against the surface until it begins to come together. Shape into a disk. Wrap in plastic wrap and refrigerate until chilled, about 1 hour.

Tip

The dough can be tightly wrapped in plastic wrap, then in foil, and frozen for up to 1 month. Thaw overnight in the refrigerator before using.

Variation

Herbed Flaky Pastry: Add 1 tsp (5 mL) fresh thyme, rosemary or parsley with the salt.

Fluffy Dumpling Batter

Makes enough batter for 12 dumplings

1¼ cups	all-purpose flour	300 mL
2 tsp	baking powder	10 mL
1 tsp	granulated sugar	5 mL
¼ tsp	salt	1 mL
3 tbsp	unsalted butter, cut into small pieces	45 mL
1	egg	1
½ cup	milk	125 mL

1. In a large bowl, combine flour, baking powder, sugar and salt. Add butter, one piece at a time, and mix with a pastry blender or your fingers until incorporated.
2. In another bowl, whisk together egg and milk. Add to flour mixture and mix just until a soft dough forms. (Do not overmix, or the dumplings will be tough.)

Tip

For instructions on cooking dumplings in soup, see Chicken and Cabbage Soup with Dumplings (page 190).

Spaetzle

Makes enough to garnish 6 to 8 servings

2	eggs	2
½ cup	milk	125 mL
½ tsp	salt	2 mL
¼ tsp	freshly ground black pepper	1 mL
Pinch	ground nutmeg	Pinch
1 cup	all-purpose flour	250 mL
2 tbsp	unsalted butter	25 mL

1. In a large bowl, whisk together eggs, milk, salt, pepper and nutmeg. Add flour and mix by hand until a smooth dough forms. Let rest, covered with a clean towel, for 15 minutes.

2. Bring a large pot of salted water to a boil. Using a spaetzle machine, a ricer, a colander with large holes or a flat grater with large holes, press about ½ cup (125 mL) of the batter at a time into the boiling water, stirring to prevent spaetzle from sticking. Cook until spaetzle float, 2 to 3 minutes. Using a slotted spoon, remove to a warmed bowl and repeat with remaining batter. Toss with butter.

Tip

Let cool and store in an airtight container in the refrigerator for up to 1 day. Reheat in a skillet over medium-low heat.

Crispy Tortilla Strips

▲▽▲▽▲▽▲▽▲▽▲▽▲▽▲▽▲▽▲▽▲▽

Makes about 3 cups (750 mL)
Enough to garnish 6 to 8 servings

- Candy/deep-fry thermometer

	Vegetable oil	
6	6-inch (15 cm) corn tortillas, halved, then cut crosswise into matchstick-sized strips	6
	Salt	

1. In a saucepan, heat $\frac{3}{4}$ inch (2 cm) oil over medium heat until it registers 350°F (180°C) on thermometer. Add tortilla strips, in 4 batches, and fry until crisp and light golden, 30 to 45 seconds. Using tongs or a slotted spoon, remove tortilla strips to a plate lined with paper towels. Season to taste with salt. Let cool and use within 3 hours.

Matzo Balls

▲▽▲▽▲▽▲▽▲▽▲▽▲▽▲▽▲▽▲▽

Makes about 20 matzo balls
Enough to garnish 10 servings

5	eggs	5
$\frac{1}{3}$ cup	vegetable oil	75 mL
$1\frac{1}{3}$ cups	matzo meal	325 mL
1 tbsp	baking powder	15 mL
$\frac{1}{4}$ tsp	salt	1 mL
$\frac{1}{4}$ tsp	freshly ground black pepper	1 mL

1. In a large bowl, whisk together eggs and oil. Using a wooden spoon, mix in matzo meal, baking powder, salt and pepper until well blended. Cover and refrigerate until firm, about 15 minutes. Meanwhile, bring a large pot of salted water to a boil.

2. Dip your hands in cold water and shape dough into balls about the size of walnuts. Gently add matzo balls to the boiling water, reduce heat and simmer, turning once, until cooked through, about 25 minutes. Using a slotted spoon, transfer directly to soup bowls.

Barley Risotto

▲▽▲▽▲▽▲▽▲▽▲▽▲▽▲▽▲▽▲▽

Makes about $2\frac{1}{2}$ cups (625 mL)
Enough to serve with 6 to 8 servings

3 cups	chicken or vegetable stock	750 mL
$\frac{1}{4}$ cup	unsalted butter	50 mL
$1\frac{1}{2}$ cups	pearl barley	375 mL
$\frac{1}{2}$ cup	whipping (35%) cream	125 mL
	Salt and freshly ground black pepper	

1. In a saucepan, bring stock to a simmer over medium heat. Reduce heat and keep at a simmer.

2. In another saucepan, melt butter over medium heat. Add barley and sauté for 2 minutes. Reduce heat to low and add stock, $\frac{1}{2}$ cup (125 mL) at a time, stirring occasionally until each addition is absorbed, about 2 minutes, before adding the next. Cook, stirring and adding stock, until barley is tender, about 20 minutes total. Stir in cream and season to taste with salt and pepper.

Tip

Store in an airtight container in the refrigerator for up to 2 days.

Wild Mushroom Risotto Cakes

▽▲▽▲▽▲▽▲▽▲▽▲▽▲▽▲▽▲▽▲▽▲▽

We always make more risotto than we need for a meal because the leftovers are so fabulous fried up in a little olive oil. But just in case you need to start from scratch, here's a recipe your family and guests will swoon over.

Makes about 8 cakes
Enough for 8 servings of soup

• Baking sheet

2 cups	beef stock	500 mL
2 cups	water	500 mL
6 tbsp	unsalted butter, divided	90 mL
1	onion, chopped	1
8 oz	cremini or other wild (exotic) mushrooms, sliced	250 g
1½ cups	Arborio rice	375 mL
½ cup	dry white wine	125 mL
½ cup	freshly grated Parmesan cheese	125 mL
¼ cup	chopped fresh flat-leaf (Italian) parsley	50 mL
¼ cup	whipping (35%) cream	50 mL
	Salt and freshly ground black pepper	
	All-purpose flour	
¼ cup	olive oil	50 mL

1. In a saucepan, bring stock and water to a simmer over medium heat. Reduce heat and keep at a simmer.

2. In a large, heavy pot, melt 3 tbsp (45 mL) of the butter over medium-high heat. Add onion and sauté until softened, about 4 minutes. Add mushrooms and sauté until they have released their liquid, about 5 minutes.

3. Reduce heat to medium. Add rice and sauté for 2 minutes. Add wine and cook, stirring constantly, until absorbed, about 3 minutes. Reduce heat to low and add stock mixture, ½ cup (125 mL) at a time, stirring occasionally until each addition is absorbed, about 2 minutes, before adding the next. Cook, stirring and adding stock, until rice is tender, about 20 minutes total. Stir in the remaining butter, cheese, parsley, cream and salt and pepper to taste.

4. Spread risotto in a thin layer on baking sheet and let cool (this allows it to cool quickly). Place in the refrigerator until chilled, about 1 hour.

5. Shape chilled risotto into patties about 4 inches (10 cm) wide and ½ inch (1 cm) thick. Dredge with flour.

6. In a large skillet, heat oil over medium-high heat. Add risotto cakes, in batches, and cook, turning once, until browned and crispy on both sides, about 3 minutes per side. Transfer to baking sheet as completed.

Tips

The risotto can be stored in an airtight container in the refrigerator for up to 2 days. The risotto cakes can be kept warm in a 200°F (100°C) oven for up to 1 hour before serving.

Steps 5 and 6 will work with any leftover risotto you have, so always make extra!

Hazelnut or Almond Biscotti

▲▼▲▼▲▼▲▼▲▼▲▼▲▼▲▼▲▼▲▼

Makes 40 biscotti

- Preheat oven to 350°F (180°C)
- Baking sheet, lined with parchment paper

2¾ cups	all-purpose flour	675 mL
1½ cups	granulated sugar	375 mL
1½ tsp	baking powder	7 mL
¾ tsp	salt	3 mL
½ cup	unsalted butter, cut into small pieces	125 mL
2	eggs	2
¼ cup	brandy	50 mL
½ tsp	almond extract	2 mL
1⅔ cups	hazelnuts, toasted, skinned and coarsely chopped, or almonds, toasted and coarsely chopped	400 mL

1. In a bowl, combine flour, sugar, baking powder and salt. Add butter, one piece at a time, and mix with a pastry blender or your fingers until coarse crumbs form.
2. In a small bowl, whisk together eggs, brandy and almond extract. Add to the flour mixture, along with nuts, and mix until dough is moist.
3. Divide dough into thirds and place 3 inches (7.5 cm) apart on prepared baking sheet. Shape into three 12- by 2-inch (30 by 5 cm) logs. Bake in preheated oven until set but still soft, about 30 minutes. Let cool completely on sheet on a wire rack. Reduce oven temperature to 300°F (150°C).
4. Place logs on a cutting board and cut crosswise into ¾-inch (2 cm) thick slices. Return to baking sheet, cut side up, and bake for 10 minutes. Turn over and bake until dry and crisp, about 15 minutes.

Tip

Store in an airtight container at room temperature for up to 2 weeks or in the freezer for up to 4 weeks.

Brownie Croutons

▲▼▲▼▲▼▲▼▲▼▲▼▲▼▲▼▲▼▲▼

Makes about 4 cups (1 L)
Enough to garnish 8 servings

- Preheat oven to 325°F (160°C)
- 8-inch (2 L) square baking pan, lined with foil, foil buttered

6 tbsp	unsalted butter	90 mL
4 oz	bittersweet or semisweet chocolate, chopped	125 g
2 oz	unsweetened chocolate, chopped	60 g
¾ cup	granulated sugar	175 mL
1 tsp	vanilla extract	5 mL
¼ tsp	salt	1 mL
2	eggs	2
½ cup	all-purpose flour	125 mL

1. In a saucepan, over low heat, whisk butter, bittersweet chocolate and unsweetened chocolate until smooth. Remove from heat and whisk in sugar, vanilla and salt. Whisk in eggs, one at a time, then fold in flour. Spread evenly in prepared pan.
2. Bake in preheated oven until a tester inserted in the center comes out with moist crumbs attached, about 30 minutes. Let cool in pan on a wire rack.
3. Turn pan upside down onto a cutting board and remove pan and foil. Using a serrated knife, cut cake into ½-inch (1 cm) squares.

Tip

Store in an airtight container at room temperature for up to 1 day.

Acknowledgments

As always, we are so grateful to our families — David, Quinn, Connor and Kyle Deeds and Ricky, Jessica, Justin and Corey Snyder — who never complained (well, almost never) about the lack of forks and knives at our dinner tables. The enthusiasm they showed for every bowl of soup (well, almost every bowl) makes us love them all the more.

Thanks go to all our recipe testers, who make our books so much better for their efforts.

For working so hard on our behalf, we'd like to thank our agent, Lisa Ekus-Saffer, and her staff at the Lisa Ekus Group.

We'd also like to thank our publisher, Bob Dees, editor Sue Sumeraj and everyone at PageWave Graphics for bringing another one of our books to life.

Library and Archives Canada Cataloguing in Publication

Snyder, Carla
    300 sensational soups / Carla Snyder, Meredith Deeds.

Includes index.
ISBN-13: 978-0-7788-0196-2
ISBN-10: 0-7788-0196-9

1. Soups. I. Deeds, Meredith. II. Title. III. Title: Three hundred sensational soups.

TX757.D43 2008   641.8'13   C2008-902436-2

Index

▲▽▲